An

Introduction to

MORAL
THEOLOGY

SECOND EDITION

An
Introduction to

MORAL
THEOLOGY

SECOND EDITION

WILLIAM E. MAY

Our Sunday Visitor Publishing Division
Our Sunday Visitor, Inc.
Huntington, IN 46750

Nihil Obstat
Rev. Basil Cole, O.P., S.T.D.
Censor Deputatus

Imprimatur
✠ Theodore Cardinal McCarrick
Archbishop of Washington
June 20, 2003

The *Nihil Obstat* and *Imprimatur* are official declarations that a book or pamphlet is free of doctrinal or moral error. No implication is contained therein that those who have granted the *Nihil Obstat* and *Imprimatur* agree with the contents, opinions, or statements expressed.

With few exceptions (including those appearing in quoted material incorporating biblical excerpts from such editions as the *New American Bible*), most Scripture texts in this work are taken from the *Catholic Edition of the Revised Standard Version of the Bible* (RSV), copyright © 1965 and 1966 by the Division of Christian Education of the National Council of the Churches of Christ in the United States of America. Used by permission. All rights reserved.

Catechism excerpts are from the English translation of the *Catechism of the Catholic Church, Second Edition,* for use in the United States of America, copyright © 1994 and 1997, United States Catholic Conference — Libreria Editrice Vaticana. Used by permission. All rights reserved.

The English translation of *Veritatis splendor* is from the Vatican website, *www.vatican.va.*

The author is grateful to all copyright holders without whose material this book could not have been completed. Every reasonable effort has been made to determine copyright holders of excerpted materials and to secure permissions as needed. If any copyrighted materials have been inadvertently used in this work without proper credit being given in one form or another, please notify Our Sunday Visitor in writing so that future printings of this work may be corrected accordingly.

Our Sunday Visitor Publishing Division
Our Sunday Visitor, Inc.
200 Noll Plaza
Huntington, IN 46750

ISBN: 1-931709-92-0 (Inventory No. T49)
LCCN: 90-60638

Cover design by Monica Haneline
Interior design by Sherri L. Hoffman

PRINTED IN THE UNITED STATES OF AMERICA

Dedicated to my grandchildren Christopher Michael May, Elizabeth Ann May, Alexandra Marie ("Sasha") Fairchok, Anastasia Teresa ("Anna") Fairchok, Kathryn Blair ("Katya") Fairchok, Megan Flora May, Peter William May, Margaret Mary ("Maggie") May, Katherine Anne ("Katie") May, Christina Marie May, Joachim Gabriel Romanosky, and to grandchildren-to-be and children of their generation.

Contents

FOREWORD TO THE FIRST EDITION

It is a pleasure for me to introduce Dr. William May's *An Introduction to Moral Theology*. In succinct and perceptive fashion, Dr. May introduces the reader to fundamental notions of Catholic moral teaching. I commend this volume to the clergy, to seminarians, to catechists, and to all who wish to discover more profoundly what it means to follow the Lord Jesus.

We live in an age that seems to have lost its moral moorings. Too many people are genuinely confused about what is right and what is wrong; some doubt that an authentic standard for judging human behavior exists. Church teachings, particularly those related to the transmission and preservation of human life, often meet with rejection. All too often, Catholic morality is regarded as a series of arbitrary obligations having nothing to do with our dignity as human persons called to eternal life in Christ Jesus.

This introduction counters such confusion with clarity and depth. It helps us understand how the Church's moral teaching is rooted in the nature of the human person created in the image and likeness of God. Indeed, as the grace of Christ takes hold of our lives we see ever more clearly the wisdom of the Church's moral teaching.

Dr. May has devoted his life to studying the Church's moral teaching and to communicating that teaching to others. He is a man of deep faith and scholarship, and we are privileged that he has shared his wisdom with us. This latest book of his deserves a very warm welcome.

✠ JAMES CARDINAL HICKEY
Archbishop of Washington

INTRODUCTION TO THE SECOND EDITION

Almost ten years have passed since this work was first revised (1994) in order to incorporate the teaching on the moral life presented in the *Catechism of the Catholic Church* and in Pope John Paul II's encyclical on "fundamental questions of the Church's moral teaching," *Veritatis splendor* ("The Splendor of Truth"). Since 1994, important new works in moral theology have appeared, and it will be useful to refer to some of these and to incorporate particularly helpful matter found in them. I will expand my own presentation of moral theology, in particular to provide a consideration of the role that virtue plays in the moral life. Although I have sought to integrate biblical teaching on the Christian moral life in the chapter "Christian Faith and Our Moral Life" (Chapter Six in this revised edition), I believe it appropriate and necessary to consider the biblical foundation of moral theology more explicitly. Consequently, I have devoted a part of a new first chapter to this question. Finally, I will correct some errors I made in the earlier editions.

In preparing the present edition, I have reorganized the text. I have incorporated the opening pages of the "Introduction to the First Edition" (1991), which was included in the 1994 edition, into a new first chapter, entitled "Moral Theology: Its Nature, Purpose, and Biblical Foundation." In this chapter, I expand considerably the brief observations made in the 1991 and 1994 editions on the subject of moral theology and also, as noted already, consider more explicitly the biblical roots of moral theology.

The chapter on human dignity, free human action, and conscience, which was Chapter One in both the 1991 and 1994 editions, is now Chapter Two; in it I have added for this edition a section on the role of virtue in the moral life.

The subsequent chapters — which are concerned with the natural law and moral life, moral absolutes (with appendices on the teaching of St. Thomas Aquinas and Pope John Paul II on this issue), sin and the moral life, Christian faith and the moral life, and the Church as moral teacher — present material covered in Chapters Two through Six of the first two editions. I have, however, made significant and substantive revisions especially in (1) the chapter devoted to natural law (Chapter Three), both to take into account important recent literature (for example, Martin Rhonheimer's *Natural Law and Practical Reason: A Thomist View of Moral Autonomy* and a recent essay of Germain Grisez that develops his own understanding of natural law) and to clarify and correct positions taken in earlier editions, and (2) the chapter on the

"Church as Moral Teacher" (Chapter Seven), where I have taken into account more recent magisterial teaching and in light thereof have made other changes.

In light of developments since 1994 — in particular, the impact of John Paul II's encyclical *Veritatis splendor* — I considered dropping the chapter on moral absolutes (Chapter Three of the 1994 edition and Chapter Four of this edition), insofar as the Holy Father's encyclical provided an incisive and authoritative critique and rejection of "consequentialist" and "proportionalist" approaches to making moral judgments and their denial of moral absolutes. However, theologians holding the views repudiated in *Veritatis splendor* uniformly (and erroneously) claim (as will be seen in the text of the chapter devoted to this encyclical included here) that their ideas were *not* those repudiated by John Paul II but rather their "caricature." Moreover, they continue to deny that there are any moral absolutes in the sense understood by the magisterium of the Church. They are, in short, still setting forth the positions rejected by John Paul II and adamantly deny that specific moral norms expressed in nonmorally evaluative language, such as the one absolutely forbidding the intentional killing of the innocent, can be absolutely binding, with no exceptions. It is thus still imperative to present their views accurately and show precisely why they are wrong and likewise, in discussing John Paul II's encyclical on the moral life, to show how seriously they have misrepresented what he said. I have thus retained the chapter on moral absolutes and, in revising the chapter on the encyclical, showed how revisionist theologians have grossly distorted its teaching.

In the 1994 edition, the chapter dealing with the moral teaching of the *Catechism of the Catholic Church* was written before the French text had been translated into English. Consequently, I had made my own translation from the French text, and it differed in places from the officially approved English translation published late in 1994. In 1997, the official Latin text of the *Catechism* was published, and subsequently minor errors in the French text and in vernacular editions based on it were corrected. I have thus revised the chapter summarizing the *Catechism*'s teaching on the moral life, making use of the official English translation as amended in light of the official Latin text. However, since my treatment of the *Catechism*'s presentation of the moral life is intended primarily to offer an overview of the *Catechism*'s teaching and not a theological analysis thereof, I have decided to place this material, with its revisions, in an appendix.

I have also revised the chapter devoted to Pope John Paul's encyclical *Veritatis splendor* by incorporating into my presentation elements of the very helpful commentary on the encyclical prepared by the Italian theologian Dionigi Tettamanzi, now the cardinal archbishop of Milan. In that chapter, I have also answered some of the major objections to the teaching of John Paul

II made by dissenting theologians. Since John Paul II's encyclical is concerned in depth with some of the major issues taken up in this book, and since in presenting his teaching I have sought to provide a theological analysis and defense of it, I have kept it as a formal chapter of this book.

Thus, the present volume includes the following chapters: (One) "Moral Theology: Its Nature, Purpose, and Biblical Foundation"; (Two) "Human Dignity, Free Human Action, Virtue, and Conscience"; (Three) "The Natural Law and Moral Life"; (Four) "Moral Absolutes" (along with two appendices, "St. Thomas and Moral Absolutes" and "Pope John Paul II and Moral Absolutes"); (Five) "Sin and the Moral Life"; (Six) "Christian Faith and Our Moral Life"; (Seven) "The Church as Moral Teacher"; (Eight) "Christian Moral Life and John Paul II's Encyclical *Veritatis Splendor*"; and an appendix, "Christian Moral Life and the *Catechism of the Catholic Church*."

In Chapter Four, I have adapted and revised material originally published in my 1989 Pere Marquette Lecture in Theology, *Moral Absolutes: Catholic Tradition, Current Trends, and the Truth* (Milwaukee: Marquette University Press, 1989). Chapter Five incorporates material first published in my article entitled "Sin," which appeared in the *New Dictionary of Theology*, edited by Joseph Komanchak and others (Wilmington, DE: Michael Glazier, 1987). Permission to use this material is gratefully acknowledged.

I want to take note of important English works on moral theology:

- In my own opinion, the most important post-Vatican II work in English in the field of moral theology is that of Germain Grisez. His multivolume work, *The Way of the Lord Jesus*, now embraces three very large volumes (each around a thousand pages): Volume 1, *Christian Moral Principles*, on which I was privileged to help him to some extent, was published in 1983 by Franciscan Herald Press of Chicago. That press is now defunct, but all three volumes are now published by the Franciscan Press of Quincy University, Quincy, Illinois. *Christian Moral Principles* deals with issues of fundamental moral theology and is most relevant to matters taken up in this book. A summary, prepared by Grisez and Russell Shaw, was published under the title *Fulfillment in Christ* by Notre Dame University Press in 1991. Grisez's Volume 2, *Living a Christian Life*, was published in 1993. It considers specific moral issues of concern to *all* Christians, lay or clergy, and takes up responsibilities pertaining to faith, hope, love, penance and reconciliation, prudence, justice and mercy, equal dignity and communication, human life and health (the chapter is a small treatise in bioethics), marriage and sexual ethics (another chapter of book length and superb quality), subhuman nature and work, and civic life. Volume 3, *Difficult*

Moral Questions, was published in 2000, and contains detailed analyses of two hundred specific questions faced by *lay* Catholics in living out their vocation to holiness. A fourth volume, concerned with responsibilities pertaining to clerical and consecrated life and service, is in preparation but will not be published until about 2008.

- In 1995, The Catholic University of America Press published an English translation, entitled *The Sources of Christian Ethics,* of the Dominican theologian Servais Pinckaers's well-respected *Les Sources de la Morale Chrètienne,* originally published in French in 1985. Père Pinckaers's work has three major parts. In the first, he discusses the nature of moral theology and the meaning of the *Christian* moral life as presented by St. Paul, St. Augustine, and St. Thomas Aquinas. Part Two provides an enlightening and comprehensive history of moral theology, and Part Three considers in depth Aquinas's understanding of human freedom and natural law. Pinckaers's book is very useful and excellent; I believe, however, that his treatment of St. Thomas's thought on natural law in Part Three is in many ways inadequate and is the weakest part of the book.

- Benedict Ashley, O.P., a very erudite Dominican theologian, published his *Living the Truth in Love: A Biblical Introduction to Moral Theology* in 1996 (Staten Island, NY: Alba House). Ashley's work not only covers issues in fundamental moral theology but also offers overviews of Catholic sexual ethics, bioethics, and social ethics. As a result, it provides a panoramic view of the Catholic moral life but lacks the depth needed for an adequate treatment of many of the matters addressed. Although subtitled "A Biblical Introduction to Moral Theology," it is in essence a presentation of moral theology according to the theological virtues of faith, hope, and charity, and the cardinal virtues of prudence, justice, temperance, and fortitude — in essence the schema adopted by St. Thomas. Ashley cleverly introduces the virtues via the biblical account of them. His book is useful and fully in accord with magisterial teaching.

- Romanus Cessario, O.P., has recently published *An Introduction to Moral Theology,* the first of a new series of texts in Catholic moral thought published by The Catholic University of America Press. Cessario provides a fine account of what moral theology is and a particularly good treatment of the virtues. However, he fails to consider in any formal way the problem of sin, and his account of Aquinas's natural law thought and of how human intentions specify the "object" of a moral act is in my opinion inadequate. This work, also fully in harmony with Catholic moral teaching, is a welcome addition to the literature.

- Fordham University Press, in 2000, brought out an excellent English translation, *Natural Law and Practical Reason: A Thomist View of Moral Autonomy*, of Martin Rhonheimer's *Natur als Grundlage der Moral*. Rhonheimer, a Swiss philosopher/theologian, is among the most important interpreters of Aquinas's thought writing today. In my chapter on natural law, I have sought to provide a summary appreciation of his contribution.

Finally, I want to thank all who have helped me in writing this work. For the earlier editions, the help given by Germain Grisez, John Finnis, and Ramón García de Háro was invaluable. In preparing this revision, I have been greatly helped once more by Germain Grisez, a true friend, and by my former student Mark Latkovic, professor of moral theology at Sacred Heart Seminary in Detroit. I also appreciate the help of two of my former students: the Rev. Paul deLadurantaye, director of religious education for the Arlington, Virginia, diocese and lecturer in moral theology at the Notre Dame Catechetical Institute of Christendom College; and the Rev. Emmanuel Afunugo, professor of moral theology at St. Vincent's Seminary, Latrobe, Pennsylvania. I also wish to thank my students for their encouragement, intelligent questions, and stimulation, and in particular Robert Plich, O.P., a Polish Dominican completing doctoral studies at the John Paul II Institute for Studies on Marriage and Family at The Catholic University of America, Washington, D.C. Father Plich, as my research assistant the past year, has been of great help to me.

KEY TO ABBREVIATIONS OF BIBLICAL BOOKS
(IN ALPHABETICAL ORDER)

Old Testament Books

Am — Amos
Bar — Baruch
1 Chr — 1 Chronicles
2 Chr — 2 Chronicles
Dn — Daniel
Dt — Deuteronomy
Eccl — Ecclesiastes
Es — Esther
Ex — Exodus
Ez — Ezekiel
Ezr — Ezra
Gn — Genesis
Hb — Habakkuk
Hg — Haggai
Hos — Hosea
Is — Isaiah
Jer — Jeremiah
Jb — Job
Jdt — Judith
Jgs — Judges
Jl — Joel
Jon — Jonah
Jos — Joshua

1 Kgs — 1 Kings
2 Kgs — 2 Kings
Lam — Lamentations
Lv — Leviticus
Mal — Malachi
1 Mc — 1 Maccabees
2 Mc — 2 Maccabees
Mi — Micah
Na — Nahum
Neh — Nehemiah
Nm — Numbers
Ob — Obadiah
Prv — Proverbs
Ps — Psalms
Ru — Ruth
Sg — Song of Songs
Sir — Sirach
1 Sm — 1 Samuel
2 Sm — 2 Samuel
Tb — Tobit
Wis — Wisdom
Zec — Zechariah
Zep — Zephaniah

New Testament Books

Acts — Acts of the Apostles
Col — Colossians
1 Cor — 1 Corinthians
2 Cor — 2 Corinthians
Eph — Ephesians
Gal — Galatians
Heb — Hebrews
Jas — James
Jn — John
1 Jn — 1 John
2 Jn — 2 John
3 Jn — 3 John
Jude — Jude
Lk — Luke

Mk — Mark
Mt — Matthew
Phil — Philippians
Phlm — Philemon
1 Pt — 1 Peter
2 Pt — 2 Peter
Rom — Romans
Rv — Revelation
1 Thes — 1 Thessalonians
2 Thes — 2 Thessalonians
Ti — Titus
1 Tm — 1 Timothy
2 Tm — 2 Timothy

CHAPTER ONE

Moral Theology: Its Nature, Purpose, and Biblical Foundation

The Moral Life — An Introductory Description

I believe that our moral life, if viewed from the perspective of a person seeking to be morally upright, can be described as an endeavor, cognitively, to come to know who we are and what we are to do if we are to be fully the beings we are meant to be, and, conatively, to do what we ourselves come to know we are to do if we are to become fully the beings we are meant to be.

Describing the moral life in this way rests, of course, on some presuppositions. It presupposes that we do not know, when we come into being, who we are and what we are to do if we are to be fully the beings we are meant to be, but that we have the capacity to find out. It further presupposes that we are not, when we come into existence, fully the beings we are meant to be, but that we are capable of becoming such. In addition, it presupposes that we have a destiny to which we are summoned in the depths of our being. And, finally, it presupposes that we are in charge of our own destiny, that we can, through our own free, self-determining choices, shape our own lives.

In both (1) our cognitive endeavor to come to know who we are and what we are to do if we are to be fully the beings we are meant to be and (2) our conative effort to do what we come to know we ought to do if we are to be fully the beings we are meant to be, we can be both crippled or disabled and helped or enabled. Sin — original, personal, social — is, as we shall see, the great disabling factor in these endeavors. The God made known in Jesus Christ is, as we shall also see, the great enabling factor in these endeavors. And an enabling factor, too, is the Church, Jesus' beloved spouse. All this is matter to be taken up in this book.

❖ ❖ ❖

THE NATURE, PURPOSE, AND RENEWAL OF MORAL THEOLOGY

1. Who We Are and Who We Are Meant to Be in the Light of Faith

The systematic effort to discover who we are and what we are to do if we are to be fully the beings we are meant to be is, when carried out exclusively by the use of human intelligence, the domain of moral philosophy or ethics. When this effort is systematically undertaken by those whose human intelligence is informed by Christian faith, it is the work of moral theology. But before considering more precisely the nature of theology and in particular the nature of moral theology, I want to first briefly indicate how Christian faith helps us in our cognitive endeavor to discover who we are and what we are to do if we are to become fully the beings we are meant to be, i.e., the beings *God himself wants us to be.*

In the light of faith, we know *who we are.* We are the only creatures made "in the image of God" (Gn 1:27), the "only creature on earth that God has wanted for its own sake" (*Gaudium et spes*, no. 24). Through faith, we know that God created man "as an intelligent and free being" and that, over and above this, man "is called as a son to intimacy with God and to share in his happiness" (*Gaudium et spes*, no. 21). We know, in other words, that we are not only unique among earthly beings in our dignity as persons made in God's image and likeness but also unique among earthly beings in being called to be God's very own children. Indeed, as the Fathers of Vatican Council II have reminded us, "it is only in the mystery of the Word made flesh that the mystery of man truly becomes clear. . . . Christ the new Adam," they continue, "in the very revelation of the mystery of the Father and of his love, fully reveals man to himself and brings to light his most high calling" (*Gaudium et spes*, no. 22).

In other words, through faith we know that we are not only persons made in God's image and likeness but, by reason of our intimate union with Christ, God's only-begotten Son made man, truly *children of God, members of the divine family, called to life eternal with Father, Son, and Spirit.* To put matters another way, through faith we know that, if we fully become the beings God wants us to be, we will be, as it were, other Christs, for the Risen Jesus is now the being we are meant to be. The Council Fathers expressed this idea in some memorable passages immediately following their affirmation that Christ "fully reveals man to himself and brings to light his most high calling." I cite them here because I believe that they provide us with Christian faith's answer to the questions "Who are we?" and "Who are we called to be?"

He [Christ], who is the "image of the invisible God" (Col 1:15), is himself the perfect man who has restored in the children of Adam that likeness to God which had been disfigured ever since the first sin. Human nature, by the very fact that it was assumed, not absorbed, in him, has been raised up in us also to a dignity beyond compare. For, by his incarnation, he, the Son of God, has in a certain way united himself with each man. He worked with human hands, he thought with a human mind. He acted with a human will, and with a human heart he loved. Born of the Virgin Mary, he has truly been made one of us, like to us in all things except sin.

As an innocent lamb, he merited life for us by his blood which he freely shed. In him God reconciled us to himself and to one another, freeing us from the bondage of the devil and of sin, so that each of us could say with the apostle: the Son of God "loved me and gave himself for me" (Gal 2:20). By suffering for us he not only gave us an example so that we might follow in his footsteps, but he also opened up a way. If we follow this path, life and death are made holy and acquire a new meaning.

Conformed to the image of the Son who is the firstborn of many brothers, the Christian man receives the "first fruits of the Spirit" (Rom 8:23) by which he is able to fulfill the new law of love. By this Spirit, who is the "pledge of our inheritance" (Eph 1:14), the whole man is inwardly renewed, right up to the "redemption of the body" (Rom 8:23). . . . The Christian is certainly bound both by need and by duty to struggle with evil through many afflictions and to suffer death; but, as one who has been made a partner in the paschal mystery, and as one who has been configured to the death of Christ, he will go forward, strengthened by hope, to the resurrection.

All this holds true not for Christians only but for all men of good will in whose hearts grace is active invisibly. For since Christ died for all, and since all men are in fact called to one and the same destiny, which is divine, we must hold that the Holy Spirit offers to all the possibility of being made partners, in a way known to God, in the paschal mystery [*Gaudium et spes*, no. 22].

Thus, in light of the Christian faith we can say that we are beings who are not only made in the image and likeness of God, but that we are also called, in Christ, *to be his very own children, members of the divine family*. And in being called to be fully the beings we are meant to be, we are called to be *other Christs*, i.e., faithful children of the Father, whose only will is, like Jesus', to do what is pleasing to the Father, and in this way share in the glory of the Risen Christ in a life of unending beauty in the communion of persons who are the Holy Trinity. And what must we do to be pleasing to the Father and to become fully what God wants us to be, i.e., other Christs? The short answer is that we must love as Christ has loved us and shape our choices and actions in accordance with his loving commands.

2. Theology and Moral Theology

I have just said that through faith we know *who we are and who we are called to be* if we are to become fully the beings we are meant to be, for through faith we know ourselves to be children of God, called to a life of eternal happiness in union with the Triune God of Father, Son, and Holy Spirit revealed to us in the life, death, and resurrection of Jesus Christ. Our faith, however, is not opposed to reason but is in harmony with it.[1] The desire of Christians to understand their faith has given birth to theology. Literally, *theology* means "talk about God," and in the sense in which this word is used by Catholic Christians it means talk about God based on the truths of Catholic faith, whose sources are Scripture and Tradition and which is mediated to us through the teaching of the magisterium of the Church.

It is customary today to divide theology into distinct areas of study, e.g., dogmatic or systematic theology, moral theology, ascetical and mystical theology or spiritual theology. Dogmatic or systematic theology[2] is concerned with truths of "faith" in the sense of revealed truths about God himself and his work of creation and redemption, e.g., the mysteries of the Trinity, the Incarnation, etc.; moral theology deals with human action; ascetical and mystical theology or spiritual theology focuses on our spiritual life, etc. Divisions of this kind, however, are legitimately made only for didactic or pedagogic purposes, and they cannot take away the radical unity of theology, nor can they be allowed to do so. The truths of salvation —which are ordinarily taken up in so-called "dogmatic" or "systematic" theology — are absolutely central to understanding the Christian moral life. Christian morality is an integral part of the doctrine of salvation and cannot be separated from the whole of divine revelation. Moreover, the Christian moral life, if lived fully, is a life of holiness or sanctity; hence, the notion that "spiritual" theology, or the theology of the spiritual life, is separate from moral theology is quite false.[3]

3. The Function and Purpose of Moral Theology

Moral theology is a systematic reflection on the Christian moral life. As Grisez says, it seeks "to make clear how faith should shape Christian life, both the lives of individuals and the life of the Church."[4] It seeks to help us come to know, through the exercise of reason enlightened by faith, what we are *to do* if we are to be faithful children of God and become fully the beings we are meant to be, i.e., other Christs, called to eternal life in and with him. It is thus concerned with human actions. It is so because, as we will see more clearly in the next chapter, we make ourselves *to be the persons we are in and through the acts we freely choose to do*. Indeed, as St. Gregory of Nyssa says in a memorable passage cited by Pope John Paul II in *Veritatis splendor*:

> All things subject to change and to becoming never remain constant, but continually pass from one state to another, for better or worse. . . . Now, human life is always subject to change; it needs to be born ever anew. . . . But here birth does not come about by a foreign intervention, as is the case with bodily beings . . .; it is the result of free choice. Thus *we are* in a certain way our own parents, creating ourselves as we will, by our decisions.[5]

It thus follows that moral theology is occupied in great measure with human conduct and with the principles and norms or moral *truths* meant to help us make good moral choices about what we are to do if we are to become fully other Christs, the beings God wants us to be as members of the divine family, within the communion of persons centered on the Blessed Trinity. Moral theology, in other words, is greatly concerned with human acts, which are like "words"[6] that we speak and in and through which we freely give to ourselves our identity.

To put it another way: We become fully the beings we are meant to be — i.e., other Christs — in and through the actions we freely choose to do. Thus, moral theology is preeminently concerned with helping us come to know, through the use of reason enlightened by faith, the *truths* that will enable us to make true moral judgments and good moral choices; it is likewise concerned with those factors that help (e.g., God's divine grace, virtues) or hinder us (e.g., sin, vices) to do so.

From this we can see that the ultimate purpose of moral theology is to be of service to the Christian faithful in their struggle, with the help of God's never-failing grace, to become holy, to become saints, to become fully the beings God wants them to be: his faithful children, fit to enter into a communion of persons with him.

I want now to consider briefly the renewal of moral theology called for by Vatican Council II forty years ago and by Pope John Paul II throughout his long pontificate.

4. The Renewal of Moral Theology

There is no need here to discuss in any detail the reasons why the Fathers of Vatican Council II, in their efforts to revitalize the Church, were very concerned with reinvigorating and "renewing" Catholic theology as a whole and, in particular, moral theology. Briefly put, one can justly say that at the time the

Council took place many had lost sight of the unity of theology and in particular of the need to "return to its sources," i.e., Sacred Scripture and Tradition. In addition, many had lost sight of the intimate bonds linking the different components of theology together, particularly the bonds uniting the truths of salvation to the moral life, and the unity of the moral and spiritual life.

The Council Fathers thus called for a revision of the studies undertaken by men preparing for the priesthood, the "ecclesiastical" disciplines of philosophy and theology. And it is important to realize that in calling for a renewal of the studies future priests should take in order to exercise properly their pastoral care of the faithful entrusted to them, the Council Fathers explicitly included the study of philosophy. They thus declared: "In the revision of ecclesiastical studies the main object to be kept in mind is a more effective coordination of philosophy and theology so that they supplement one another in revealing to the minds of the students with an ever-increasing clarity the Mystery of Christ, which affects the whole course of human history, exercises an unceasing influence on the Church, and operates mainly through the ministry of the priest" (*Optatam totius*, no. 14). Insisting on the fact that theology can be done well only if rooted in a sound philosophy, they continued by saying:

> Philosophical subjects should be taught in such a way as to lead the students gradually to a solid and consistent knowledge of man, the world, and God. . . . The teaching method adopted should stimulate in the students a love of rigorous investigation, observation and demonstration of the truth, as well as an honest recognition of the limits of human knowledge. . . . *The students themselves should be helped to perceive the connection between philosophical arguments and the mysteries of salvation which theology considers in the higher light of faith* [ibid., no. 15].

I have emphasized the final sentence of this paragraph because it shows us that there is a bond between the philosophical study of human morality (ethics) and moral theology. In light of the truths of faith, we can, to be sure, show that certain philosophical moral theories are false insofar as they are incompatible with the faith, and we can also show the limitations of some philosophical ethical theories and positions. Nonetheless, sound philosophical analyses of human acts, of the sources of their morality, and the meaning of a virtuous life are an indispensable help to the development of moral theology. The law of love or of the gospel in no way annuls or sets aside the natural law; rather, it helps us to come to a better grasp of the truths of the natural law and at the same time "fulfills" or "perfects" it in a wondrous way (as will be seen later in this book).

John Paul II has developed this great teaching of Vatican Council II, particularly in his encyclical *Fides et Ratio*, where we read, for instance, the following at the conclusion of Chapter III, entitled "Credo ut Intelligam" ("I believe that I may understand"):

> [The] truth, which God reveals to us in Jesus Christ, is not opposed to the truths philosophy perceives. On the contrary, the two modes of knowledge lead to truth in all its fullness. The unity of truth is a fundamental premise of human reasoning, as the principle of non-contradiction makes clear. Revelation renders this unity certain, showing that the God of creation is also the God of salvation history. It is the one and same God who establishes and guarantees the intelligibility and reasonableness of the natural order of things upon which scientists confidently depend, and who reveals himself as the Father of our Lord Jesus Christ . . . [no. 34].

John Paul II then devotes Chapter IV of *Fides et Ratio*, entitled "The Relationship Between Faith and Reason," to the relationship between revealed truth and philosophical learning. At the end of this very important chapter, he says that when reason is deprived of what revelation has to offer, "reason has taken sidetracks which expose it to the danger of losing sight of its final goal [to help us come to know more fully the meaning of life]." But, he continues, "deprived of reason, faith has stressed feeling and experience, and so runs the risk of no longer being a universal proposition. *It is an illusion to think that faith, tied to weak reasoning, might be more penetrating; on the contrary, faith then runs the grave risk of withering into myth or superstition*" (ibid., no. 48; emphasis added). He therefore makes an appeal "that faith and philosophy recover the profound unity which allows them to stand in harmony with their nature without compromising their mutual autonomy. The *parrhesia* [= freedom] of faith must be matched by the boldness of reason" (ibid.).

Vatican Council II, moreover, drew specific attention to the need to renew the study of moral theology. The Council Fathers declared:

> Special care should be given to the perfecting of moral theology. Its scientific presentation should draw more fully on the teaching of holy Scripture and should throw light upon the exalted vocation of the faithful in Christ and their obligation to bring forth fruit in charity for the life of the world [*Optatam totius*, no. 16].

Although this is the only explicit reference to moral theology made in the sixteen documents of the Council, Matthew Gutowski, in a fine study entitled *Vatican Council II and the Renewal of Moral Theology*,[7] points out:

From that which the Council Fathers say here in *Optatam totius*, a few items are evident about their directions for the renewal of moral theology. The use here of the phrase "the lofty vocation of the Christian faithful and their obligation to bring forth fruit in charity" parallels the Council's pronouncement that all Christians are called to holiness, which is one of the principal teachings of Vatican II and is found particularly in *Lumen gentium*, the Dogmatic Constitution on the Church (nos. 39-42). And the insistence that moral theology "draw more fully on the teaching of Holy Scripture," for the purpose of emphasizing the vocation to holiness, reflects two other key facets of the Council's teaching: first, the point that *Lumen gentium* recognizes that this call is central to the Scriptures (nos. 39-40) and, second, the proclamation that Sacred Scripture is to be the very heart and soul of theology, as stated earlier in *Optatam totius* (no. 16) and as found in *Dei Verbum*, the Dogmatic Constitution on Divine Revelation (no. 24). The Council Fathers make it clear that a Catholic moral theology true to its mission, by rooting itself in Scripture, should cast light on the vocation of all Christians to holiness, to sanctity; in other words, a genuine moral theology must be a genuine spiritual theology that is first nourished by Scripture [pp. 1-2].

In order to show more fully how Vatican II regarded moral theology, Gutowski then studied in depth (1) the *Acta* of the Council, where we find the reactions of various Council Fathers to the preparatory schema, *De ordine morali*, and likewise their criticisms of the way moral theology was in fact being presented; and (2) different conciliar documents, in particular *Gaudium et spes*, in which the Council Fathers addressed various moral issues. Gutowski then extrapolates from these sources the elements that the Council Fathers were eager to see included in a renewed moral theology as well as their content.

From his examination of the *Acta*, Gutowski was able to extrapolate five pedagogical and methodological elements that constitute what the Council Fathers considered to be integral to the renewal of moral theology:

These five elements are the following: (1) a pastoral and positive presentation; (2) a reliance upon divine revelation as the primary theological source; (3) a Christocentrism and an acknowledgment of the role of the Holy Spirit and grace in the moral life; (4) a personalistic approach; and (5) a highlighting of the vocation to charity by stressing the Lord's commandment of love [p. 95].

Gutowski emphasizes, in expanding on the second element (a reliance upon divine revelation), that the Council Fathers, while insisting that Scripture is the source of moral theology's vitality, made it clear that divine revelation includes more than reference to Scripture alone: "The written word of God is inseparably linked to Sacred Tradition; both together as the supreme rule of the Church's faith are authentically interpreted by the Magisterium, whose definitive teachings are to be faithfully assented to" (p. 97). Moreover, as Gutowski notes, the Fathers also directed that in understanding divine revelation the teaching of the Church Fathers — and in particular, the teaching of St. Thomas Aquinas — provides indispensable help and insight (p. 97).

In seeking to follow the directions of Vatican Council II and Pope John Paul II, therefore, I will try to show the sound philosophical foundations that help the Christian faithful come to a deeper and richer understanding of the truths of the moral life mediated through Christian faith and also to show how the truth about human existence definitively revealed in and through the saving mission of Christ and the new law of grace and love "perfect" and "fulfill" the "natural law" written on our hearts. As we have seen already, it is indeed Jesus, God's eternal Word-made-man, become, like us, a "created word" of the Father, who reveals to us who we really are. And one way of coming to know Jesus is to meditate on the Scriptures — in particular, the New Testament, wherein the promises made through the prophets of the Old Testament come to fulfillment. I thus hope to root the moral theology presented in this book in the Scriptures — in particular, the New Testament. I seek to do this primarily in Chapter Six, below, which treats of Christian faith and the moral life — and in particular, with Jesus as the foundation of our moral life and with his Sermon on the Mount as the "*magna carta*" of the Christian moral life. It will, however, be useful to conclude this opening chapter by briefly considering how moral theology is rooted in Sacred Scripture.

MORAL THEOLOGY AND HOLY SCRIPTURE

The Church teaches that *all Scripture* is inspired by the Holy Spirit and that it provides us with the truths necessary for our salvation. "We must acknowledge," Vatican Council II instructs us, "that the books of Scripture firmly, faithfully and without error, teach that truth which God, *for the sake of our salvation*, wished to see confided to the sacred Scriptures. Thus 'all Scripture is inspired by God, and profitable for teaching, for reproof, for correction and for training in righteousness, so that the man of God may be complete, equipped for every good work' (2 Tm 3:16-17, Gk text)" (*Dei Verbum* [Dogmatic Constitution on Divine Revelation], no. 11; emphasis added). This means that it includes the moral truths necessary for our salvation. In particular, the gospels, although not intended to give us a "biography" of Jesus, present an accurate portrait of him and offer him as the model of the moral life required of his disciples. Thus, the Church insists on the historical accuracy of the gospel narratives, as this passage from Vatican Council II makes very clear:

> Holy Mother Church has firmly and with absolute constancy held, and continues to hold, that the four Gospels just named, whose historical character the Church unhesitatingly asserts, faithfully hand on what Jesus Christ, while living among men, really did and taught for their eternal salvation until the day he was taken up into heaven (see Acts 1:1-2). Indeed, after the ascension of the Lord the apostles handed on to their hearers what he had said and done. This they did with that clearer understanding which they enjoyed after they had been instructed by the events of Christ's risen life and taught by the light of the Spirit of truth. The sacred authors wrote the four Gospels, selecting some things from the many which had been handed on by word of mouth or in writing, reducing some of them to a synthesis, explicating some things in view of the situation of their churches, and preserving the form of proclamation but always in such fashion that they told us the honest truth about Jesus. For their intention in writing was that either from their own memory and recollections, or from the witness of those who themselves "from the beginning were eyewitnesses and ministers of the word" we might know "the truth" concerning those matters about which we have been instructed (cf. Lk 1:2-4) [Dei Verbum, no. 19].

The Pontifical Biblical Commission's 1964 *Instruction on the Historical Truth of the Gospels* is instructive here. In this document, the Commission affirmed: "From the results of the new investigations it is apparent that the doctrine and the life of Jesus were not simply reported for the sole purpose of being remembered, but were 'preached' so as to offer the Church a basis of faith *and of morals*" (emphasis added).[8]

Jesus definitively reveals to us God's wise and loving plan for human existence and redeems us from sin, establishing with us a new and lasting covenant. But the way for Jesus had been prepared in and through God's covenant with the people Israel. Thus, here I will review the nature of this covenant and its requirements in order to show how the moral life was understood in the Old Testament.[9]

In the ancient Near East, the spoken word was invested with great solemnity and could not be annulled or retracted.[10] The covenant was a solemn ritual agreement guaranteed by the spoken word.[11] The covenanting parties bound themselves by a treaty or an alliance that included severe sanctions on the party who should violate its stipulations. Such covenants among men appear throughout much of the Old Testament, and the relationship among men thereby established was transferred by the Israelites to identify the relationship between Yahweh and the people Israel. There were covenants between Yahweh and Noah (Gn 6:18) and between Yahweh and Abraham (Gn 15:lff); but the covenant between Yahweh and the people Israel was the covenant of Sinai (Ex 19:1ff),[12] and the laws that are placed in the book of Exodus after this event are called the covenant code (Ex 20-24).[13] The major stipulations of the covenant are the Ten Commandments (Ex 20:1-17), which require the people's exclusive loyalty to God and also regulate relationships among God's people, who must preserve unity to remain in common allegiance to their covenant Lord. Chapter 24 of Exodus completes the account of the covenant. The agreement between Yahweh God and his people is read, the people accept it, the covenant is sealed with the blood of bulls, sprinkled upon both the people and the altar. This blood is life, the vital principle (see Gn 9:4), and thus it brings the covenant to life and puts it in force.[14]

Through the covenant, which he initiates, God calls Israel to partnership with him. He will be their God, their protector, and they will be his people. Their relationship, as prophets like Hosea, Jeremiah, and Ezekiel show us, is analogous to that of husband and wife in marriage: it is a love-based union and requires utmost fidelity. Israel's entire existence is rooted in Yahweh's choice to give himself to this people, the descendants of Abraham with whom he had made a personal covenant. By his sovereign power, Yahweh speaks, and Israel comes into being as *his people.*

Yahweh's act of love is that of a unique, wholly other sovereign, the only God there is, the one who is to be loved and worshipped above everything. The people to whom he has espoused himself, in receiving his offer of faithful love and friendship, respond in awe and gratitude for the unexpected generosity given them. This relationship naturally brings with it the expectations and requirements of the sovereign God who initiated it. As a covenant partner of Yahweh, Israel is a people defined by obedience. They must listen to God, hear his voice, and become a light to the nations, bearing witness in their lives to his merciful love and fidelity.[15]

The covenant requires obedience to the commandments given to the people by God through Moses on Sinai. The stipulations of the covenant, summarized in the Ten Commandments or "ten words" (cf. Ex 20:1), require the people to love Yahweh God above all and to have no strange gods before him, to honor their parents, to forbear killing the innocent and the just (Ex 20:13 in light of Ex 23:7), not to commit adultery or bear false witness or steal, etc. But the requirements of the covenant, epitomized in the Decalogue, affected the whole of Israel's life. The God who had espoused himself to them wanted sacrifice, to be sure, but more than this he required them to care for the widowed and orphaned and to love the stranger in the land (cf. Dt 10:17-19). Indeed, as Walter Bruggemann so well says, "It is clear that in these most radical injunctions [to execute justice for the orphan and the widows, etc.], understood as Israel's covenantal obligations, the wealth and social resources of Israel are understood not in privatistic or acquisitive ways, but as common resources that are to be managed and deployed for the enhancement of the community by the enhancement of its weakest and most disadvantaged members."[16]

It is essential to keep in mind that although the covenant contains stipulations requiring a certain way of life, their fulfillment is not a condition for entering the covenant with God but rather a demand arising from the relationship with God freely accepted by the people. As Germain Grisez points out, "God provides a law so that his people can cooperate freely in their valued personal relationship with him. Law is not a burden but a blessing and a real necessity for developing an orderly life in common, especially for people recently freed from slavery and used to arbitrary treatment."[17] Continuing, Grisez makes a most important observation, central to understanding what the moral life, as understood in Scripture, is like. He writes:

> The reason why the requirements of life within the covenant are not impositions is that they follow from what God's people are. Humankind is made in God's image and shares in responsibility for creation (see Gn 1.26-29). Even after sin, the children of Man share in God's glory and enjoy an almost godlike status (see Ps 8.5-10). Under the covenant, the challenge of being like God persists and is heightened for his people: "You shall be holy; for I, the Lord your God am holy" (Lv 19.2). Created in God's image and recalled from sin to his friendship, human persons are expected to be as pure and holy in their lives as God is in his. God's people are expected to follow him.[18]

Yes, God's people are to be "holy." The God of Israel, utterly unlike the "no-gods" of their pagan neighbors, is a holy God, and he wills that his people be, like him, holy. John G. Gammie has provided a comprehensive presentation of the holiness theme in his book *Holiness in Israel*, a volume in the "Overtures to Biblical Theology" series.[19] "Holiness in Israel," Gammie says, "was not first and foremost something for human beings to achieve, but rather that characteristic of ineffability possessed only by God, the Lord of Hosts, the Holy One of Israel." But this all-holy God summoned the people Israel to be holy, and this vocation was a call to aspire to the justice and compassion of Yahweh himself so that his glory could be made manifest. This noble mission given to the people obliged Israel to a "social conduct and individual morality befitting the majesty and dignity of the Most High." The kind of purity or cleanness it required varied according to different authors. The prophets demanded cleanness of social justice; the priests, a cleanness of proper ritual and maintenance of separation; the sages, a cleanness of inner integrity and individual moral acts.[20]

The major idea common to all the Old Testament sources — given God's sovereign holiness and the vocation of his people to be holy so that his glory could be made manifest — is that holiness requires morally upright conduct: justice and mercy, concern for the poor and the weak, personal integrity and fidelity.

The covenant relationship between God and his people in the Old Testament deepens and transforms morality. Grisez well summarizes what this entails:

> All human life is drawn into its context. . . . The [covenantal] relationship causes God's people to share in his qualities, including those which are more than human. Moral insights are deepened, and the richness of human goods [which are indeed God's gifts to his creature man] is unfolded. A fresh perspective is provided for criticizing all conventional morality.[21]

Nonetheless, the covenant between God and the Chosen People was but the preparation for the new and definitive covenant to be made between God and humankind in and through the redemptive work of his only-begotten Son, Jesus Christ. God simply could not complete his redemptive work all at once, but through this covenant he prepared the way for the fulfillment of his promises in Jesus.[22] The new covenant initiated by Jesus "fulfills" and "perfects" the old covenant. As St. Paul makes clear (cf. Rom 7), the old law could not justify sinful mankind. God indeed could save by his grace not only Abraham and the patriarchs but also the Israelites subject to the old law. Nonetheless, the old law did not empower those under it to live good and holy lives. As St. Paul so poignantly reminds us (see Rom 7), the law made the people aware of their moral responsibilities, but it did not give them the power to fulfill them. By contrast, the new covenant in Jesus, true God and true man, does empower the people of the new covenant not only to know but to do what God wants them to do if they are to be the beings they are meant to be, i.e., other Christs, co-redeemers with the Son of God made man. How the new covenant does this will be taken up in depth in Chapter Six of this work, where we will examine the way in which the new "law," the new "covenant," fulfills and perfects the old. But it is important here to reflect briefly on this central teaching of the Bible and its relevance to the moral life.

The New Testament shows us that Jesus of Nazareth, born of a woman and like us in all things save sin, is indeed the only-begotten Son of God made man, the eternally begotten "Word" of God become man, become flesh (*sarx*) (cf. Jn 1:14). In Jesus of Nazareth, God comes personally to visit his people, to become one with them by sharing their human nature, and to redeem them by his saving death and resurrection. Jesus invites us to become one with him, to share in his saving death and resurrection, and to become new creatures through the gift of his Spirit. The epistle to the Ephesians begins by summarizing God's plan for our salvation:

> Blessed be the God and Father of our Lord Jesus Christ, who has blessed us in Christ with every spiritual blessing in the heavenly places, even as he chose us in him before the foundation of the world, that we should be holy and blameless before him. He destined us in love to be his sons through Jesus Christ, according to the purpose of his will, to the praise of his glorious grace which he freely bestowed on us in the Beloved. In him we have redemption through his blood, the forgiveness of our trespasses, according to the riches of his grace which he lavished upon us [Eph 1:3-8].

Indeed, through baptism we "put on" Christ and become new creatures, God's very own children, members of the divine family, living Christ's very own life — a truth developed marvelously and in different ways by various New Testament authors, e.g., by St. Paul, with his teaching on the Church as the "body" of Christ with its many members, and by St. John, with his teaching on the vine and the branches.

As God's adopted children — and so we are by virtue of our union with his only-begotten Son, Jesus Christ (cf. 1 Jn 3:1-2), we are given a new commandment: to love even as Jesus loves us. "This is my commandment, that you love one another as I have loved you" (Jn 15:12). And we can love in this way only if we keep Jesus' commandments and seek, like him, to do only what is pleasing to the Father, who calls us to be holy.

In short, the moral life as understood by the people of the new and eternal covenant is a living imitation or following of Jesus Christ. He is "the way, and the truth, and the life" (Jn 14:6), and if we abide in his love he will abide in us. Our moral task is to complete the work God has begun in us by making us the very brothers and sisters of Christ. By reason of our baptism, we have, as St. Paul tells us, "put on" Christ, and our sublime mission and the meaning of our moral lives as Christians is to keep putting Christ on until we are fully one with him. In Chapter Six, we will develop these key themes of the New Testament understanding of our lives as moral beings.

We need remember, too, that a life lived in union with Christ is possible because he is with us and for us. Thus, with St. Paul we can be "sure that neither death, nor life, nor angels, nor principalities, nor things present, nor things to come, nor powers, nor height, nor depth, nor anything else in all creation, will be able to separate us from the love of God in Christ Jesus our Lord" (Rom 8:38-39).[23]

Conclusion

This chapter has given a concise description/definition of moral theology; its nature, function, and purpose; the kind of renewal of moral theology called for by Vatican Council II and Pope John Paul II; and its relationship to Sacred Scripture. In concluding, it is important to keep in mind the words of Vatican Council II regarding the relationship between the sources of the truths of faith (Scripture and Tradition) and the magisterium. In its Dogmatic Constitution on Divine Revelation (*Dei Verbum*) the Council declared:

> The task of giving an authentic interpretation of the Word of God, whether in its written form or in the form of Tradition, has been entrusted to the living teaching office of the Church alone. Its authority in this matter is exercised in the name of Jesus Christ. Yet this magisterium is not superior to the Word of God, but is its servant. It teaches only what has been handed on to it. At the divine command and with the help of the Holy Spirit, it listens to this devotedly, guards it with dedication and expounds it faithfully. All that it proposes for belief as being divinely revealed is drawn from this single deposit of faith [no. 10].

It can thus be said, with John Paul II, that the "proximate and obligatory norm in the teaching of the faith . . . belongs to the hierarchical magisterium" (*Familiaris Consortio*, no. 73).

Notes for Chapter One

1. This conviction, central to Catholic faith, was developed by the Fathers of the Church and beautifully summarized by St. Anselm of Canterbury in his famous declarations "I believe that I may understand" (*Credo ut intelligam*) and "I understand that I may believe" (*Intelligo ut credam*). It was a major theme of Vatican Council I and was addressed in depth by Pope John Paul II in his encyclical *Fides et Ratio* (1998), in particular in Chapters II, III, and IV.

2. Germain Grisez quite properly, in my opinion, believes that systematic theology ought not be limited to dogmatic theology, insofar as moral theology is systematic, too. He prefers to use the term "contemplative" for "dogmatic." The contemplative theologian seeks to work out a single, coherent view of all of reality in the light of faith. Moral theology, like contemplative theology, is a systematic reflection on the truths of faith, but as Grisez says, "it is less concerned to round out the Christian view of reality than to make clear how faith should shape Christian life, both the lives of individual Christians and the life of the Church" (*The Way of the Lord Jesus*, Vol. 1, *Christian Moral Principles* [Chicago: Franciscan Herald Press, 1983], pp. 5-6).

3. The unity of theology is of critical importance in order to properly understand what moral theology is all about. Many contemporary authors emphasize the unity of theology and the inseparability of contemplative or dogmatic theology from moral theology. On this, see Grisez, *Christian Moral Principles*, pp. 3-7; Ramón García de Háro, *La Vita Cristiana* (Milan: Edizioni Ares, 1995), pp. 16-22; Servais Pinckaers, O.P., *The Sources of Christian Ethics*, trans. Sister Mary Thomas Noble, O.P. (Washington, DC: The Catholic University of America Press, 1995), pp. 1-14; Romanus Cessario, O.P., *An Introduction to Moral Theology* (Washington, DC: The Catholic University of America Press, 2001), pp. 2-16 (Cessario presents in some detail the way St. Thomas Aquinas showed the unity of theology and moral theology's integral role within it).

4. Grisez, *Christian Moral Principles*, p. 6.

5. St. Gregory of Nyssa, *De Vita Moysis*, II, 2-3; *PG* 44, 327-328; cited in *Veritatis splendor*, no. 71.

6. One of the most stimulating post-Vatican II accounts of moral theology speaks of human acts in this way — as "words" that we speak, and we ought to speak words worthy of those to whom God addressed his eternal Word, the Word who gives us life. See Herbert McCabe, O.P., *What Is Ethics All About?* (Cleveland/Washington: Corpus Books, 1969).

7. Matthew Gutowski, *Vatican Council II and the Renewal of Moral Theology*, unpublished S.T.L. thesis at the John Paul II Institute for Studies on Marriage and Family, Washington, DC, 1998.

8. The text of this important document is given in full in a translation provided by Joseph A. Fitzmyer, S.J., in his article "The Biblical Commission's Instruction on the Historical Truth of the Gospels," *Theological Studies* 25 (1964), 386-408 (402-408 provide text of document).

9. A very helpful *theological* reflection on the centrality of the covenant in both the Old and New Testaments and on the way the new covenant in Jesus "fulfills" and "perfects" the old covenant is provided by Germain Grisez in his *Christian Moral Principles*, Chapter 21. I have found his presentation of great value and here liberally make use of it.

10. On the dynamic power of the spoken word in the ancient Semitic world, see the short but powerful article of John L. McKenzie, "Word," in his *Dictionary of the Bible* (Milwaukee: Bruce Publishing Company, 1965), pp. 938-941.

11. On covenant, see Delbert R. Hillers, *The History of a Biblical Idea* (Baltimore: Johns Hopkins University Press, 1969), pp. 28-70; G.E. Mendenhall, "Covenant," *The Interpreter's Dictionary of the Bible* (Nashville, TN: Abingdon, 1962), 1.714-723.

12. Scholars point out that the treaty form of covenant is more perfectly illustrated by Deuteronomy, Chapters 5-28, but the account of the covenant in Exodus in many ways offers parallels with the forming of the new covenant at the Paschal meal of Christ with his disciples in the New Testament and thus serves better for the purposes of moral theology. On the treaty form of covenant, see Dennis J. McCarthy, S.J., *Treaty and Covenant: A Study in Form in the Ancient Oriental Documents and in the Old Testament* (Rome: Pontifical Biblical Institute, 1963), pp. 109-140.

13. For this, see McKenzie, article "Covenant," in his *Dictionary of the Bible*, pp. 153-155.

14. See F. Laubach, "Blood," and G.R. Beasley-Murray, "Sprinkle," *New International Dictionary of New Testament Theology* (Grand Rapids, MI: Zondervan, 1982), 1.220-225.

15. On this, see Walter Brueggemann, *Theology of the Old Testament: Testimony, Dispute, Advocacy* (Minneapolis: Fortress Press, 1997), pp. 414-440.

16. Ibid., p. 422.

17. Grisez, *Christian Moral Principles*, pp. 509-510. Grisez adds an interesting and important footnote at the end of passage cited, in which he says: "For a good treatment of this point and criticism of the excessive polemic of Luther against the law, see Karl Barth, *Ethics*, ed. Dietrich Braun, tr. Geoffrey W. Bromiley (New York: Seabury Press, 1981), 89-93."

18. Ibid., p. 510.

19. John G. Gammie, *Holiness in Israel* (Minneapolis: Fortress, 1989).

20. Ibid., pp. 195-198.

21. Grisez, *Christian Moral Principles*, p. 520; see p. 511.

22. On this, see Pierre Grelot, "Relations between the Old and New Testaments in Jesus Christ," in *Problems and Perspectives of Fundamental Theology*, ed. René Latourelle and Gerald O'Collins, tr. Matthew O'Connell (New York: Paulist Press, 1982), pp. 186-199. For a fine treatment of the limitations of Old Testament morality, see Luke Johnston, "Old Testament Morality," *Catholic Biblical Quarterly* 20 (1968), 19-25.

23. Among sources regarding the Pauline and Johannine way of envisioning the moral life, I believe the following relatively brief essays very helpful: Manuel Miguens, "On Being a Christian and the Moral Life," in *Principles of Catholic*

Moral Life, ed. William E. May (Chicago: Franciscan Herald Press, 1981), pp. 89-112; Francis Martin, "The Integrity of Christian Moral Identity: The First Letter of John and *Veritatis Splendor*," *Communio* 31 (1994), 265-285; William F. Murphy, Jr., "The Pauline Understanding of Appropriated Revelation as a Principle of Christian Moral Action," *Studia Moralia* 39 (2001), 371-409. On St. Paul's teaching on the moral life, one of the finest studies, in my opinion, remains that of George T. Montague, S.M., *Maturing in Christ: St. Paul's Program for Christian Growth* (Milwaukee: Bruce Publishing Company, 1965). Good general works concerned with the moral teaching of the New Testament are Rudolph Schnackenburg, *The Moral Teaching of the New Testament* (New York: Seabury, 1973) and Frank J. Matera, *New Testament Ethics: The Legacies of Jesus and Paul* (Louisville, KY: Westminster John Knox Press, 1996).

CHAPTER TWO

Human Dignity, Free Human Action, Virtue, and Conscience

1. Three Kinds of Human Dignity

According to the Catholic tradition — as found, for example, in St. Thomas Aquinas[1] — there is a threefold dignity proper to human persons: (1) the first is intrinsic, natural, inalienable, and an endowment or gift; (2) the second is also intrinsic, but it is an achievement, not an endowment — an achievement made possible, given the reality of original sin and its effects, only by God's unfailing grace; (3) the third, again an intrinsic dignity, is also a gift, not an achievement, but it is a gift far surpassing man's nature and literally divinizing him — it is, moreover, given to him as a treasure he must guard and nurture and which he can lose by freely choosing to sin gravely.

The first dignity proper to human beings is the dignity that is theirs simply as living members of the human species, which God called into being when, in the beginning, he "created man in his own image . . . male and female he created them" (Gn 1:27).[2] Every living human body, the one that comes to be when new human life is conceived, is a living word of God. Moreover, in creating man, male and female, God created a being inwardly capable of receiving our Lord's own divine life (see below on the third dignity predicable of human beings). God cannot become incarnate in a pig or cow or an ape because these creatures of his are not inwardly capable of being divinized. But, as we know from God's revelation, he can become incarnate in his human creature, and in fact he has freely chosen to become truly one of us, for his Eternal and Uncreated Word, true God of true God, became and *is* a human being, a man. Thus, every human being can rightly be called a "created word" of God, the created word that his Uncreated Word became and is precisely to show us how deeply we are loved by the God who formed us in our mothers' wombs (cf. Ps 139:11-18). Every human being, therefore, is intrinsically valuable, surpassing in dignity the entire material universe, a being to be revered and respected from the very beginning of its existence.[3]

This intrinsic, inalienable dignity proper to human beings is God's gift, in virtue of which every human being, of whatever age or sex or condition, is a being of moral worth, an irreplaceable and nonsubstitutable person. Because of this dignity, a human person, as Karol Wojtyla has said, "is the kind of good that does not admit of use and cannot be treated as an object of use and as such a means to an end." Because of this dignity, a human person "is a good toward which the only adequate response is love."[4]

When we come into existence, we *are* already, by reason of this intrinsic dignity, *persons*; we do not "become" persons after a period of development. As God's "created words," as persons, we are endowed with the capacity to discover the truth and the capacity to determine our own lives by freely choosing to conform our lives and actions to the truth. A baby (born or preborn) does not, of course, have the *developed* capacity for deliberating and choosing freely, but it has the natural capacity to do so because it is human and personal in nature.[5] Yet when we come into existence we are *not yet* fully the beings we are meant to be. And this leads us to consider the second sort of dignity proper to human beings, a dignity that is also intrinsic but is an achievement, not an endowment.

The second kind of dignity is the dignity to which we are called as intelligent and free persons capable of determining our own lives by our own free choices. This is the dignity we are to *give to ourselves* (with the help of God's never-failing grace) by freely choosing to shape our choices and actions in accord with the truth. In other words, we give to ourselves this dignity and inwardly participate in it by making good moral choices, and such choices are in turn dependent upon true moral judgments.

The nature of this dignity has been beautifully developed by the Fathers of Vatican Council II and by Pope John Paul II, particularly in his encyclical *Veritatis splendor*, and a summary of their teaching will help us grasp the crucial importance of making true moral judgments and good moral choices if we are to respect our God-given dignity and participate in the dignity to which we are called as intelligent and free persons.

In a document hailed by almost everyone as one of the most important of the entire Council — namely, the Declaration on Religious Liberty (*Dignitatis humanae*) — the Council Fathers declared: "The highest norm of human life is the divine law — eternal, objective, and universal — whereby God orders, directs, and governs the entire universe and all the ways of the human community according to a plan conceived in wisdom and in love." Immediately after affirming this truth, the Council Fathers went on to say: "Man has been made by God to participate in this law, with the result that, under the gentle disposition of divine providence, he can come to perceive ever increasingly the unchanging truth" (no. 3). Precisely because he can come "to perceive ever increasingly the unchanging truth," man "has the duty, and therefore the right, to seek the truth" (ibid.). The truth in question here is evidently not a contemplative or speculative truth but a truth that is to shape and guide human choices and actions, i.e., a *practical* truth.

This passage concludes by saying: "On his part, man perceives and acknowledges the imperatives of the divine law through the mediation of conscience" (ibid.). The role of conscience in helping us to know the "unchanging truth" of God's divine and eternal law and its "imperatives" is developed in another document of the Council, the Pastoral Constitution on the Church in the Modern World (*Gaudium et spes*). There we find the following important passage:

> Deep within his conscience man discovers a law which he has not laid upon himself but which he must obey. The voice of this law,[6] ever calling him to love and to do what is good and to avoid evil, tells him inwardly at the right moment, do this, shun that. For man has in his heart a law written by God. *His dignity lies in observing this law*, and by it he will be judged. His conscience is man's most secret core, and his sanctuary. There he is alone with God, whose voice echoes in his depths. By conscience, in a wonderful way, that law is made known which is fulfilled in the love of God and of one's neighbor [no. 16; emphasis added].

Fidelity to conscience means a "search for the truth," and for "true solutions" to moral problems. Conscience, this passage notes, can indeed err "through invincible ignorance without losing its dignity" (so long as there is sufficient "care for the search for the true and the good"); but "to the extent that a correct conscience holds sway, persons and groups turn away from blind choice and seek to conform to the objective norms of morality" (ibid.).

Such, according to Vatican Council II, is the second kind of dignity proper to human persons. This dignity is acquired by diligently seeking the truth about what we are to do if we are to be fully the beings we are meant to be and by shaping our lives freely in accordance with this truth. According to the Council, the human person has the capacity of inwardly participating in God's divine and eternal law — the "highest norm of human life." It maintains that this capacity of human persons is related to their "conscience," for it is through the "mediation" of conscience that human persons come to know ever increasingly the "imperatives" of God's law.

Reflecting on conscience as "man's most secret core" where "he is alone with God," Pope John Paul II writes as follows in his encyclical *Veritatis splendor*:

> The importance of this interior *dialogue of man with himself* can never be adequately appreciated. But it is also a *dialogue of man with God*, the author of the law. . . . It can be said that conscience bears witness to man's own rectitude or iniquity to man himself, but, together with this and indeed even beforehand, conscience is the *witness of God himself*, whose

voice and judgment penetrate the depths of man's soul, calling him *forti-ter et suaviter* to obedience [no. 58].

John Paul II likewise insists that "it is always from the truth that the dignity of conscience derives" (ibid. no. 63).

Later in this chapter, after considering the reality of free choice and the role of virtue in the moral life, I will return to the subject of conscience in order to consider it more fully; and in the following chapter I will examine in depth the meaning of natural law as humankind's participation in God's divine and eternal law. Before considering free choice and the role of virtue in the moral life in this chapter, however, it is necessary to reflect on the third kind of dignity predicable of human persons.

This is the dignity we have as "children of God," brothers and sisters of Jesus, members of the divine family. This kind of dignity is a purely gratuitous gift from God himself, who gives this to us when, through baptism, we are "re-generated" as God's very own children and given the vocation to become holy, even as the heavenly Father is holy, and to be co-workers with Christ, his collaborators in redeeming the world. This dignity is a treasure entrusted to us, and we can lose it by freely choosing to do what is gravely evil. There is a close bond between this kind of dignity and the second kind of dignity proper to us as intelligent and free persons. This kind of dignity, our dignity as God's very own children, will be developed at length in Chapter Six, "Christian Faith and Our Moral Life."

I now will look more closely at the meaning of free choice, for it is by freely choosing to observe God's law — his wise and loving plan for human existence — as this is made known to us that we acquire the dignity to which we are called as intelligent and free persons, and which is inextricably linked, as will be seen later, to our incomparable dignity as God's children.

2. Free Choice

A central truth of Christian revelation is that human persons, created in the image and likeness of God, have the power of free choice. In order to create a being to whom he could give his own life, God created persons (angelic and human) who have the power to make or break their own lives by their own free choices. Persons are of themselves, *sui iuris*, i.e., in their own power or dominion. Their choices and actions are their own, not the choices and actions of others. If God's offer of his own life and friendship is to be a gift, it must be freely received; it cannot be forced on another or settled by anything other than the free choices of the one who gives and the one who receives.

The truth that human persons have the capacity to determine their own lives through their own free choices is a matter of Catholic faith. It is central to the Scriptures, as the following passage from the book of Sirach, cited by the Fathers of Vatican II in *Gaudium et spes* (no. 17), shows:

> Do not say, "Because of the Lord I left the right way"; / for he will not do what he hates. / Do not say, "It was he who led me astray"; / for he has no need of sinful man. / The Lord hates all abominations, / and they are not loved by those who fear him. / It was he who created man in the beginning, / and he left him in the power of his own inclination. / If you will, you can keep the commandments, / and to act faithfully is a matter of your own choice. / He has placed before you fire and water: / stretch out your hand for whichever you wish. / Before a man are life and death, and whichever he chooses will be given to him. / For great is the wisdom of the Lord; / he is mighty in power and sees everything; / his eyes are on those who fear him, / and he knows every deed of man. / He has not commanded any one to be ungodly, / and he has not given any one permission to sin [Sir 15:11-20].

The reality of free choice, so central to the biblical understanding of man, was clearly affirmed by Church Fathers such as Augustine[7] and by all the great Scholastics. As St. Thomas put the matter, it is only through free choice that human persons are masters of their own actions and in this way beings made in the image and likeness of God.[8] The great truth that human persons are free to choose what they are to do and, through their choices, to make themselves *to be* the persons that they are was solemnly defined by the Council of Trent.[9] Vatican Council II stressed that the power of free choice "is an exceptional sign of the divine image within man" (*Gaudium et spes*, no. 17).

Germain Grisez, who, in collaboration with others, has authored an important work defending the reality of free choice against the attacks of contemporary determinist philosophers,[10] rightly notes that free choice is an existential principle or source of morality. It is an existential principle of moral good and evil because moral good and evil depend for their being on the power of free choice. This is so because what we do is *our* doing and can be *evil* doing or its opposite only if we freely choose to do it.[11] A dog or a cat or a chimp cannot be morally good or evil; human persons can, and they can because they have the power of free choice. It is through free choice that human persons make themselves *to be* the sort of persons that they are, that they make themselves *to be* morally good or morally bad persons. It is for this reason that free choice is an existential principle of morality.

Pope John Paul II also emphasizes the self-determining character of free choice, its significance as the existential principle of morality. Thus, he writes that "freedom is not only the choice for one or another particular action; it is also, within that choice, a *decision about oneself* and a setting of one's own life for or against the Good, for or against the Truth, and ultimately, for or against God" (*Veritatis splendor*, no. 65).

Free choice is experienced when one is aware of a conflict. Different possible alternatives of action are present to one, but they cannot all be realized simultaneously. One deliberates about these possibilities, but deliberation cannot settle the matter. Deliberation cannot determine which of the alternatives promises unambiguously the greater good (although, as we shall see later, one can determine which alternatives are *morally good* and which are not), and it cannot do so precisely because each alternative, to be appealing and eligible as a possibility of choice, must promise participation in some good that is simply incommensurable with the good promised by other alternatives.

For example, if one is thinking about buying a house and wants a house (a) within a certain price category, (b) with four bedrooms and a family room, (c) within walking distance of church and school, and (d) proximate to good public transportation, and if one house out of four that are examined promises all these benefits (a, b, c, d), whereas none of the other three houses do so, then no choice is possible or even necessary, so long as one is still willing to buy a house fulfilling these conditions. Of the alternatives available, only one has all the benefits one is looking for; hence, the appeal of the other houses — what makes them alternatives of choice — simply disappears. They are no longer eligible or choosable because they promise no good that is not present in the house that has all the benefits one is looking for. But if one is in the market for buying a house, and indeed must buy a house, and none of the houses available has *all* the "goods" or benefits one wants, then one will have to make a choice from among those that offer some of these benefits; each of these houses is choosable because each offers some good or benefit incommensurable with the good or benefit offered by the other houses. And ultimately the matter is settled by the choice itself. As Grisez says: "One makes a choice when one faces practical alternatives, believes one can and must settle which to take, and takes one. The choice is free when choosing itself determines oneself to seek fulfillment in one possibility rather than another. Inasmuch as one determines oneself in this way, one is of oneself."[12]

The experience of free choice can be summarized in the following way. First, a person is in a situation where he or she is attracted by alternative possibilities and there is no way to eliminate the incompatibility of the different alternatives or to limit the possibilities to only one. A person can do this or do that, but not both; they are real, i.e., choosable but incompatible possibilities. Second, the person realizes that it is up to him or her to settle the matter and determine which possibility is realized. Third, the person is aware of making the choice and aware of nothing that "makes" him or her make it. In other words, one is aware that one is free in settling the matter, in making the choice among the alternative possibilities.

The *Catechism of the Catholic Church* devotes a section (nos. 1730-1748) to the subject of free choice.

3. The Significance of Human Action and the Meaning of Character

Free choice bears upon actions that we can do. But the actions in question are not simply physical events in the material world that come and go, like the falling of rain or the turning of the leaves. The actions at stake are not something that "happen" to a person. They are, rather, the outward expressions of a person's choices, the disclosure or revelation of a person's moral identity, his or her being as a moral being. For at the core of an action, as human and personal, is a free, self-determining choice, which as such is something spiritual and abides within the person, determining the very being of the person. The Scriptures, particularly the New Testament, are very clear about this. Jesus taught that it is not what enters a person that defiles him or her; rather, it is what flows from the person, from his or her heart, from the core of his or her being, from his or her choice (cf. Mt 15:10-20; Mk 7:14-23). We can say that a human action — i.e., a free, intelligible action, whether good or bad — is the adoption by choice of some intelligible proposal and the execution of this choice through some exterior act. But the core of the action is the free, self-determining choice that abides within the person, making him or her *to be* the kind of person he or she is. Thus, I become an adulterer, as Jesus clearly taught (Mt 5:28), when I look at a woman with lust, i.e., when I adopt by choice the proposal to commit adultery or to think with satisfaction about doing it, even if I do not execute this choice externally.

This illumines the *self-determining* character of free choice. It is in and through the actions we freely choose to do that we give to ourselves an identity, for weal or for woe. This identity abides in us until we make other, contradictory kinds of choices. Thus, if I choose to commit adultery, I make myself *to be* an adulterer, and I remain an adulterer until, by another free and self-determining choice, I have a change of heart (*metanoia*) and repent of my deed. Even then I remain an adulterer, for I have, unfortunately, given myself that identity; but now I am a *repentant* adulterer, one who has, through free choice, given to himself a new kind of identity, the identity of one who repudiates his freely chosen adultery, repents of it, and is now determined, through free choice and with the help of God's never-failing grace, to amend his life and *to be* a faithful, loving spouse.

The significance of human acts as self-determining is beautifully brought out by Pope John Paul II. After noting that "it is precisely through his acts that man attains perfection as man," he goes on to say: "Human acts are moral acts because they express and determine the goodness or evil of the individual who performs them. They do not produce a change merely in the state of affairs outside of man, but, *to the extent that they are deliberate choices* [emphasis added], they give moral definition to the very person who performs them, determining his *profound spiritual traits*" (*Veritatis splendor*, no. 71).

Continuing, John Paul calls attention to a remarkably perceptive passage from St. Gregory of Nyssa's *De Vita Moysis*, II, 2-3: "All things subject to change and to becoming never remain constant, but continually pass from one state to another, for better or worse. . . . Now human life is always subject to change; it needs to be born ever anew. . . . But here birth does not come about by a foreign intervention, as is the case with bodily beings . . . ; it is the result of free choice. Thus we are in a certain way our own parents, creating ourselves as we will, by our decisions" (cited in *Veritatis splendor*, no. 71).

The *Catechism of the Catholic Church* (no. 1749) speaks of the significance of human action.

We might say that our actions are like "words" that we speak and through which we give to ourselves our moral character, our identity as moral beings.[13] Character, as Grisez notes, "is the integral existential identity of the person — the entire person in all his or her dimensions as shaped by morally good and bad choices — considered as a disposition to further choices."[14] We shape our character, our identity as moral beings, by what we freely choose to do. We are free to choose what we are to do and, by so choosing, to make ourselves *to be* the kind of persons we are. But we are not free to make what we choose to do to be good or evil, right or wrong. Our choices are good or bad insofar as they conform to what Vatican Council II called "the highest norm of human life" (*Dignitatis humanae*, no. 3), God's divine and eternal law and its "imperatives," which are made known to us by the mediation of conscience. But before examining the role of conscience in our moral life we need first to examine the role of virtue, which is rooted in free choice, in that life.

4. Virtue and Our Moral Life

We have just considered free choice and its existential significance and the meaning of "character" as the "integral existential identity of the person — the entire person in all his or her dimensions as shaped by morally good and bad choices." From what has been said regarding free choice and its existential significance, we can conclude that the free, self-determining choices at the core of a human act *abide within the person as dispositions inclining the person to make similar kinds of choices in the future unless contradictory choices are made*. Thus, if a person freely chooses to tell the truth, to reject immediately proposals to commit adultery, he or she makes himself or herself *to be* the kind person willing to tell the truth and to be faithful to his or her marital commitment, whereas the person who freely chooses to lie or to commit adultery makes himself or herself *to be* the kind of person disposed to lie or to commit adultery.

Moreover, among the choices we make, some of them serve to organize a person's life. Grisez calls these kinds of choices "large" choices or "commitments,"[15] which put us in the position of having to carry them out by many "smaller" choices — for example, in choosing to marry we commit ourselves to a way of life and to integrate other, smaller choices into this central commitment. Similarly, Pope John Paul II in *Veritatis splendor* emphasizes the "importance of certain choices which 'shape' a person's entire moral life, and which serve as bounds within which other particular everyday choices can be situated and allowed to develop" (no. 65). The role of those choices — which we can call "commitments" — in the development of a person's character is well summarized by Grisez in the following passage: "The enduring, spiritual reality of one's choices, especially the larger ones which mainly shape one's identity, is the principle of an integrated moral self. Character simply is this self, regarded as the source of further acts."[16] This will be set forth more fully below. But from what has been said already regarding the existential significance of freely chosen human acts and "character" as shaped by free choices, we can easily understand what Grisez had to say in a book he co-authored with Russell Shaw:

> Typically, we say of good people that they have good character. "Character" here signifies nothing less than the totality of a person integrated around good choices. And virtues? They are the different aspects of a good character. Looking at the matter from one point of view — relationships with other persons — we say that the individual of good character is fair or just; considering the individual from the aspect of sexuality, we say that he or she is chaste or modest; from the aspect of response to dangerous situations, that the individual is brave or steadfast; and so on. These virtues . . . are different aspects of a good character, considered in light of different problems and challenges.[17]

In other words, we can regard virtues — and their opposites, vices — as both a residue of a person's prior acts and dispositions to engage in further acts similar in moral quality to those that gave rise to the dispositions. "St. Thomas," as Grisez points out, "and many later Catholic writers called virtues and vices 'habits,' but in an unusual sense. In ordinary speech a habit is what shapes an unthinking routine of behavior. Thomas and his successors did not mean that virtues and vices are habits in this sense; they considered them aspects of character that make for consistency in deliberate behavior done by free choice."[18]

From what has been said thus far, we can gain an initial appreciation of the role that moral virtues have to play in our moral life. They give the person the facility to do what is good with facility and readiness. They make the person's "work" — i.e., his or her actions — good, and in addition make the person himself or herself morally good.[19] We must, however, understand properly what all this means. We must not "hypostasize" the virtues, i.e., erect them into agents of some sort. It is rather the *person* (with God's never-failing help, I must add immediately) who makes himself or herself, and his or her "work" or action, good by making good moral choices; but virtues are dispositions that the person gives to himself or herself (again, with God's never-failing help) by consistently making morally good choices, and these dispositions facilitate "doing" the good well.

Note, too, that in the preceding paragraph I have referred to "moral" virtues as the dispositions or "habits" engendered by consistently choosing freely to do what is good by shaping one's choices and actions in accordance with the truth that makes the person, as well as his or her "work," good. There are other "virtues" that persons can acquire that enable them to do some things well which do not make the persons themselves good. These are virtues in a "relative" sense, and among them the Catholic tradition, particularly as represented by St. Thomas, includes the "intellectual" virtues of understanding, scientific knowledge, and metaphysical wisdom that perfect the intellect in its speculative inquiry and through which those who have acquired, say, the intellectual virtue of scientific knowledge of medicine can do what doctors are supposed to do; and the "intellectual" virtue of art, concerned with making things, such as speeches, poems, symphonies, etc., beautiful and well. But such virtues do not necessarily make the medical doctor or research scientist or great painter a morally good person.[20]

Virtuous, morally upright persons know how to shape their choices and actions in accordance with the truth and to take care to form their consciences in an upright way. They know how to choose well among alternatives of choice and to distinguish those that are morally good from those that are morally bad, even if, at times, they might find it difficult to articulate reasoned arguments to support their moral judgments. They nonetheless have an authentic kind of moral knowledge, and, unlike some professional moral philosophers or theologians who might be capable of presenting cogent arguments in support of the judgments these morally upright persons make, they are ready and willing to choose in accordance with their moral judgments and not devise clever rationalizations in order to avoid doing what ought to be done because doing so might have undesirable consequences for themselves.

These morally upright women and men "know" what they are to do if they are to become fully the beings they are meant to be, and they are ready to "do" it because they are virtuous, either because they have, with God's never-failing grace, acquired virtues, or because God in his great love and mercy has infused virtues into their being when they turned from sin, repented it, and changed their hearts. Their knowledge is "connatural," that is, it is knowledge mediated by a love for the good, a love for God and their neighbor, a love for the truth. Their knowledge is analogous to the knowledge that close friends, for instance, husbands and wives, have of each other, a knowledge different from that of disinterested observers, a knowledge rooted in love.[21]

Grisez, upon whose work (along with that of St. Thomas) this book depends greatly, maintains that it is possible to "distinguish among virtues in different ways, by using as a principle of distinction any intelligible set of factors relevant to choices. Thus, virtues (or vices) can be distinguished by the different dimensions of the acting person, by different fields of behavior, and so on. No one of these accounts is definitive to the exclusion of others. Each is a way, helpful for some purposes, of dividing the same whole into intelligible parts."[22] Grisez's own way of distinguishing among virtues is different from St. Thomas's way of doing so, although both agree in distinguishing naturally acquired virtues (e.g., chastity, courage, justice) from the theological virtues of faith, hope, and charity.

The principle used by St. Thomas in distinguishing the naturally acquired virtues is based on the distinction among the different "operative powers" of the human person that are subject to perfection — the intellectual and appetitive powers — and among the appetitive powers the distinction between the sensitive powers of simple emotions of desire for food, drink, sex, etc. (the emotions of what he called the "concupiscible" appetite) and of emotions evoked in the presence of danger or difficulty (the emotions of what he termed the "irascible" appetite) and finally the "intellectual appetite" or the will. The principle used by Grisez to differentiate among the moral virtues is the kind of fundamental moral truth in light of which persons can discriminate among alternatives of choice in order to discern which alternatives are morally good and which are morally bad.

I will first briefly outline Grisez's way of distinguishing among virtues, noting that further aspects of his teaching on virtue will be set forth in the following chapter (on natural law) and in the chapter devoted to the specific nature of the Christian moral life. I will then summarize St. Thomas's way of distinguishing among virtues insofar as it has become classical and, moreover, offers us valuable insights into the nature of our moral life that are surely compatible with and complementary to the light Grisez's analysis of virtue sheds on the moral life. I will conclude by briefly commenting on the contemporary debate — a misplaced one, I believe — that sees a dichotomy between a "virtue"-based ethics and a "normative"-or "principle"-based ethics.

A. Grisez on Virtue

Earlier in this section, I spoke of "commitments," i.e., of certain kinds of choices committing us to a way of life into which lesser, everyday choices, are to be integrated. Reflecting on this, Grisez maintains that "virtues are aspects of personality as a whole when all the other dimensions of the self are integrated with morally good commitments. . . . Commitments establish one's existential identity: a whole personality integrated with a morally good self is virtuous. **Since such a personality is formed by choices which are in accord with the first principle of morality and the modes of responsibility, the virtues embody the modes.** In other words, the modes of responsibility shape the existential self of a good person, this self shapes the whole personality, and so good character embodies and expresses the modes."[23]

To understand what Grisez is saying here, it is necessary to anticipate matter to be taken up in the following chapter on "natural" law. There we will see that the great moral issue is this: in order for us to choose well — i.e., to choose those alternatives of choice that are morally good — we must in some way *know*, prior to choice, which alternatives are morally good. In other words, we need moral *truths* to guide our choices. In the following chapter, we will see that the natural moral law — written in our hearts by God — is precisely a set of such truths, beginning with the first principle of morality (religiously expressed in the commandments that we are to love God above all things and our neighbor as ourselves) and its specifications, principles such as the Golden Rule, and that in the light of this first basic moral principle and its specifications we can indeed make true moral judgments and good moral choices.

Grisez, as we will see, calls the specifications of the first moral principle — principles such as the Golden Rule — "modes of responsibility." These fundamental moral truths can be known in some way by everyone — as the Church and such Christian saints and doctors as St. Thomas teach.[24] Thus, ordinary persons who seek to act in a morally upright way can come to know them, perhaps not explicitly formulating them but recognizing them and appealing to them if asked to give basic reasons for making the kind of choices they make — analogously to the way ordinary persons know such principles or starting points of speculative inquiry as the principle of non-contradiction. If they then choose to shape their choices and actions — and in particular, their "big" choices or "commitments — in accord with these truths, they will become virtuous, i.e., inwardly disposed to choose well and to do what is morally good with facility. Grisez thus concludes that virtues embody these truths, i.e., the first principle of morality and its specifications or "modes of responsibility."

His way, then, of identifying the natural or acquired moral virtues is, as will be seen more fully in the following chapter, closely related to his way of identifying and articulating the "modes of responsibility," and he thus speaks of virtues such as "diligence," "self-control," "courage," "fairness," or "justice" etc. Grisez, moreover, believes, as will be seen in Chapter Six, that the beatitudes of our Lord's Sermon on the Mount can rightly be regarded as "Christian modes of response," and that those who choose in harmony with these divinely revealed moral principles — principles rooted in the new commandment that we are to love others as Jesus has loved us — acquire and are given with God's grace such Christian virtues as "humility," "detachment," "Christian fortitude," " mercy," "single-minded devotion to God," etc.

The virtuous person is the person whose reason, as Grisez expresses the matter, is "unfettered" — i.e., he or she is the one who shapes his choices and actions in accordance with the truth, the one who is in possession, through the virtues, of his or her desires and emotions and is not possessed by them.[25]

B. St. Thomas Aquinas on Virtue

St. Thomas's teaching on virtue is provided in many of his writings,[26] and there are several excellent studies of his thought on this matter.[27]

I have noted already that the principle St. Thomas uses for distinguishing among virtues — or the stable dispositions through which the acting person is able to do the good well — is based on the distinction among the operative "powers" or "faculties" of the human person. St. Thomas says that the proper subject or seat of virtue, as an operative habit (i.e., a quality disposing us to act well, i.e., to choose in accord with the truth), is some power of the soul. But the human soul has different powers; those properly the subject of virtue are those from which human acts proceed: (1) the intellect (whose operation concerns the truth, in light of which we can make choices), (2) the will (whose operation concerns choice and intention of end), and the (3) irascible and (4) concupiscible appetites, not insofar as they are sensitive powers of the soul but insofar as they "participate" in reason by obeying it, so that we can say that "the virtue which is in the irascible and concupiscible powers is nothing else but a certain habitual conformity of these powers to reason."[28]

"Qualities" or "*habitus*" of the intellect through which it can carry out its operations well are intellectual virtues. As we have seen already, some of these are virtues in a *relative sense* inasmuch as they enable the person *to do some things well,* i.e., (1) to *understand* (the virtue of understanding or *intellectus,* which embraces not only "intellectus" — understood as our grasp of the first principles of speculative inquiry — but also what St. Thomas called *synderesis* or our habitual grasp of the first principles of *practical* reasoning), (2) to *know things in their causes* (knowledge or *scientia*), (3) to *grasp the deepest causes of things* (wisdom or *sapientia*), and (4) to *make things* (art). Virtue in the strict sense, however, not only enables a person *to do things well* but also *makes its possessor good and his work [human act] good likewise.* This kind of virtue also exists in the intellect insofar as it is moved by the will. A supernatural virtue of this kind perfects the speculative intellect, namely, the virtue of faith. The natural virtue perfecting the intellect is the virtue of *prudence,* which perfects reason as practical, not speculative.[29] And prudence, St. Thomas insists, requires *moral* virtue and is itself moral virtue.

"Since prudence is the right reason of things to be done," he writes:

> It is a condition thereof that man be rightly disposed in regard to the principles of this reason of things to be done, that is, in regard to their ends, to which man is rightly disposed by the rectitude of the will. . . . Therefore, just as the subject of [the virtue] of science or understanding, which is right reason with respect toward beings whose truth is to be contemplated, is the speculative intellect in its relationship to the agent intellect [through whose light we can come to grasp the essences of things], so the subject of [the virtue] of prudence is the practical intellect in its relationship to a rectified will.[30]

Of the virtues perfecting a person through his intellect, then, the only one that is a moral virtue — one that makes not only the person's "work" good but also the person himself or herself — is that of prudence.

In *Summa theologiae* (q. 58, a.2), Thomas further discusses more fully how moral virtue differs from a purely intellectual virtue. There he writes:

> . . . for a man to act rightly, it is requisite not only that his reason be well disposed by means of a habit of intellectual virtue, but also that his appetitive power [and he has three such appetitive powers: the will, and two sensitive appetites, the concupiscible and irascible] be well disposed by means of a habit of moral virtue. And so moral virtue differs from intellectual virtue, even as appetite differs from reason. Hence, just as appetite is the principle of human acts in so far as it partakes of reason in some way, so a moral habit has the meaning of human virtue insofar as it is in conformity with reason.[31]

This text prepares the way for Aquinas's division of the moral virtues perfecting the appetites into the classical "cardinal" virtues, namely, those of prudence (perfecting one's practical reason), justice (perfecting the appetite of the will), temperance (perfecting the concupiscible appetite), and fortitude (perfecting the irascible appetite).[32]

Prudence, in other words, presupposes that a person be rightly disposed inwardly to the "ends" or "goods" of human action, because a person's moral choices involve affective knowledge or judgments to which assent is given on the basis of appetitive dispositions. Consequently, a person's appetites must be rightly disposed toward the "ends" or "goods" of human conduct if he or she is to make prudent judgments.[33] Prudence is "*right* reason about things that are to be done" (*recta ratio agibilium*),[34] because it is reason *rectified by right appetite:* the appetite of the will being rectified by the virtue of justice, the concupiscible appetite by the virtue of temperance, and the irascible appetite by the virtue of courage or fortitude.

In an illuminating passage in which he shows that fortitude is a virtue necessary for a good moral life, St. Thomas clearly expresses his thought on the cardinal virtues and their role in the moral life. In it he writes:

> As Aristotle says, "a virtue is what makes the one who has it good, and good too his activity." But the good of man is to be in accord with reason. . . . It follows that it pertains to human virtue that it make a human being and his activity to be in accord with reason. But this happens in three ways. In one way insofar as reason itself is made right, and this is done through the intellectual virtues (of which prudence is chief). In another way, insofar as the very rectitude of reason is instituted in human affairs, and this belongs to justice. In a third way, insofar as impediments to this rectitude are removed. But the human will can be hindered in two basic ways from putting the order required by reason into human affairs. In one way, from the fact that it is so strongly attracted by some delightful good that it fails to bring about the good required by reason; and this impediment is removed by the virtue of temperance. In another way, from the fact that it is kept from doing what is good on account of some terrible difficulty that it encounters. And for removing this impediment the virtue of fortitude is required, a fortitude or courage of the mind or spirit, whereby the person resists this difficulty, just as through bodily courage he overcomes and resists bodily impediments. It is thus evident that fortitude is a virtue insofar as it makes man conform to reason.[35]

The foregoing offers a summary of the teaching of St. Thomas on the acquired natural virtues. I will not here consider his teaching on the theological virtues of faith, hope, and charity and his teaching that, with charity, God infuses supernatural moral virtues of prudence, justice, fortitude, temperance, etc. These aspects of his teaching are well set forth by Romanus Cessario in *The Moral Virtues and Theological Ethics* and *Virtue or the Examined Life*. An excellent brief account of Thomas's teaching on the virtues can be found in T. C. O'Brien's article on virtue in the *New Catholic Encyclopedia*.[36]

C. Virtue-based Ethics and Principles-based Ethics

Some today oppose a "virtue-based ethics" to a "normative" or "principle-based ethics." This debate is in my opinion misplaced. The following passage from Grisez indicates the proper relationship between virtues and moral principles: "What," he asks, "is the connection . . . between moral principles and virtues? Do we have two distinct, perhaps even competing, approaches to morality — an ethics of moral truth versus an ethics of virtue? Not at all. Take the Golden Rule. One who consistently chooses fairly and works consistently to carry out such choices is a fair person — a person, that is, with the virtue of fairness or justice. *A virtue is nothing other than an aspect of the personality of a person integrated through commitments and other choices made* in accord with relevant moral norms derived from the relevant modes of responsibility. In other words: living by the standard of fairness makes a person fair. *Moral norms and virtues are not separate standards of morality; virtues grow out of norms in the lives of people who consistently live by them; righteousness and holiness are fruits of truth in hearts recreated by God's grace* (see Eph 4:24)."[37] The same truth can be expressed by saying that "virtues do not constitute moral norms distinct from the basic principle of morality and its 'modes of specification.'" Quite to the contrary, virtues embody this principle and its specifications. For "virtues are aspects of a personality integrated around good commitments, and the latter are choices in accord with the first principle of morality and the modes of responsibility."[38]

Some of Grisez's critics have complained that he ignores the role of virtue in the moral life and is "Kantian" because of his emphasis on normative principles. I believe that here it has been shown that he does not neglect the role of virtue, and more of his thought on this matter will be considered in later chapters.[39]

Moreover, at times virtuous persons disagree, and disagree in a contradictory way, with regard to specific moral issues on which the magisterium of the Church has not made a firm judgment. For example, some (including bishops) argue that ordinarily one is required to provide food and hydration to persons in the so-called "persistent vegetative state" unless it is clear that doing so fails to nourish the person or imposes unnecessarily harsh burdens, whereas others (again including bishops) vigorously maintain that there is no moral duty to do so. One of the parties to this debate must be wrong and the other right, insofar as contradictory views are championed. One presumes that the parties to the debate are equally virtuous (or are the bishops of Pennsylvania, who hold the first view, morally more virtuous than the bishops of Texas, who hold the second? — and this seems impossible to prove). Hence, the debate can only be resolved by examining the arguments advanced and the moral norms invoked to support the different views.

I will conclude this chapter with an examination of conscience and the moral life.

The *Catechism of the Catholic Church* gives an extensive treatment of virtues and the moral life in Article 7 of Chapter One, Section One, of Part Three, "Life in Christ," nos. 1804-1829.

5. Conscience and Our Moral Life

Today the term "conscience" has many meanings, among them, that of a "psychological conscience." When conscience is understood in this way, it is frequently identified with the Freudian superego, which is, as it were, the distillate of parents' influence upon their children. The superego is described by Freud in the following way: "The long period of childhood during which the growing human being lives in dependence on his parents leaves behind it a precipitate, which forms within his ego a special agency in which this parental influence is prolonged. It has received the name of 'superego.' The parents' influence naturally includes not only the personalities of the parents themselves but also the racial, national, and family traditions handed on through them, as well as the demands of the immediate social milieu which they represent."[40]

Conscience understood in this sense is essentially related to feelings of moral approval or disapproval. In this sense, conscience is the result of a process of psychological conditioning; and the spontaneous reactions, impulses, and feelings associated with conscience understood in this sense may be either realistic and healthy or illusory and pathological. Conscience in this sense is shaped largely by nonrational factors, and it is frequently found to condemn what is not wrong or to approve what is not right. "Psychological conscience," therefore, cannot of itself provide a person with moral guidance, and there can be no obligation to follow conscience understood in this sense.

Obviously, the Fathers of Vatican Council II, in using the term "conscience" to designate the agency whereby human persons participate in God's eternal and divine law, were using it in a much different sense. For them, conscience designates first and foremost our *awareness of moral truth*. The documents from which passages have been cited, moreover — namely, *Dignitatis humanae* and *Gaudium et spes* — make it clear that there are different levels of our awareness of moral truth. These documents use the term "conscience" to designate different levels of our awareness of moral truth.

In order to grasp properly the different levels of awareness of moral truth to which *conscience,* as used in the documents of Vatican Council II, refers, it will be helpful, I believe, to take into account some perceptive comments on conscience made by the noted Scottish theologian John Macquarrie and to relate his observations to the Council documents' use of the term "conscience."

Macquarrie, after noting the ambiguity that at times surrounds the term "conscience," observes that it is possible to distinguish several basic levels of conscience when the term is used to designate a person's awareness of moral truth. At one level, it refers to a practical judgment terminating a process of moral deliberation. At this level, it designates one's personal and reasoned judgment that a particular course of action is right and therefore morally permissible or that a particular course of action is wrong and therefore morally excluded.[41] *Gaudium et spes* uses *conscience* in this sense when it says that at times the voice of God's law, made known to us through our conscience, tells us "to do this, shun that" (no. 16). Conscience in this sense does not refer to one's "feelings" of approval or disapproval, nor to some mysterious nonrational agency; rather, here it refers to reflective moral judgment that serves to bring to a conclusion a process of moral deliberation. Since the judgment of conscience is the result of a person's reasoned and thoughtful evaluation about the morality of a particular course of action, conscience in this sense can be called "particular moral conscience." The judgment that one makes can be about an action that one is considering doing or not doing (and in this instance, some theologians rightly speak of *antecedent* conscience); or it can be about the morality of an action that one has already done (and in this instance, it is referred to as *consequent* conscience).[42] As John Paul II points out, "the judgment of conscience is a *practical judgment,* a judgment which makes known what man must do or not do, or which assesses an act already performed by him" *(Veritatis splendor,* no. 59).

Here it is important to stress that conscience, understood at this level of moral awareness, is a judgment or an act of the intellect. It thus cannot be a mere subjective feeling or option to act and live in a certain way. In saying this, I am in no way denying the importance that affections and feelings can have in our moral life, nor am I saying that they are irrelevant in making judgments of conscience.[43] My point is simply that upright moral life requires one's personal conviction that given acts are or are not in accord with correct moral standards. Concern for the truth is essential here. Intelligent judgment, not nonrational feelings or preferences, should direct human choices and actions. A person is obliged to act in accord with his or her conscience precisely because one of the central meanings of conscience is that it is one's own best judgment about what one ought or ought not to do.[44] This matter will be taken up more fully after other legitimate meanings of conscience have been examined.

At another level, Macquarrie writes, conscience can mean a "broader . . . more generalized knowledge of right and wrong, of good and bad."[45] In this sense, conscience is one's personal awareness of basic moral principles or truths. Vatican Council II refers to conscience in this sense when it affirms that it is through the mediation of conscience that man comes to perceive ever increasingly the unchanging truth and comes to recognize the demands of God's divine and eternal law (*Dignitatis humanae*, no. 3). It is to conscience at this level that *Gaudium et spes* refers when it says that the voice of God's law, made known through conscience, calls upon man to "love and to do what is good and to avoid evil" (no. 16). It is in this sense of the term that one's conscience can be said to be an awareness of the law of God written in the human heart (cf. Rom 2:14-16 and *Gaudium et spes*, no. 16). At this level, conscience can rightly be called "general moral conscience," for it is an awareness of moral truth not at the level of particular actions and situations but at the level of general principles. Medieval theologians such as St. Thomas had a special term for designating this level of awareness of moral truth, namely, *synderesis* or our habitual awareness of the first principles of practical reasoning and of morality.[46]

Particular moral conscience, or conscience at the level of a practical judgment that one makes about the morality of given acts, is the termination of a process of moral deliberation. General moral conscience, or conscience at the level of one's awareness of the basic principles of morality, is concerned with the moral truths that serve as the starting points or principles for moral deliberation, principles to which one can appeal in order to show the truth of the particular moral conclusions reached in the judgments terminating the process of moral deliberation.

In *Veritatis splendor*, Pope John Paul II neatly shows how the practical judgment of conscience is related to what I have here called "general moral conscience" or "our awareness of the basic principles of morality." Centering his attention on what I have here called "particular moral conscience" or "conscience at the level of a practical judgment" about the morality of given acts, the Holy Father observes that this judgment "applies to a concrete situation the rational conviction that one must love the good and avoid evil. This first principle of practical reason is part of the natural law; indeed it constitutes the very foundation of the natural law inasmuch as it expresses that primordial insight about good and evil, that reflection of God's creative wisdom which, like an imperishable spark (*scintilla animae*), shines in the heart of every man.

But whereas the natural law discloses the objective and universal demands of the moral good, conscience is the application of the law to a particular case; this application of the law thus becomes an inner dictate for the individual, a summons to do what is a good in this particular situation" (*Veritatis splendor*, no. 59).

The third level of conscience to which Macquarrie refers is "a special and very fundamental mode of self-awareness — the awareness of 'how it is with oneself.'"[47] At this level, conscience is indeed, as the Fathers of Vatican Council II, following Pope Pius XII, put it, "the most secret core and sanctuary of a man, where he is alone with God" (*Gaudium et spes*, no. 16).[48] The character of "conscience" as a special mode of self-awareness is indicated by the etymology of the word. Our English term derives from the Latin *conscientia*, which means both "consciousness" and "conscience." As a special mode of self-awareness, conscience has as its basic function the disclosure of ourselves to ourselves as moral beings. As Macquarrie puts it: "Specifically, conscience discloses the gap between our actual selves and that image of ourselves that we have already in virtue of the 'natural inclination' toward the fulfillment of man's end. Thus, conscience is not merely a disclosure; it is also . . . a call or summons. It is a call to that full humanity of which we already have some idea or image because of the very fact that we are human at all, and that our nature is to exist, to go out beyond where we are at any given moment. Although we commonly think of conscience as commanding us to *do* certain things, the fundamental command of conscience is to *be*."[49]

At this level, in other words, conscience is a mode of self-awareness whereby we are aware of ourselves as moral beings, summoned to give to ourselves the dignity to which we are called as intelligent and free beings. This is the level of conscience to which *Dignitatis humanae* referred when it declared that ". . . all men . . . are by their own nature impelled, and are morally bound, to seek the truth" about what they are to do (no. 2). It is our realization that we are not yet fully the beings God calls us to be, and that we are capable of becoming by shaping our lives and actions in accord with the truth. It is the summons, deep within our being, to be fully the beings God wills us to be and to make ourselves to be, by our own choices and actions, lovers of the true and the good. At this level, conscience is a dynamic thrust within the person for moral truth.

Because conscience at this level dynamically orients the person to transcend himself or herself by continually progressing to a fullness of being, it is called *transcendental conscience* by some. This is indeed a valid meaning of conscience. Here, too, as at the level of particular moral conscience and general moral conscience, "conscience" is concerned with our awareness of moral truth, of the truth that we are called to conform our lives and actions to objective standards of morality so that we can be fully the beings we are meant to be.

There are, however, some theologians who develop a theory of "transcendental conscience" that is seriously flawed. The leading representative of these theologians is Walter Conn. He rightly says that "transcendental" conscience is "the dynamic thrust toward self-transcendence at the core of a person's very subjectivity, revealing itself . . . as a demand for responsible decision in accord with reasonable judgment."[50] However, he goes on to claim that authentic moral living "is determined neither by absolute principles nor by arbitrary creativity relative to each situation; authentic living, rather, is defined by a normative structure of consciousness which demands that a person respond to the values in each situation with creativity that is at once sensitive, critical, responsible, and loving."[51]

Conn is correct, of course, in denying that authentic moral living is determined by "arbitrary creativity relative to each situation." However, in this passage he denies that there are basic moral criteria or principles in terms of which one can determine whether one's response is indeed "sensitive," "critical," "responsible," and "loving." His understanding of transcendental conscience seems to make it completely autonomous and unrelated to the other meanings of conscience that have already been considered. By rejecting the crucial role played by the basic moral principles that are made known to us through the mediation of conscience at the level previously considered, Conn makes "transcendental conscience" more similar to a "funny internal feeling" than to a mode of awareness of moral truth. Unless there are basic moral principles, made known to us through the mediation of conscience, it is difficult to see how the "dynamic thrust toward self-transcendence" could be directed toward those goods that are truly perfective of the human person. In my opinion, it is this "creative" understanding of conscience that John Paul II firmly repudiates in *Veritatis splendor*. He notes that some authors, emphasizing the " 'creative' character of conscience" (*Veritatis splendor*, no. 55), have been led to stress "the priority of a certain more concrete existential consideration" beyond "the doctrinal and abstract level." This concrete existential consideration, according to these authors, "could legitimately be the basis of certain *exceptions to the general rule*. . . . A separation, or even an opposition, is thus established in some cases between the teaching of the precept, which is valid in general, and the norm of the individual conscience, which would in fact make the final decision about what is good and what is evil" (ibid., no. 56).

A person has the obligation to follow his or her conscience — i.e., to act in accordance with his or her own best judgment of what he or she is to do — precisely because this judgment of conscience is the final judgment that a person makes about the moral goodness or badness of the alternatives possible for him or her. If one were willing to act contrary to this judgment, one would be willing to do what one had personally judged one ought not choose to do. One would thus be willing to be an evildoer if one were willing deliberately to act contrary to one's own best judgment.

There is, indeed, a relationship between the various levels of conscience that have already been considered, and by looking at this relationship we can see clearly why we have the obligation to "follow" our conscience in the sense of acting in accord with the judgment of conscience. We have seen that, at one of its levels, conscience is our awareness of ourselves as moral beings, as persons summoned to act in accordance with the truth and to show ourselves to be lovers of the true and the good and in this way to become fully the beings God wills us to be. But to become what we are meant to be, to become more fully human, we are to do good and avoid evil. The judgment that we make, conscientiously, that *this* act here and now is the good that I am obliged to do or the evil that I am obliged to avoid if I am to be faithful to the "me" that I am in virtue of being human to begin with, is our own personal way of knowing what we must do if we are to answer the call or summons to become what we are meant to be. Moreover, we make the judgment about what we are to do here and now in light of the basic norms of morality of which we are aware. Thus, all three levels of conscience are inherently interrelated, and their interrelationship helps us to see why we are obligated to act in accordance with our own best reasoned judgment. The Catholic theological tradition and, as we have seen, the Fathers of Vatican Council II emphatically affirm that this indeed is a serious moral obligation.[52] "The judgment of conscience," John Paul II stresses, "has an imperative character: man must act in accordance with it. If man acts against this judgment or, in a case where he lacks certainty about the rightness and goodness of a determined act, still performs that act, he stands condemned by his own conscience, *the proximate norm of personal morality*. The dignity of this rational forum and the authority of its voice and judgments derive from the *truth* about moral good and evil, which it is called to listen to and to express" (*Veritatis splendor*, no. 60).

Yet our own judgments about what we are to do can be mistaken. There is thus the serious obligation, stressed by the Fathers of Vatican Council II and John Paul II, to seek the truth. Our judgment of conscience does not make what we choose to do *to be* morally right and good; in other words, we are not, through our judgment of conscience, the arbiters of good and evil. Our obligation is to conform our judgments of conscience to objective norms of morality, norms that have as their ultimate source, as *Dignitatis humanae* put it, "God's divine law — eternal, objective, and universal" (no. 3). It is for this reason that the Council Fathers spoke of a "correct" conscience, declaring, "the more a correct conscience prevails, the more do persons and groups turn aside from blind choice and try to be guided by objective standards of moral conduct" (*Gaudium et spes*, no. 16).

If the error or mistake in one's judgment of conscience is not attributable to the person, then acting in accordance with such a judgment of conscience does not make the person to be an evildoer or an evil person, for the person has not, in his or her conscience, ratified or endorsed the evil in the course of action that is chosen. The action will still be wrong, and one who learns later that his or her judgment of conscience was erroneous will have cause for regret (not remorse), and must, of course, reorder his or her life in accord with the knowledge of the truth. Speaking of errors of this kind, the Fathers of Vatican Council II noted: "It often happens that conscience goes astray through ignorance which it is unable to avoid, without thereby losing its dignity" (*Gaudium et spes*, no. 16). But, as they went on to say, "this cannot be said of the man who takes little trouble to find out what is true and good, or when conscience is by degrees almost blinded through the habit of committing sin" (ibid.). As John Paul II says, "Conscience, as the ultimate concrete judgment, compromises its dignity when it is *culpably erroneous*. . . . Jesus alludes to the danger of the conscience being deformed when he warns: 'The eye is the lamp of the body. So if your eye is sound, your whole body will be full of light; but if your eye is not sound, your whole body will be full of darkness. If then the light in you is darkness, how great is the darkness!' (Mt 6:22-23)" (*Veritatis splendor*, no. 65). In such instances, remorse, not regret, is called for, or what the gospels call *metanoia* or repentance.[53] In their pastoral letter on the moral life, *To Live in Christ Jesus*, the bishops of the United States put the matter this way:

> We must have a rightly informed conscience and follow it. But our judgments are human and can be mistaken; we may be blinded by the power of sin in our lives or misled by the strength of our desires. "Beloved, do not trust every spirit, but put the spirits to a test to see if they belong to God" (1 Jn 4.1). Clearly, then, we must do everything in our power to see to it that our judgments of conscience are informed and in accord with the moral order of which God is creator. Common sense requires that conscientious people be open and humble, ready to learn from the experience and insight of others, willing to acknowledge prejudices and even change their judgments in light of better instruction.[54]

Here the bishops speak of the obligation to have an "informed" conscience. Thus, to bring to a close this discussion of conscience, it will be necessary to offer some observations on the meaning of an *informed Catholic conscience*.

The purpose or goal of particular moral conscience, or conscience in the sense of one's best judgment about what one is to do here and now, is true knowledge of what ought to be done in this particular situation. If one is to make a true judgment of this kind, one needs to be aware, first of all, of the basic principles of morality and how these relate to the situation at hand. One thus needs to know the facts of the situation. Thus, forming one's conscience involves the following: first, one must grasp the implications of the basic principles of morality; second, alert to all the morally significant features of the situation, one must learn how to apply these norms so as to form reasonable judgments of conscience.

The person eager to make true moral judgments will, of course, be anxious to learn what he or she can from moral advisers who can be trusted. Thus, the person who is seeking to make a truly informed judgment of conscience will be willing to listen to the truth and to seek it from sources where it is most likely to be found. The Catholic, aware that the Church is God's gift to him or her, that it is indeed the pillar of truth, will therefore be ready to accept the moral teachings of the Church, for the Catholic realizes that Christ speaks to him or her through the authoritative teaching of the Church that is the bride and body of Christ. Indeed, as the Fathers of Vatican Council II remind us, "in forming their consciences the faithful must pay careful attention to the sacred and certain teaching of the Church. For the Catholic Church is by the will of Christ the teacher of truth. It is her duty to proclaim and teach with authority the truth which is Christ and, at the same time, to declare and confirm by her authority the principles of the moral order which spring from human nature itself" (*Dignitatis humanae*, no. 14). John Paul II, after citing this important conciliar text, has this to say: "It follows that the authority of the Church, when she pronounces on moral questions, in no way undermines the freedom of conscience of Christians. This is so not only because freedom of conscience is never freedom 'from' the truth but always and only freedom 'in' the truth, but also because the Magisterium does not bring to the Christian conscience truths which are extraneous to it; rather it brings to light the truths which it ought already to possess, developing them from the starting point of the primordial act of faith. The Church puts herself always and only at the *service of conscience*, helping it . . . especially in more difficult questions, to attain the truth with certainty and to abide in it" (*Veritatis splendor*, no. 64).

The Catholic, therefore, will be connaturally inclined to embrace as true what the Church teaches in the moral order. For the Catholic, the moral teachings of the Church are not some kind of legalistic code imposed arbitrarily upon the Catholic from without. Rather, the Catholic regards, or ought to regard, the moral teachings of the Church as truths intended to remind us of our dignity as beings made in the image and likeness of God and called to shape inwardly our choices and actions in accordance with the truth. The moral teachings of the Church are meant to help Catholics walk worthily in the vocation to which they have been called as children of God and adopted brothers and sisters of the Lord, whose reign makes sovereign claims upon them, requiring them to love even as they have been and are loved by God in Christ.

Today some look upon the moral teachings of the Church as a set of legalistic and arbitrary norms, imposed on persons from without. They regard these teachings as a "party line" that the "official" Church proposes. This way of looking at the moral teachings of the Church is totally erroneous. When a person becomes, through an act of living faith, a member of the Church, Christ's bride and body, that person commits himself or herself to a life in unity with Christ and his Church. The Catholic accepts, as part of his or her own identity, the identity of a Catholic, of one to whom life in Christ is mediated through the Church. And central to this life is the moral teaching of that Church. The Catholic, thus, will be eager to embrace as true what this Church proposes and will be anxious to shape his or her life in conformity with the moral truths that the Church proclaims.

We have seen that in forming conscience one needs to be aware, first of all, of the basic principles of morality. Indeed, one of the levels of conscience examined in this chapter is the awareness of moral truth at the level of principles or starting points for moral deliberation. In the following chapter, devoted to the subject of natural law, we will be concerned with identifying these principles.

In this chapter, we have seen that a Catholic, in forming his or her conscience, can do so only by paying "careful attention to the sacred and certain teaching of the Church." In the final chapter of this work, the role of the Church as moral teacher and the issue of dissent from authoritative teachings of the Church on moral questions will be taken up in detail. Here it suffices to note that for the Catholic the authority of those who teach in Christ's name is a more-than-human authority, and the truths these teachers propose are to be taken to heart so that one's life in Christ may be deepened and enriched. (On conscience and the moral life, see the *Catechism of the Catholic Church*, nos. 1776-1802.)

Notes for Chapter Two

1. St. Thomas Aquinas, *Summa theologiae*, 1, 93, 4. In this article, St. Thomas distinguishes a threefold human dignity proper to human persons. The first is the dignity human beings have by virtue of being made in God's image and likeness; the second is their dignity as beings who know and love God by conforming to his grace, but in an imperfect way as sojourners in this life; the third is their dignity as beings now living in complete union with God, and this is the dignity of the blessed.

2. On the "beatifying beginnings" of human existence, see the probing analyses of Pope John Paul II in *The Original Unity of Man and Woman: Catechesis on Genesis* (Boston: St. Paul Editions, 1981).

3. The Church has always taught that human life, precisely because it is a gift from God and is destined for life everlasting in union with him, is priceless and merits the most profound respect from its beginning. Perhaps the most profound and eloquent presentation of this great truth is given by Pope John Paul II in his 1995 encyclical *Evangelium vitae* ("The Gospel of Life"), in particular in Chapter II. A useful collection of earlier Church documents on the sanctity of human life extending from the time of the *Didache* in the early second century up to the 1976 pastoral letter of the U.S. bishops, *To Live in Christ Jesus*, is the anthology *Yes to Life* (Boston: St. Paul Publications, 1977). See also Congregation for the Doctrine of the Faith, *Instruction on Respect for Human Life in Its Origins and on the Dignity of Human Procreation (Donum vitae)* (1987).

4. Karol Wojtyla, *Love and Responsibility*, trans. H. Willetts (New York: Farrar, Straus, and Giroux, 1981), p. 41.

5. On this matter, see my book *Catholic Bioethics and the Gift of Human Life* (Our Sunday Visitor: Huntington, IN, 2000), Chapter 3; see also Patrick Lee, *Abortion and the Unborn Child* (Washington, DC: The Catholic University of America Press, 1996), Chapter 1; Germain Grisez, "When Do People Begin?" in *Proceedings of the Annual Convention of the American Catholic Philosophical Association* (Washington, DC: The American Catholic Philosophical Association, 1986). See also Mortimer Adler, *The Difference of Man and the Difference It Makes* (Cleveland/New York: Meridian Books, 1968).

6. In the Abbott edition of *The Documents of Vatican Council II* (New York: America Press, 1965), this passage from *Gaudium et spes* (no. 16) is incorrectly translated as "the voice of conscience." The Latin text is *cuius vox*, with the antecedent of *cuius* being *lex* ("law"), not *conscientia* ("conscience").

7. St. Augustine devoted one of his earliest works after his baptism to the subject of free choice, namely, *De Libero Arbitrio*. The apostolic Fathers, such as Justin Martyr, stressed free choice in the face of pagan determinism. Early in Christianity, Justin developed a line of reasoning to be used over and over again by such writers as Augustine, John Damascene, and Aquinas. He wrote: "We have learned from the prophets and we hold it as true that punishments and chastisements and good rewards are distributed according to the merit of each man's actions. Were this not the case, and were all things to happen according to the decree of fate, there would be nothing at all in our power. If fate decrees that this man is to be good, and that one wicked, then neither is the former to be praised nor the latter to be blamed. Furthermore, if the human race does not have the power of freely deliberated choice in fleeing evil and in choosing good, then men are not accountable for their actions"

(*The First Apology*, 43; trans. W. A. Jurgen, *The Faith of the Early Fathers* [Collegeville, MN: Liturgical Press, 1970], Vol. 1, no. 123).

8. St. Thomas Aquinas, *Summa theologiae*, 1-2, Prologue.

9. The Council of Trent solemnly defined the truth that human persons, even after the Fall, are gifted with free choice. For the text, see Henricus Denzinger and Adolphus Schönmetzer, *Enchiridion Symbolorum Definitionum et Declarationum de Rebus Fidei et Morum* (35th ed., Rome: Herder, 1975), no. 1555. This source will henceforth be referred to as DS.

10. Joseph Boyle, Germain Grisez, and Olaf Tollefsen, *Free Choice: A Self-Referential Argument* (Notre Dame, IN: University of Notre Dame Press, 1976).

11. Germain Grisez, *The Way of the Lord Jesus*, Vol. 1, *Christian Moral Principles* (Chicago: Franciscan Herald Press, 1983), p. 41. On this, see also St. Thomas Aquinas, *Summa theologiae*, 1, 83, 1; 1-2, 1, 1; 1-2, 6, 1; 1-2, 18, 1.

12. Grisez, *Christian Moral Principles*, p. 50.

13. On this, see the interesting account of human action as language in Herbert McCabe, O.P., *What Is Ethics All About?* (Washington, DC: Corpus Books, 1969), pp. 90-94.

14. Grisez, *Christian Moral Principles*, p. 59.

15. Ibid., pp. 60-61.

16. Ibid., p. 193.

17. Germain Grisez and Russell Shaw, *Fulfillment in Christ: A Summary of Christian Moral Principles* (Notre Dame, IN: University of Notre Dame Press, 1991), pp. 23-24.

18. Grisez, *Christian Moral Principles*, p. 58. *Grisez* provides a reference to St. Thomas, *Summa theologiae*, 1-2, 49, 1-3 and 55, 1-2, for the way in which Aquinas understood virtues and vices to be "habits" or, in Latin, *habitus*.

19. See St. Thomas Aquinas, *Summa theologiae*, 1-2, 55, 4.

20. On the difference between intellectual virtues of this kind, which he calls virtues in a relative sense, and moral virtue, see St. Thomas, *Summa theologiae*, 1-2, 57-58.

21. On knowledge by connaturality, see my article, "Knowledge, Connatural," in *New Catholic Encyclopedia* (New York: McGraw-Hill, 1967), Vol. 8, pp. 228-229.

22. Grisez, *Christian Moral Principles*, p. 59.

23. Ibid., p. 192; boldface in the original text.

24. On this, see Vatican Council II, Declaration on Religious Liberty (*Dignitatis humanae*), no. 3; Pastoral Constitution on the Church in the Modern World (*Gaudium et spes*), no. 16; St. Thomas Aquinas, *Summa theologiae*, 1-2, 94, 2, 4.

25. On this, see in particular the essay co-authored by Grisez, Joseph Boyle, and John Finnis, "Practical Principles, Moral Truth, and Ultimate End," *Ameri-*

can Journal of Jurisprudence 32 (1987), 121. See also Chapter Three, below, pp. 104-105.

26. In *Summa theologiae* (1-2, questions 55-67), St. Thomas offers an extended treatment of virtue and its kinds (intellectual, moral, cardinal, theological), its causes, duration, etc. In *Summa theologiae* (2-2), he considers in depth (1) the theological virtues of faith (questions 1-16), hope (questions 17-22), and charity (questions 23-46); and (2) the cardinal virtues of prudence (questions 47-57), justice (questions 58-122), fortitude (questions 123-140), and temperance (questions 141-170).

27. Among the more significant are the following: (1) Josef Pieper's "classical" presentation of *The Four Cardinal Virtues* (Notre Dame, IN: University of Notre Dame Press, 1965), a reprint of three books — one on prudence, another on justice, and the other on fortitude and temperance — published originally in the 1950s by Pantheon Books, New York; (2) Romanus Cessario, O.P., *The Moral Virtues and Theological Ethics* (Notre Dame, IN: University of Notre Dame Press, 1991); *The Virtues or the Examined Life* (New York: Continuum, 2002); (3) Jean Porter, *The Recovery of Virtue* (Philadelphia: Westminster, 1993). See also Pieper, *Belief and Faith* (New York: Pantheon, 1963); Pieper, *Hope* (San Francisco: Ignatius, 1986); Pieper, *About Love* (Chicago: Franciscan Herald Press, 1978). In 1997, Ignatius Press published the three titles of Pieper listed here in one volume, entitled *Faith, Hope, and Love.*

28. St. Thomas Aquinas, *Summa theologiae,* 1-2, 56, 1-6; the citation is taken from 56, 4.

29. See ibid., 57, 1-5.

30. Ibid., 56, 3. The Latin text, which I translated freely above, reads as follows: "Cum enim prudentia sit recta ratio agibilium, requiritur ad prudentiam quod homo se bene habeat ad principia huius rationis agendorum, quae sunt fines; ad quos bene se habet homo per rectitudinem voluntatis, sicut ad principia speculabilium per naturale lumen intellectus agentis. Et ideo sicut subiectum scientiae, quae est ratio recta speculabilium, est intellectus speculativus in ordine ad intellectum agentem, ita subiectum prudentiae est intellectus practicus in ordine ad voluntatem rectam." See the excellent treatment of virtue and in particular of prudence in St. Thomas in John Finnis, *Aquinas: Moral, Political, and Legal Theory* (New York: Oxford, 1998), pp. 163-170.

31. Ibid., 58, 2: ". . . ad hoc quod homo bene agat, requiritur quod non solum ratio sit bene disposita per habitum virtutis intellectualis; sed etiam quod vis appetitive sit bene disposita per habitum virtutis moralis. Sicut igitur appetitus distinguitur a ratione, ita virtus moralis distinguitur ab intellectuali. Unde sicut appetitus est principium humani actus secundum quod participat aliqualiter rationem, ita habitus moralis habet rationem virtutis humanae, inquantum rationi conformatur."

32. See, e.g., ibid., 61, 2.

33. See ibid., 65, 1.

34. Ibid.

35. Ibid. 2-2, 123, 1. ". . . secundum Philosophum, 'virtus est quae bonum facit habentem et opus eius bonum reddit' (*Nicomachean Ethics*, 3.8, 1116a16); unde 'virtus hominis,' de qua loquimur, 'est quae bonum facit hominem, et opus eius bonum reddit.' Bonum autem hominis est secundum rationem esse. . . . Et ideo ad virtutem humanam pertinet ut faciat hominem et opus eius secundum rationem esse. Quod quidem tripliciter contingit. Uno modo, secundum quod ipsa ratio rectificatur: quod fit per virtutes intellectuales. Alio modo, secundum quod ipsa rectitudo rationis in rebus humanis instituitur: quod pertinet ad justitiam. Tertio, secundum quod tolluntur impedimenta huius rectitudinis in rebus humanis ponendae. Dupliciter autem impeditur voluntas humana ne rectitudinem rationis sequatur. Uno modo, per hoc quod attrahitur ab aliquo delectabili ad aliud quam rectitudo rationis requirat: et hoc impedimentum tollit virtus temperantiae. Alio modo, per hoc quod voluntatem repellit ab eo quod est secundum rationem, propter aliquod difficile quod incumbit. Et ad hoc impedimentum tollendum requiritur fortitudo mentis, qua scilicet huiusmodi difficultatibus resistat: sicut et homo per fortitudinem corporalem impedimenta corporalia superat et repellit. Unde manifestum est quod fortitudo est virtus, inquantum facit hominem secundum rationem esse."

36. T.C. O'Brien, "Virtue," *New Catholic Encyclopedia* (New York: McGraw-Hill, 1967), Vol. 15, pp. 704-708.

37. Grisez and Shaw, *Fulfillment in Christ*, pp. 84-85.

38. Grisez, *Christian Moral Principles*, p. 195.

39. On this, see Grisez and Boyle, "Response to Our Critics and Our Collaborators," in *Natural Law & Moral Inquiry: Ethics, Metaphysics and Politics in the Work of Germain Grisez*, ed. Robert P. George (Washington, DC: Georgetown University Press, 1998), pp. 213-237, at 235-236.

40. Sigmund Freud, *An Outline of Psychoanalysis*, trans. James Strachey (London: Hogarth Press, 1949), pp. 3-4.

41. John Macquarrie, *Three Issues in Ethics* (New York: Harper and Row, 1971), p. 111.

42. In the New Testament, the use of *conscience* was apparently limited to consequent conscience or the judgment of one's past actions. On this, see James Turro, "Conscience in the Bible," in *Conscience: Its Freedom and Limitations*, ed. W.C. Bier, S.J. (New York: Fordham University Press, 1971), pp. 3-8. But see Eric D'Arcy, *Conscience and Its Right to Freedom* (New York: Sheed and Ward, Inc., 1961), pp. 8-12, for an interesting argument that St. Paul has a directive or antecedent sense of conscience as well.

43. In his *Themes in Fundamental Moral Theology* (Notre Dame, IN: University of Notre Dame Press, 1977), p. 211, Charles E. Curran mistakenly argues that the traditional view of conscience as one's best moral judgment cannot account for the legitimate role of affectivity in conscience. For a more adequate account, see Grisez, *Christian Moral Principles,* ch. 10, q. D; ch. 31, q. E.

44. On this, see St. Thomas Aquinas, *Dc Veritate,* q. 17, a. 3. See D'Arcy, *Conscience and Its Right to Freedom,* pp. 87-112, for a commentary on St. Thomas's position.

45. Macquarrie, *Three Issues in Ethics,* p. 111.

46. On this, see St. Thomas Aquinas, *Summa theologiae,* 1, 79, 12.

47. Macquarrie, *Three Issues in Ethics,* p. 114.

48. Pope Pius XII, "Radio Message on Rightly Forming Conscience in Christian Youth," March 23, 1952, *Acta Apostolicae Sedis* 44 (1952), 271.

49. Macquarrie, *Three Issues in Ethics,* p. 114.

50. Walter Conn, *Conscience: Development and Self-Transcendence* (Birmingham, AL: Religious Education Press, 1981), p. 205.

51. Ibid., p. 213.

52. See St. Thomas Aquinas, *De Veritate,* q. 17, a. 3.

53. St. Thomas Aquinas, *Summa theologiae,* 1-2, 19, 6.

54. *To Live in Christ Jesus: A Pastoral Letter of the American Bishops on the Moral Life* (Washington, DC: USCC, 1976), p. 10.

CHAPTER THREE

The Natural Law and Moral Life

Introduction

Vatican Council II, as we have already seen, taught that the "highest norm of human life is God's divine law — eternal, objective, universal — whereby God orders, directs, and governs the entire universe and all the ways of the human community according to a plan conceived in wisdom and in love." In addition, it held that "man has been made by God to participate in this law, with the result that, under the gentle disposition of divine providence, he can come to perceive ever increasingly the unchanging truth" (*Dignitatis humanae,* no. 3). Man's participation in God's divine and eternal law is precisely what the Catholic theological tradition understands by "natural law," the law that he discovers "deep within his conscience" (*Gaudium et spes,* no. 16). Although they did not use the expression "natural law" to designate man's participation in God's divine and eternal law in these passages from *Dignitatis humanae* and *Gaudium et spes,* the Council Fathers clearly had the natural law in mind, for right after saying that "man has been made by God to participate in this law," they explicitly referred to three texts of St. Thomas; and of these one was obviously uppermost in their mind, for in it Aquinas affirms that all human beings know the immutable truth of the eternal law at least to this extent, that they know the universal principles of the natural law.[1]

But what is the natural law? I propose that we begin our investigation of this topic by examining the teaching of St. Thomas on the natural law. We shall then examine the teaching of Vatican Council II, the teaching of Pope John Paul II, and the thought of some contemporary writers who seek to build on the foundations established by St. Thomas. We will consider at length the natural law position developed by Germain Grisez, John Finnis, and Joseph Boyle, taking into account Grisez's latest views (pp. 110-111), and briefly summarize the theory set forth by Martin Rhonheimer.

NATURAL LAW IN ST. THOMAS AQUINAS

St. Thomas considered the subject of natural law formally in his *Summa theologiae,* but references to natural law and to such allied notions as conscience, synderesis, providence, as well as eternal and divine law are found throughout his writings, from his early "Commentary" or *Scriptum* on Peter Lombard's *Libri Sententiarum* onward.[2]

In his master work, the *Summa theologiae,* Thomas discusses law in general, the different kinds of law (including natural law), and God's eternal law before offering a more extensive exposition of his ideas about natural law and its relationship both to human positive law and the law of God as divinely revealed. Since natural law is "law" in a real and proper sense, it is important to begin our consideration of Thomas's thought on natural law in the *Summa theologiae* by briefly summarizing his teaching on the meaning of law as such. I then propose to note succinctly his understanding of God's eternal law. I will then turn to a consideration of his more detailed presentation of natural law.

1. The Basic Understanding of Law in the *Summa Theologiae*

In this work, Thomas begins by saying that law is an extrinsic principle of human acts, in distinction to virtues and vices, which are intrinsic principles of such acts. He initially describes law as "a rule or measure of acts whereby one is induced to act or is restrained from acting." Since this is so, he says that law pertains to reason, insofar as "reason, which is the first principle of human acts, is the rule and measure of human acts."[3] Law as such is thus something that is brought into being by reason: it is an *ordinatio rationis,* an ordering of reason. In an enlightening response to an objection that law cannot pertain to reason because St. Paul had spoken of a "law" in his "members" (Rom 7:23), Thomas notes that law can be said to be "in" something or "pertain to" something in two ways: "In one way [law is said to be 'in' something] as it is in that which rules and measures. And because this is proper to reason, it follows that in this way law exists exclusively in reason." He continues by saying that law can be said to be "in" something in a more passive, participative way, in whatever is ruled and measured by a law: "And it is in this way that law is 'in' all those things that are inclined toward something in virtue of some law, not essentially, but as it were in a participative sense."[4]

The fact that law belongs essentially and formally to reason and is, indeed, the result of an act of intelligence is made even clearer by St. Thomas in a response that he gives to another objection. According to this objection, law cannot belong to reason since it can be neither the power of reason itself nor one of its habits or faculties, nor one of its acts. In replying to this objection, St. Thomas says that practical reason — i.e., reason as ordered to action — brings into being "universal propositions directed to action." These universal propositions of practical reason play a role in practical thinking comparable to the role played in speculative inquiry by the universally true propositions of speculative reason relative to the conclusions that it reaches. And, Aquinas continues, "universal propositions of this kind, namely, of the practical reason as ordered to actions, have the meaning of law" (*et huiusmodi propositiones universales rationis practicae ordinatae ad actiones habent rationem legis*).[5]

From all this, it is luminously clear that in the mind of St. Thomas *law as such not only belongs to reason but consists of true propositions or precepts brought into being by reason.*

In subsequent articles of the *Summa theologiae* (1-2, 90), Thomas describes other qualities of law in the general sense. It must be ordered to the common good,[6] it must come from the whole people or from someone having charge of the whole people and acting on their behalf,[7] and it must be promulgated or made known.[8]

2. Eternal Law

Thomas taught that all creation — the cosmos and all things within it — is under the governance of God's intelligence. Thus, the eternal law is the *ratio* or divine plan of the governance of all things insofar as this *ratio* or divine plan exists within the mind of God himself as the ruler of the universe.[9] The eternal law directs the entire created universe and the activity of all created things, including the activity of human persons. Eternal law is thus the "*ratio* of the divine wisdom insofar as it is directive of all acts and movements."[10] The end to which the eternal law directs all of creation is the universal common good of the entire created universe, and it is promulgated along with creation.[11]

3. Natural Law: Its Central Meaning and Character

Thomas teaches that *all* created realities "participate" in the eternal law. But they do so differently, in accordance with their natures. Nonrational beings participate in the eternal law in a purely passive way insofar as from it they receive an "impression" whereby "they have inclinations toward their proper acts and ends."[12] The eternal law is "in" them inasmuch as they are ruled and measured by it.[13] But human persons, inasmuch as they are intelligent, rational creatures, participate *actively* in the eternal law, and their active, intelligent participation is precisely what the natural law is.[14] The eternal law is "in" them both because they are ruled and measured by it *and* because they actively rule and measure their own acts in accordance with it. It is thus "in" them properly and formally as "law." Contrasting the different ways in which nonrational and rational creatures participate in God's eternal law, Aquinas says: "Even nonrational animals participate in the eternal *ratio* in their own way, just as does the rational creature. But because the rational creature participates in it by intelligence and reason (*intellectualiter et rationaliter*), therefore the participation of the eternal law in the rational creature is *properly* called law: for law is something pertaining to reason. . . . But in the nonrational creature it is not participated in rationally; hence it cannot be said to be law [in the nonrational creature] except by way of a similitude."[15]

Natural law, as it exists in the rational creature, is entitatively distinct from the eternal law that exists in God, the superintelligent Creator. But it is not something "other than" the eternal law. It *is* this eternal law itself mediated to or shared by the rational creature.[16] Natural law characterizes both the nobility of the rational creature as the being created in the image of God and the great love that God has for the rational creature, whom he wills to share actively in his own provident wisdom.

Thomas clarifies the way that the eternal law is "in" the rational creature when he considers the position, held by many of his medieval predecessors, that the natural law is a power or a habit, in particular the habit of synderesis or of the first principles of practical reasoning.[17] He grants that natural law may, in a secondary and derived sense, be regarded as a habit insofar as the judgments of practical reason that together go to constitute it are habitually kept in mind. But in its proper sense, natural law is *not* a habit, nor is it a power. Rather, it is a reality brought into being (*constitutum*) through reason; it is a work of human intelligence as ordered to action (*ratio practica*), just as a proposition of the speculative intellect is an achievement of human intelligence as ordered to knowing for the sake of knowing. Natural law, therefore, is something that we ourselves naturally bring into being by the spontaneous exercise of our own intelligence as ordered to action. It is something that we bring into being by our doing (what Thomas calls a *quod quis agit*), not something enabling us to bring something into being by our own doing (what he calls a *quo quis agit*).[18]

As such and properly, then, natural law is for St. Thomas an achievement of practical reason. It consists of a body or ordered set of true propositions formed by practical reason about what-is-to-be-done.[19] But what are these propositions, and how do they constitute an ordered set?

Thomas begins to address this issue in the important second article of question 94 of the *Prima Secundae* of his *Summa theologiae*. In this article, he is concerned with the "starting points" or "first principles" of natural law, the first set of practical propositions or precepts that go to make it up. In this article, he begins by making an important analogy between the precepts of natural law, which pertain to reason as ordered to action (*ratio practica*), and the first principles of demonstration, which pertain to reason as ordered to speculative inquiry or knowledge for the sake of knowledge (*ratio speculativa*). He says that just as *being* is the first thing that our intellect grasps with regard to its knowledge of reality, so *good* is what is first of all grasped by our intelligence as directed to action. He then declares: "Therefore, the first principle in practical reason is that which is founded upon the meaning (*ratio*) of the good, which meaning is, *the good is that which all things desire.* Therefore, this is the first precept of [natural] law, namely, that *good is to be done and pursued, and evil is to be avoided.* And upon this [precept or 'proposition' of practical reason] are based all other precepts of natural law, namely, that all those things belong to natural law that practical reason naturally grasps as goods to be done [or evils to be avoided]."[20]

Continuing, Thomas says that "good" has the meaning of an end, whereas "bad" has the opposite meaning. It thus follows that "reason naturally apprehends as goods, and consequently to be pursued in action, all those things to which man has a natural inclination, and things contrary to them [reason naturally apprehends] as evils to be avoided."[21]

It is most important here to note that Thomas does not say that these "natural inclinations" constitute natural law. Rather, he is saying that the real goods of human existence to which human beings are naturally oriented are grasped "naturally" — i.e., nondiscursively — by human reason as the "good" that is to be done and pursued. Practical reason apprehends in these goods the "ends" or "points" of human choices and action. To put matters another way, the basic practical principle that *good is to be done and pursued, and that its opposite, evil, is to be avoided* is specified by identifying real goods of human persons. According to Thomas, there exist within us "natural inclinations" dynamically directing us toward specific aspects of human well-being and flourishing, and our practical intelligence "naturally" apprehends as good, and therefore to be pursued in human choice and action, the realities to which these natural inclinations direct us. When he says that practical reason "naturally" apprehends the goods to which human beings are naturally inclined, Thomas means that there is no need for discursive, syllogistic reasoning in order for us to know them as good. Knowledge of these goods is not innate, but it is direct and nondiscursive, given human experience.

But what are our "natural inclinations" and the basic human goods or aspects of human well-being corresponding to them? In q. 94, a. 2, Thomas distinguishes three levels of basic, natural inclinations and basic human goods. On the first level, there is in us a natural inclination to the good in accordance with the nature that we have in common with all substances. The good to which we are naturally inclined at this level is that of being itself, and since, as Thomas elsewhere notes, the being of living things is life itself,[22] the relevant human good here is life itself. At another level, there is in us a natural inclination "to more special goods according to the nature" we have "in common with other animals." The relevant good here is the union of male and female and the handing on of new life and the education of human persons. Finally, there is in us, Thomas says, an "inclination to the good according to the nature of reason, which is a nature proper to man: thus man has a natural inclination to know the truth about God, and to live in society; and in this respect whatever pertains to this inclination belongs to natural law, for example, that man avoid ignorance, that he not give offense to others with whom he must live (*conversari*), and other such things."[23] In other words, the relevant human goods to which this inclination points us are such goods as knowledge about God, fellowship and friendship with other persons, and the like.

The list of basic human goods given by Thomas in this article is not intended by him to be taxative or exhaustive; it is rather an illustrative list, as is indicated by the fact that he uses such expressions as "and the like" (*et similia*) and "of this kind" (*huiusmodi*) in speaking about the goods that he names. Moreover, in the very next article Thomas explicitly says that "there is a natural inclination in every human being to act in accord with reason. And this is to act in accord with virtue." Thus, here the good to which we are naturally inclined is the good of virtue.[24]

It seems that one can legitimately say, on the basis of q. 94, a. 2 of the *Prima Secundae*, that the goods to which we are naturally inclined, when grasped by practical reason, serve as starting points or principles of practical reason, of natural law, of deliberating about what-is-to-be-done, and that these primary principles could be articulated as: *life is a good to be preserved and protected; marriage and the education of children are goods to be pursued; knowledge of the truth, particularly the truth about God, is a good to be pursued;* etc. Such principles or precepts specify the basic precept — *good is to be done and pursued and its opposite, evil, avoided* — by identifying the goods that are to be pursued in action. Surprisingly, however, Thomas himself does not articulate primary precepts of natural law in this way. Rather, in the body of q. 94, a. 2, he articulates precepts such as "man is to avoid ignorance" (*homo ignorantiam vitet*) and "one is not to offend others with whom one must live" (*alios non offendat cum quibus debet conversari*).

Summary: From the texts studied thus far, it is clear that in the *Summa theologiae* St. Thomas regards the natural law as follows: (1) it is the active participation by the rational creature in God's eternal law; (2) it pertains to reason insofar as it is something that practical reason constitutes or brings into being; (3) the "something" that practical reason brings into being are "precepts" or practical propositions about what-is-to-be-done, beginning with the "first" or "primary" precept of practical reason, a precept founded upon the concept of the "good." I now propose to look more closely at the teaching of Thomas in this work on the different sorts of precepts that, taken together, constitute the natural law.

4. 'Primary' Precepts of Natural Law, Precepts 'Close to' Primary Precepts, and Other Precepts of Natural Law

According to St. Thomas, there are three "grades" or "levels" of natural law precepts. The first grade or set of natural law precepts consists of "those common and first principles,"[25] "of which there is no need for any other 'edition' inasmuch as they are written in natural reason and are, as it were, self-evidently known (*per se nota*)."[26] Belonging to this set of natural law precepts are principles already examined, namely, the precept that *good is to be pursued and done, and its opposite, evil, is to be avoided,* such precepts as "man is to avoid ignorance" and "one is not to offend others with whom one must live," and such like. In addition, as noted above, one can articulate as primary precepts of natural law such principles as *life is a good to be preserved and protected, knowledge of the truth is to be pursued,* and others of like kind.

Thomas also includes, among the primary and common precepts of natural law, such precepts as "evil is to be done to no one,"[27] "do unto others as you would have them do unto you; do not do unto others as you would not have them do unto you,"[28] and "you are to love the Lord your God and you are to love your neighbor."[29] And one loves one's neighbor by willing that the goods of human existence, of which we have already spoken, flourish in him.

Among the *first, nondemonstrable principles or precepts of natural law,* some direct us to do and pursue the good and avoid its contrary (e.g., *good is to be done and pursued and its opposite, evil, is to be avoided,* and, as suggested above, such principles as *human life is a good to be preserved and protected, knowledge of the truth is a good to be pursued, ignorance is to be avoided,* etc.), whereas others concern our way of pursuing such goods (e.g., we are to do so by acting fairly [the Golden Rule], by refusing to do evil to anyone, and by loving God and neighbor). In fact, St. Thomas affirms that the precept to love God and neighbor is precisely the precept or principle from which those precepts that make up the second grade or set of natural law precepts are derived, or in whose light these precepts are known to be true.[30]

This second grade or set of natural law precepts includes those "that the natural reason of every man immediately and of itself (*per se*) judges to be done or not done."[31] Such precepts are proximate conclusions from the first nondemonstrable precepts of natural law,[32] and they can be understood to be true "immediately, with a modicum of consideration."[33] They are "more determinate" than the primary precepts of natural law, but they can be easily grasped by the intelligence of the most ordinary individual.[34] These precepts, which are proximate conclusions from the primary principles of natural law, "are absolutely of the natural law."[35] These precepts, it is true, can become perverted in a few instances because of sin and bad habits, and it is for this reason that they have need of a further "edition," namely, through the divine (positive) law,[36] for these precepts are those that we find in the Decalogue.

The third grade or set of natural law precepts, according to Thomas, are truths about human action that are known only "by the more subtle consideration of reason."[37] They are like conclusions derived from the second set of natural law precepts,[38] and they are known only by the "wise," i.e., for Aquinas, by those in whom the virtue of prudence is perfected. To know these precepts of natural law, "much consideration of different circumstances" is required, and to consider these diligently is something that pertains to the wise. Those not perfected in virtue need to be instructed in these precepts by those who are wise.[39]

Thus, according to Thomas, there is a definite structure to the natural law. It consists of (1) certain fundamental, nondemonstrable, primary principles; (2) normative precepts that flow immediately, and with very little consideration, from these primary precepts; and (3) normative precepts that can be known only after considerable thought and only by the wise, or those perfected in the virtue of prudence.

This structure of natural law is brought out in several passages of the *Summa theologiae*.[40] One of the most striking is 1-2, q. 100, a. 3, where Thomas asks whether all the moral precepts of the old law can be reduced to the ten precepts of the Decalogue. According to Thomas, all the precepts of the Decalogue, while revealed by God, are capable of being known by the exercise of natural human reason — with the exception of the third commandment, regarding the Sabbath, whose determination of a specific day is not knowable by natural reason.[41] The precepts of the Decalogue, in other words, belong to natural law. But they are not among the primary precepts of natural law. The following kind of schema shows the structure of natural law as described by Thomas in this question:

Primary Precepts	Proximate Conclusions	Remote Conclusions
	Among the precepts of the Decalogue, two kinds of precepts are not counted.	
Those, namely, which are first and common, of which there is no need of further "edition," inasmuch as they are written in natural reason, as it were self-evidently known		
		and also those that are discovered to be fitting to reason through diligent inquiry of the wise: for these come from God to the people by means of the discipline of the wise.[42]

Here Thomas explicitly says that there are two kinds of precepts that are distinct from the precepts of the Decalogue. The primary precepts of natural law, since they are self-evidently true, are written in human reason and do not require divine revelation. Also not among the precepts of the Decalogue are those more specific precepts that need considerable thought for their truth to be grasped. Yet both of these kinds of natural law precepts are intimately related to the precepts of the Decalogue. Indeed, Thomas's argument here is that the Decalogue in some way does "contain" both these kinds of precepts of natural law. Thomas puts it this way:

Primary Precepts	Proximate Conclusions	Remote Conclusions
But both of these kinds of precepts are contained in the precepts of the Decalogue, but differently.		
For those that are first and common are contained [in the precepts of the Decalogue] as principles		
	are contained in their proximate conclusions,	
		while those that are known by the wise
	are contained in them	
conversely,		
		as conclusions
	in their principles.[43]	

I believe that by now Thomas's understanding of natural law should be quite clear. For him, natural law is a "work" of human reason, consisting in an ordered series or set of "precepts." The first set of natural law precepts embraces the self-evidently true propositions about what-is-to-be-done that are grasped by practical reason. These primary precepts or first principles of natural law include two sorts of precepts. One sort directs us to do and pursue the good and avoid its contrary (and principles logically related to this basic principle direct us to pursue the real goods perfective of us and toward which we are naturally inclined, goods such as life itself, marriage and the education of children, knowledge of the truth etc). The other sort concerns our way of pursuing these goods: we are to do so by acting fairly (the Golden Rule), by loving God and neighbor, by refusing to do evil to anyone. These primary precepts or principles of natural law can never be obliterated from the (developed) human mind. All moral agents are aware of them, for they are written in the human heart.[44]

The second set or grade of natural law precepts includes those that are "proximate" to the primary principles. They are so close to them, in Thomas's view, that they can easily be known by everyone, even the simplest person, unless one's practical reason is perverted by sin or one lives in a perverse society.[45] These *derivative* but easily known (according to Aquinas) precepts of natural law are the moral precepts of the Decalogue. According to Aquinas, these natural law precepts are moral absolutes, exceptionless norms, from which not even God can grant a dispensation.[46]

Finally, the third set or grade of natural law precepts includes more remote moral norms, derived from the precepts of the Decalogue as from their principles, and known only after much consideration by the "wise" — i.e., persons perfected in the virtue of prudence or, in Christian terms, saints.

This is clearly the structure of natural law according to St. Thomas.

EXCURSUS 1:
St. Thomas and Ulpian's Definition of Natural Law

Ulpian, a second-century Roman lawyer, defined natural law as "that which nature has taught all animals." Several contemporary Catholic moral theologians — among them Charles E. Curran, Timothy E. O'Connell, and Richard M. Gula — claim that the teaching of St. Thomas on natural law is highly ambiguous. On the one hand, it stresses the role that reason has to play in constituting natural law. On the other hand, they say, his thought, because of the influence of Ulpian, definitely tends "to identify the demands of natural law with physical and biological processes"[47] and leads to what they consider a "physicalistic" understanding of natural law.[48] Because of this claim by some contemporary Catholic theologians, it will be worthwhile to examine the way in which Aquinas accommodated Ulpian's definition of natural law into his own thought.

In one of his earliest writings, his *Scriptum super IV Libros Sententiarum,* Thomas takes up the question of natural law in connection with his discussion of a problem that had plagued his predecessors in their attempts to relate natural law to the teaching of Scripture. How could the polygyny of the Old Testament patriarchs be reconciled with natural law?[49] My concern is not with this specific problem but rather with Thomas's thought on natural law and his use of Ulpian's definition of natural law.

In his analysis of this issue, Thomas first notes that all beings have within themselves, by their very nature, principles whereby they can not only bring about the actions proper to themselves but also direct them to their proper ends. Beings that lack knowledge act in a necessary way, but in beings that have knowledge, the principles of operation are knowledge and appetite. In beings capable of knowledge, consequently, there must be a natural concept (*naturalis conceptio*) in the cognitive faculty and a natural inclination (*naturalis inclinatio*) in the appetitive faculty, whereby these beings are ordered to the actions and ends appropriate to them. Since man differs radically in kind from other animals, however, in his ability to know the end as such and the relationship of means to ends, the "natural concept" in his case "is called natural law, whereas in other animals it is called a natural estimation (*aestimatio*)." Nonrational animals "are impelled by a force of nature to perform actions proper to them rather than acting by being regulated, as it were, by any kind of judgment properly so called." Aquinas then continues: "Therefore natural law is nothing other than the concept naturally impressed upon man whereby he is directed to acting suitably in the actions that are proper to him, whether these actions pertain to his generic nature, such as generating life, eating, and so forth, or whether they pertain to his specific nature as man, such as thinking and things of this kind."[50]

What is most important about the notion of natural law expressed in this passage from an early writing of St. Thomas is that natural law is explicitly related to human intelligence, to the fact that the human person, alone of all animals, is capable of knowing the end as such and of relating means to ends. The thought expressed here and elsewhere in St. Thomas's *Commentary on the Sentences* is surely in accord with the thought set forth in the passages from the *Summa theologiae* that we have already considered: natural law, as law, is exclusively proper to human persons, and, precisely as law, natural law is related to human cognition.

As already noted, the discussion of natural law in this passage from the *Commentary on the Sentences* was prompted by the polygyny of the patriarchs. The question posed was "whether having many wives is contrary to natural law." In the body of the article, from which the citations given above are taken, Thomas asserts that polygyny is indeed against the natural law in the sense that it impedes at least partially the marital good of fidelity and the peace and harmony that ought to reign in the family. He also notes that it completely destroys the good of the "sacrament" of marriage. He concedes, however, that it is not destructive of the principal end of the institution of marriage — namely, the procreation and education of children — and in this sense is not against natural law.[51] One of the objections to the view (which Thomas held) that polygyny is against natural law had urged that a plurality of wives is in no way against natural law, inasmuch as the natural law is that which nature has taught all animals — i.e., Ulpian's definition of natural law — and obviously in the animal kingdom it is by no means unnatural for one male to have more than one mate. In replying to this objection, Thomas distinguishes several ways in which natural law could be understood; and in commenting on these ways of understanding natural law, Thomas takes up the celebrated definition of Ulpian.

Thomas says that natural law can be understood, first, to refer to something that is natural *by reason of its principle* or source. It is in this way that Cicero understood natural law, for to him it was a kind of innate source or power, a principle intrinsic to things (*ius naturae est quod non opinio genuit, sed quaedam innata vis inseruit*). He goes on to note that the principle from which natural law springs can be extrinsic to the being regulated by natural law, and in this sense he makes room for the definition given by Gratian (incorrectly attributed, in Thomas's text, to Isidore), that natural law is what is contained in law and gospel (*ius naturale est quod in lege et in Evangelio continetur*). Finally, he notes that natural law may be understood to refer to what is natural, not by reason of its source or principle but rather by reason of "nature," i.e., *by reason of the subject matter with which natural law is concerned* (*tertio dicitur ius naturale non solum a principio, sed a natura, quia de naturalibus est*). If natural law is taken in this sense, nature is contrasted with or is opposed to reason. Consequently, "taking natural law in its most restricted or limited sense" (*strictissimo modo accipiendi ius naturale*),[52] "those things that pertain only to men, although they follow from the dictate of reason, are not said to be of the natural law; but only those things that natural reason dictates about matters that are common to man and to other animals; and thus the aforesaid definition is given, namely, that 'natural law is what nature has taught all animals.' "[53]

It is most important to be clear about Aquinas's thought here. He is definitely *not* claiming that natural law, as *law*, is something infrarational, an instinct that human persons share with other animals. After all, in the body of the article he had stressed that natural law as such is unique to human beings and that it is a *naturalis conceptio*. In nonrational animals, he taught in the body of the article, there is no natural law; there is only a natural "estimation," a power or force of nature impelling them to act in ways appropriate to achieve the ends for which they are made. Thus, in this celebrated passage, Thomas in no way repudiates what he has just said in the body of the article (or what he was to say subsequently in the texts from the *Summa theologiae* that we have already examined) about natural law as something brought into being or constituted by reason. He is making room for Ulpian's understanding of natural law in only a limited way, namely, *in the sense that it refers to the subject matter with which or about which natural law is concerned*, for this is what he explicitly says. In other words, he is saying that the tendencies that human beings share with other animals are fitting objects of natural law taken in its proper sense as an achievement of reason — they are fit matter to be brought under the rule of law, i.e., under natural law understood as an achievement of human reason. This is evident from the text, for Thomas explicitly says that the natural law, understood in Ulpian's sense, has to do only with those things that *"natural reason dictates* about matters that are common to man and to other animals" (*illa tantum quae naturalis ratio dictat de his quae sunt homini aliisque communia*).

Thomas also makes room for Ulpian's definition in his later works, in passages in the *Summa theologiae*[54] and in his commentary on Aristotle's *Nicomachean Ethics*.[55] But in all these places, the room given by Thomas to Ulpian's definition of natural law as the law that nature has taught all animals is limited to fit in with his own teaching on natural law as the work of reason. Natural law as defined by Ulpian never has the meaning of an *ordinatio* or *dictamen rationis,* the achievement of practical reason, that Thomas always considers to be the essential element of law and of natural law in the formal, proper sense.[56] Ulpian's definition can never be used in reference to natural law as that which is in something as ruling and measuring. It uniformly refers to natural law only in an accommodated sense, as found in something only "participatively, as it were."[57] In short, Ulpian's definition of natural law, as St. Thomas appropriates it, refers to the tendencies or inclinations that human beings possess by virtue of being, in truth, animals, albeit animals of a special and unique kind — tendencies that can be grasped by practical reason along with the real goods toward which they incline the human person, and thereby formally brought under the dominion of reason and capable of being expressed in principles or propositions that serve as starting points for thinking about what is to be done in and through human action — that serve, in other words, as the principles that go to make up the content of natural law as law.[58]

There was good reason, I believe, why Thomas took pains to make room for Ulpian's definition of natural law within his thought. Aquinas was no dualist. For him, a human being is not an incarnate spirit, a "separated substance" in some way accidentally united to a material body. For him, a human being is first and foremost an animal, a very special kind of animal to be sure, different in kind from all other animals by reason of his intelligence and power to determine his life by his own free choices, but an animal nonetheless. Thus, the tendencies that humans possess in virtue of their animality are basic *human* tendencies, fundamental *inclinationes naturales,* and the goods correlative to these tendencies, goods such as the procreation and education of children, are basic *human* goods meriting the respect of human intelligence.

This analysis of the way in which Thomas incorporated Ulpian's definition of natural law into his own thought on the subject shows that he never accepted Ulpian's understanding of natural law as a nonrational kind of instinct. Rather, he consistently held that natural law, formally and properly as *law*, is the work of practical reason. He accepted Ulpian's definition only as a very restricted or limited way of understanding natural law, as referring to those tendencies that human beings share with other animals and which, in the human animal, must be brought under the rule of reason, under the tutelage of natural law.

EXCURSUS 2:
St. Thomas's Teaching on Natural Law in the
Summa Contra Gentes

In addition to his formal treatment of natural law in his most mature work, the *Summa theologiae*, St. Thomas also had much to say about the reality of natural law in another major work, the *Summa Contra Gentes*. In this important work, written as a handbook for preachers attempting to win intelligent Muslims over to the Catholic faith, St. Thomas devotes much of Book 3 to a study of divine providence. In Chapters 111-129 of this book, he is concerned primarily with the way in which God, through his providence, governs the intellectual and rational creature, man. The expression "natural law" is used sparingly in these chapters, but the reality to which this expression refers is central to the ideas developed in them. My observations will center on the following matters: (1) the understanding of natural law central to Thomas's thought in this work; (2) the "divine" law and the way in which the rational creature is subject to it; (3) the end or purpose of the divine law; and (4) the requirements of this law and of "nature."

1. The Central Meaning of Law in *Summa Contra Gentes*, Book 3, Chapters 111 and Following: These chapters make it evident that for Thomas the primary and formal meaning of "law" is a certain *ratio* or intelligent "plan" of operation or action. It is the rule or measure of an action, as Thomas says time and time again.[59] The meaning of law for Thomas in this work is very clear: it is an intelligent plan existing in the mind of the lawgiver directing the actions of agents toward their end. As can be seen, this notion of "law" is the same as that set forth in the texts from the *Summa theologiae*.

2. The "Divine" Law and the Subjection of Rational or Intelligent Creatures to It: Chapters 111 and following of Book 3 make it clear that for St. Thomas the highest law and indeed the source of all true law is the "divine law," i.e., a *"ratio* of divine providence in its governing capacity."[60] God's providence and the divine law extend to everything that God has made, for he directs all things to their proper ends. But, in a special way, God's intelligent creature, man, is subject to divine providence and to divine law. This is the theme of Chapters 113-114, and their core idea is luminously set forth in the following passage: "The intelligent creature is subject to divine providence in such a way that he is not only governed thereby, but is also able *to know the rational plan of providence* in some way. . . . Through his possession of the capacity to exercise providence [over his own actions and those of lower creatures], man may also direct and govern his own acts. So the rational creature participates in divine providence, not only by being governed passively, but also by governing actively, for he governs himself in his personal acts, and even others."[61]

St. Thomas's thought here can be easily summarized. The highest law is the divine law, an intelligent plan in God's mind ordering all things toward their proper ends. Nonintelligent creatures are subject to divine providence and to the divine law in a purely passive way, inasmuch as they are ruled by it. But rational creatures are subject to divine providence and divine law in a special way. They are endowed with the capacity to know the end to which they are ordered and the suitability of their freely chosen acts for attaining this end.[62] They are thus subject to divine providence and divine law not only insofar as they are ruled by divine law but, more importantly, because they can inwardly participate in the divine law by knowing it and its requirements and freely ordering their lives and actions in accord with it. Indeed, this divine law is "given" to them,[63] and they are to use their freedom of choice rightly by choosing in accord with this divine law as this is inwardly known by them. Although the term "natural law" is not used in these chapters (113-114) that I have been summarizing, the reality of natural law is precisely what Aquinas has in mind. One could say that the active participation by men in the divine law, whereby they order their own actions, is the natural law, the "divine law" as "given" or communicated to men. Note that in this work Aquinas uses the expression "divine law" to refer to what he calls "eternal law" in the *Summa theologiae.*

3. The End or Purpose of the Divine Law: The final end or purpose for the sake of which God has given mankind a share in his divine law is that they may cling to him in love.[64] Indeed, as Thomas puts it most eloquently, the "chief intent of the divine law" is that "man be subject to God and that he should offer special reverence to him, not merely in his heart, but also orally and by bodily works."[65]

But in addition to directing man to God by "works" — i.e., "actions" that are fitting — the divine law (in which man participates in some degree by his own knowledge of what he is to do) also directs him to love of his neighbor.[66] It does so by directing or ordering man to "live in relationship to other men according to the order of reason." This in turn requires that man live in harmony and peace with his fellows, that he render to them what is their due, honoring his parents and refraining from injuring his neighbor, either by killing him or harming him in other ways (such as by committing adultery, stealing, or bearing false witness).[67]

4. The Requirements of This Law and of "Nature": The final paragraphs of the preceding section have already, to some extent, covered this theme. The divine law, in which human beings participate through their intelligence, directs them to "act in accordance with reason."[68] It requires them to render to God, first of all, the adoration that is due to him and to him alone.[69] It requires man to respect his neighbors, to live at peace and harmony with them, rendering to them what is their due — and this requires honoring one's parents and respecting the life, marriage, good name, and property of one's neighbor.[70]

It also requires man to use created things lower in the hierarchy of creation in a way befitting his own needs,[71] and likewise demands that man subordinate his lower powers (his feelings, passions, etc.) to the requirements of reason or of intelligence, managing them so that the "activity of reason and the human good are least hindered, and instead are helped."[72]

It is also evident, from his discussion of fornication and marriage in Chapter 122, that the divine law in which man participates and his own "nature" require him to respect the goods or purposes to which certain specific kinds of human actions are ordered, e.g., the deliberate choice to exercise one's power of genital sexuality.[73] All these are, in Aquinas's judgment, demands or requirements of the "divine" law and of the "nature" that has been given to man.

Summary: This brief account of St. Thomas's teaching in Book 3 of the *Summa Contra Gentes* allows us to have a clear idea of the way he conceived natural law in this work. It is something pertaining to human intelligence. Indeed, it is the way human beings *actively* participate in the divine law, ordering their own actions in accordance with this law insofar as this law is inwardly known by them. This law directs man to live in accordance with reason, i.e., to respect the "end" or "ends" for which he has been made and to which he is naturally inclined. These "ends" include, first of all, God, whom man must adore and to whom he must cling in love. But, in a somewhat different way, these "ends" include life in fellowship and amity with others, proper respect for one's personal integrity and dignity, and proper respect for the goods or purposes to which specific sorts of human activity — e.g., genital sex — are ordered. The account in the *Summa Contra Gentes*, while differently expressed than the account found in the *Summa theologiae*, is fundamentally the same.

From all that has been said thus far, the understanding of natural law in Thomas Aquinas should now be quite clear. I shall now consider the teaching of Vatican Council II and Pope John Paul II on natural law.

NATURAL LAW, VATICAN COUNCIL II, AND POPE JOHN PAUL II

1. Natural Law and Vatican Council II

We have already seen, in Chapter One, some aspects of the teaching of Vatican Council II that are relevant to the subject of natural law. The Council affirmed, first of all, that "the highest norm of human life is God's divine law — eternal, objective, and universal — whereby God orders, directs, and governs the entire universe and all the ways of the human community according to a plan conceived in his wisdom and love" (*Dignitatis humanae*, no. 3). It likewise affirmed, and in doing so explicitly referred to the thought of St. Thomas,[74] that "God has enabled man to participate in this law of his, so that, under the gentle disposition of divine providence, man may be able to arrive at a deeper and deeper knowledge of unchanging truth" (ibid.). In other words, it affirmed the reality of natural law, which is precisely humankind's participation in God's divine and eternal law. It likewise affirmed that man discovers this law of God "deep within his conscience," and that this law summons man to "love and to do what is good and to avoid evil" (*Gaudium et spes*, no. 16). My intention now is to examine the teaching of Vatican Council II relevant to natural law more fully.[75]

According to the Council Fathers, "all men, because they are persons, that is, beings endowed with reason and free will and therefore bearing personal responsibility, are both impelled by their nature and bound by a moral obligation to seek the truth" (*Dignitatis humanae*, no. 2). The truth at stake here is, moreover, not an abstract or speculative truth. Indeed, men "are bound to adhere to the truth once they come to know it and to direct their whole lives in accordance with the demands of truth" (ibid.). Their duty is to "prudently form right and true judgments of conscience" (ibid., no. 3). The truth in question, in other words, is *moral truth*, truth known by practical reason — and in knowing it men participate in God's divine and eternal law.

Clearly, the demands of God's divine and eternal law are one and the same as the requirements of natural law. This is made clear by the Council Fathers in several key passages. For instance, in *Dignitatis humanae*, after reminding the Catholic faithful that they are obliged, in forming their consciences, to pay careful heed to the "sacred and certain teachings of the Church," the Council Fathers go on to say: "The Catholic Church is by the will of Christ the teacher of truth. It is her duty to proclaim and teach with authority the truth which is Christ and, at the same time, to declare and confirm by her authority *the principles of the moral order which spring from human nature itself*" (no. 14).

Note that this passage refers to *principles* of the moral order or of natural law. This obviously means that in the minds of its authors the moral order (which, ultimately, is identified with God's divine and eternal law and which, ultimately, is identified with natural law or humankind's intelligent participation in God's eternal law) embraces not simply one fundamental principle but a number of universally binding principles. This is a subject to which I shall return.

In another passage, God's divine law is explicitly linked to the natural law, for in it the Council Fathers say, "The Church, in preaching the Gospel to all men and dispensing the treasures of grace in accordance with its divine mission, makes a contribution to the strengthening of peace over all the world and helps to consolidate the foundations of brotherly communion among men and peoples. *This it does by imparting the knowledge of the divine and natural law*" (*Gaudium et spes*, no. 89).

It is worth observing, in connection with these passages, that Vatican Council II recognized the difficulty people have in coming to know the truth. Their struggle to arrive at a deeper and deeper knowledge of the demands of God's divine and eternal law can be impeded because of their own biases and passions and because of the prejudices and misconceptions common to the cultures in which they live. The heart of the problem is human sinfulness, which afflicts the whole human race and each individual personally. As a result, human beings need help in coming to know the moral truths to which they must cleave and in whose light they are to shape inwardly their choices and actions. This help, the Council teaches (cf., e.g., *Gaudium et spes*, no. 17) is given humankind by God, who has deigned to reveal to us the basic truths of the moral order and who has given his Church the competence and authority to impart knowledge of the "divine and natural law."[76]

What sort of "principles" pertain to natural law according to the teaching of Vatican Council II? In the magnificent passage in *Gaudium et spes* on the dignity of personal conscience that we have already examined, the Council Fathers insisted that the voice of God's law, which man discovers deep within his conscience, always summons him "to love and to do what is good and to avoid evil" (no. 16). Thus, the principle that good is to be done and pursued and evil avoided is explicitly affirmed by the Council Fathers.

In addition, the documents of the Council clearly specify what they mean by the "good," for in other passages we learn that the good fruits of our nature as human persons include the goods of "truth and life, holiness and grace, justice, love, and peace" and that these goods perfective of human persons will be found again, "transfigured," in the heavenly kingdom (*Gaudium et spes*, no. 39). The Council Fathers, like Aquinas, obviously think that there are real goods of human persons, aspects of their full being or well-being, and that among these are the goods of life itself, knowledge of the truth, harmonious relationships with others (justice, peace) and with God (holiness). It would thus seem to follow that each of such goods, when intelligently grasped, serves as a *principle* of human choice and action. These are the goods that are to be done and pursued, and their opposites are the evils that are to be avoided.

In another significant passage of *Gaudium et spes*, the Council Fathers first point out the significance of human action as self-determining. They then go on to propose a *norm* or criterion for human action. Obviously, this proposed norm is subordinate to the ultimate norm of human life already identified in *Dignitatis humanae*, namely, God's divine, eternal law. Yet this norm is proposed by the Council as a true norm for guiding human choices and actions. This norm, the Council Fathers assert, "is that in accord with the divine plan and will, *human activity should harmonize with the genuine good of the human race*, and allow men as individuals and as members of society to pursue their total vocation and fulfill it" (no. 35).

This, I believe, is an exceptionally important passage. In it, the Council Fathers are asserting that human persons, in making good moral choices, are to choose in such a way that they reverence and respect, in each and every choice and action, whatever is really a good of human persons. It is in this way that human beings fulfill the command to love, for by doing so they manifest (a) their love of God, who is the author of the goods of human existence, and (b) their love of neighbor, in whom these God-given gifts are meant to flourish.

The texts already examined make it clear that Vatican Council II affirmed that human beings are to do and pursue what is good and avoid what is evil, and that they are to choose in such a way that they respect every true good of human persons. But, in addition, the Council insisted that there are some very specific moral norms which are *universally binding*, transcending historical and cultural conditions. Thus, in a crucial section of *Gaudium et spes*, where the Council Fathers judge it necessary "first of all" to recall to mind for all human beings "the permanent binding force of universal natural law and its all-embracing principles," they go on to declare that "actions which deliberately conflict with these same principles, as well as orders commanding such actions, are criminal" (no. 79). In other words, according to this text there are certain sorts or kinds of actions that are opposed to universally binding or absolute principles of natural law. The Council Fathers, in this context, immediately go on to say that "every act of war directed to the indiscriminate destruction of whole cities or vast areas with their inhabitants is a crime against God and man, and merits firm and unequivocal condemnation" (ibid., no. 80).

The same kind of thought is central to another section of the same document, in which the subject matter is respect for human persons and the goods meant to flourish in them. In this section, the Council Fathers brand as absolutely criminal and immoral very specific sorts of human acts, for they say: "All offenses against life itself, such as murder, genocide, abortion, euthanasia and willful self-destruction; all violations of the integrity of the human person, such as mutilation, physical and mental torture, undue psychological pressures; all offenses against human dignity, such as subhuman living conditions, arbitrary imprisonment, deportation, slavery, prostitution, the selling of women and children, degrading working conditions where men are treated as mere tools for profit rather than free and responsible persons; all these and their like are criminal; they poison civilization; and they debase their perpetrators more than their victims and militate against the honor of the Creator" *(Gaudium et spes,* no. 27).

From this it is abundantly clear that the Fathers of Vatican Council II are firmly convinced that God's divine and eternal law, in which human persons intelligently participate through the natural law, includes some very specific moral norms which are absolutely and universally binding. The natural law, in other words, contains both common or first principles (e.g., good is to be done and pursued and evil avoided; human actions are to harmonize with the authentic good of human persons) and specific moral precepts (e.g., it is absolutely immoral to abort, to commit euthanasia, to kill oneself, to destroy entire cities with their populations). I believe that the teaching of Vatican Council II relevant to natural law can be summarized in the following set of propositions:

1. The highest norm of human life is God's divine law — eternal, objective, and universal *(Dignitatis humanae,* no. 3).
2. Human persons have been so made by God that they are able, by exercising their intelligence, to come to know ever more securely the unchanging truths meant to guide human choices and actions contained in God's law *(Dignitatis humanae,* no. 3; *Gaudium et spes,* no. 16).
3. The human search for unchanging truth is not easy, and it is for this reason that God has, through divine revelation, made his law and its unchanging truths known to mankind and has given his Church the competence and authority to teach mankind the requirements of his divine and natural law *(Gaudium et spes,* nos. 17, 51; *Dignitatis humanae,* no. 14).
4. Nonetheless, the unchanging truths of the moral order can be known by human intelligence insofar as these truths are rooted in the being of human persons and in the constitutive elements of human nature *(Dignitatis humanae,* nos. 3, 14; *Gaudium et spes,* nos. 16, 17, 51).
5. The divine, eternal law, which is the natural law insofar as it comes to be in the minds of human beings, contains (a) first or common prin-

ciples and (b) more particular and specific norms transcending historical and cultural situations precisely because they are rooted in constitutive elements of human nature and human persons and conform to the exigencies of human nature and human persons. Among the (a) first or common principles are such principles as *good is to be done and pursued and evil is to be avoided* (cf. *Gaudium et spes,* no. 16) and *human activity should harmonize with the genuine good of the human race* (cf. ibid., no. 35). Among the (b) more particular and specific norms are those moral absolutes proscribing the killing of the innocent, suicide, torture, and similar kinds of actions (cf. *Gaudium et spes,* nos. 27, 51, 79-80).

2. Natural Law in the Teaching of Pope John Paul II

With St. Thomas and the Fathers of Vatican Council II, Pope John Paul II clearly affirms that the highest norm of human action is God's divine law: eternal, objective, and universal, whereby he governs the entire universe and the human community according to a plan conceived in wisdom and in love (cf. *Veritatis splendor,* no. 43). Again, along with St. Thomas and Vatican Council II, he emphasizes that the "natural law" is our intelligent participation in God's eternal law (cf. ibid., nos. 12, 40). Moreover, with St. Thomas, whom he cites extensively, particularly on this point (cf. his citation from *Summa theologiae,* 1-2, 91, 2 in no. 42), John Paul II emphasizes that the natural law, inasmuch as it is the participation of *intelligent, rational* creatures in God's eternal law, is properly a *human law.* Thus, he says that "this law is called the natural law . . . not because it refers to the nature of irrational beings but because the reason which promulgates it is proper to human nature" (*Veritatis splendor,* no. 42). The moral law (i.e., the natural law), John Paul II affirms, "*has its origin in God and always finds its source in him.*" Nonetheless, "by virtue of natural reason, which derives from divine wisdom," the natural law must also be recognized as "*a properly human law*" (ibid., no. 40).

Moreover, precisely because the natural law finds its origin in God's divine and eternal law, the pope insists, its normative requirements are *truths* meant to help us choose rightly. John Paul II, in fact, speaks of our moral life as a "*theonomy, or participated theonomy,* since man's free obedience to God's law effectively implies that human reason and human will participate in God's wisdom and providence. By forbidding man to 'eat of the tree of the knowledge of good and evil,' God makes it clear that man does not originally possess such 'knowledge' as something properly his own, but only participates in it by the light of natural reason and of Divine Revelation, which manifest to him the requirements and promptings of eternal wisdom. Law must therefore be considered an expression of divine wisdom: by submitting to the law, freedom submits to the truth of creation" (ibid., no. 41).

John Paul II takes up the normative requirements or truths of the natural law in his presentation, in Chapter One of *Veritatis splendor,* of the essential link between obedience to the Ten Commandments and eternal life. In his presentation of this essential link, John Paul II makes it clear that the primordial moral requirement of the natural law is the twofold love of God and neighbor, and that the precepts of the second tablet of the Decalogue are based on the truth that we are to love our neighbor as ourselves.

He begins by noting that our Lord, in responding to the question posed to him by the rich young man, "Teacher, what good must I do to have eternal life?" (Mt 19:16), makes it clear that the answer to the question can be found "only by turning one's mind and heart to the 'One' who is good. . . . *Only God can answer the question about what is good, because he is the Good itself*" (no. 9; cf. nos. 11, 12). He continues by saying that "God has already given an answer to this question: he did so *by creating man and ordering him* with wisdom and love to his final end, through the law which is inscribed in his heart (cf. Rom 2:15), the 'natural law.' . . . He also did so *in the history of Israel,* particularly in the 'ten words,' the *commandments of Sinai*" (ibid., no. 12). The pope then reminds us that our Lord then told the young man: "If you wish to enter into life, keep the commandments" (Mt 19:17). By speaking in this way, John Paul II continues, Jesus makes clear "the close connection . . . *between eternal life and obedience to God's commandments* [which] . . . show man the path of life and lead to it" (no. 12). The first three of the commandments of the Decalogue call "us to acknowledge God as the one Lord of all and to worship him alone for his infinite holiness" (no. 11). But the young man, in responding to Jesus' declaration that he must keep the commandments if he wishes to enter eternal life, demands to know "which ones" (Mt 19:18). As the pope notes, "he asks what he must do in life in order to show that he acknowledges God's holiness" (no. 13). In his answer to this question, Jesus reminds the young man of the Decalogue's precepts concerning our neighbor. "From the very lips of Jesus," the pope observes, "man is once more given the commandments of the Decalogue" (no. 12). These Ten Commandments, the Holy Father insists, are rooted in the commandment that we are to love our neighbor as ourselves, a commandment expressing "*the singular dignity of the human person,* 'the only creature that God has wanted for its own sake' " (no. 13, with an internal citation from *Gaudium et spes,* no. 24).

It is at this point that John Paul II develops a matter of crucial importance for understanding the truths of the natural law and the relationship between the primordial command to love our neighbor as ourselves and the specific commandments of the second tablet of the Decalogue. His point is that we can love our neighbor and respect his dignity as a person only by cherishing the real goods perfective of him and by refusing to damage, destroy, or impede these goods. Appealing to the words of Jesus, John Paul II emphasizes the truth that "the different commandments of the Decalogue are really only so many reflections on the one commandment about the good of the person, at the level of the many different goods which characterize his identity as a spiritual and bodily being in relationship with God, with his neighbor, and with the material world. . . . The commandments of which Jesus reminds the young man are meant to safeguard *the good* of the person, the image of God, by protecting his *goods*" (no. 13). He goes on to say that the negative precepts of the Decalogue — "You shall not murder; you shall not commit adultery; you shall not steal; you shall not bear false witness" — "express with particular force the ever urgent need to protect human life, the communion of persons in marriage," and so on (no. 13). In addition, John Paul II insists that the negative precepts of the Decalogue, which protect the good of human persons by protecting the goods perfective of them, are moral absolutes admitting of no exceptions. (This issue will again be addressed in Chapter Four of this book.)

John Paul II likewise emphasizes that the natural law, whose specific normative requirements have been revealed through the "ten words" given on Sinai and reaffirmed by the lips of Jesus himself, is ultimately fulfilled and perfected only as "*a gift of God*: the offer of a share in the divine Goodness revealed and communicated in Jesus" (no. 11). We will return to the question of the "fulfillment" of the natural law by the law of divine grace given in Jesus in Chapter Six.

Summary: The thought of John Paul II on natural law, as set forth in his encyclical *Veritatis splendor,* can be summarized as follows. The highest law is God's divine, eternal law. The natural law is our human, intelligent participation in this eternal law, which we can come to know through the exercise of our practical reasoning. Its basic normative requirement is that we are to love God and neighbor. Love of neighbor requires us to respect and protect the good of our neighbor by protecting the goods perfective of him and by being unwilling ever to damage, destroy, or impede these goods. The natural law is fulfilled and perfected by the "offer of a share in the divine Goodness revealed and communicated in Jesus."

A brief treatment of the eternal and natural law is given in the *Catechism of the Catholic Church* (nos. 1950-1960).

NATURAL LAW IN THE THOUGHT OF GERMAIN GRISEZ, JOHN FINNIS, AND JOSEPH BOYLE

Among contemporary Catholic authors, three in particular have sought to develop the understanding of natural law on the foundations erected by St.

Thomas Aquinas, namely, Germain Grisez, John Finnis, and Joseph Boyle.[77] Here I intend, first, to summarize their understanding of natural law, relating it to that of St. Thomas and showing how it clarifies and develops his thought. I will then offer an assessment of their contribution to the development of natural law theory.

1. The First Principle of Practical Reasoning and Its General Specifications

These authors, in company with St. Thomas, distinguish between speculative and practical reasoning, not in the sense that we have two different intellectual powers, one speculative and the other practical, but in the sense that there are two distinct forms or types of thinking, each with its own non-demonstrable, underived *first* principles or "starting points." In speculative inquiry, our concern is with *what is,* whereas in practical deliberation our concern is with *what-is-to-be-done.*[78] Our authors, therefore, again in company with Aquinas, hold that the very first principle or starting point of practical reasoning is that *good is to be done and pursued, and evil is to be avoided.*[79] This is a directive for intelligent, purposeful human activity: this principle is immediately known to be true once one understands the meaning of "good" and "evil." "Good" here means not only what is morally good but also whatever can be understood to be truly perfective of human persons, while "evil" or "bad" has the meaning of whatever deprives human persons of their perfection or fullness of being.[80]

This first principle of practical reasoning directs human persons to the fulfillment to be realized in and through human acts. Grisez, Finnis, and Boyle, again following the lead of St. Thomas, hold that this first principle is specified or given its general determinations by identifying those real goods which in truth fulfill human persons. In other words, the general determinations of this first principle of practical reasoning take the form, "such and such a basic human good is to be done and/or pursued, protected, and promoted."[81] In presenting the thought of St. Thomas on natural law, I noted that he had distinguished various sorts of basic human goods, corresponding to "natural inclinations" of the human person, goods such as life itself, the handing on of human life and its education, knowledge of the truth about God, and living in friendship and fellowship with others. I also noted that Thomas did not consider his list of basic human goods to be exhaustive or taxative but rather illustrative. He consequently used such expressions as "and the like" and "things of this kind" to describe them.[82]

In their efforts to develop St. Thomas's thought, Grisez, Finnis, and Boyle seek to identify *all* the basic goods of human persons. They hold that these goods can be distinguished by noticing the assumptions implicit in the practical reasoning of ordinary people, by considering the "ends" or "purposes" for whose sake people ultimately engage in various activities. The basic human goods, while diverse, are alike in that each is a good *of* persons, not a good *for* persons. The basic goods perfect different aspects or dimensions of human persons in their individual and communal flourishing. In their different works, our authors have, to some degree, varied slightly their list of fundamental human goods.[83] They now agree that there are eight categories of such basic goods.

Four of these have *harmony* as their common theme, and the relevant goods are the following: (1) self-integration or "inner peace," which consists in harmony among one's judgments, feelings, and choices; (2) "peace of conscience and consistency between one's self and its expression," a good in which one participates by establishing harmony among one's judgments, choices, and performances; (3) "peace with others, neighborliness, friendship," or harmony between and among individuals and groups of persons; and (4) "peace with God . . . or some more-than-human source of meaning and value," a good that can be called the good of religion.[84]

Grisez, Finnis, and Boyle call these basic human goods "reflexive" or "existential" because they fulfill persons precisely insofar as they are able to make choices and are thus capable of moral good and evil. Choice is included in the very meaning of these goods, because the choice by which one acts for them is included in their realization or "instantiation." For example, one cannot participate in the good of friendship without making a choice whose object includes harmony between that choice itself and the will of another person, whose friend one wills to be.

It would be a mistake, however, to regard these goods, which have harmony as their common theme, as having *moral* value as such. That is, we ought not, in conceiving these goods, to import moral value into them.[85] It is a mistake to do so because one can choose to establish these diverse goods whose common theme is harmony in immoral ways. For example, one can seek to establish the good of harmony between judgments and choices by rationalizing immoral choices; one can seek to participate in the good of friendship and peace with others by compromising moral principles or by cooperating with others in immoral enterprises. Thus, not all choices to participate in these reflexive goods are *morally* good choices, although, as we shall see later, true and lasting fulfillment in them must be.[86]

In addition to these existential or reflexive goods of human persons, Grisez, Finnis, and Boyle identify three basic goods that they call "substantive." These are goods of human persons in whose definitions choice is not included insofar as they fulfill aspects or dimensions of human persons other than the existential or reflexive. There are three categories of such basic substantive human goods: (1) human life itself, including health and bodily integrity and the handing on and educating of human life, a good that fulfills human persons as bodily beings; (2) knowledge of the truth and appreciation of beauty, goods that fulfill human persons as intelligent beings; and (3) playful activities and skillful performances, goods that fulfill human persons as simultaneously bodily and intelligent beings and as makers and sharers in culture.[87]

Grisez identifies *marriage* as the eighth basic good, irreducibly distinct. He and his associates had not considered marriage as such in writings prior to 1993. However, in preparing his chapter on marriage for Volume 2 of *The Way of the Lord Jesus* — namely, *Living a Christian Life* — Grisez came to recognize, primarily because of the teaching of the Church's magisterium on marriage, that this human reality is a basic human good irreducible to any other good. He describes this good as follows: "Marriage is a basic human good, and the married couple's common good is, not any extrinsic end to which marriage is instrumental, but the communion of married life itself. The *communion of married life* refers to the couple's *being* married, that is, their being united as complementary, bodily persons, so really and so completely that they are two in one flesh. This form of interpersonal unity is actualized by conjugal love when that love takes shape in the couple's acts of mutual marital consent, loving consummation, and their whole life together, not least in the parenthood of couples whose marriages are fruitful."[88]

Grisez considers the basic good of marriage unique in that it is both "reflexive," in so far as it includes marital friendship and fidelity, and "substantive," in so far as the core of the good of marital communion is the "*sacramentum*" or indissoluble one-flesh unity, and also because it is open to the good of human life.[89]

This account of both "reflexive" and "substantive" human goods should make it evident that our authors, in identifying the basic human goods that are to be "done, pursued, protected, and promoted" and whose opposites are to be avoided, are essentially taking the lead of St. Thomas. Their endeavor is to specify more clearly the kinds of goods to which he referred when he distinguished between goods pertaining to human beings as substantive entities, as bodily beings, and as intelligent and choosing persons.

Like Aquinas, they speak at times of basic or natural inclinations dynamically orienting us to these goods, and they appeal to the work of cultural anthropologists and others to support their views.[90] They likewise note, in company with St. Thomas, that very often people engage in activities that enable them to participate in these goods for no other purpose than to participate in them. These goods, in other words, are regarded as "ends" or "points" of human activity. One can study precisely in order to participate in the good of learning (knowledge of the truth), and one can do so for no ulterior purpose; one goes to the doctor to preserve one's health and life, and can do so for no further purpose; one can watch a sunset or listen to a symphony just to participate in the good of beauty, etc. These goods, in other words, are "ends" for whose sake human beings act to begin with,[91] although, of course, people can subordinate these goods to other purposes — e.g., one can study in order to learn, in order to pass an exam, in order to graduate, etc., *ad infinitum.*

None of the goods in question is the highest good or absolute good; none, in other words, is the *Summum Bonum,* for God alone is this good. But each of these goods is a *real* good of human persons, a good that human persons *prize* and do not *price,* an aspect or dimension of the fullness of being human. Each of these goods, when grasped by practical reason, serves as a principle or starting point for thinking about what-is-to-be-done. Moreover, in seeking to render their choices and actions intelligible both to themselves and to others, people frequently appeal to these goods as the *raison d'être* of their choices and actions.

One further point about these basic goods needs to be noted. This has to do with their "incommensurability," i.e., with the fact that they cannot be meaningfully arranged in any hierarchical order and compared or measured with respect to each other. Here two kinds of incommensurability need to be distinguished. The first is the incommensurability between goods of different categories, e.g., between the good of life and the good of knowledge of the truth or the good of inner peace. Grisez, Finnis, and Boyle clearly explain why there is this kind of incommensurability. "If they [the goods of diverse categories] were commensurable," they write, then "they would have to be homogeneous with one another or reducible to something prior by which they could be measured. If they were homogeneous with one another, they would not constitute diverse categories. If they were reducible to something prior, they would not be primary principles. Thus, they are incommensurable. No basic good considered precisely as such can be meaningfully said to be better than another. . . . Hence, the basic goods of different categories are called 'good' only by analogy."[92]

In other words, there is no rational way of comparing, say, the good of life with the good of knowledge of the truth or of friendship or of religion and of judging which is "greater." It is like comparing apples and oranges or the number 33 with the width of this page. Each is *incomparably* good in its own way, and there is no possibility of reducing them to a common denominator so that we can have some uniform measure in terms of which we could compare them — as we can, for instance, compare the number 33 with the width of this page by reducing both to a common denominator, say a millimeter, in terms of which we can meaningfully judge that the width of this page is "greater" than the number 33.

In addition to this incommensurability between the goods of diverse categories, there is an incommensurability between the realizations or "instantiations" of one and the same good. There is no way, for example, of comparing the good of *my* life with the good of *your* life. Each is incomparably good. Thus, and this is most important — as we shall see more clearly in the following chapter when we discuss the method of making moral judgments known as "proportionalism" — "when one has a choice, no option includes in the instantiation of the good it promises everything promised by its alternatives — even when the alternative would instantiate the very same basic good."[93]

2. The First Principle of Morality and the Ideal of 'Integral Human Fulfillment'

Before presenting and discussing the formulation of the "first principle of morality" proposed by Grisez, Finnis, and Boyle, it is important and necessary to recall that one can distinguish two sorts of propositions or precepts that St. Thomas included among the "first and common precepts of natural law." The first type includes the precept that good is to be done and pursued and its opposite avoided and, by extension, the precepts that life, marrying and raising children, knowledge of the truth, etc., are the "goods" that are to be done and pursued insofar as these are the goods to which we are naturally inclined and which practical reason "naturally" apprehends as the goods to be pursued in action (see *Summa theologiae*, 1-2, q. 94, a. 2). Moreover, we saw that Aquinas did not seek, in this article, to provide an exhaustive list of the goods to which we are naturally inclined. In addition, as was noted previously (in 94, 3), Aquinas explicitly names the good of virtue as one toward which we are naturally inclined.

We have now seen how Grisez, Finnis, and Boyle develop and clarify the thought of St. Thomas on this matter. *With St. Thomas,* they hold that these principles or precepts of natural law are not as yet *moral* principles. That is, they do not enable us to discriminate between alternatives of choice that are morally good and morally bad. Everyone, the morally upright and the morally bad, appeal to these principles of practical reasoning in order to render their choices and actions intelligible and to justify ("rationalize," on the part of the morally bad) their choices and actions to themselves and others. After all, one chooses to do what is morally bad only because one thinks that by doing so one will ultimately participate in some good and avoid some evil.[94] Thus, even immoral choices and actions respond in some measure to the principle that good is to be done and pursued and evil avoided.[95]

But, as we have seen, St. Thomas included a second set of practical propositions among the first and common principles or precepts of natural law.

These had to do with the *way* we are to pursue and do good and avoid evil. Among this second set of first or common principles of natural law, it will be recalled, St. Thomas included the twofold command of love of God and neighbor, as well as the Golden Rule and the precept that we are to do injury to no one.[96] Although both these kinds of propositions — namely, those directing us to pursue and do the good and identifying the good we are to pursue and do, and those concerned with the *way* we are to pursue and do these goods — were included by St. Thomas among the primary or most common principles or precepts of natural law, he did not himself explicitly draw attention to the difference between them.

Grisez, Finnis, and Boyle, in their effort to clarify and develop the thought of St. Thomas, explicitly distinguish between the first principles of natural law that are *principles of practical reasoning* — i.e., principles directing us to pursue and do good and avoid evil and identifying the goods we are to pursue and do — and the first principles of natural law that are *moral* principles. They show that there must be a first principle of *morality* or of practical reasonableness analogous to the first principle of *practical reasoning*. The function of the first principle of practical reasoning is to direct human persons to the goods perfective of them and to rule out pointlessness or purposelessness in human choice and action. The function of the first principle of morality, on the other hand, is to provide a way of distinguishing between alternatives of choice that are morally good and alternatives of choice that are morally bad. Its purpose is to provide the basis for guiding choices and actions toward integral human fulfillment.

Grisez, Finnis, and Boyle note that St. Thomas considered the twofold command of love to be the *first principle of morality: You are to love the Lord your God and you are to love your neighbor.* St. Thomas insisted that this is the moral principle from which the moral precepts of the Decalogue are derived.[97] And St. Thomas, as a Christian, had very good grounds for saying that this is the first and greatest commandment upon which all others are based, for this is, after all, what Jesus taught (Mt 22:37-40 and par.). Our authors also note that the Fathers of Vatican Council II, as we have already seen, had proposed a basic or fundamental moral norm: "The norm of human activity is this: that in accord with the divine plan and will, it should harmonize with the authentic good of the human race and allow men as individuals and as members of society to pursue their total vocation and fulfill it" (*Gaudium et spes*, no. 35).[98]

Grisez, Finnis, and Boyle do not deny that St. Thomas (following Scripture) and Vatican Council II have formulated the basic or first moral principle in a sound way. Referring to the biblical articulation of this principle (adopted by St. Thomas) — namely, that we are to love God above all things and our neighbor as ourselves — they note that "for Jews and Christians, God is the supreme good and source of all goods." Thus, "loving him requires the cherishing of all goods . . . [including] the basic human goods. . . . And loving one's neighbor as oneself at least excludes egoism and means accepting the fulfillment of others as part of one's own responsibility"[99] — i.e., one loves one's neighbor by willing that the goods of human existence flourish in him or her. They clearly recognize that the love commandments of the Bible authentically express the basic or first principle of morality in religious language.

In other words, they believe that the biblical (and Thomistic) and Vatican II formulations of the first or basic moral principle are sound when viewed from the perspective of religious faith. Nonetheless, they think that these formulations of this principle are not entirely satisfactory "for purposes of ethical reflection and theology." "To serve as a standard for practical judgment," Grisez writes, "a formulation must refer to the many basic human goods which generate the need for choice and moral judgment."[100] It should do so because the function of the first principle of morality is to provide us with a criterion for distinguishing which alternatives of choice are morally good and which are morally bad. The first principle of morality is expressed more clearly and fully if it is more closely related to the first principles of practical reasoning; this means that it should articulate "the integral directiveness of the first principles of practical reasoning, when they are working together harmoniously in full concert"[101] or what also might be called the directiveness of "right reason" or "unfettered practical reason."[102]

Consequently, they believe that the first principle of morality, expressed religiously by the twofold command to love, can be more precisely formulated for philosophical and theological purposes as follows: "In voluntarily acting for human goods and avoiding what is opposed to them, one ought to choose and otherwise will those and only those possibilities whose willing is compatible with a will toward integral human fulfillment."[103]

The matter can be put this way. If we are to be morally upright persons, our basic, fundamental attitude ought to be that of persons who are eager to embrace, revere, and honor the real goods perfective of human persons and the persons in whom these goods are meant to flourish. It is to these goods that we are directed by the first principles of practical reasoning. Our "heart" ought to be open to them. A person about to choose in a morally upright way is open to *all* the real goods perfective of human persons and listens to *all* the appeals they make through the principles of practical reasoning. A morally upright person is a person whose practical reason is "unfettered." A person like this is one responsive to the "integral directiveness of all the first principles of practical reasoning," precisely insofar as he or she is willing to affirm, embrace, revere, and honor all the real goods of human existence in his or her self-determining choices.

A person about to choose immorally, on the other hand, is one who does *not* have this attitude toward these goods and the persons in whom they are meant to flourish. Such a person is willing to adopt by choice proposals that in one way or another neglect, ignore, slight, damage, destroy, or impede these goods or treat them and the persons in whom they are meant to flourish in ways that are unfair and arbitrary. Morality comes from the heart, and our hearts ought to be open to what is really good.[104] All this is central to understanding this formulation of the first principle of morality.

It is important to note here that the "integral human fulfillment" to which we are directed by the first principle of morality is *not* itself a basic human good alongside of or in addition to the basic goods already identified. While it is by no means individualistic self-fulfillment, it is not "some sort of super-good transcending all other categories of goodness"[105] or "some gigantic synthesis of goods in a vast state of affairs, such as might be projected as the goal of a worldwide billion-year plan."[106] Unlike the basic goods, it is not a *reason* for acting. It is, rather, an ideal whose attractiveness depends on *all* the goods that can appeal to persons and serve as reasons for acting.[107] This ideal guides human persons in making choices by directing them "to avoid unnecessary limitation and so maintain openness to further goods."[108]

By doing so, the ideal of integral human fulfillment, while not itself a basic good, constitutes the "object" of a good will and as such "rectifies" the will, i.e., it is the object of "right" or "unfettered human reason." The will of a person committed to choosing and acting in accord with the requirements of integral human fulfillment is the will of a person inwardly disposed to choose well, to choose in accord with unfettered or "right" reason. In short, it is the ideal community of all human persons richly fulfilled in all human goods, for whose realization a virtuous person wishes; this ideal guides such a person's choices in pursuing particular benefits for particular persons and communities.[109]

In the previous chapter, in the section on virtue and the moral life, differences and similarities in the accounts of virtue given by St. Thomas and Grisez were noted. Here I want to show how the thought of Grisez, Finnis, and Boyle on the first principle of morality and the "ideal" of integral human fulfillment is related to the thought of St. Thomas on the moral virtues and on the connection between the "intellectual" moral virtue of prudence and the "appetitive" moral virtues of justice, temperance, and fortitude.

For St. Thomas, the moral appetitive virtues inwardly dispose persons rightly toward the "ends" of human existence, i.e., toward the basic goods perfective of them as individuals and as members of a community.[110] As we saw in the previous chapter, the principle used by Grisez to differentiate among the moral virtues is the kind of fundamental moral truth in light of which persons can discriminate among alternatives of choice in order to discern which alternatives are morally good and which are morally bad. And the most fundamental moral truth is that directing us to choose and otherwise will those and only those alternatives compatible with a will toward integral human fulfillment. This principle, as Grisez, Finnis, and Boyle emphasize, requires that one be "entirely reasonable" in one's practical thinking;[111] they insist, as we have just seen, that this principle demands reason to be "right" or "unfettered." But reason can be "right" or "unfettered" only if the person whose reason it is is inwardly disposed well toward the "ends" or "goods" of human existence to which the first practical principles direct us. Such a person is the virtuous person. He or she can judge rightly (i.e., with prudence) because his or her appetites have been "rectified" (i.e., well disposed to the goods of human existence). Thus, the thought of Grisez, Finnis, and Boyle on "unfettered" or "right" reason seems, to me at least, quite analogous to the teaching of St. Thomas on prudence. For Grisez, Finnis, and Boyle, the first principle of morality, when embodied in the acting person, generates, as it were, the virtue of prudence.

At the conclusion of the next section, where I briefly summarize the thought of Grisez, Finnis, and Boyle on the "modes of responsibility" — i.e., moral truths that specify or "pin down" the first principle of morality — I will show how in their thought these moral truths, as embodied in the acting person, generate different kinds of moral virtues.

3. The Specifications of the First Principle of Morality: The Modes of Responsibility

Just as the first principle of practical reasoning — namely, *good is to be done and pursued and evil is to be avoided* — is specified by identifying the real goods of human persons that are to be done and pursued, so too the basic moral principle of practical reasonableness can be specified by identifying ways of choosing that do, in fact, fail to honor and respect "integral human fulfillment," i.e., the whole range of real goods perfective of human persons. St. Thomas identified some of these specifications of the first moral principle (formulated by him in the twofold command to love) when he referred to the principle of the Golden Rule (do unto others as you would have them do unto you; do not do unto others as you would not have them do unto you) and the principle that we are to do injury to no one (principles he included among the "first and common" precepts of natural law).

Grisez, Finnis, and Boyle, in an effort to develop in a more systematic and clearer fashion what St. Thomas was up to in articulating these basic moral principles, seek to identify with more precision the specifications of the first moral principle. These specifications of the first normative principle can be called "modes of responsibility," requirements of unfettered practical reason or of practical reasonableness.[112] Their purpose is to specify, "pin down," the primary moral principle by excluding as immoral those actions which involve willing in certain specific ways incompatible with a will toward integral human fulfillment.[113] These modes exclude specific kinds of choices involving various immoral relationships between the acting person and the goods perfective of human beings.

In their earlier writings, Grisez, Finnis, and Boyle expressed these specifications of the first moral principle in affirmative and negative ways. Affirmatively, they noted that, if we are to act rightly, we are required to take the real goods of human persons into account in judging and choosing what to do; simply to disregard them, to be unconcerned and lazy about them, is to manifest a will that is not truly open to them. In addition, we are required to pursue these real goods of human existence and to seek them rather than such pseudo-goods as pleasure. Moreover, each one of these goods demands of us that, when we can do so easily as not, we avoid ways of acting that inhibit their realization and prefer ways of acting that contribute to their realization. In addition, each of these goods requires us to make an effort on its behalf (and on behalf of the person or persons in whom it is meant to flourish), when its significant realization in some other person or persons is in peril — e.g., if someone is about to drown and thus be deprived of the good of life and we are capable of preventing his or her drowning, we are morally obligated to do so.

Other requirements necessary if we are to shape our lives in accord with the first principle of morality include the principle of fairness or the Golden Rule (which, as we have seen, is one of the specifications of the first moral principle identified by St. Thomas). And one requirement that is surely crucial is that we ought not freely choose, with deliberate intent, to set aside these goods, to destroy, damage, or impede them either in ourselves or in others. We might be tempted to do so out of hostility toward some good that we arbitrarily do not wish to accept; or, more commonly, we may be tempted to do so because the continued flourishing of one or another good either in ourselves or in others inhibits our participation in some other good that we unreasonably erect as "greater." We are, in short, not to do evil so that good may come about — an instruction that St. Paul gave Christians in Romans (3:8), and that St. Thomas expressed when he said that one of the first and common precepts of natural law is that we are to do injury to no one.[114]

In their more recent writings, Grisez, Finnis, and Boyle express all the modes of responsibility negatively rather than expressing some affirmatively and others negatively. They do so because formulating these modes negatively shows that it is impossible for them to come into conflict, because one can simultaneously forbear choosing and acting in an infinite number of ways.[115] They distinguish eight specific modes of responsibility (the final two describing two different reasons for choosing to destroy, damage, or impede a basic human good), and the precise but somewhat cumbersome way our authors formulate these modes negatively is provided in the accompanying note.[116] Put in more simple language, these modes of responsibility rule out choices motivated by laziness, impatient individualism, emotionalism, preferences based on feelings alone, hostility toward some good, or nonrationally based preference for one good over another.

The specifications of the first moral principle taken together guide human choices and actions positively toward the ideal of integral human fulfillment. Together with the first moral principle that they "pin down," they enable human persons to have a vision of moral truth — a world view that opens them to transcendent sources of meaning and value. Although, as Grisez observes, "alternative world views tempt people to turn from the vision of moral truth," anyone "who deals uprightly with this temptation makes a more or less explicit commitment to integral human fulfillment. *Such a commitment is basic in the sense that it shapes the whole life of the one who makes it.* For Christians, their act of faith constitutes such an upright commitment; for those who have not heard the gospel, their basic commitment [to shape their lives in accord with moral truth] serves as an implicit act of faith"[117] (emphasis added). This, as we shall see more fully below in discussing "moral priorities, religion, and God," is of paramount importance.

However, before considering how Grisez, Finnis, and Boyle understand the movement from modes of responsibility to specific moral norms and how they establish moral priorities, it is fitting to conclude this section by briefly showing how Grisez relates the "modes of responsibility" to virtues.

Recall what was said in the previous chapter, that for Grisez "virtues are aspects of personality as a whole when all the other dimensions of the self are integrated with morally good commitments. . . . Commitments establish one's existential identity: a whole personality integrated with a morally good self is virtuous. *Since such a personality is formed by choices that are in accord with the first principle of morality and the modes of responsibility, the virtues embody the modes.* In other words, the modes of responsibility shape the existential self of a good person, this self shapes the whole personality, and so good character embodies and expresses the modes."[118] Thus, just as the person whose character is formed by choices in accord with the first principle of morality is the one whose reason is "unfettered" or "right" — i.e., the prudent person — so the person whose character is shaped by choices in accord with the eight modes of responsibility is the one marked by the virtues corresponding to these modes. Grisez identifies these as the virtues of "diligence" (corresponding to the first mode), "team spirit" (corresponding to the second), "self-control" or "discipline" (corresponding to the third), "courage" (corresponding to the fourth), "fairness" (corresponding to the fifth), "sincerity" or "clearheadedness" (corresponding to the sixth), "patient/forgiving" (corresponding to the seventh), and "reverence" (corresponding to the eighth).[119]

4. From Modes of Responsibility to Specific Moral Norms

Recall that St. Thomas, who considered the precept to love God above all things and one's neighbor as oneself as the first moral principle of natural law, thought that it is possible to infer "immediately, with little consideration," some very specific moral norms on the basis of this fundamental moral principle; for he held that the precepts of the Decalogue follow as immediate and proximate conclusions from the precept to love God and neighbor.[120]

Grisez, Finnis, and Boyle think that it is necessary here to clarify and develop Thomas's thought on natural law by making explicit those matters that he treated more or less implicitly. They point out that he included, among the first and common precepts of natural law, not only the love commandment but also such normative principles as the Golden Rule and the injunction that we are to do injury to no one — principles included in their modes of responsibility or specifications of the first moral principle (modes five, seven, and eight). Their point is that principles of this kind — the principle of fairness or the Golden Rule, the principle that we ought not intentionally damage, destroy, or impede basic human goods, etc. — enable us to show the truth of more specific moral norms, such as those requiring us to keep promises, not to kill the innocent, not to commit adultery, etc. That is, they enable us to show why these specific moral norms indeed follow as conclusions from the first moral principle or norm.[121] The modes of responsibility, in other words, are normative principles more specific than the first principle of morality, but they are more general than specific moral norms identifying kinds of human choices as morally good or morally bad. Such specific norms are discovered by considering the ways a proposed human action relates a person's will to basic human goods and by considering such a proposed human action in light of the first principle of morality and its specifications.

For example, one specific moral norm is that we ought to keep promises. The truth of this specific moral norm can be seen if we consider the action at stake, keeping a promise, in the light of the first moral principle and of the Golden Rule or mode of responsibility requiring us to be fair and treat others as we would have them treat us. Similarly, we can grasp the truth of the specific moral norm requiring us not to kill the innocent intentionally if we consider this type of action — one that intentionally destroys the good of innocent human life — in the light of the first moral principle and of the modes of responsibility requiring us not to destroy, damage, or impede basic human goods, either in ourselves or in others, whether out of hostility toward that good or because we consider its continued flourishing an inhibition to our participation in some other good that we arbitrarily prefer.

Many specific moral norms, while true, are not absolute or exceptionless. These norms are nonabsolute because they are open to further specification in light of the same moral principles from which they were derived in the first place. Promise-keeping is an example. We are obliged to keep our promises in light of the good of interpersonal harmony, the basic moral norm, and the Golden Rule or principle of fairness that excludes arbitrary partiality (the fifth mode of responsibility). However, promises and the cooperation they foster very often concern goods other than interpersonal harmony. When keeping a promise would harm these goods, and if these goods could be protected by breaking the promise *without being unfair or violating the Golden Rule*, then the obligation to keep the promise ceases. Thus, for example, if I promise a friend to play tennis on a specific morning and, on awakening that morning, discover that I have a temperature and am sick with the flu, I would not be obliged to keep the promise — and my friend would understand why, for my friend would not regard it unfair for me to break the promise in order to protect the good of health and life.[122] In other words, the principle of fairness or the Golden Rule generated the norm that promises are to be kept; the same principle or mode of responsibility generates exceptions to this norm.

But some specific moral norms, in the understanding of natural law developed by our authors, are absolute or exceptionless. For example, the specific moral norm proscribing the intentional killing of innocent human life, which violates either the seventh or eighth modes of responsibility, is absolute. This norm and others like it are absolute because nothing which can further specify the kind of action which the norm concerns would prevent it from violating the relevant mode of responsibility and the first principle of morality itself. In short, any norm which so specifies an object of human choice so that no further condition or circumstance could so modify it that it no longer violated a relevant mode of responsibility and, therefore, the first principle of morality, is absolute. In choosing such an object — willing such a proposal — we are not acting in accord with the ideal of integral human fulfillment, the object "rectifying" the will. We are not to "do" evil — i.e., to make ourselves will that evil be — no matter what the further circumstances may be or no matter what good we may seek to realize by our willingness to do what we know to be evil.[123]

5. Moral Priorities, Religion, and God

In order to complete the presentation of the natural law theory of Grisez, Finnis, and Boyle, it is imperative to set forth their thought on moral priorities, religion, and God.

Before summarizing their thought on these issues, I think it pertinent to note a passage from Vatican Council II, insofar as it expresses a truth that is, as shall be seen, central to their understanding of natural law, of the requirements imposed by the ideal of integral human fulfillment and expressed in the first principle of morality. The Council Fathers declared: "It is in accordance with their dignity that all men, because they are persons, that is, beings endowed with reason and free will, and therefore bearing personal responsibility, are both impelled by their nature and bound by a moral obligation to seek the truth, especially religious truth. They are also bound to adhere to the truth once they come to know it and to direct their whole lives in accordance with the demands of truth" (*Dignitatis humanae*, no. 2).

How is this truth expressed in the thought of Grisez, Finnis, and Boyle on natural law, and why is it so central? This is what I hope to show here.

One might think that the position developed by our authors does not offer any way to account for moral priorities and for the overarching significance of the obligation to seek moral and religious truth. After all, do they not insist, as we have seen, that the basic human goods and the principles of practical reasoning based on them are incommensurable and that, therefore, there is no rational way of arranging them in a hierarchy and judging that any one basic good, including that of religion or of harmony between human persons and God or "some more-than-human source of meaning and value," is "greater" than another?

In one of their most important essays, Grisez, Finnis, and Boyle acknowledge that "*some* statements in *some* of our previous works may *appear* to suggest" that it is impossible to establish moral priorities. However, they insist that this way of viewing their thought "is incorrect and incompatible with constant features of the theory developed in all our works."[124] Although the basic human goods and principles of practical reasoning are incommensurable and impossible to arrange in a hierarchy, it does not follow that they are "an unordered crowd which offer no objective standard for setting moral priorities in life," insofar as "unfettered practical reason," prior to anyone's free choice, "establishes some priorities among one's interests in the different basic aspects [goods] of fulfillment."[125]

What do they mean by this? Recall that, as we saw earlier, integral human fulfillment is the ideal toward which we are directed by the first principle of morality, and that it in turn expresses the requirements of "right reason," "unfettered practical reason," i.e., the integral or full directiveness of *all* the principles of practical reasoning. Among these requirements of unfettered practical reason is the requirement that we develop an intelligent or rational plan of life and not live haphazardly from moment to moment, drifting along aimlessly from day to day. In addition, as we have seen already, commitment to the ideal of integral human fulfillment provides us with a vision of moral truth, a "world view" that is so basic it shapes the whole life of the one who makes it. And one cannot shape one's whole life or develop an intelligent plan of life without having moral priorities. But what are these priorities, and why is the obligation to pursue moral and religious truth so overarching among them?

The reflexive goods of human persons (inner peace, peace of conscience, peace and friendship with others, harmony with God or some "more-than-human source of meaning and value"), as we have seen, do not, of themselves, have *moral* value, insofar as one can participate in them immorally by compromising moral principles. Nonetheless, as Grisez, Finnis, and Boyle make clear, interest in these reflexive goods takes priority whenever they are at stake precisely because these goods fulfill human persons *insofar as they are moral beings, i.e., deliberating, choosing agents "who can strive to avoid or overcome various forms of personal and interpersonal conflict."*[126] Thus, for example, the good of peace of conscience or harmony among one's judgments, choices, and performances can be realized immorally by harmonizing one's judgments and performances with one's immoral choices, i.e., one can rationalize one's own immoral choices. But, as our authors say, "if one considers this good morally — that is, with practical reason unfettered — one sees that the only way to realize it is consistent with integral human fulfillment is by making sure that one's judgments are morally true, conforming one's choices to them, and striving to make one's performances carry out one's choices as perfectly as possible."[127] A human person's very existence *as a moral being, an agent of deliberation and choice,* in other words, is at stake whenever these goods of personal and interpersonal harmony come into focus. And among them is the good of religion or of harmony between human persons and God or some "more-than-human source of meaning and value." As a result, the integral directiveness of practical knowledge as expressed in the first moral principle requires us to establish priorities in our interests in the basic human goods and to put order into our lives in accordance with these priorities. In short, the demands of moral truth require us to integrate our lives and choices by ordering our interests in the basic human goods. We do this by unifying our lives and choices in view of an overarching purpose.

This overarching purpose, our authors argue, "can be established by a religious commitment and cannot be established without it."[128] Their argument can be put this way. Practical knowledge — the kind of knowledge involved, as we have seen, in the "natural law" — is knowledge of what-is-to-be, i.e., of what-is-to-be-done in and through human agency. The principles of practical knowledge, as we have likewise seen (namely, "good is to be done and pursued and its opposite avoided," together with the practical principles identifying the goods that are to be done and pursued), are the *underived* principles or starting points for thinking about what-is-to-be, and we *know* that these principles are underived. Their integral directiveness that, as we have seen, is expressed in the first moral principle, preconditions all human self-direction and fulfillment. It is a directiveness that human beings discover and do not give to themselves. As such, therefore, the *"is-to-be* of the directiveness of practical knowledge *points to its transcendent source,"* which, since it is a transcendent source of directiveness, "can only be thought of as if it were a person anticipating human fulfillment and leading human persons to it."[129] Harmony with this transcendent source is, indeed, *one* of the basic goods fulfilling, perfecting, human persons — the good of religion or of harmony with God or some "more-than-human source of meaning and value." It thus follows that one of the natural responsibilities of human persons "is the duty to seek religious truth, embrace what appears to be the truth, and live according to it."[130] What all this shows is that it is possible for a person to integrate his or her whole moral life only by committing himself or herself to the search for religious truth, for the transcendent source of meaning and value — in a word, for God.

In addition, we know, from our own experience, that realizing the ideal of integral human fulfillment to which the first principle of morality directs us is not, unfortunately, within our power. "Therefore," our authors argue, "in intending an anticipated and hoped-for benefit, every human person in every action wills . . . that the benefit come about both through the action [one rightly chooses] and through whatever causality is required, insofar as that fulfillment is beyond the agent's own knowledge and power."[131] Ultimately, the "causality" other than one's own that is required in order to achieve the ideal of integral human fulfillment is the cooperation of the "more-than-human source of meaning and value," i.e., of God. Trust in this more-than-human source of meaning and value provides hope that one's morally good choices will, indeed, enable one to achieve the ideal of integral human fulfillment.[132]

Unfettered practical reason or the integral directiveness of the principles of practical reason expressed in the first moral principle, is, therefore, the principle both enabling and requiring us to establish priorities in our interests in the basic human goods. Its demands require us to plan our lives intelligently by having a harmonious set of purposes in life, conceived not on the model of technological "blueprints," but in the sense of life-determining commitments. And among these, the commitment that is of primordial importance, overarching significance, is the commitment to discover religious truth, the truth about our relationship with God, the "more-than-human source of meaning and value." In short, "harmony with the divine [the 'more-than-human source of meaning and value'], however misconceived, will be thought to condition one's hopes of achieving every other purpose in life."[133]

Moreover, as experience so poignantly bears witness, the effort to shape one's life in accord with the demands of moral truth — with the demands of the ideal of integral human fulfillment, of unfettered practical reason — is at times frustrated. One does one's best, but still the anticipated benefit is not realized. Thus, our authors conclude, "In experiencing and accepting failure, morally good people submit to the intention of God, who could have granted them success, but did not, obviously for some reason of his own. In this submission, human persons will God's fulfillment insofar as it fulfills him — [that is, they] love him as a person. For morally good persons, their religious commitment [therefore] will provide at least one purpose to integrate their other commitments."[134]

More recently, Grisez has presented very helpful clarifying remarks concerning the overarching religious commitment that can organize one's entire life.[135] In his most recent consideration of this issue, Grisez first stresses that the incommensurability of the basic goods of different categories implies that one cannot organize one's entire life by a commitment to a substantive good such as life or knowledge of the truth because committing oneself to such a purpose simply cannot be relevant to every choice one might make. He then shows that a commitment to the reflexive goods of harmony with other persons is simply not at stake in every choice and that harmony within oneself is at stake only when one or more appealing alternatives is morally acceptable. Only the good of religion, among the reflexive goods, can be at stake in every choice one can make. Therefore, he concludes, "only some prospective realization of that good [religion] could provide an overarching purpose to unify one's entire life."[136]

This overarching purpose is "to maintain and promote harmony in an ongoing cooperative relationship [with God]," and for this purpose "one might commit himself to act always in accord with all the guidance God provides." Grisez then offers reasons why such a commitment should be made:

> First, because harmony with God is self-evidently good, and always following his guidance in an ongoing cooperative relationship will maintain and promote this harmony. Second, because God guides human individuals and communities toward their own good. So, consistently following his guidance is likely to safeguard and promote not only harmony with him but every other aspect of one's well-being and flourishing. In choosing, it is not entirely within one's power to achieve the benefits one intends; other conditions must concur, and the reality both of those conditions and of one's own power depends on God. So, one depends on him for everything and always must hope for his cooperation. Mutuality requires that one consistently cooperate with him.[137]

He concludes with a paragraph of great importance, declaring:

> A person's life would be an integrated whole if he or she consistently acted in accord with all the guidance God provides. Harmony with God would be the single ultimate end intended in every choice such a person made. Because God guides everyone toward fulfillment in human goods, that ultimate end would lead everyone committed to it to authentic self-fulfillment, including good interpersonal relationships. And because God guides different individuals to use their diverse gifts in diverse ways to meet their own and others' diverse needs, that single ultimate end would lead different persons to organize their lives in somewhat different ways. Major elements in the structure of most people's lives would be settled by their commitments to participate in certain enduring relationships and communities, and to make a living in a particular way. Those major commitments, in turn, would serve as the criterion for discerning among the remaining morally acceptable options in respect to the less central elements of one's life. If an entire community made and carried out such an overarching religious commitment, its members would thank God for the diverse gifts each person had received and would cooperate in using their diverse gifts to protect and promote the common good.[138]

In sum, the integral directiveness of the demands of practical reason, "unfettered" practical reason, as expressed in the first principle of morality, ultimately leads persons to order their lives by an overarching commitment to religious truth, to a search for the "more-than-human source of meaning and value," and to the hope that their struggle to live uprightly, despite failures, will ultimately contribute to achieving integral human fulfillment. In Chapter Six, when we come to a consideration of our life in Christ, we will see how this natural law and its requirements are fulfilled, perfected, and completed by the evangelical law made known to us in the redemptive work of Christ.

6. A Summary of the Natural Law Teaching of Grisez, Finnis, and Boyle

Before offering an assessment of the thought of these authors on natural law, I think it may be helpful to provide a summary of their thought on this subject. I will do so by first presenting a summary of this position as set forth by Finnis in 1980 and then by setting forth a restatement of it in the light of the greater precision that he, Grisez, and Boyle have made in their efforts to deepen and clarify the meaning of natural law.

In 1980, Finnis offered the following brief overview of the essential features of a theory of natural law:

> There is (i) a set of basic practical principles which indicate the basic forms of human flourishing as goods to be pursued and realized, and which are in some way or another used by everyone who considers what to do, however sound his conclusions; (ii) a set of basic methodological requirements of practical reasonableness (itself one of the basic forms of human flourishing) which distinguish between acts that (always or in particular circumstances) are reasonable all-things-considered (and not merely relative-to-a-particular-purpose) and acts that are unreasonable all-things-considered, i.e., between ways of acting that are morally right or morally wrong — thus enabling one to formulate (iii) a set of general moral standards.[139]

In light of the developments in the thought of Grisez, Finnis, and Boyle since 1980 (many of which have simply made explicit elements of their thought implicit in writing prior to that time and which I have sought to integrate into the preceding summary of their ideas), this synoptic presentation of natural law can now be expressed as follows:

> The natural law consists of an ordered set of true propositions of practical reason. The first set (i) consists of first principles of practical reasoning, of which the fundamental principle is that *good is to be done and pursued and evil is to be avoided,* a principle that is given specific determinations by identifying the basic forms of human flourishing which are the goods that are to be pursued and realized. These principles of practical reasoning are used in one way or another by everyone who considers what to do, however unsound his conclusions. The second set (ii) consists of (a) the first principle of morality — which expresses the integral directiveness of *all* the principles of practical reasoning — and (b) its specifications or modes of responsibility. The first principle is that *in voluntarily acting for human goods and avoiding what is opposed to them, one ought to choose and otherwise will those and only those possibilities whose willing is compatible with a will toward integral human fulfillment.* Its specifications — the modes of responsibility — exclude ways of choosing that ignore, slight, neglect, arbitrarily limit, or damage, destroy, or impede basic human goods. In the light of the first principle of morality and its specifications, human persons are able to distinguish between acts reasonable all-things-considered (and not merely relative-to-a-particular-purpose) and acts that are unreasonable all-things-considered, i.e., between

ways of acting that are morally right and morally wrong. The third set (iii) of natural law propositions, formulated in light of the first and second sets, consists of specific moral norms — of which some are absolute, whereas others admit of exceptions in light of the principles that gave rise to them to begin with.

In addition, the integral directiveness of the first principles of practical reasoning — expressed in the first principle of morality that directs us toward the ideal of integral human fulfillment — provides us with the criterion for establishing moral priorities among our interests in the basic goods of human existence. When these goods are considered from the perspective of this integral directiveness — the directiveness of unfettered practical reason — the good of religion, or of harmony between human persons and God or the "more-than-human source of meaning and value," is seen to have a priority insofar as commitment to this good offers to human persons an overarching purpose in terms of which they can order their lives as a whole.

In fact, a commitment to act always in accord with all the guidance God provides ultimately emerges as the commitment that can integrate the whole of human life when this is conceived in light of the demands of moral truth. Because of such a commitment, harmony with God would be the single ultimate end intended in every choice a person committed to this purpose makes.

7. An Assessment of the Thought of Grisez, Finnis, and Boyle on Natural Law

Although it is not possible here to attempt a full assessment of the work of Grisez, Finnis, and Boyle regarding natural law (to do so would take us far beyond the purposes of this chapter), I think it is important to offer a brief evaluation of their thought. I will do so by relating it to the thought of St. Thomas and by briefly commenting on some of the reactions that their work has elicited from others.

In my opinion, the thought of Grisez, Finnis, and Boyle on natural law has great significance and is very helpful in any effort to understand what is meant by "natural law." While their thought is rooted in that of St. Thomas, they have clearly sought not only to clarify and develop basic features of St. Thomas's work but also to make their own contributions to natural law theory. First of all, St. Thomas did not attempt to identify all the basic goods of human persons; he rather provided an illustrative list — something that has been made clear earlier in my summary of St. Thomas's teaching on natural law. Grisez, Finnis, and Boyle, on the other hand, seek to identify all the basic goods of human persons and to distinguish between those that are "reflexive" or "existential" and those that are "substantive."

Second, they clearly distinguish two sorts of propositions that St. Thomas had included, without any explicit distinction, among the "first and common principles of natural law": (1) the first sort of propositions of this kind direct us to do and pursue the good and avoid evil and identify the real goods, toward which we are naturally inclined, which are to be done and pursued — goods such as life itself, knowledge of the truth, friendship and fellowship with others — the "principles of practical reasoning"; and (2) the second sort of propositions concern the way we are to pursue these goods — the "principles of morality." The very first of these principles — which St. Thomas had formulated in religious biblical language as the commandments to love God and neighbor — they think is better formulated for philosophical theological purposes in terms of making choices in accordance with a will toward integral human fulfillment.

Third, St. Thomas had identified, in addition to the first moral principle (formulated in the love commandments), such moral principles as the Golden Rule and the principle that we are to do injury to no one. Grisez, Finnis, and Boyle seek to identify all such moral principles that further specify the first moral principle. They call them the "modes of responsibility." They are principles enabling us to move from the very first principle of morality to specific moral norms, such as those we find in the Decalogue. St. Thomas regarded the precepts found in the Decalogue as "conclusions" from the first moral principle (and from such principles as the Golden Rule), but he did not clearly show the process of moral reasoning from the first principle to these more specific moral norms. Grisez, Finnis, and Boyle have much more clearly shown this in their development of natural law thought.

In my judgment, the work of Grisez, Finnis, and Boyle on the three issues noted here (the identification of the basic goods, the distinction between "principles of practical reasoning" and "principles of morality," and the process of moral deliberation proceeding from the first principle of morality to specific moral norms by means of the modes of responsibility that further specify the first moral principle) marks a significant contribution to natural law theory and substantively builds on the foundations of St. Thomas.

Finally, they also, in my opinion, throw light on the relationship between natural law, which is a participation in the eternal law, and the eternal law. They do so because they show why the first principle of morality, which expresses the integral directiveness of all the principles of practical thinking, and the ideal of integral human fulfillment to which it directs us, requires us to adopt an intelligent plan of life, one in which commitment to religious truth is of overarching importance. By doing this, they show how the natural law opens us to God, the transcendent source of meaning and value.

The work of Grisez, Finnis, and Boyle has been ignored or quite inadequately considered by the leading representatives of "revisionist" Catholic moral theologians, i.e., by such leading representatives of the "proportionalist" school of thought as Richard A. McCormick, S.J., Joseph Fuchs, S.J., and Louis Janssens. The thought of these revisionists, who deny that there are any intrinsically evil acts in the strong sense and, corresponding to them, specific moral absolutes, will be considered in the next chapter. However, younger representatives of "revisionist" theology — in particular, Todd A. Salzman — have written critiques of the thought of Grisez, Finnis, and Boyle.[140]

Several authors — philosophers and theologians — who accept magisterial teaching on moral absolutes and intrinsically evil actions sharply criticize Grisez, Finnis, and Boyle on allegedly Thomistic grounds. Among these, the most notable are Russell Hittinger, Ralph McInerny, and Henry Veatch, who charge them with failing to ground the precepts of natural law in human nature itself.[141]

Grisez, Finnis, and Boyle, however, have responded fully to this kind of criticism.[142] In their responses, they have clearly shown that St. Thomas considered the principles of natural law to be *underived,* i.e., that one comes to know these principles without the need to derive them from some prior knowledge of human nature (this is something I have tried to show in my own presentation of St. Thomas's natural law thought). But, at the same time, they have shown that erroneous understandings of the human person can indeed block or inhibit one's ability to grasp rightly the goods of human existence and the principles based on them. It is obvious that the goods perfective of human persons would be different from what they are if human persons had a different kind of nature than they do. Still this does not mean that one comes to know these goods and the principles based on them by deriving them from one's speculative understanding of human persons. It is, nonetheless, necessary to defend, by dialectical argument, the truth of these first principles, and this Finnis, Grisez, and Boyle have sought to do.

In addition, other scholars have shown that the kind of criticism raised by Hittinger and others against the thought of our authors is misplaced and inaccurate, based at times on misunderstandings or misinterpretations of their thought. Among such scholars are Robert George, William Marshner, and Aurelio Ansaldo.[143]

More recently, Benedict Ashley, O.P., has raised challenging objections to the natural law thought of Grisez, Finnis, and Boyle; and as yet they have not responded to his objections.

Ashley calls the understanding of natural law developed by Grisez, Finnis, Boyle and their collaborators a "polyteleologism" and identifies three "theses" it affirms, which in his judgment are erroneous.[144] The three "theses" are the following: "(1) Ethics is independent of a philosophical anthropology; (2) the human person, even if as Christians believe it now has a supernatural ultimate end, still also has a natural end; (3) the ultimate end of the human person is not a single good, but integral human fulfillment jointly constituted by several incommensurable basic goods."[145]

It is, first of all, not accurate to call the new natural law theory "polyteleologism" or "plural-goals-ism." It is not accurate and actually misrepresents the position. Grisez et al. do say that the diverse human goods are *ends* in the sense that people recognize that they are worth pursuing *for their own sake*. But they avoid calling these ends "goals," precisely because "goal" suggests a sought-after state of affairs that can be attained once and for all, at which point one's desire is satisfied. But the basic goods of human persons are not ends in this sense. They are *not* concrete states of affairs one seeks to bring about as a result of one's actions. A sign of this is that one *never* reaches a point of having "enough" knowledge, friendship, health, etc.

With regard to the three "theses," which Ashley says he finds in the new natural law theory, I maintain in the following analysis that its authors hold *none* of the theses he attributes to them:

- **Re Thesis 1:** As we have seen already, Grisez and his associates hold, *with St. Thomas*, that *the first principles of practical reason* are *underived*, gnoseologically or epistemologically independent of prior known truths of the speculative intellect or of prior knowledge of human nature, from which their truth could be derived. However, as we have already seen, they never deny but rather vigorously affirm that there is an *ontological* and *anthropological* foundation of ethics or natural law. This is so because the *goods* perfective of human persons would be other than what they are were human *nature* other than what it is; and these are the goods which, when grasped by practical reason, function as starting-points or principles for thinking about human action (what-am-I-to-do). In fact, Grisez clearly affirms that "moral thought must remain grounded in a sound anthropology which maintains the bodiliness of the person. Such moral thought sees personal biological, not merely generically biological, meaning and value in human sexuality. The bodies which become one flesh in sexual intercourse are persons; their unity in a certain sense forms a single person, the potential procreator from whom the personal, bodily reality of a new human individual flows in material, bodily, personal continuity."[146] Ashley would find it difficult to reconcile passages like this with his claim.

• **Re Thesis 2:** Grisez et al. make it clear that they do *not* think that man has a natural end in any strong sense of that term, i.e., some definite good which of itself fully perfects man. The "integral human fulfillment" to which the first moral principle directs one is *not* a supergood, *not* the ultimate reason why one chooses or should choose all one chooses; it is, rather, an ultimate end in the sense that it is the object of a rectified will, the object of "unfettered practical reason."[147]

• **Re Thesis 3:** Grisez, Finnis, and Boyle explicitly teach, as we have seen, that a good life is a complex, not of incommensurable goods connected together, but rather of *morally good actions* in and through which human persons give themselves their identity as moral persons, in and through which they give themselves their moral *character*. Such a life is unified by the commitment one makes to seek the truth about God or the more-than-human source of meaning and value and to shape one's entire life in accord with that truth.[148]

Another objection that might be raised against the thought of Grisez, Finnis, and Boyle is that they fail to include the *moral good* among the basic goods of human persons. Is not there in man, the human person, a natural inclination to the *moral good, or the good of virtue*? Is not this a perfection of the human person, and does not the moral good function as a *basic reason* for acting? And are not these characteristics of the basic goods of human persons in the thought of Grisez, Finnis, and Boyle? Moreover, the moral good was included by St. Thomas among the basic goods of human persons, toward which we have a natural inclination, as noted above. Commenting on this text in 1a-2ae, John Finnis emphasizes that this good, of which Aquinas speaks often and centrally, is precisely "the good of [practical] reasonableness [*bonum rationis; bonum secundum rationem esse*], the good of ordering one's emotions, choices, and actions by intelligence and reason. The *bonum rationis*," Finnis says, "is both an intelligible good *and* the good of that person's being interested in it and sufficiently well integrated [mind integrated with will and each with subrational desires and powers] to choose it and put it into practice. Another name for it, then, is the good of virtue."[149]

It thus seems that the good Aquinas identified as the good according to reason, the good of virtue, is indeed a basic good of human persons and one to which they are naturally inclined. Yet it is not among the basic goods of human persons according to Grisez, Finnis, and Boyle. One can ask, why not?

It turns out that Grisez, in one of his most recent writings, has considered this objection carefully and responded to it. He acknowledges that people sometimes choose to do what is morally good even when aware of no reason for choosing other than it is morally good to do so. Hence, one might claim that moral goodness is another category of basic human good, "with the corresponding primary principle that moral good is to be done and moral evil to be avoided." After posing this problem, Grisez responds to it as follows:

> However, people in general do not manifest any inclination to choose moral goodness for its own sake; only virtuous people manifest that inclination. And it is easy to see why this is so. Everyone understands the goods of inner composure and inner consistency and is naturally inclined to them, but virtuous people overlook the distinction between these goods considered as principles and their morally good instantiations, which pertain to moral virtues; so, they always are inclined to choose what is morally good, even when unaware of any ulterior reason for their choice. If, however, there were a self-evident principle of practical reason directing that moral good be done and moral evil be avoided, that principle would presuppose a natural inclination of some human capacity toward moral goodness; and, since an inclination toward moral goodness would not be toward the object of any single human capacity, it would have to be in the person as a whole. If there is an inclination toward moral goodness in a person as a whole, however, that person is virtuous. Thus, if people had a natural inclination toward moral goodness, they would be virtuous by nature. But in fact they are not; they become virtuous only by consistently making and perseveringly carrying out morally good free choices.[150]

I have some difficulties with Grisez's rejection of the moral good as a basic good of the person. It does not follow, as Grisez argues, that a person is virtuous if there is an inclination toward moral goodness in a person as a whole. After all, he himself recognizes that all human persons have a natural inclination to know the truth, but it does not follow from this that human persons actually know the truth. It seems odd to me that the moral good, which makes a person unqualifiedly good, is not an intrinsic perfection of the person. I have thus come to disagree with Grisez on this matter.

We have now examined in detail natural law in the thought of Grisez, Finnis, and Boyle, considering some of the major objections raised against them.

NATURAL LAW IN THE THOUGHT
OF MARTIN RHONHEIMER[151]

Another important contemporary author noted for his presentation of the natural law thought of St. Thomas is the Swiss philosopher/theologian Martin Rhonheimer, whose very important study of natural law in St. Thomas's writings has recently been made available for English-speaking readers. Here I will briefly consider his work on Thomistic natural law. I cannot do justice to his very valuable work in this short section. What I will do, in order to convey some idea of his work and its importance, is to compare it with the natural law theory developed by Grisez, Finnis, and Boyle, showing where Rhonheimer is in basic agreement with these authors and major areas where he differs from them.

1. Areas of Agreement Between Rhonheimer and Grisez, Finnis, and Boyle

Rhonheimer agrees with Grisez et al. in holding that according to Aquinas — and reality — our knowledge of the truths of natural law is *not* derived from metaphysics or anthropology or any speculative knowledge. With them, he opposes those who maintain the opposite, explicitly acknowledging his debt to Grisez on this matter.[152] In fact, a substantive portion of his study is a critique of leading representatives (e.g., Josef Pieper) of the view that truths of natural law are derived from our knowledge of metaphysics and human nature.[153] With Grisez and his associates, Rhonheimer emphasizes that natural law is a "work" of practical reason, something "constituted" (i.e., brought into being) by the activity of practical reason, having its own "principles" or starting points.[154]

With Grisez et al., Rhonheimer also opposes strongly those Catholic moralists who deny moral absolutes (an issue to be considered in depth in the following chapter). Insisting that natural law is man's active, intelligent participation in God's eternal law, Rhonheimer provides a strong critique of contemporary Catholic moralists who advocate an "autonomous" morality, in which the natural law, accessible to human reason, serves as the *ultimate* norm, speaks of a legitimate kind of "participated theonomy" as the kind of morality proper to human persons. Although the natural law is entitatively distinct from the eternal law, it is in essence the eternal law itself insofar as it is shared by human practical intelligence.[155]

Rhonheimer, moreover, agrees with Grisez, Finnis, and Boyle, in holding that practical reason spontaneously (i.e., naturally, without discursive reasoning) apprehends the goods (*bona*) to which we are naturally inclined as intelligible goods — the goods that are to be pursued and done. He does not, like

Grisez et al., seek to provide an exhaustive list of the goods constitutive of the whole human good; rather, he speaks of the ones considered explicitly by St. Thomas in 1-2, q. 94, a. 2. However, like Finnis, he calls special attention to the teaching of St. Thomas in 1-2, q. 94, a. 3, where the Common Doctor speaks of our *natural inclination* to act in accordance with reason or to act according to virtue.[156] Indeed, as we shall see, Rhonheimer goes on — and here he differs from Grisez et al. — to insist that practical reason imposes a moral order on all of our natural inclinations and the goods toward which they orient us, insisting that the natural law is a law leading us to and being fulfilled in the virtues.

2. Areas of Disagreement Between Rhonheimer and Grisez, Finnis, and Boyle

But Rhonheimer's work, which he proposes precisely as the proper understanding of St. Thomas's theory of natural law, offers an understanding of natural law different from that proposed by Grisez, Finnis, and Boyle in their endeavor to develop a natural law *rooted* in St. Thomas but *developing* matters relevant to the natural law that, in their opinion, were not adequately addressed by St. Thomas himself. Here I will focus attention on three major elements in Rhonheimer's presentation of natural law where he differs from Grisez et al.: (a) the distinction between the perceptive-practical and descriptive-reflexive levels of practical reason; (b) the relationship between natural law and virtue; and (c) the movement from the first or common principles of natural law to its "proximate" or "immediate" conclusions.

A. Two Levels of Practical Reason: The Perceptive-Practical and the Descriptive-Reflexive

According to Rhonheimer, there are two levels of practical knowledge concerned with behavior. This distinction, which Rhonheimer acknowledges is only implicit in St. Thomas himself,[157] is that between the level on which the practical judgments of reason are carried out and that on which one reflects on these acts of practical reason or the level of moral philosophy.

As we have seen, law, for Aquinas, is the "product" of practical reason, something "constituted by practical reason." Rhonheimer maintains that the "product" of practical reason at the first level is a "command" or "precept." The *"propositio"* constituted by practical reason at this level, he insists, "is not a 'statement' but rather a 'command' or 'precept' (*praeceptum*)" or *dictamen rationis*.[158] According to Rhonheimer, at the first or "preceptive" level of practical reason, the "product" of practical reason "must not be thought of in a reified fashion: as a preceptive subject-matter of the reason (or 'object' of practical reason) . . . it is really the *content* of this act [of practical reason]. This *praeceptum* . . . can be expressed only as a command: 'Do that!' The adequate expression of the practical judgment as *praeceptum* appears only to be *an act of the will itself* . . . stamped by the perceptive content of this judgment . . . or the *action itself* thus willed. The intersubjectively encountered 'language' of the perceptive act of the reason is, finally, *behavior* itself."[159]

Rhonheimer maintains that it is only at the second level, the "descriptive-reflexive" level, that "normative statements" or *enuntiationes* of natural law are produced. Thus, he declares:

> A *normative statement* such as "good is to be done" (*bonum est faciendum*) or "evil is to be avoided" (*malum est vitandum*) is not a statement made by the practical reason at the level where it actually *makes* such "precepts" or commands, but rather is a statement of *reflection upon* this preceptive act of the practical reason. . . . The practical reason constitutes the command (*praeceptum*) and not a "normative statement"; the latter is a "statement" (*enuntiatio*) in a prescriptive or "ought" mode, and not a precept. . . . The practical good becomes objectified as commandment, norm, or duty only in reflection — and then a *normative statement* arises such as "good is to be pursued" (*bonum prosequendum est*).[160]

And again he writes, "The discovery of this natural law in man — its cognitive objectification, one might say — occurs *only on the level of reflection*, where the order of precepts of the natural law is recognized as an order of right actions established by the practical reason"(emphasis added).[161] He likewise maintains that the terms of *per se notae* judgments of practical reason

> consist . . . of a good (*bonum:* from the most universal *bonum communissimum* to the concrete *bonum operabile*) and a practical predicate, "to be pursued" or "to be avoided." Such a description of practical judgments — as "normative statements" — is in any case meaningful only in reflection on the act of the practical reason — on the level, that is, where practical judgments are capable of a linguistic formulation. At the level of their original execution [the "perceptive-practical"] they are not accessible to such formulation, since they then involve either an appetitive-preceptive *affirmatio* of what is recognized as "good" or a corresponding *negatio*.[162]

I find this feature of Rhonheimer's interpretation of Aquinas difficult to understand. He himself admits that the distinction is not explicit but only implicit in St. Thomas.

B. The Relationship Between Natural Law and Virtue

One of the principal features of Rhonheimer's work is his attempt to articulate the harmony that St. Thomas understood to exist between reason, law, and virtue. In *Summa theologiae* (1-2, q. 94, a. 3) — a text central to Rhonheimer's interpretation — Thomas considers the question, "whether all acts of the virtues are of the natural law." Reflecting on this key text, Rhonheimer insists that action virtuously carried out "corresponds to a 'dictate of the natural reason' (*dictamen rationis naturalis*). . . ." Indeed, the good of man, as St. Thomas says in *De virtutibus* (a. 9), consists in this: "that reason sufficiently recognize the truth and that lower urges be ordered in accordance with the rule of reason."[163] Thus, within the unity of the person, the natural law is not only a part of the order of reason that has its ground in the natural inclinations; in its preceptive function, the natural law also puts virtuous order into the inclinations. Because of the diversity of human goods, man does not possess a determination (*determinatio*) toward a single thing (*inclinatio ad unum*) through a natural form (*forma naturalis*), but must freely orient himself toward the good through a form conceived by reason (*forma a ratione concepta*).[164]

Rhonheimer argues that "in the course of moral philosophical reflection, the natural law is recognized to be nothing other than the preceptive activity of the practical reason, as it constitutes the order of the virtues (*ordo virtutum*) and as it constitutes the content of this order — itself an *ordo rationis*."[165]

According to Rhonheimer, the goods toward which the natural inclinations orient us, "once they have been apprehended as natural inclinations that belong to the person, are brought into (that is, integrated within) reason's own order by the reason and thereby become the object of the will's *intellective* seeking. And *only as such* are they in each case the content of a *praeceptum* and a *prosequendum* and belong to the natural law [emphasis added]. 'All inclinations of any part of human nature, that is, both of the concupiscible and irascible parts, belong to natural law [*pertinent ad legem naturalem*] insofar as they are regulated by reason' (I-II, q. 94, a. 2, ad 2um). This is because reason is 'ordering principle of everything that has to do with human beings' (*ordinativa omnia quae ad homines spectant*; ibid., ad 3um)."[166]

All this makes it evident that Rhonheimer considers the "good of acting in accordance with reason" or the "moral good" one of the basic goods of the human person. In fact, this shows that for Rhonheimer this good — the moral good, the good of virtue — is the good that serves to provide unity to the moral life and the criterion in light of which actions can be judged morally good or bad. As we have seen, Grisez et al. do not regard the moral good or the good of virtue as a basic good of human persons. They assign to the good of religion the function of integrating and unifying the moral life. Here they and Rhonheimer part company.

In my opinion, it is on this issue more than any other that Rhonheimer's position differs from that of Grisez, Finnis, and Boyle. In considering the view of Grisez et al., I noted that in their very important 1987 essay "Practical Principles, Moral Truth, and Ultimate Ends," they acknowledged that one ought not regard reflexive goods such as self-integration or inner peace and peace of conscience as having *moral* value, even though they themselves, in some previous writings, had imported moral value into them. This, I believe, is particularly true of John Finnis in an earlier work, *Natural Law and Natural Rights*. In that work, he had called attention to the key text of 1-2, 94, 3, where St. Thomas speaks of our natural inclination to act in accord with reason, i.e., with virtue. In fact, he devoted in that work a complete chapter to a consideration of what he called there the "good of practical reasonableness" and its "requirements," a term used in that work to designate the function of what he later on called, with Grisez, "modes of responsibility." In other words, the Finnis of 1980 would seem to hold the same view of this good and its centrality in our moral life as does Rhonheimer; but Finnis, in the 1987 article jointly authored with Grisez and Boyle, abandoned this position.

However, Finnis, in his comprehensive study published in 1998, *Aquinas: Moral, Political, and Legal Theory* (New York/Oxford: Oxford University Press), again comments on St. Thomas's teaching in 1a-2ae 94, 3 on the moral good and clearly makes this teaching his own. It thus seems to me that Finnis has returned to the view he set forth in his 1980 book and would hence be in agreement with Rhonheimer. As noted earlier, I also hold that the moral good is one of the basic goods of the human person and thus differ on this issue from Grisez.

C. The Movement From the First or Common Principles of Natural Law to Its 'Proximate' or 'Immediate' Conclusions

Rhonheimer, summarizing St. Thomas's thought regarding the "first and common principles" of natural law writes as follows:

> The natural law, fundamentally and essentially, is the ensemble of those most general principles that the practical reason recognizes by an "insight into first principles" (*intellectus principiorum*) and in an instantaneous-intuitive manner . . .; these principles, as something "naturally known" (*naturaliter cognitum*) form a so-called "natural habit of first principles," or *synderesis*. This is a spontaneous and "natural" source of light, acquired without any discursive movement, but belonging to the practical reason and thus "bringing movement" and forming the "seeds" of all subsequent knowledge — containing knowledge potentially and implicitly — so that Thomas can also call it the habit of the "natural principles of natural law."[167]

But how do we go from these first and common principles to their proximate and more remote conclusions? According to Rhonheimer, these conclusions or implications are "discovered" in the first and common principles through the discursive process of the natural reason, thereby providing the proximate rule or measure for actions. The basic movement that initiates this process of discovery is grounded in *synderesis*. As the *habitus* of first principles, it "provides a 'natural' source of light, acquired without any discursive movement, but belonging to the practical reason and thus 'bringing movement' and forming the 'seeds' of all subsequent knowledge. . . ."[168]

Although the conclusions that result from this "inventive" process (and the precepts of the Decalogue are, we should recall, its immediate and proximate conclusions) are considered secondary, this does not mean they are relatively insignificant; they are secondary in the sense of their subsequent cognitive explication. In the order of actions, however, they are less remote and therefore have more legislative significance than the first principles, due to their being closer to the object of action.[169] Thus, these secondary principles, as part of the natural law itself, provide the proximate determination of the first principles as rule and measure of an action under consideration. Nonetheless, the concrete judgment of action (*iudicium electionis*) that provides the proximate rule (*regula proxima*) comes from prudence as right reason about things to be done (*recta ratio agibilium*). This proximate rule has for its object "the action to be done here and now" (*hic et nunc*), the concrete "doable" (*operabile*). Thus, the secondary principles are "proximate determinations of the first principles as they pertain to [the regulation of] our concrete actions" whereas the proximate rule of action itself comes from prudence.[170]

Rhonheimer does not, however, explicitly show how the primary principles of natural law serve as premises in the light of which one can show the truth of the "proximate and immediate" conclusions. In this, he seems to follow St. Thomas himself. As we have seen, Grisez, Finnis, and Boyle argue — correctly in my opinion — that one must show clearly how the so-called "proximate conclusions" are shown to be true in the light of prior principles. They believe that St. Thomas neglected to do this and argue for the need of "intermediary principles" midway between the first moral principle of the natural law and specific precepts such as those found in the Decalogue, and they call these intermediary principles the "modes of responsibility."

Conclusion

This chapter has reviewed in depth the teaching of St. Thomas on natural law. In addition, it has summarized relevant teachings of Vatican Council II and of Pope John Paul II on this subject. Finally, it has provided an extensive account of the thought of Germain Grisez, John Finnis, and Joseph Boyle on natural law and a briefer account of the position on natural law taken by Martin Rhonheimer. From the material presented here, readers should now be able to understand, in a more precise and comprehensive way, what is meant by "natural law" and its role in our moral lives. It is not a mystery, a funny internal feeling, a fuzzy concept. It is, rather, an ordered set of true propositions about what we are to do if we are to be fully the beings we are meant to be. Among the goods to which it directs us is the moral good, the good of practical reasonableness or of virtue.

As already noted, it is the natural law that is perfected, fulfilled, and completed by the evangelical law of love, of a more-than-human kind of love, the love that God himself has for us. In Chapter Six, where we will be concerned with our life as moral persons in Christ, we shall seek to show how the evangelical law of love fulfills and completes the natural law.

Notes for Chapter Three

1. St. Thomas Aquinas, *Summa theologiae*, 1-2, 93, 2; the other texts of St. Thomas to which *Dignitatis humanae* refers are 1-2, 91, 1, and 93, 1.

2. For the historical development of Thomas's thought on natural law, see the following: Odon Lottin, *Le droit naturel chez Saint Thomas d'Aquin et ses prédécesseurs* (Bruges: Beyaert, 1931); Michael Bertram Crowe, *The Changing Profile of the Natural Law* (The Hague: Martinus Nijhoff, 1977), pp. 136-191; R.A. Armstrong, *Primary and Secondary Precepts in Thomistic Natural Law Thinking* (The Hague: Martinus Nijhoff, 1966), pp. 56-114. Lottin, Armstrong, and Crowe in an earlier article ("St. Thomas and the Natural Law," *Irish Ecclesiastical Record* 76 [1951], 293-305) follow the chronology of Aquinas's works proposed by Grabmann and Mandonnet, and consequently consider the discussion of natural law in St. Thomas's *Commentary on the Nicomachean Ethics* (written, according to Grabmann, c. 1261-64, or, according to Mandonnet, c. 1266) chronologically prior to the presentation in the *Summa theologiae*. In his *Changing Profile of the Natural Law*, Crowe adopts the more accurate chronology proposed by R. Gauthier ("La date du commentaire de saint Thomas sur l'éthique a nicomaque," *Recherches de théologie ancienne et médiévale* 18 [1951], 66-105 and *Sententia Libri Ethicorum* [*Sancti Thomae de Aquino Opera Omnia*], t. xlvii, Romae, 1969, praefatio, p. 201), who suggests the years 1271-72 for the composition of the *Commentary on the Nicomachean Ethics*, making it either contemporary with or perhaps a little after the composition of the *Prima Secundae* of *Summa theologiae*. See also John Finnis, *Aquinas: Moral, Political, and Legal Theory* (New York: Oxford University Press, 1998).

3. *Summa theologiae*, 1-2, 90, 1: "Lex quaedam regula est et mensura actuum, secundum quam inducitur aliquis ad agendum vel ab agendo retrahitur . . . Regula autem et mensura humanorum actuum est ratio, quae est primum principium actuum humanorum. . . . rationis autem est ordinare ad finem, qui est principium in agendis. . . . Unde relinquitur quod lex sit aliquid pertinens ad rationem."

4. Ibid., ad 1: "cum lex sit regula quaedam et mensura, dicitur dupliciter esse in aliquo. Uno modo, sicut in mensurante et regulante. Et quia hoc est proprium rationis, ideo per hunc modum lex est in ratione sola. Alio modo, sicut in regulato et mensurato. Et sic lex est in omnibus quae inclinantur in aliquid ex aliqua lege, potest dici lex, non essentialiter, sed quasi participative."

5. Ibid., ad 2: "sicut in actibus exterioribus est considerare operationem et operatum . . . ita in operibus rationis est considerare ipsum actum rationis, qui est intelligere et ratiocinari, et aliquid per huiusmodi actum constitutum. Quod quidem in speculativa ratione primo quidem est definitio; secundo, enunciatio; tertio vero, syllogismus vel argumentatio. Et quia ratio practica utitur quodam syllogismo in operabilibus . . . ideo est invenire aliquid in ratione practica quod ita se habeat ad operationes, sicut se habet propositio in ratione speculativa ad conclusiones. Et huiusmodi propositiones universales rationis practicae ordinatae ad actiones habent rationem legis. Quae quidem propositiones aliquando actualiter considerantur, aliquando vero habitualiter a ratione tenentur."

6. Ibid., 90, 2.

7. Ibid., 90, 3.

8. Ibid., 90, 4.

9. Ibid., 91, 1: "nihil est aliud lex quam quoddam dictamen practicae rationis in principe qui gubernat aliquam communitatem perfectam. Manifestum est autem . . . quod tota communitas universi gubematur ratione divina. Et ideo ipsa ratio gubernationis rerum in Deo sicut in principe universitatis existens, legis habet rationem."

10. Ibid., 93, 1: "lex aeterna nihil aliud est quam ratio divinae sapientiae, secundum quod est directiva omnium actuum et motionum."

11. Ibid., 91, l, ad 1 and ad 2; 93, l, ad 2.

12. Ibid., 91, 2: "lex, cum sit regula et mensura, dupliciter potest esse in aliquo . . . alio modo, sicut in regulato et mensurato, quia inquantum participat aliquid in regula vel mensura, sic regulatur et mensuratur. Unde cum omnia quae divinae providentiae subduntur, a lege aeterna regulentur et mensurentur . . . manifestum est quod omnia participant aliqualiter legem aeternam, inquantum scilicet ex impressione eius habent inclinationes in proprios actus et fines."

13. Ibid., 91, 2 and ad 3. The text cited in note 12 (91, 2) and the response to the third objection, ad 3: "in creatura irrationali non participator rationaliter; unde non potest dici lex nisi per similitudinem."

14. Ibid., 91, 2: "Inter cetera autem rationalis creatura excellentiori quodammodo divinae providentiae subiacet, inquantum et ipsa fit providentiae particeps, sibi ipsi et aliis providens. Unde et in ipsa participatur ratio aeterna, per quam habet naturalem inclinationem ad debitum actum et finem. Et talis participatio legis aeternae in rationali creatura lex naturalis dicitur. Unde cum Psalmista dixisset (Ps 4.6), 'Sacrificate sacrificium iustitiae,' quasi quibusdam quaerentibus quae sunt iustitiae opera, subiungit: 'Multi dicunt, Quid ostendit nobis bona?' cui quaestioni respondens, dicit: 'Signatum est super nos lumen vultus tui, Domine,' quasi lumen rationis naturalis, quo discernimus quid sit bonum et malum, quod pertinet ad naturalem legem, nihil aliud sit quam impressio divini luminis in nobis. Unde patet quod lex naturalis nihil aliud est quam participatio legis aeternae in rationali creatura."

On this issue, it is worth noting what D. O'Donoghue says in his helpful article, "The Thomist Concept of the Natural Law," *Irish Theological Quarterly* 22 (1955), 93-94: "There are two ways of understanding rational participation: We might see it as a *receptive* participation: created reason is receptive of Eternal Law just as irrational nature is . . . though in a higher way. . . . *Or* we might see rational participation as *legislative*, as participation in the very activity of legislating. . . . That we must understand rational participation in the second sense, seeing human reason as regulative rather than regulated, is clear from the fact that St. Thomas identifies the Natural Law with the 'propositions' or 'precepts' of natural reason [see below, notes 18-21]. The matter is put beyond doubt by the discussion in Q. 93, a. 6, where a sharp distinction is drawn between participation in Eternal Law by way of *inclinatio naturalis ad id quod est consonum legi aeternae* and *ipsa naturalis cognitio boni*. . . . That which differentiates Natural Law from natural inclination, and makes it law in the proper sense, is the fact that it is the work of reason, expression rather than impression. It comes from God, as [do] all human things . . . but the mind receives it, not as itself an object which is revealed by it, but as becoming a source of light, discerning and declaring the truth for human activity (cf. 1-2, 91, 2)."

On this matter, see also Martin Rhonheimer, *Natural Law and Practical Reason: A Thomist View of Moral Autonomy*, trans. Gerald Malsbary (New York: Fordham University Press, 2000), pp. 61-64.

15. *Summa theologiae*, 1-2, 91, 1, ad 3: "etiam animalia irrationalia participant rationem aeternam uno modo, sicut et rationalis creatura. Sed quia rationalis creatura participat earn intellectualiter et rationaliter, ideo participatio legis aeternae in creatura rationali proprie lex vocatur: nam lex est aliquid rationis. . . . In creatura autem irrationali non participatur rationaliter; unde non potest dici lex nisi per similitudinem."

16. Ibid., 91, 2, ad 1. On this matter, see Rhonheimer, *Natural Law and Practical Reason*, pp. 62-63.

17. On the views of Thomas's predecessors regarding the relationship between synderesis and natural law, see Crowe, *The Changing Profile of the Natural Law*, pp. 111-135. Also see Crowe, "The Term *Synderesis* and the Scholastics: St. Thomas and *Synderesis*," *Irish Theological Quarterly* 23 (1956), 228-245.

18. *Summa theologiae*, 1-2, 94, 1: "aliquid potest dici esse habitus dupliciter. Uno modo, proprie et essentialiter; et sic lex naturalis non est habitus. Dictum est enim supra quod lex naturalis est aliquid per rationem constitutum. . . . Non est autem idem quod quid agit, et quo quis agit. . . . Cum igitur habitus sit quo quis agit, non potest esse quod lex aliqua sit habitus proprie et essentialiter. Alio modo potest dici habitus id quod habitu tenetur. . . . Et hoc modo, quia praecepta legis naturalis quandoque considerantur in actu a ratione, quandoque autem sunt in ea habitualiter tantum, secundum hunc modum potest dici quod lex naturalis sit habitus."

19. Here it is important to stress the role that practical reason plays for St. Thomas and the significance of the difference between speculative and practical reason. According to Thomas, there are *not* two reasons in man, speculative and practical, but there *are* two basically different ways in which intelligence or reason is exercised. In speculative inquiry, its concern is with *what is*. In practical inquiry, its concern is with *what-is-to-be-done-or-made* by rational or intelligent beings. And in both realms, there are nondemonstrable starting points or principles. On this matter, see Germain Grisez, *Contraception and the Natural Law* (Milwaukee: Bruce Publishing Co., 1964), Chapter 3, and the literature cited there.

20. *Summa theologiae*, 1-2, 94, 2: "Sicut autem ens est primum quod cadit in apprehensione simpliciter, ita bonum est primum quod cadit in apprehensione practicae rationis, quae ordinatur ad opus: omne enim agens agit propter finem, qui habet rationem boni. Et ideo primum principium in ratione practica est quod fundatur supra rationem boni, quae est, *Bonum est quod omnia appetunt*. Hoc est ergo primum praeceptum legis, quod *bonum est faciendum et prosequendum, et malum vitandum*. Et super hoc fundantur omnia alia praecepta legis naturae: ut scilicet omnia illa facienda vel vitanda pertinent ad praecepta legis naturae, quae ratio practica naturaliter apprehendit esse bona humana."

21. Ibid.: "Quia vero bonum habet rationem finis, malum autem rationem contrarii, inde est quod omnia illa ad quae homo habet naturalem inclinationem, ratio naturaliter apprehendit ut bona, et per consequens ut opere prosequenda, et contraria eorum ut mala et vitanda."

22. See ibid., 1, 18, 2.

23. Ibid., 1-2, 94, 2: "Inest enim primo inclinatio homini ad bonum secundum naturam in qua communicat cum omnibus substantiis; prout scilicet quaelibet substantia appetit conservationem sui esse secundum suam naturam. Et secundum hanc inclinationem pertinent ad legem naturalem ea per quae vita hominis conservatur, et contrarium impeditur. Secundo inest homini inclinatio ad aliqua magis specialia, secundum naturam in qua communicat cum ceteris animalibus.

Et secundum hoc, dicuntur ea esse de lege naturali, *quae natura omnia animalia docuit*, ut est coniunctio maris et feminae, et educatio liberorum, et similia. Tertio modo inest homini inclinatio ad bonum secundum naturam rationis, quae est sibi propria; sicut homo habet naturalem inclinationem ad hoc quod veritatem cognoscat de Deo, et ad hoc quod in societate vivat. Et secundum hoc, ad legem naturalem pertinent ea quae ad huiusmodi inclinationem spectant; utpote, quod homo ignorantiam vitet, quod alios non offendat cum quibus debet conversari, et cetera huiusmodi quae ad hoc spectant."

24. Ibid. and 94, 3: "naturalis inclincatio inest cuilibet homini ad hoc quod agat secundum rationem. Et hoc est agere secundum virtutem."

25. Ibid., 100, 1: "illa communia et prima praecepta."

26. Ibid., 100, 8: "quorum non oportet aliquam editionem esse, nisi quod sunt scripta in ratione naturali quasi per se nota." See also 100, 11.

27. Ibid., 95, 2: "nulli esse malum faciendum."

28. Ibid., 94, 4, ad 1: "Unde cum dixisset Gratianus quod *ius* naturale est quod in Lege et Evangelio continetur, statim, exempli-ficando, subiunxit, *quo quisque iubetur alii facere quod sibi vult fieri.*"

29. Ibid., 100, 3, 1st objection: "Diliges Dominum Deum tuum, et Diliges proximum tuum."

30. Ibid., 100, 3, ad 1: "illa duo praecepta [Diliges Dominum Deum tuum, et Diliges proximum tuum] sunt prima et communia praecepta legis naturae, quae sunt per se nota rationi humanae, vel per naturam vel per fidem. Et ideo omnia praecepta decalogi ad illa duo referuntur sicut conclusiones ad principia communia." See also 100, 11.

31. Ibid., 100, 1: "quae statim per se ratio naturalis cuiuslibet hominis diiudicat esse facienda, vel non facienda."

32. Ibid., 3 and 100, 11.

33. Ibid., 100, 1: "statim, cum madica consideratione."

34. Ibid., 100,11.

35. Ibid., 100, 1: "sunt absolute de lege naturali."

36. Ibid., 100, 11: "Quaedam vero sunt magis determinata, quorum rationem statim quilibet, etiam popularis, potest de facili videre; et tamen quia in paucioribus circa huiusmodi contingit iudicium humanum perverti, huiusmodi editione indigent; et haec sunt praecepta decalogi."

37. Ibid., 100, 1: "subtiliori consideratione rationis."

38. Ibid., 100,3 and 100, 11.

39. Ibid.

40. The principal texts bringing out this structure of natural law according to St. Thomas are *Summa theologiae*, 1-2, 100, 1; 100, 3; and 100, 11. R.A. Armstrong, *Primary and Secondary Precepts in Thomistic Natural Law Teaching*, pp. 98-114, offers a very illuminating presentation of these texts with commentary.

41. On this, see Armstrong, *Primary and Secondary Precepts*, p. 109.

42. *Summa theologiae*, 1-2, 100, 3: "Inter praecepta ergo decalogi non computantur duo genera praeceptorum, illa scilicet, quae sunt prima et communia, quorum non oportet aliquam editionem esse, nisi quod sunt scripta in rationi naturali quasi per se nota, et iterum illa, quae per diligentem inquisitionem sapientum inveniuntur rationi convenire; haec enim proveniunt a Deo ad populum mediante disciplina sapientum."

43. Ibid.: "Utraque tamen horum praeceptorum continentur in praeceptis decalogi, sed diversimode. Nam illa quae sunt prima et communia, continentur in eis sicut principia in conclusionibus proximis; illa vero quae sapientes cognoscuntur continentur in eis e converso, sicut conclusiones in pnincipiis."

44. Ibid., 94, 6: "ad legem naturalem pertinent primo quidem quaedam praecepta communissima, quae sunt omnibus nota; quaedam autem secundaria praecepta magis propria, quae sunt quasi conclusiones propinquae principiis. Quantum ergo ad illa praecepta communia, lex naturalis nullo modo potest a cordibus hominum deleri in universali. Deletur tamen in particulari operabili, secundum quod ratio impeditur applicare commune praeceptum ad particulare operabile, propter concupiscentiam vel aliquam aliam passionem."

45. Ibid.: "Quantum vero ad alia praecepta secundaria, potest lex naturalis deleri de cordibus hominum, vel propter malas persuasiones, eo modo quo etiam in speculativis errores contingunt circa conclusiones necessarias, vel etiam propter pravas consuetudines et habitus corruptos."

46. Ibid., 100, 8. On this matter, see Patrick Lee, "The Permanence of the Ten Commandments: St. Thomas and His Modern Commentators," *Theological Studies* 42 (1981), 422-433.

47. Charles E. Curran, "Natural Law and Contemporary Moral Theology," in his *Contemporary Problems in Moral Theology* (Notre Dame, IN: Fides, 1970), p. 106. See his "Absolute Norms in Moral Theology," in his *A New Look at Christian Morality* (Notre Dame, IN: Fides, 1968), pp. 75-89.

48. Timothy E. O'Connell, *Principles for a Catholic Morality* (New York: Seabury, 1978), p. 138. See Richard M. Gula, *Reason Informed by Faith: Foundations of Catholic Morality* (New York: Paulist Press, 1989), pp. 223-228.

49. On St. Thomas's use of Ulpian, see my "The Meaning and Nature of the Natural Law in Thomas Aquinas," *American Journal of Jurisprudence* 22 (1977), 168-189, especially 175-185.

50. *In IV Sent.*, d. 33, q. 1, a. 1 (reprinted as q. 65, a. 1 of the *Supplementum* of the *Pars Tertia* of the *Summa theologiae*): "Lex ergo naturalis nihil est aliud quam conceptio homini naturaliter indita, qua dirigitur ad convenienter agendum in actionibus propriis, sive competunt ei ex natura generis, ut generare, comedere, et huiusmodi, sive ex natura speciei, ut ratiocinari, et similia."

51. Ibid.: "Pluralitas ergo uxorum neque totaliter tollit neque aliqualiter impedit primum finem . . . sed secundum finem etsi non totaliter tollat, tamen multum impedit, eo quod non facile potest esse pax in familia ubi uni viro plures uxores iunguntur. . . . Tertium autem finem totaliter tollit, eo quod sicut Christus est unus, ita Ecclesia una; et ideo patet ex dictis quod pluralitas uxorum quodammodo est contra legem naturae, et quodammado non."

52. The expression "strictissimo modo accipiendi ius naturale" is *not* to be understood as "taking natural law in its *most precise (or formal) sense*" but rather as "taking natural law in its *most restricted and limited* sense." Whenever Thomas wishes to express the *formal, essential* meaning of something, he uses the terms "proprie" or "essentialiter," as we have seen repeatedly in his insistence that natural law, as *law*, is found essentially and properly only in the rational creature. In *A Lexicon of St. Thomas Aquinas based on the Summa Theologiae and selected passages of his other works*, Roy J. Deferrari et al. (Washington, DC: The Catholic University of America Press, 1949) 5.1055, show us that the participial adjective *strictus* (with its comparative and superlative) is frequently used in the sense of what is "most rigid in interpretation," and this very text is used to illustrate this meaning.

53. *In IV Sent.*, d. 33, q. 1, a. 1, ad 4: "ius naturale multipliciter accipitur. Primo enim ius aliquod dicitur naturale ex principio, quia a natura est inditum; et sic definit Tullius . . . dicens, 'ius naturae est quod non opinio genuit sed quaedam innata vis inseruit.' Et quia etiam in rebus naturalibus dicuntur aliqui motus naturales, non quia sunt ex principio intrinseco, sed quia sunt a principio superiori movente . . . ideo ea quae sunt de iure divino, dicuntur esse de iure naturali, cum sint ex impressione et infusione superioris principii, scilicet Dei, et sic accipitur a Isidoro . . . qui dicit quod 'ius naturale est quod in lege et in Evangelio continetur.' Tertio dicitur ius naturale non solum a principio, sed a natura, quia de naturalibus est. Et quia natura contra rationem dividitur, a qua homo est homo, ideo strictissimo modo accipiendi ius naturale, illa quae ad homines tantum pertinent, etsi sint de dictamine rationis naturalis, non dicuntar esse de iure naturali; sed illa tantum quae naturalis ratio dictat de his quae sunt homini aliisque communia; et sic datur dicta definitio, scilicet, 'ius naturale est quod natura omnia animalia docuit.'"

54. In the *Summa theologiae*, Thomas refers (at least by implication) to Ulpian's definition in 1-2, 94,2; 95,4, ad 1.

55. Here the pertinent text is *In V Ethicorum*, lec. 12, no. 1019.

56. *Summa theologiae*, 1-2, 90, 1; 90, 1, ad 1 and ad 2; 91, 2.

57. Ibid., 1-2, 90, l, ad 1; 91, 2 , ad 3.

58. For further discussion of St. Thomas's use of Ulpian, see my work referred to in note 49 and Michael Bertram Crowe, "St. Thomas and Ulpian's Natural Law," *St. Thomas Aquinas 1274-1974 Commemorative Studies* (Toronto: Pontifical Institute of Mediaeval Studies, 1974), pp. 26 1-282.

59. See, for example, *Summa Contra Gentes,* 3.114: "lex nihil aliud sit quam quaedam ratio et regula operandi"; ibid.: "lex nihil aliud sit quam ratio operis."

60. Ibid., 115: "Lex . . . est quaedam ratio divinae providentiae gubernantis."

61. Ibid., 113: "Creatura rationalis sic providentiae divinae subiacet quod non solum ea gubernatur, sed etiam rationem providentiae utcumque cogmoscere potest: unde sibi competit etiam aliis providentiam et gubernationem exhibere. . . . Per hoc autem quod aliquis facultatem providendi habet, potest etiam suos actus dirigere et gubernare. Panticipat igitur rationalis creatura divinam providentiam non solum secundum gubernari, sed etiam secundum gubernare. Gubernat enim se in suis actibus propriis, et etiam aliis."

62. Ibid., 111, 113, and 114.

63. Ibid., 114.

64. Ibid., 116.

65. Ibid., 120: "haec est principalis legis divinae intentio, ut homo Deo subdatur, et ei singularem reverentiam exhibeat non solum corde, sed etiam ore et opere corporali."

66. Ibid., 117.

67. Ibid., 128.

68. Ibid.: "Secundum legem divinam homo inducitur ut ordinem rationis servet in omnibus quae in eius usum venire possunt."

69. Ibid., 120.

70. Ibid., 128.

71. Ibid., 129.

72. Ibid.

73. Ibid., 122.

74. The texts referred to are *Summa theologiae,* 1-2, 93, 2; 91, 1; and 93, 1. I should note here that for some reason neither the Abbott nor the Flannery translations of the documents of Vatican Council II include this important note. Yet it is found in the official Latin text of *Dignitatis humanae.*

75. An excellent study of the teaching of Vatican Council II on natural law is John M. Finnis, "The Natural Law, Objective Morality, and Vatican Council II," in *Principles of Catholic Moral Life,* ed. William E. May (Chicago: Franciscan Herald Press, 1981), pp. 113-150.

76. The Church teaches that human beings are able, by the exercise of their own intelligence, to come to the knowledge of some truths about God and human existence. It thus teaches that men can come to know the truth that God exists by the use of reason unaided by revelation. Similarly, men can come to know the moral truths set forth in the Decalogue by the use of their reason. We have seen that this was indeed the teaching of St. Thomas in our review of his thought on natural law. Yet St. Thomas himself, as we also saw in our review of his thought, taught in common with all Catholic theologians that God had gra-

A) GOAL SEARCH

1) Name your dream. Write it down. If I didn't have to do it perfectly,
If it didn't matter to me what other people
thought about it,
if it wasn't about the money,
if I was allowed to change my mind

I would love to do or be a _____

2) What would it look like in my life if I reached my goal - (give as much detail as you can dream of)

_____

3) What action can I take, this year, to move closer to that goal?

_____

4) What action can I take this month? This week? This day? Right now?

_____

_____

ciously revealed these moral norms to us insofar as they are so necessary for our salvation and insofar as knowledge of them is made difficult by reason of sin (cf. *Summa theologiae*, 1, 1, 1; 1-2, 98, 5). Vatican Council I (1870-72) clearly taught that God chooses to reveal himself and his moral law to us partially so that "even in the present condition of the human race, those religious truths which are by their nature accessible to human reason can readily be known by all men with solid certitude and no trace of error" (Vatican Council I, DS 3005/1786; cf. Vatican Council II, *Gaudium et spes*, no. 17).

77. Frequently, this understanding of natural law is attributed only to Germain Grisez and John Finnis. While they have surely been its principal exponents, the contributions of Joseph Boyle to the development of this understanding must, in justice, be taken into account. He has collaborated with Grisez in several works, including Grisez's most comprehensive study on moral principles, and he has co-authored major books and articles with Grisez and Finnis. Here I will list first major sources authored individually by Grisez, Finnis, and Boyle, and then works in which they have jointly collaborated. I will include only material relevant to the issue of natural law and not all the writings of these authors.

(1) Works by Grisez alone: *Contraception and the Natural Law* (Milwaukee: Bruce Publishing Co., 1964); *Abortion: The Myths, the Realities, and the Arguments* (New York: Corpus, 1970); *The Way of the Lord Jesus*, Vol. 1, *Christian Moral Principles* (Chicago: Franciscan Herald Press, 1983) [although Grisez is the exclusive author of this work, he notes in the preface that Joseph Boyle devoted over a half a year of full-time work in helping him with this centrally important work, and that he could even be regarded as a co-author; Finnis also provided help in preparing it]; "The First Principle of Practical Reasoning: A Commentary on the *Summa theologiae*, I-II, Q. 94, A. 2," *Natural Law Forum* 10 (1965), 168-196; "Toward a Consistent Natural Law Ethics of Killing," *American Journal of Jurisprudence* 15 (1970), 64-96; "Against Consequentialism," *American Journal of Jurisprudence* 23 (1978), 21-72; "Suicide and Euthanasia," in *Death, Dying, and Euthanasia*, ed. Dennis Horan and David Mall (Frederick, MD: University Publications of America, 1980), pp. 742-817; "Moral Absolutes: A Critique of the View of Josef Fuchs, S.J.," *Anthropos* (now *Anthropotes*): *Rivista di Studi sulla Persona e la Famiglia* 1 (1985), 155-201.

In collaboration with Russell Shaw, Grisez also wrote a work of relevance to his natural law theory, *Beyond the New Morality* (Notre Dame, IN: University of Notre Dame Press, 1st ed., 1974; 2nd ed., 1980; 3rd ed., 1988).

(2) Works by John Finnis alone: *Natural Law and Natural Rights* (Oxford and New York: Oxford University Press, 1980); *Fundamentals of Ethics* (Washington, DC: Georgetown University Press, 1985); *Moral Absolutes: Tradition, Revision, and the Truth* (Washington, DC: The Catholic University of America Press, 1991); "Natural Law and Unnatural Acts," *Heythrop Journal* 11 (1970), 366-372;

"The Rights and Wrongs of Abortion: A Reply to Judith Thomson," *Philosophy and Public Affairs* 2 (1972), 119-147; "... Objectivis criteriis ex personae eiusdemque actuum desumptis...," in *Ética y Teología ante la crisis contemporánea: Actas del I Simposio Internacional de Teología: Facultad de Teología de la Universidad de Navarra* (Pamplona: EUNSA, 1980), pp. 633-642; "The Natural Law, Objective Morality, and Vatican Council II," in *Principles of Catholic Moral Life*, ed. William E. May (Chicago: Franciscan Herald Press, 1981), pp. 113-150; "The Act of the Person," *Persona, Verità e Morale* (Rome: Città Nuova Editrice, 1987), pp. 159-176; "Natural Inclinations and Natural Rights: Deriving 'Ought' from 'Is' According to Aquinas," in *Lex et Libertas: Freedom and Natural Law According to St. Thomas* (Studi Tomistici, 30), ad. L.J. Elders and K. Hedwig (Vatican City: Libreria Editrice Vaticana, 1987), pp. 43-55; "The Consistent Ethic of Life: A Philosophical Analysis," in Joseph Cardinal Bernardin et al., *Consistent Ethic of Life* (Shawnee Mission, KS: Sheed and Ward, Inc., 1988), pp. 140-181; "Absolute Moral Norms: Their Ground, Force, and Permanence," *Anthropotes: Rivista di Studi sulla Persona e la Famiglia* 4 (1988), 287-303.

(3) Works by Joseph Boyle alone: "Aquinas and Prescriptive Ethics," in *Proceedings of the American Catholic Philosophical Association* 49 (1975), 82-95; "'Practer Intentionem' in Aquinas," *Thomist* 42 (1978), 649-665; "Toward Understanding the Principle of Double Effect," *Ethics* 90 (1980), 527-538; "Moral Reasoning and Moral Judgment," in *Proceedings of the American Catholic Philosophical Association* 58 (1984), 37-49; "Aquinas, Kant, and Donagan on Moral Principles," *The New Scholasticism* 58 (1984), 391-408.

(4) Works jointly authored by Grisez and Boyle: *Life and Death with Liberty and Justice: A Contribution to the Euthanasia Debate* (Notre Dame, IN: University of Notre Dame Press, 1978).

(5) Works jointly authored by Grisez, Finnis, and Boyle: *Nuclear Deterrence, Morality, and Reality* (Oxford and New York: Oxford University Press, 1987); "Practical Principles, Moral Truth, and Ultimate Ends," *American Journal of Jurisprudence* 32 (1987), 99-151.

In a later note, I will refer to more recent writings of these authors in which they respond to some of the criticism that has been raised about their work.

78. On reason as practical, see in particular Grisez, "The First Principle of Practical Reason: A Commentary on *Summa Theologiae*, I-II, Q. 94, A. 2," esp. 170-175; Finnis, *Natural Law and Natural Rights*, pp. 33-36; Finnis, *Fundamentals of Ethics*, pp. 1-25; Grisez, Boyle, and Finnis, "Practical Principles, Moral Truth, and Ultimate Ends," esp. 115-117.

79. See works cited in note 78. Also see Grisez, *Christian Moral Principles*, pp. 178-180.

80. *Christian Moral Principles*, p. 179.

81. Ibid., p. 180.

82. See above, p. 48.

83. In *Contraception and the Natural Law,* pp. 63-64, Grisez listed life itself, mating and raising children, experiences worthwhile in themselves, play, knowledge of the truth, fellowship with others, harmony with unknown higher powers, and the use of intelligence in guiding actions (practical reasonableness). In *Abortion: The Myths, the Realities, and the Arguments,* pp. 312-313, he listed life itself, activities engaged in for their own sake, experiences sought for their own sake, knowledge pursued for its own sake, interior integrity, genuineness, justice and friendship, and worship and holiness. In *Natural Law and Natural Rights,* pp. 83-91, Finnis listed life, knowledge, play, aesthetic experience, sociability or friendship, practical reasonableness, and religion. The more recent articulation of the basic human goods is provided in Grisez's *Christian Moral Principles,* pp. 121-124, and the essay jointly authored by Grisez, Finnis, and Boyle, "Practical Principles, Moral Truth, and Ultimate Ends," 107-108. The goods identified as basic in these last two works are substantially the same as those listed in previous writings, but our authors have attempted to bring their terminology into harmony and to make as clear as possible the sorts of goods that are fundamental. They have also sought to describe the "reflexive" goods — i.e., those involving harmony — without importing moral value into them. In some of their earlier writings, such moral value was imported, e.g., in describing the good of harmony within the person as "practical reasonableness."

84. Internal citations in the text are from "Practical Principles, Moral Truth, and Ultimate Ends," 108; a very similar formulation of the four reflexive goods having harmony as their theme is given in *Christian Moral Principles,* p. 123.

85. In their most recent joint article, "Practical Principles, Moral Truth, and Ultimate Ends," Grisez, Finnis, and Boyle draw explicit attention to the fact that the reflexive goods, as such, are not moral goods, i.e., that it is a mistake to import moral value into them, insofar as one can realize them in immoral ways. They observe, as I pointed out in note 83, that in some of their previous writings they had not, at times, avoided importing moral value into them. Thus, they had called the harmony between judgments and choices "practical reasonableness"; the harmony between choices and performances they called "authenticity"; and the harmony between humankind and God they referred to as "holiness." Cf. "Practical Principles, Moral Truth, and Ultimate Ends," 139-140.

86. On this, see ibid., 108.

87. Ibid., 107; *Christian Moral Principles,* p. 124.

88. Grisez, *Living a Christian Life,* Vol. 2 of *The Way of the Lord Jesus* (Quincy, IL: Franciscan Press, 1993), p. 568.

89. Ibid., footnote 43.

90. E.g., Grisez, *Contraception and the Natural Law,* p. 54, and p. 74 (notes 19 and 20), refers to the work of psychologist Ernest R. Hilgard and the anthropologists

Robert H. Lowie and Alexander MacBeath regarding tendencies or inclinations universally found in human beings. Likewise, Finnis, in *Natural Law and Natural Rights*, pp. 83, 97-98, refers to the work of a number of anthropologists and psychologists on the same subject.

91. For this, see Grisez (with Shaw), *Beyond the New Morality* (3rd ed., 1988), pp. 77-79; Finnis, *Natural Law and Natural Rights*, pp. 38-39.

92. "Practical Principles, Moral Truth, and Ultimate Ends," 110.

93. Ibid.

94. Thus, St. Thomas says that *"nullus enim intendens ad malum operatur"* ("no one intentionally does evil"), *Summa theologiae*, 1-2, 72, 1. Sin is not irrational, although it is unreasonable.

95. "Practical Principles, Moral Truth, and Ultimate Ends," 121. Immoral acts, however, do not, as Grisez, Finnis, and Boyle explicitly note at this point, respond as fully to the first practical principle as do morally good acts.

96. See above, p. 76, and accompanying notes.

97. For St. Thomas, see *Summa theologiae*, 1-2, 100, 3, 1 and ad 1. Note, however, that here Aquinas explicitly says that the love commands are *"per se nota rationi humanae, vel per naturam vel per fidem"* ("*per se* known to human reason, either through nature *or through faith"*). On this, see *Christian Moral Principles*, p. 183; *Nuclear Deterrence, Morality, and Reality*, p. 284.

98. *Christian Moral Principles*, p. 184, citing *Gaudium et spes*, no. 35.

99. *Nuclear Deterrence, Morality, and Reality*, p. 284.

100. *Christian Moral Principles*, p. 184.

101. "Practical Principles, Moral Truth, and Ultimate Ends," 128.

102. Ibid., 121.

103. In his earlier writings, Grisez did not articulate this basic moral principle clearly. Rather, he said that all the principles of practical reasoning taken together constitute the norm; e.g., in *Contraception and the Natural Law*, p. 76. In *Abortion*, p. 315, he spoke of choosing with an "attitude of openness to goods not chosen," and of respecting "equally all of the basic goods." Similarly, Finnis, in *Natural Law and Natural Rights*, pp. 23, 101, spoke of bringing all the principles of practical reasoning to bear upon definite ranges of action or particular actions. But in later writings, Grisez, Finnis, and Boyle have clearly articulated this moral norm. The formulation given in the text is found in *Christian Moral Principles*, p. 184; it is also found in *Nuclear Deterrence, Morality, and Reality*, p. 283. On this whole point, see what Grisez, Finnis, and Boyle have to say in "Practical Principles, Moral Truth, and Ultimate Ends," 128.

104. On this, see, for instance, Grisez and Boyle, *Life and Death with Liberty and Justice*, pp. 365-366.

105. "Practical Principles, Moral Truth, and Ultimate Ends," 132.

106. "Nuclear Deterrence, Morality, and Reality," p. 283.

107. "Practical Principles, Moral Truth, and Ultimate Ends," 132.

108. *Christian Moral Principles*, p. 186.

109. "Practical Principles, Moral Truth, and Ultimate Ends," 127-132.

110. St. Thomas, *Summa theologiae*, 1-2, 58, 5; cf. 58, 3, ad 2.

111. Grisez, Finnis, and Boyle, "Practical Principles, Moral Truth, and Ultimate Ends," p. 137.

112. In *Natural Law and Natural Rights*, pp. 100-127, Finnis called these the "requirements of practical reasonableness." "Modes of responsibility" is now the proper way to refer to these. See *Christian Moral Principles*, pp. 205-228.

113. *Christian Moral Principles*, p. 189.

114. On this, see *Christian Moral Principles*, pp. 215-221.

115. See ibid., p. 191.

116. Ibid., p. 225: "These are the eight modes of responsibility. (1) One should not be deterred by felt inertia from acting for intelligible goods. (2) One should not be pressed by enthusiasm or impatience to act individualistically for intelligible goods. (3) One should not choose to satisfy an emotional desire except as part of one's pursuit and/or attainment of an intelligible good other than the satisfaction of the desire itself. (4) One should not choose to act out of an emotional aversion except as part of one's avoidance of some intelligible evil other than the inner tension experienced in enduring that aversion. (5) One should not, in response to different feelings toward different persons, willingly proceed with a preference for anyone unless the preference is required by intelligible goods themselves [this is Grisez's way of formulating the principle of fairness or the Golden Rule]. (6) One should not choose on the basis of emotions which bear upon empirical aspects of intelligible goods (or bads) in a way which interferes with a more perfect sharing in the good or avoidance of the bad. (7) One should not be moved by hostility to freely accept or choose the destruction, damaging, or impeding of any intelligible human good. (8) One should not be moved by a stronger desire for one instance of an intelligible good to act for it by choosing to destroy, damage, or impede some other instance of an intelligible good."

117. *Christian Moral Principles*, p. 226.

118. Grisez, *Christian Moral Principles*, p. 192.

119. Ibid., p. 225.

120. See above, pp. 77-79, and accompanying notes.

121. *Christian Moral Principles*, pp. 251-274.

122. Ibid., pp. 256-257.

123. Ibid., pp. 257-258.

124. "Practical Principles, Moral Truth, and Ultimate Ends," 137; emphasis added.

125. Ibid., 137, 138-139.

126. Ibid., 107.

127. Ibid., 137.

128. Ibid., 141.

129. Ibid., 142.

130. Ibid.

131. Ibid., 144.

132. Ibid., 143-145.

133. Ibid., 145.

134. Ibid., 146.

135. Grisez, "Natural Law, God, Religion, and Human Fulfillment," *American Journal of Jurisprudence* 46 (2001), 3-35.

136. Ibid., 15-17.

137. Ibid., 16.

138. Ibid., 17.

139. *Natural Law and Natural Rights*, p. 23.

140. Todd A. Salzman, *What Are They Saying About Roman Catholic Ethical Method?* (Paramus, NJ: Paulist Press, 2002). See also Salzman's series of articles: "The Basic Goods Theory and Revisionism: A Methodological Comparison on the Use of Reason and Experience as Sources of Moral Knowledge," *Heythrop Journal* 42 (2001), 423-450; "The Basic Goods Theory and Revisionism: A Methodological Comparison on the Use of Scripture as a Source of Moral Knowledge," *Louvain Studies* 26 (2001), 117-146; and "The Basic Goods Theory and Revisionism: A Methodological Comparison on the Use of Tradition as Source of Moral Knowledge," *Studia Moralia* 40 (2002), 171-209.

141. On this, see the following: Ralph McInerny, "The Principles of Natural Law," *American Journal of Jurisprudence* 25 (1980), 1-15 (substantially reprinted as the third chapter of his *Ethica Thomistica* [Washington, DC: The Catholic University of America Press, 1982]); Henry Veatch, "Review of *Natural Law and Natural Rights* by John Finnis," *American Journal of Jurisprudence* 26 (1981), 247-259; Vernon Bourke, "Review of *Natural Law and Natural Rights* by John Finnis," *American Journal of Jurisprudence* 26 (1981), 247-259; Russell Hittinger, *A Critique of the New Natural Law Theory* (Notre Dame, IN: University of Notre Dame Press, 1987); Hittinger, "The Recovery of Natural Law and the 'Common Morality,'" *This World*, No. 18 (Summer, 1987), 62-74.

142. On this, see the following: Grisez, "A Critique of Russell Hittinger's Book, *A Critique of the New Natural Law Theory*," *New Scholasticism* 62 (1988), 62-74; Grisez and Finnis, "The Basic Principles of Natural Law: A Reply to Ralph McInerny," *American Journal of Jurisprudence* 26 (1981), 21-31; Finnis, "Natural Law and the Is-Ought Question: An Invitation to Professor Veatch," *Catholic Lawyer* 26 (1980-81), 265-277; Finnis, "Observations de M.J.M. Finnis," *Archives de Philosophie du Droit* (1981), 425-427; Finnis, "Practical Reasoning, Human Goods, and the End of Man," *Proceedings of the American Catholic Philo-*

sophical Association 58 (1984), 23-36, also published in *New Blackfriars* 66 (1985), 438-449.

It is pertinent to observe here that McInerny took note of the "Reply to Ralph McInerny," referred to above, in his book *Ethica Thomistica: The Moral Philosophy of Thomas Aquinas*. As already noted (note 141, above), Chapter 3 of that work includes substantively the material from his article, "The Principles of Natural Law." In a "Bibliographic Note" appended to his book, McInerny refers to the Grisez-Finnis "Reply." He then says: "Alas, this book was already in proof before I became aware of their response and thus I am unable to give it the attention it deserves here. The two authors now seem reluctant to be assessed in terms of fidelity to St. Thomas. That of course was the angle from which I read them" (p. 128). McInerny here clearly leaves his readers with the impression that Grisez and Finnis concede that McInerny's interpretation of St. Thomas's understanding of natural law is correct and that they simply do not wish to be judged on Thomistic grounds. This, unfortunately, is a very erroneous impression, for in the "Reply" Finnis and Grisez take great pains to show that on a key matter, namely, the underivability of the first principles of practical reasoning, they, and *not* McInerny, are being faithful to St. Thomas. In short, McInerny simply misleads his readers. In addition, McInerny has nowhere sought to answer the arguments given by Grisez and Finnis — he has not, in other words, given their reply "the attention it deserves." In my opinion, McInerny, in order to be fair, ought to have omitted the final two sentences of his observations as cited above insofar as they seriously misrepresent the nature of the "Reply" given to his article by Grisez and Finnis. In the 1987 revised edition of his book, McInerny deleted the offensive note.

143. Robert George, "Recent Criticism of Natural Law Theory," *The University of Chicago Law Review* 55 (1988), 1371-1429; William Marshner, "A Tale of Two Beatitudes," *Faith & Reason* 16.2 (1990), 177-199; and Aurelio Ansaldo, *El Primer Principio del Obrar Moral y Las Normas Morales Específicas en el Pensamiento de G. Grisez y J. Finnis* (Rome: Pontificia Universita Lateranense, 1990).

144. Benedict Ashley, O.P., "What Is the End of the Human Person?" in *Moral Truth and Moral Tradition: Essays in Honor of Peter Geach and Elizabeth Anscombe*, ed. Luke Gormally (Dublin: Four Corners Press, 1994), pp. 68-96.

145. Ibid., p. 70.

146. Grisez, "Dualism and the New Morality," in *Atti del Congresso sul settimo centenario di San Tommaso d'Aquino*, Vol. 5, *L'agire morale* (Naples: Edizioni Domenicane, 1975), p. 325.

147. Grisez, Finnis, and Boyle, "Practical Principles, Moral Truth, and Ultimate Ends," 131-132.

148. Ibid., 135-136, 145-146.

149. Finnis, *Natural Law and Natural Rights*, pp. 83-84.

150. Grisez, "Natural Law, God, Religion, and Human Fulfillment," 8, n. 9.

151. On Rhonheimer's work, see the very comprehensive and helpful essay of William Murphy, "Martin Rhonheimer's Natural Law and Practical Reason," *Sapientia* 55 (2001), 517-548.

152. Martin Rhonheimer, *Natural Law and Practical Reason: A Thomist View of Moral Autonomy*, trans. Gerald Malsbary (New York: Fordham University Press, 2000), p. 44, n. 7.

153. Ibid., pp. 16-22.

154. Ibid., pp. 22-42.

155. Ibid., pp. 194-256, especially, pp. 234-256.

156. Ibid., pp. 74-78.

157. Ibid., pp. 147-148, no. 5.

158. Ibid., p. 62.

159. Ibid., p. 63.

160. Ibid., p. 59.

161. Ibid., p. 58.

162. Ibid., p.71.

163. Ibid., p.81.

164. Ibid., p. 85.

165. Ibid., p. 59.

166. Ibid., p.76.

167. Ibid., p. 279; cf. *De veritate*, 16, 1.

168. Ibid., p. 279.

169. Ibid., pp. 279-280.

170. Ibid., p. 280.

CHAPTER FOUR

Moral Absolutes

Introduction

In the previous chapter, we saw that the natural law is an ordered set of true propositions about what we are to do if we are to be the beings God wills us to be. The first set of natural law propositions includes the *principles of practical reasoning*. The first principle of practical reasoning is that *good is to be done and pursued, and its opposite, evil, is to be avoided.* The other *principles of practical reasoning* are specifications of this principle, i.e., principles identifying basic aspects of human flourishing as goods to be done and pursued — i.e., goods such as life itself (including bodily health and integrity and the handing on of human life), knowledge of the truth, appreciation of beauty, play, harmonious relationships within the self (the goods of integrity and practical reasonableness or peace of conscience), harmonious relationships with other human persons (the goods of friendship, justice, and peace), and harmonious relationships with God (the good of religion).

The second set of natural law propositions embraces the *first principles of morality or moral choice*. The first *principle of moral choice*, expressed religiously in the twofold command of love of God and of neighbor, can be articulated more philosophically and theologically as follows: "In pursuing the good and avoiding what is opposed to it, one ought to choose and otherwise will those and only those possibilities whose willing is compatible with integral human fulfillment," i.e., with a heart open to everything that is really good and to the persons in whom whatever is really good is meant to flourish. Just as the first principle of practical reasoning is specified by identifying the basic goods perfective of human persons, so too this first principle of moral choice is specified by identifying ways in which a choice would be incompatible with integral human fulfillment. The specifications of the first principle of moral choice, which can be called "modes of responsibility," exclude choices motivated by nonrational desires or in which one ignores, slights, neglects, damages, destroys, or impedes basic human goods or acts in ways that arbitrarily and unfairly limit the participation of any person in these goods.

The third set of natural law propositions is made up of more specific moral norms, namely, those that identify specific kinds of human action that ought either to be done (e.g., to keep one's promises, to honor one's parents) or not done (e.g., to break one's promises, deliberately to kill innocent people). St. Thomas, it will be recalled, taught that some of these specific norms — for instance, those that we find in the Decalogue — are absolute or exceptionless. Grisez and Finnis likewise, as we have seen, hold that some specific norms are absolute (e.g., that proscribing the deliberate killing of the innocent) whereas others are not.

This chapter will investigate in depth the question of moral absolutes. It is therefore most important to understand clearly what this expression means. The expression "moral absolutes" is used here to refer to moral norms identifying certain types of action, which are possible objects of human choice, as *always* morally bad, and specifying these types of action without employing in their description any morally evaluative terms.

Deliberately killing babies, having sex with someone other than one's spouse, contracepting, and making babies by artificial insemination are examples of types of action specified by norms of this kind. Such norms are called "absolute" because they unconditionally and definitively exclude specifiable kinds of human action as morally justifiable objects of choice. They are said to be true always and for always, under every circumstance (*semper et pro* [or *ad*] *semper*). The types of actions specified by such norms are called "intrinsically evil acts."[1] Although exceptions to these norms are logically possible (one can, of course, deliberately kill babies or have sex with persons other than one's spouse), they are morally excluded. Thus, these norms are also called "exceptionless." The magisterium of the Church proposes some norms as absolutes, including norms unconditionally proscribing the deliberate killing of the innocent, adultery, remarriage after divorce, fornication, contraception, the generating of human life in the laboratory, etc., and the magisterium proposes these norms as true. Today, however, many people, including some very prominent and influential Catholic moral theologians, deny that there are absolute norms of this kind.

In this chapter, I will (1) summarize the major reasons why some contemporary Catholic theologians (henceforth called "revisionists" or "revisionist theologians") deny that there are moral absolutes as understood here, (2) criticize the revisionist position, and (3) show why human dignity and basic moral principles require moral absolutes. Two appendices present the teaching of St. Thomas and John Paul II.

❖ ❖ ❖

1. The Revisionist Rejection of Moral Absolutes

The roots of the rejection of moral absolutes can be found in the reasoning advanced by the authors of the celebrated "Majority Report" of the Papal Commission for the Study of Population, the Family, and Natality. This commission had been established by Pope John XXIII and, after his death, had been increased in size by Pope Paul VI. Its original purpose was to advise the Holy See about what to say in international organizations about the population problem and proposed solutions to it. But the expanded body undertook to study the whole issue of contraception. The documents of this commission — which were intended, in accord with the mandate given to the commission, solely for the use of the Holy Father, who had the responsibility to assess their worth — were leaked to the public in 1967, plainly with the intent of putting pressure on Pope Paul VI to change the teaching of the Church on contraception.

In the papers comprising what came to be called the "Majority Report" of the commission, the authors presented arguments to justify the practice of contraception by married couples. Nevertheless, they insisted, in company with all Catholic moral theologians of the time, that there are moral absolutes, for they vehemently denied the charge, made by theologians on the commission who held that the norm against contraception was unchangeable, that the reasoning they employed to justify contraception by married couples could also be used to justify such acts as anal and oral sex.[2] The authors of the "Majority Report" expressed outrage over this charge, and by doing so showed that they did indeed accept as true some moral absolutes. Despite their protests, however, it soon became clear that the reasoning they advanced to support their view that married persons could, under given conditions, rightly practice contraception could also be used to justify exceptions to other norms that had been regarded up to that time as absolute by Catholic moral theologians. This point has been conceded by revisionist theologians such as Charles E. Curran.[3]

But what was the reasoning used by the authors of the "Majority Report" to justify contraception? Two passages found in the documents comprising the "Majority Report" are, in my judgment, absolutely crucial. I shall first cite these passages and then offer brief comments on them. The first reads as follows:

> To take his or another's life is a sin not because life is under the exclusive dominion of God, but because it is contrary to right reason *unless there is question of a good of a higher order*. It is licit to sacrifice a life for the good of the community. It is licit to take a life in capital punishment for the sake of the community.[4]

According to the principle set forth in this passage, it is morally permissible to destroy human life (or other human goods), if doing so is necessary for the sake of a greater good. I call this the "Caiaphas" principle. Revisionist theologians today refer to it as the "preference principle" or the "principle of proportionate good," and we shall examine the nature and significance of this principle more fully below.

A second crucially important passage from the documents of the "Majority Report" occurs in a section where the authors claim that married couples may rightly contracept individual marital acts provided that these contracepted marital acts are ordered to the expression of marital love, a love that culminates in fertility responsibly accepted. This passage states:

> When man intervenes in the procreative purpose of individual acts by contracepting, he does this with the intention of regulating and not excluding fertility. Then he unites the material finality toward fecundity which exists in intercourse with the formal finality of the person and renders the entire process human. . . . Conjugal acts which by intention are infertile,[5] or which are rendered infertile [by the use of artificial contraceptives], are ordered to the expression of the union of love; that love, moreover, reaches its culmination in fertility responsibly accepted. For that reason other acts of union are in a sense incomplete and receive their full moral quality with ordination toward the fertile act. . . . Infertile conjugal acts constitute a totality with fertile acts and have a single moral specification [namely, the fostering of love responsibly toward generous fecundity].[6]

This passage is important because it presents an understanding of the "totality" of human acts that is, as we shall see, central to the denial of moral absolutes. The argument holds that there is a "material privation" (or what will later be called an "ontic," "premoral," or "nonmoral" evil) in contraceptive activity insofar as it deprives a conjugal act of its procreative potential. However, the contraceptive intervention is only a partial aspect of a whole series of contracepted marital acts, and this entire ensemble "receives its moral specification from the other finality, which is good in itself [namely, the marital union] and from the fertility of the whole conjugal life."[7] According to this line of reasoning, married couples that rightly use contraception are not choosing to exclude children selfishly from their marriage, or expressing what the authors elsewhere call a "contraceptive mentality."[8] Rather, *what* they are doing — the moral "object" of their act — is "the fostering of love responsibly toward a generous fecundity." And this is obviously something good, not bad.

This line of argumentation is very significant for the question of moral absolutes because it foreshadows the revisionist theologians' understanding of human action as a whole that receives its moral specification from the end for whose sake it is done. Revisionists, as will be seen, claim that the specific moral absolutes defended in the Catholic tradition and affirmed by the magisterium isolate partial aspects of human acts and, on the basis of such isolated aspects, render decisive moral judgments about them. Their claim is that reason, objectivity, and truth require that an action be evaluated as right or wrong only as a *totality* that includes all the circumstances and motivations, considered in relation to *all* the "premoral" (but morally relevant) goods and bads involved in that totality, for the purpose of identifying the behavior that will further human self-realization and self-development[9] or at least will not contradict or negate its own good purpose.[10]

I have presented and commented briefly on these critically important passages from the documents of the "Majority Report" because, as noted already, they are the roots from which the denial of moral absolutes by revisionist theologians developed.

A. Clarifying the Terminology

Before proceeding to a presentation of the principal arguments that revisionist theologians developed from these roots, a brief discussion of the terminology employed by these theologians will be helpful.

First of all, revisionist theologians — among them Franz Böckle, Charles E. Curran, Josef Fuchs, Bernard Häring, Louis Janssens, Richard McCormick, Timothy E. O'Connell, Richard Gula, Franz Scholz, and Bruno Schüller — while denying the existence of moral absolutes in the sense previously described, acknowledge that there are other kinds of moral absolutes. They admit, first of all, that there are absolutes in the sense of "transcendent principles" that direct us to those elements of our existence whereby we transcend or surpass the rest of material creation. Thus, they acknowledge the absoluteness of such principles as "One must always act in conformity with love of God and neighbor" and "One must always act in accordance with right reason."[11] Similarly, they regard as absolute the norms they call "formal." These norms articulate what our inner dispositions and attitudes ought to be. It is thus always true that we should act justly, bravely, chastely, and so on.[12] Such formal norms express the qualities that ought to characterize the morally good person. They are *not* concerned with specific human acts and choices but rather with the moral *being* of the agent.[13]

In a way they are, as Josef Fuchs has said, "exhortations rather than norms in the strict sense,"[14] and, as Louis Janssens has noted, they "constitute the absolute element in morals."[15] Finally, these theologians admit that norms using morally evaluative language to refer to actions that human persons ought never freely choose to do are absolute. Thus, we ought never to *murder,* because to murder is by definition to kill a person *unjustly.* Likewise, we ought never to have sex with the *wrong* person, because such sex is also wrong by definition. Yet norms like this are tautological and do not help us know which specific kinds of killing are unjust or what specific kind of sex is sex with the wrong person, etc. As Fuchs observes, these "absolute" norms are "parenetic," not instructive, and simply serve to remind us of what we already know and exhort us to avoid morally wrong actions and to engage in morally right ones.[16]

While acknowledging "absolutes" of the foregoing kind, revisionist theologians deny that there are moral absolutes in the sense of norms universally proscribing specifiable sorts of human action described in morally neutral language. They call such norms "material" or "behavioral/material" norms. According to them, such norms identify "physical acts" or "material acts" or "behavior," including, in some cases, the "direct" or immediate effects of such acts, described independently of *any* of the acting subject's purposes.[17] As one revisionist theologian, Richard Gula, puts it, such "material norms," "when stated negatively, point out the kind of conduct which ought to be avoided *as far as possible*," but all such norms "ought to be interpreted as containing the implied qualifiers, 'if there were no further intervening factors,' or 'unless there is a proportionate reason,' or 'all things being equal.'"[18] Later I wish to examine more closely this way of describing the "absolute" or "exceptionless" norms that the Catholic tradition has affirmed.

B. Arguments to Support the Revisionists' Denial of Moral Absolutes

To support their claim that there are no moral absolutes in the sense of specific moral norms proscribing actions described in morally neutral language, revisionist theologians advance several lines of reasoning. Among the more important are the following: (I) the requirements of the "preference principle" or "principle of proportionate good"; (II) the nature of a human act as a totality; and (III) the historicity of human existence.

I. The 'Preference' Principle or Principle of 'Proportionate Good'

A principal line of reasoning advanced by revisionist theologians to support their denial of the truth of moral absolutes is that such a denial is entailed by the requirements of the basic principle of morality, the "preference principle" or the "principle of proportionate good."

According to revisionist theologians, "material" or "behavioral" norms, although not absolute, are intended to guide our choices. Their purpose is to help us distinguish right from wrong and to understand how human actions relate to human goods and values. Consequently, in articulating material norms, such as those proscribing the killing of the innocent, sex with persons other than one's spouse, etc., it is essential to take into account the way that human goods and values will be affected by possible courses of actions. By human goods and values revisionist theologians have in mind the kind of goods basic to human persons and considered in the previous chapter, goods such as life itself, knowledge of the truth, appreciation of beauty, and the like.[19] Revisionist theologians maintain that these human goods and values (and their deprivations, or evils or disvalues) are not, of themselves, moral in nature. Rather, they are described by these theologians as being "premoral," "nonmoral," or "ontic."[20] The crucial question is how we should determine, in developing material norms and in judging which acts are legitimate exceptions to them, which acts are morally right and which acts are morally wrong, i.e., which acts promote and enhance these nonmoral goods and values and which do not. There is need, in other words, for a basic moral norm or criterion to help us distinguish morally acceptable alternatives from unacceptable ones.

Recall now the principle to which the authors of the "Majority Report" appealed, namely, that it is against right reason to take the life of an innocent person (a nonmoral good) or to destroy other goods, "unless there is question of a good of a higher order."[21] As formulated by leading revisionist theologians, the principle has come to be known as the "preference principle" or the "principle of proportionate good" or "proportionate reason." Bruno Schüller puts it this way: "Any ethical norm whatsoever regarding our dealings and omissions in relation to other men . . . can be only a particular application of that more universal norm, 'The greater good is to be preferred.'"[22]

According to this principle, it is morally right to intend a nonmoral evil, such as the death of an innocent person, if this evil is required by a "proportionately related greater good." Thus, as Richard A. McCormick says, "Where a higher good is at stake and the only means to protect it is to choose to do a nonmoral evil, then the will remains properly disposed to the values constitutive of human good. . . . This is to say that the intentionality is good even when the person, reluctantly and regretfully to be sure, intends the nonmoral evil if a truly proportionate reason [i.e., good] for such a choice is present."[23]

This principle does not, according to revisionist theologians, mean that a good end can justify morally evil means. But they do hold that the intending and doing of any nonmoral evil — i.e., the deprivation of any nonmoral good — can be justified if such intending and doing of evil is ordered to a "proportionately greater" nonmoral good.[24]

From this it follows that every material norm is subject to an exception clause: It is wrong to kill an innocent person, to lie, to have sex with someone other than one's spouse, and so forth, *except* when doing so is required in order to attain a proportionately greater good. Thus some acts of direct abortion, mercy killing, contraception, remarriage after divorce, etc., can be morally right acts *if* such acts are done for the sake of a proportionately greater good.[25]

Note that revisionist theologians hold that it is morally right deliberately to intend a "nonmoral" evil for the sake of a proportionately greater "nonmoral" good.[26] Here it is interesting to recall that one of these theologians, Richard A. McCormick, acknowledged in an essay written in 1973 that there is a significant moral difference between a will that intends evil and a will that merely permits evil. At that time, McCormick wrote: "The will relates differently to what it intends and what it permits . . . the intending will (hence the person) is more closely associated with the evil than is a permitting will. This bespeaks (in some admittedly obscure way) a greater willingness that it [the evil] occur."[27]

Thus, at that time, McCormick held that a "greater" proportionate good is required if one is to intend the nonmoral evil than if one only "permits" or "indirectly intends" the nonmoral evil associated with one's action.

Bruno Schüller, on reading this essay of McCormick, insisted that "the person who is prepared to realize the good even by intending evil is more willing that the evil exist, but only because he is more willing that the good exist."[28] He went on to say that "if someone is ready to bring the good into existence only by permitting the evil, it has been suggested [by McCormick] that he is less willing that the evil exist. Yet it must also be said that he is less willing that the good exist."[29] From this Schüller concluded: "Therefore, I am strongly inclined to believe that in point of fact *'intend as a means' and 'permit,' when referring to a non-moral evil, denote exactly the same mental attitude.*"[30] In other words, according to Schüller there is, contrary to McCormick's belief in 1973, *no* significant moral difference between an intending and a permitting will.

When apprised of Schüller's view, McCormick changed his mind and abandoned his position that an intending will more closely relates the person to evil than does a permitting will. Declaring that Schüller's objection to his original position was "fatal,"[31] McCormick now agrees with Schüller. Their common point is this: Since there is no moral difference between deliberately intending a "nonmoral" evil and merely permitting it, the person who intends and does evil for the sake of a proportionately greater good has a greater love for the good than does a person who refuses to intend and do evil and yet at times does permit it. And in their judgment, this is an admirable trait of moral character.

The foregoing account of the "preference principle" or "principle of proportionate good" summarizes one of the major reasons why revisionist theologians deny that there are any moral absolutes. According to these theologians, the refusal to intend and do the ("nonmoral") evil these absolutes proscribe would be a moral weakness when intending and doing such evil is demanded by the "preference principle." It is, after all, the basic norm of morality, holding primacy in moral judgment.[32]

II. The Nature of a Human Act as a Totality

Another line of reasoning, closely related to the former, is that based on the nature of a human act as a whole or totality. This line of reasoning, like the previous one, was also central to the "Majority Report" of the Papal Commission. Readers will recall that in the report the majority had argued that a moral judgment about contraception could only be made in terms of the purposes of contracepted marital acts and the whole of the married life. The "Majority Report" claimed that if a couple deliberately prevents conception in individual marital acts in order to express their marital union and orders these contracepted marital acts toward generous fecundity, then one could properly say that *what* the couple was doing — the "object" of their moral choice — was "fostering love responsibly toward generous fecundity," even, though this required the "material privation" (= nonmoral evil) of individual acts of marital union of their openness to human life.[33]

One major supporter of this "Majority Report," it should be noted, was Josef Fuchs. In subsequent writings, Fuchs insisted that it is not possible to make a moral judgment about the intending and doing of "premoral" evil as such, because, he claimed, "an action cannot be judged morally in its materiality (killing, wounding, going to the moon) without reference to the intention of the agent; without this, we are not dealing with a human action, and only of a human action may one say in a true sense whether it is morally good or bad."[34]

It is important to recall here that Fuchs and other revisionists identify the moral absolutes they deny with "material" or "concrete behavioral" norms specifying "physical acts" or "material acts," including, in some cases, their "direct" effects, described independently of *any* purpose of the agent.[35] Revisionists claim that the tradition affirming such absolutes arbitrarily abstracted *some* elements of an action from its total, concrete reality and rendered a moral judgment on this abstraction and not on the total human act. In their view, such judgments simply ignored the moral reality of the act as a whole.

According to revisionists, therefore, if one properly evaluates the whole act and not merely partial aspects of it, one will arrive at the correct moral judgment. Thus, for example, one will see that contraceptive intercourse, if done by married persons for a truly proportionate good, is only a partial aspect of a whole human act that can rightly be described as "fostering love responsibly toward a generous fecundity." Likewise, if a married couple resorts to contraceptive sterilization (tubal ligation or vasectomy) because any further pregnancy might endanger the mother's life, the choice to sterilize, when seen within the totality of what the couple is doing, can be truthfully described as a "marriage-stabilizing" act.[36] Accordingly, in the view of revisionists, to absolutize norms proscribing contraception and contraceptive sterilization is to be blind to the wholeness of the concrete human act. And the same is true, they claim, of other alleged moral absolutes, such as those proscribing the deliberate killing of the innocent, having sex with someone who is not one's spouse, etc. Such material norms, while useful and valid for the most part, ought to be set aside when the action as a concrete whole demands that this be done if the greater good is to be served.

III. The Historicity of Human Existence

According to revisionist theologians, material norms are useful generalizations alerting us, as Gula says, to the "kind of conduct that ought to be avoided as far as possible."[37] We come to the knowledge of these norms by the collaborative exercise of human intelligence by persons living together in communities and reflecting on shared human experiences.[38] Since material norms are discovered in this way, it follows that they are affected by human historicity and the open-ended, ongoing character of human experience. Revisionists recognize that there is a "transcendent," "transhistorical," and "transcultural" dimension of human persons, insofar as human persons are called to "a steadily advancing humanization."[39] Nonetheless, "concrete" human nature, by reason of its historicity, is subject to far-reaching changes. It thus follows that no specific material norm, articulated under specific historical conditions, can be true and applicable universally and unchangeably.

Nor does it follow from this that these norms are merely subjective and relative. Their objective truth corresponds to the actions they proscribe or prescribe insofar as these are related to the "whole concrete reality of man" and of the particular, historical society in which people live.[40] Nonetheless, while these norms are true and objective, they cannot be absolute in the sense of being universally true propositions about what human persons ought or ought not to do in every conceivable situation. In fact, as Fuchs has said, "a strict behavioral norm, stated as a universal, contains unexpressed conditions and qualifications which as such limit its universality."[41] Since human experience, reflection upon which leads to the formulation of material norms, is itself an ongoing, open-ended process, it follows, as Francis Sullivan put it, that "we can never exclude the possibility that future experience, hitherto unimagined, might put a moral problem into a new frame of reference which would call for a revision of a norm that, when formulated, could not have taken such new experience into account."[42]

As a result, material norms are "valid only for the most part."[43] Some describe actions that for all practical purposes ought never to be freely chosen — for instance, raping a retarded child[44] or dropping nuclear bombs on civilian centers of population[45] — and can be regarded as "practical absolutes" or "virtually exceptionless" norms.[46] Nonetheless, because of the historicity of human existence and the ongoing character of human experience, all material norms must be regarded as open in principle to exceptions in the light of new historical conditions and new human experience.

I believe that the foregoing sections have summarized the principal lines of reasoning advanced by revisionist theologians to support their claim that there are no moral absolutes. I turn now to a critical assessment of their views.

2. A Critique of Revisionist Denial of Moral Absolutes

Here I will show that the lines of reasoning advanced by revisionists to support their claim that there are no exceptionless specific moral norms (= moral absolutes) are fatally flawed. But before offering a critique of their principal modes of argumentation I want first to note how they prejudice matters by their way of describing these moral norms.

Revisionist theologians, as we have seen, uniformly refer to moral absolutes as "material" or "concrete behavioral" norms. They say that these norms identify "physical acts" or "material acts," including, in some instances, the direct effects of these acts. They maintain that such "material" acts are physical or material events considered in abstraction of *any* purpose or intention of their agents.[47]

But Catholic theologians who today defend the truth of moral absolutes and those who did so in the past, including St. Thomas Aquinas (whose thought on this matter will be taken up later), offer a much different account of these "material" or "behavioral" norms, which they *never* call "material" or "behavioral" norms. According to these theologians, the human acts identified and morally excluded by such norms are not specified independently of the agent's will. Rather, they are specified "by the object" (*ex obiecto*), and by "object" they mean exactly *what the agent chooses*, i.e., the act to be done or omitted and the proximate result sought in carrying out the choice to do this act.[48] Thus, for example, Pope John Paul II, in *Reconciliatio et Poenitentia*, referred to a "doctrine, based on the Decalogue and on the preaching of the Old Testament, and assimilated into the *kerygma* of the Apostles and belonging to the earliest teaching of the Church, and constantly reaffirmed by her up to this day." What doctrine? The doctrine that "there exist acts which *per se* and in themselves, independently of circumstances, are *always* seriously wrong *by reason of their object (propter obiectum)*."[49]

The Catholic tradition affirming these moral absolutes held that these norms do not bear upon acts "in their *natural* species" but rather upon them "in their *moral* species (or genus)."[50] The "form" or "intelligibility" of such acts is not given by their nature as physical or material events in abstraction from the agent's understanding and willing but from their intelligibly chosen objects.[51] In this tradition, moreover, "direct" does not mean merely causal, material, or behavioral immediacy but rather the adoption by the will of what serves as either end or means.[52] For example, the very same *physical* or *material* act (the "natural" species of an act) — namely, sexual intercourse — can be, by reason of its intelligibly chosen "object," either a marital act, which is good in its *moral* species, or an act of incest or of adultery or of fornication, all of which are evil in their moral species.[53]

I will return later to this subject. I note it here, at the beginning of my critical assessment of revisionist thought, to show how great is the difference in the way traditional Catholic thought conceived of the exceptionless norms or moral absolutes that are the subject of our inquiry and in the way that revisionist theologians conceive of them. I now turn to an examination of the major lines of reasoning advanced by revisionists to support their denial of moral absolutes.

I. The 'Preference' Principle or Principle of 'Proportionate Good'

According to revisionist theologians, the basic moral principle that is to guide us both in formulating "material" norms, which are, after all, useful guidelines that are valid for the most part, and also in determining when there are exceptions to these norms is the "preference principle" or "principle of proportionate good." This principle maintains that moral judgments should be made by a comparative evaluation of the "nonmoral" goods or evils promised by the various alternatives of choice, and that the alternative promising the greater balance or proportion of nonmoral good over nonmoral evil is the one that ought to be chosen because it is the morally right action or sort of action. This principle justifies the deliberate intention to do a nonmoral evil for the sake of a proportionately greater nonmoral good. Some revisionist theologians — for instance, Josef Fuchs and Peter Knauer — claim that one does not, in any morally relevant sense, "intend" evil when one chooses to do evil only as a proportionate means to a greater good. But most revisionists frankly acknowledge that the "preference" principle provides moral warrant for directly intending evil when this is done for the sake of a greater good. In fact, as we have seen, Schüller and McCormick deny that there is any morally relevant difference between a will that only "permits" evil and a will that deliberately or directly "intends" evil, and they consider it a commendable character trait to be willing deliberately to intend a lesser evil for the sake of a higher good insofar as this manifests a greater love of the good.[54]

Revisionist theologians seem to consider the "principle of proportionate good" to be self-evidently true. According to it, we are to choose the alternative promising the greater balance of good over evil. If this principle is not true, they say, then the absurdity seems to follow that we ought to choose the alternative promising the greater proportion of evil over good. Thus, McCormick states the "preference principle" negatively to show how it is used in "conflict" situations in which evil inevitably results no matter what one chooses to do. He put the matter this way: "The rule of Christian reason, if we are to be governed by the *ordo bonorum*, is to choose the lesser evil. This general statement, it would seem, is beyond debate, for the only alternative is that in conflict situations we should choose the greater evil, which is patently absurd."[55]

Although the "preference principle" has some initial plausibility, closer examination shows that this plausibility rests on the ambiguity of the word "good." The morally upright person naturally wants to do the greater good, in the sense of what is morally good. But the revisionist "principle" assumes that it is possible to determine, prior to choice, which among various alternatives is *morally* good by balancing or measuring or commensurating in some way the different nonmoral goods and evils in these different options. The insuperable problem here, as Germain Grisez, John Finnis, and Joseph Boyle have shown,[56] is that there can be no unambiguous or homogeneous measure according to which the goods in question (such goods as human life itself, health, knowledge of the truth, appreciation of beauty, friendship) can be compared with one another or according to which individual instances of these goods (e.g., the life of Mary Smith and the life of Peter Jones) can be weighed or measured or "commensurated." Although none of these goods is absolute — only God, the *Summum Bonum*, is absolute — each is in truth a priceless good of human persons and, as such, a good to be prized, not priced, a good participating in the incalculable goodness of the human person.

The effort to commensurate them, to determine which is in every way "greater," is like trying to compare the number 87 with the length of this page. One simply cannot do so. One could do so if they could be reduced to some common denominator, as one can compare the number 87 with the length of this page if one compares these items by means of a common denominator such as centimeters, inches, or feet, scales adopted not by discovering a truth about these realities but by an arbitrary act of the will. But the goods involved in moral choice are not reducible to some common denominator. They are simply different and incomparable goods of human persons. Thus, the presupposition upon which the alleged "preference principle" rests is false: one cannot determine, prior to choice, which alternative unambiguously promises the "greater" good. One cannot determine, in a nonarbitrary way, which human goods are greater or lesser. They are all incomparably good, irreducible aspects of human flourishing and well-being.[57] And the same is true of individual instances of these basic goods of human persons. Who could judge whether Jane Smith's life is a "greater good" than the life of John Jones?

As a matter of fact, most revisionists have simply ignored this criticism and continue to say that in making moral judgments the goods and evils at stake in the available alternatives are commensurable. Those revisionists who have sought to respond to this objection have not done so satisfactorily.

McCormick, for instance, has been forced by this criticism to acknowledge that it is, in the strict sense, impossible to commensurate goods of different categories "against" each other. Thus, he now says that "while the basic goods are not commensurable (one against the other), they are clearly associated." He then claims that one can, by considering these goods in their interrelatedness or association, commensurate them and judge that the deliberate choice to destroy an instance of one good in present circumstances will not undermine respect for that good and that destroying or impeding it here and now is necessary to foster the flourishing of related goods.[58]

McCormick's response, however, is in reality no response at all. It amounts to saying that, although there is no nonarbitrary way to commensurate goods, we somehow succeed in doing so by "relating" or "associating" them. McCormick himself admits as much, for he speaks of assessing the greater good as a "prudent bet" and of commensurating in "fear and trembling" by *adopting a hierarchy*.[59] By saying this, he is admitting that the commensuration required by the "preference principle" is accomplished by an act of choice. But the *principle* was proposed so that we could determine, *prior* to choice, which alternatives are morally good and which are morally bad by commensurating the goods and evils in these alternatives. Now McCormick says that in order to commensurate the goods so that a judgment can be made as to which alternative promises the greater proportion of good over evil, we must first adopt a hierarchy of goods and make prudent bets. This kind of response simply will not do, nor does it face squarely the criticism that the goods in question are simply not commensurable in the way that proportionalism requires them to be.[60]

Garth Hallett claims that comparison of goods is possible because the intelligibly appealing features of the various alternatives of choice can be said to have more or less "value," in some sense of "value" that remains the same as one moves from one feature to another. By comparing goods in this way, he alleges, one can discover the alternative promising the greater good, for it will have *all* the "value" promised by any other alternative *and more*.[61]

But this reply is not coherent. As John Finnis has noted, "if one option seems to a deliberating agent to offer all that the alternatives offer *and some more*, the alternatives simply fall away; they completely lose the intelligible appeal which made them options. . . . Morally significant choices . . . are not and cannot be made in situations where the alternatives to option X have *nothing* intelligibly attractive which X does not have, and X has *everything* the alternatives have, *and some*."[62]

Two philosophers, Robert McKim and Peter Simpson (who are not, so far as I know, followers of revisionist thought), have argued that one who has identified, on the basis of the "preference principle," the option promising the greater proportion of good over evil can still choose an alternative excluded by the principle, perhaps out of selfishness.[63] Their objection misses the point of the criticism. The revisionist principle is not offered as a way for discerning the moral alternatives to selfishness or other immoral character traits. Nor is it the futile attempt to identify the morally right option *after* one has identified alternatives as selfish. Its purpose is to discover the morally right choice from among alternatives, each of which has some intelligible appeal. And the insuperable difficulty it faces is that if it could succeed in doing so, the choice it was proposed to exclude as morally unacceptable would simply fade away, for only one alternative would be left that would be *intelligibly* appealing. It is possible for us to make immoral choices not only because we can follow feelings against reason but also because the intelligible goods promised by available options are simply not commensurable or reducible to some common denominator. Immoral choices made in pursuit of intelligible goods are *unreasonable,* but they are not *irrational.*

In their effort to support the "preference principle," Schüller and McCormick, as we have seen, claim that a person who is willing to intend a lesser "nonmoral" evil for the sake of a greater "nonmoral" good has a greater willingness or love of the good — an admirable character trait — than does one who refuses to do such evil. But this claim, as Finnis has noted, involves equivocal uses of the term "willing." Schüller and McCormick use it to designate emotional attitudes, not intelligent choices. But, as Finnis observes, "the moral life is in large measure a struggle to *integrate* one's feelings and attitudes, one's 'willingness and unwillingness,' with intelligent commitments . . . and choices."[64] On the Schüller-McCormick understanding of "willingness," it would seem to follow that a nation threatened by a ruthless adversary would have a greater love or will for the good if it is willing to execute the adversary's children in order to deter the adversary from carrying out planned injustices than if it is willing to defend itself by attacking the adversary but unwilling to hold the adversary's children as hostages and executing them. Or a man willing to swear to a document setting forth beliefs that he does not hold in order to stay alive, care for his wife and family, and do noble deeds has a greater love of the good than, say, St. Thomas More, who was unwilling to do so. Such examples (and others could be given) show the fallacy of the Schüller-McCormick thesis, which equivocates in its use of the term "willing."

Another telling argument against the "preference principle" is advanced by Bartholomew Kiely, who emphasizes that this principle fails to consider seriously the reflexive or immanent consequences of human acts as self-determining choices.[65] As Kiely notes, we make ourselves to be the persons we are by the actions we freely choose to do. In choosing to do evil, even for the sake of some alleged "greater good," we make ourselves *to be* evildoers. I shall return to this matter later, when defending the truth of moral absolutes.

The reasons given here are sufficient to show that the alleged "preference principle" must be rejected, and with it the rationale it offers for rejecting the truth of moral absolutes.[66]

II. The Nature of a Human Act as a Whole or Totality

Revisionists claim that we cannot judge whether a given act is morally good or bad unless we consider this act in its wholeness or totality; because we cannot do so, it follows that there can be no moral absolutes insofar as such absolutes arbitrarily abstract the "material" or "physical" character of the act from its human totality, without any reference to the agent's purposes or intentions.

I have already shown that this claim rests upon a prejudiced description of moral absolutes. For, as we have seen, theologians who defend the truth of moral absolutes do not ignore the purposes or intentions of the agents; rather, they insist that both the "remote" or "ulterior" end and the "proximate" end of the agent's action — i.e., both the purpose for whose sake the deed is done and the deed willingly chosen as a means to that purpose — must be taken into account. It is true that an act must be good in its "totality" or "wholeness" if it is to be morally good (*bonum ex integra causa*). But it is not true that we cannot judge that a proposed act is morally bad without taking into account *all* of its elements, for if we know that *any* of its elements is bad, we know that the *whole* act is morally vitiated (*malum ex* quocumque *defectu*). Consequently, human acts already known to be bad by reason of their "objects" (i.e., the intelligible subject matter upon which the agent's will must bear as a chosen means to some ulterior end) remain morally bad even if the circumstances in which they are chosen or the end for whose sake they are adopted as means are good. Revisionists, in their arguments based on the "wholeness" or "totality" of the human act, focus on the agent's "remote" or "ulterior" end or "further intention," i.e., on the good that the agent hopes to realize by choosing to do *x* here and now, or the evil that the agent hopes to avoid by choosing to do *x* here and now. But they fail to take seriously — indeed, they even ignore — the moral significance of the *x* that is chosen to realize this end and the fact that the agent freely wills this *x* as a chosen means, for it is the "proximate" end of his will act and the "present intention" that shapes his moral being.

Revisionists are thus led to *redescribe* human actions in terms of their hoped-for results. Thus, as we have seen, they describe a series of contracepted marital acts *not* as acts of contraception but as a single act of "fostering love responsibly toward a generous fecundity." Similarly, they describe the choice of contraceptive sterilization as a "marriage-stabilizing" act. To do this is like describing an act of embezzlement, when done in order to gain money to build a park for children, as "obtaining money for a children's park." It conceals, rather than reveals, *what* the person is doing.[67]

The argument to support the denial of moral absolutes based on the "totality" or "wholeness" of a human act is, thus, fallacious. It fails, first of all, to recognize that, although one cannot definitively say that a human act is morally good unless one takes into account all of the elements that enter into it (insofar as all aspects of a human act must be morally good if the act as a whole is to be good), one can definitively say that a given human act is morally bad as soon as one knows that *any* of its elements is morally bad. Secondly, it falsely redescribes actions in terms of their anticipated results and by doing so fails to reveal and at times even conceals *what* moral agents are in fact choosing and doing.

III. The Historicity of Human Existence and Moral Absolutes

A key tenet of revisionist theologians is that we come to know "material norms" inductively by the collaborative effort of persons living in communities, reflecting together on common human experience. Since such experience is open-ended and ongoing, it follows, they say, that "we can never exclude the possibility that future experience, hitherto unimagined, might put a moral problem into a new frame of reference which would call for a revision of a norm which, when formulated, could not have taken such experience into account."[68]

There is no doubt that morality is in some ways relative to contingent social and historical reality. Thus, societies, like individuals, make choices that both generate and limit moral responsibilities; new alternatives become available as societies and technologies develop; better factual judgments often give rise to new insights into moral responsibilities; and moral judgment is frequently blocked by cultural biases and opened by changed conditions.[69] But it does not follow from this that *all* specific moral norms are relative to changing social and historical reality. Revisionists themselves seek to avoid a radical historical and cultural relativism by appealing to the "transcendental" standard of "a steadily advancing 'humanization'" or to the self-realization of persons and of the communities in which they live.[70] But this vague standard, as Germain Grisez (among others) has noted, lacks the content needed "to determine what should and what should not count as morally determinative when one fills the formal concept of human self-realization [or 'humanization'] with the whole concrete reality of persons in society and their world."[71]

The claim that the open-ended and ongoing character of human experience precludes the possibility of permanently true specific moral norms is undoubtedly verified with reference to *some* moral norms — not all moral norms, after all, are absolute. But this claim presumes that an action can be morally evaluated only as a totality for the purpose of identifying the behavior that will foster human self-realization and self-development,[72] or that will not contradict or negate its own good purpose.[73] But this assumption, as has already been shown in our discussion of the wholeness or totality of a human act, is simply not true. Once an action has been properly identified — for instance, as an act of rape — one need not delay judgment about its morality until one knows why the rapist is choosing to do it, where it is done, in what century or millennium it occurs, and so forth. One can, on the basis of relevant moral *principles,* at once declare that it is simply the sort of act that an upright human person, one whose heart is open to the goods perfective of human persons, ought not freely choose to do.

Revisionist theologians claim that specific moral norms must be based on "concrete" human nature, which is subject to radical change, as opposed to "transcendent" human nature, on which the formal norms that revisionists recognize as absolute are based. They then claim no specific moral norms based on concrete human nature can be universally and irreversibly true.[74] But revisionist theologians do not explain clearly what "concrete," as opposed to "transcendent," human nature means. They do not show how fundamental human goods — such as life itself, knowledge of the truth, friendship, and so forth — might cease to be good and perfective of human persons, nor do they explain how their claim about radical change in human nature is compatible with the unity of the human race and our solidarity with Christ. They fail to show how this claim can be harmonized with such basic truths of Catholic faith as, for instance, that "all human beings . . . have the same nature and the same origin,"[75] a "common nature,"[76] and the "same calling and destiny," and so, being fundamentally equal both in nature and in supernatural calling, can be citizens of the one people of God regardless of race or place or time.[77] Thus, the denial of moral absolutes on the alleged claim that there is a radical change in concrete human nature because of human "historicity" simply cannot be sustained.

For all the reasons given in this section, I believe that the revisionist attack on the truth of moral absolutes has been shown to be based on seriously defective arguments. The failure of revisionists to support their denial of moral absolutes by reasoned arguments is itself evidence that there are moral absolutes.

Before presenting a defense of the truth of moral absolutes, however, it is necessary to consider the position taken by some philosophers and theologians who repudiate the revisionist or "proportionalist" method of making moral judgments but who nonetheless think that "prudence" can at times justify the choice of an act judged bad by reason of its object.[78] These moralists emphasize the fact that the norms excluding such acts are universal, whereas the acts one chooses are absolutely individual, unique, unrepeatable. They think that a prudent person must consider not only the universal norm but also the existential and unique features characteristic of this particular act here and now. They believe that when a prudent — i.e., virtuous — person, does take into account these unique and unrepeatable features he may reach the judgment that here and now, in these particular circumstances, an act that would normally be judged immoral by reason of its object is morally justified.

The principal difficulty with this position — advanced, it needs to be noted, by moralists who repudiate the kind of moral reasoning employed by revisionist theologians to justify their denial of moral absolutes — is that it misconceives the meaning of prudence as a virtue and the sense in which particular human acts are indeed unique and unrepeatable. The virtue of prudence does indeed enable human persons to determine the situations in which there are genuine exceptions to moral norms. Not all moral norms, as previously noted, are absolute. For example, the norms requiring us to keep promises and to return things that we have borrowed to their owners are not absolute; and the prudent person, the virtuous person, is the one who is capable of determining the existential situation in which norms of this kind are not binding. He or she is able to judge that in these particular circumstances norms of this kind are not obligatory insofar as the moral principles giving rise to them likewise justify exceptions to them here and now.

Nonetheless, some moral norms are absolute, without exceptions, insofar as the sorts or kinds of actions specified by them are actions in which one cannot *not* intend evil, i.e, choose to damage, destroy, or impede what is really good. Thus, prudence, the virtue disposing one to choose rightly the means to achieving the good, can never justify a choice to *do* evil, to adopt by choice a proposal to damage, destroy, or impede what is really good.

For all the reasons given in this section, I conclude that the revisionist attack on the truth of moral absolutes has been shown to be based on seriously defective arguments. The failure of revisionists to support their denial of moral absolutes by reasoned arguments is itself evidence that there are moral absolutes. I will now offer positive reasons to support the truth of such norms.

3. A Defense of the Truth of Moral Absolutes

I will begin my defense of the truth of moral absolutes by reflecting briefly on the significance of human acts as free, self-determining choices. As we have already seen, one of the criticisms advanced against revisionist moral theology is that it fails to consider seriously the reflexive or immanent consequences of human acts as free, self-determining choices. As we saw in Chapter Two, human acts, while involving physical performances, are not transient physical events in the material world that come and go. At their core is a free, self-determining choice that abides within the person, giving to him or her an identity and disposing him or her to choose in similar ways in the future.[79] In short, we make ourselves to be the kind of persons we are, in and through the actions we freely choose to do.

Many revisionist theologians, it is important to observe, maintain that the terms "good" and "bad" refer most properly to human persons as moral beings, whereas the proper terms to use in referring to human acts are "right" and "wrong." They regard "transcendent formal" norms, which they recognize as absolute, as norms expressing the qualities, dispositions, and attitudes that ought to characterize the morally good person. These norms, they note, are concerned *not* with human acts but rather with the *being* of the human person.[80] So-called "material" norms, on the other hand, are not concerned with the *being* of the person but with the rightness or wrongness of human acts.[81]

In addition, many revisionist theologians hold to some form of a theory of "fundamental option" or "basic freedom" that *relocates* self-determination from the free choices we make every day (including such basic commitments as getting married or entering the priesthood or religious life) to an alleged exercise of a fundamental option or basic freedom at the core of our being whereby, it is said, we take a stance "for" or "against" God and basic human values. It is in the exercise of this basic freedom that we determine ourselves and make ourselves *to be* the persons we are. According to these theologians, we do *not* determine ourselves and make ourselves *to be* the persons we are through the everyday exercise of free choice, which, they maintain, is concerned with actions on the "periphery" of our existence.[82] Some even claim that a person *can* at times freely choose to do what he or she believes to be gravely immoral — for instance, to have intercourse with the "wrong" person or to kill an innocent person without a proportionate reason — and still remain, in the core of his or her being, a morally good person whose fundamental option is still one "for" God. In short, for revisionists the everyday deeds we choose to do in exercising our "categorical" freedom of choice "horizontally" in our daily relationships are of a fundamentally different moral character from the option we make (apparently, in the thought of at least some revisionists, without even being consciously aware of doing so[83]) deep within our being in our "transcendental" relationship with God.

Revisionists maintain that our relationship with God, established by the exercise of our fundamental option, is directly related to our salvation. They grant that our everyday, "categorical" free choices are related to salvation but only "indirectly," insofar as our many acts of free choice must be finally integrated into our fundamental option and bring it to maturity.[84]

But the Catholic tradition affirms the saving (or damning) significance of our daily deeds — of the free choices we make every day. Vatican Council II affirmed that we will find perfected in heaven the very good fruits of human nature and work that we nurture here on earth.[85] The New Testament teaches us that redemption includes all human goods and the cosmos itself (see Rom 8:21; 1 Cor 3:22-23; Eph 1:10), and the Church proclaims that the spiritual and temporal orders, while distinct, are so intimately linked in God's plan that he intends in Christ to appropriate the whole universe into a new creation, "beginning here and now on earth and finding its fulfillment on the last day."[86]

The truth, in short, as we have seen in Chapter Two, is that we determine ourselves, our *being* as moral persons, in and through the actions we freely choose to do every day. When, for example, I choose to lie to my wife, perhaps about a minor matter and perhaps because I hope by doing so to preserve the "greater good" of family harmony, I make myself *to be* a liar; and I remain a liar, disposed to lie again in similar circumstances, until, by another free choice, I become a repentant one. At the core of a human act is a free, self-determining choice.

Therefore, if we are to become fully the beings God wills us to be, we must make good moral choices. Choices are possible only when there are alternatives, and our task is to discover, prior to choice, which alternatives are morally good and which are morally bad. Moral norms are thus "truths" intended to guide us in our choices.

Revisionists claim that the basic moral norm or first moral principle is the preference principle or principle of proportionate good. According to this principle, we are to adopt by choice that alternative that promises the greater proportion of nonmoral good over nonmoral evil. We have now seen the fallacious character of this alleged principle.

In Chapter Three, following the lead of St. Thomas and of Vatican Council II, I proposed, in company with Germain Grisez and others, a different basic moral norm or first moral principle. Here I will briefly summarize what was said in Chapter Three. According to St. Thomas, the first moral principle is that we should choose in accordance with love of God and of neighbor.[87] The Fathers of Vatican II taught that the "norm of human activity is this: that in accord with the divine plan and will, it should harmonize with the genuine good of the human race, and allow men as individuals and as members of society to pursue their total vocation and fulfill it" (*Gaudium et spes*, no. 35). As formulated by Grisez, this first principle of morality can be expressed as follows: "In voluntarily acting for human goods and avoiding what is opposed to them, one ought to choose and otherwise will those and only those possibilities whose willing is compatible with a will toward integral human fulfillment."[88] Or, to put it another way, in making choices we ought to choose those and only those alternatives whose willing is compatible with a love for all the goods of human persons and of the persons in whom those goods are meant to flourish. A person who chooses in a morally bad way does not respect and love the good gifts of God and the persons in whom these gifts are meant to exist. He or she chooses to act in a way that fails to honor the basic goods of human persons and the persons whom these goods perfect and ennoble.

This first principle of morality can be specified by various "modes of responsibility," which identify specific ways in which human persons can fail, in their choices and actions, to respect and honor the goods of human existence and the persons in whom these goods are meant to subsist. Among the modes of responsibility, as we saw in Chapter Two, are those requiring us *not* to adopt by choice proposals to damage, destroy, or impede these goods, either in ourselves or in others, whether out of hostility toward a good (the seventh mode) or because the continued flourishing of a good in ourselves or others inhibits our participation in some other good that we arbitrarily prefer (the eighth mode). From these modes of obligation we can derive more specific moral norms, such as those proscribing the deliberate choice to kill innocent human life, to commit adultery or to substitute, for the person whom we have made nonsubstitutable by our choice to be married, some other person, etc. In short, these modes of responsibility are the basis of specific moral norms proscribing actions in which, of necessity, our will — our heart, our person — ratifies the doing of evil, deliberately damaging, destroying, or impeding what is really good. Such norms are absolute or exceptionless because they are rooted in modes of responsibility that in turn simply specify the moral requirements of the first principle of morality.

Although moral absolutes are negative, they allow human persons to keep themselves open to be fully the beings they are meant to be. They remind us that some kinds of human choices and actions, although responsive to *some* aspects of human good, make us persons whose hearts are closed to the full range of human goods and to the persons in whom these goods are meant to exist. We simply *cannot* have a heart open to and responsive to what is really good if, through choices and actions, we are willing that evil — i.e., the intentional deprivation of these goods from the persons in whom they are meant to subsist — *be*. Because the human person's vocation is to love, even as he or she has been and is loved by God in Christ, it is not possible to say, affirmatively, precisely what love requires, for its affirmative obligations must be discovered by us in our creative endeavor to grow daily in love of God and neighbor. But moral absolutes show us what love *cannot* mean: it cannot mean that we deliberately set our wills *against* the good gifts that God wills to flourish in his children and close our hearts to our neighbors.

Each true specific moral absolute summons each person to revere the goods intrinsic to human persons. Human persons, each in his or her corporeal and spiritual unity (*Gaudium et spes*, no. 14), are the only earthly creatures God has willed for themselves (*Gaudium et spes*, no. 24). Respect for human persons, each for his or her own sake, is therefore required by the Creator's design, and is a primary element in love of God and of one's neighbor as oneself. Such a respect and reverence is, moreover, a primary demand of that divine dignity to which Christ has raised human nature by assuming it (*Gaudium et spes*, no. 22).

Each true specific moral absolute excludes every moral choice in which, by adopting and striving after that choice's precise object, one would necessarily integrate into one's will and character some violation of, or other disrespect for, a good intrinsic to human persons — oneself or another or others. Choices that conform to these moral norms enable us to live worthily the vocation to which we have been called. Since they show reverence for human persons, they provide the materials for the building up of the kingdom (cf. *Gaudium et spes*, no. 38). Whatever their earthly fortune or failure, these choices cultivate human personal goods (the goods of "truth and life, holiness . . ., justice, love, and peace") and will, with those goods, be found again in the completed kingdom (cf. *Gaudium et spes*, no. 39) — like Christ's adherence to his vocation in the face of earthly failure, suffering, and death. The reality of this kingdom, which is being built up on earth in mystery but is not to be equated with earthly fulfillment and will not be completed save in the new heavens and new earth (cf. *Gaudium et spes*, no. 39), is a reality which relativizes every earthly horizon which one might hope to use as a "measure" for weighing the worth of possible choices. Thus, the prospect of the kingdom replaces every alternative horizon against which a violation of human dignity can seem "necessary" or "the greater good" or "the lesser evil."

In fact, the norms that identify such violations of the goods intrinsic to human dignity liberate man from servitude to every partial, fragmentary, and illusory horizon, from servitude to every aspiration to assume the role proper to divine Providence itself. Instead, these norms leave each person to the creativity of his or her own vocation, within the all-embracing vocation to holiness, the holiness which alone is adequate to the gift and promise of divine sonship and to giving and reflecting God's true glory.

In and through the deeds we freely choose to do, we give to ourselves our identities as moral beings. Moral absolutes remind us that by freely choosing to damage, destroy, or impede what is really good either in ourselves or in others — even for the noblest motives — we make ourselves to be evildoers. But human persons, made in the image of the holy and triune God, are to be, like him, absolutely innocent of evil. God wills properly and *per se* — i.e., as end or means — only what is good. He permits evil, but he does not choose to do evil or intend that evil *be*.[89] Likewise, we, his children, ought never freely choose to do evil, to intend that evil *be*. Moral absolutes, therefore, are required by our *being* as moral beings, as persons capable of making ourselves to be the persons we are, in and through the choices we freely make every day of our lives. The *Catechism of the Catholic Church* takes up the issue of intrinsically evil acts and moral absolutes in the part of the work devoted to the Christian moral life, presenting a teaching fully in harmony with that set forth in this chapter. For a brief presentation of the *Catechism's* teaching on this matter, see the Appendix of this work, wherein I provide an account of the moral teaching of the *Catechism*.

Notes for Chapter Four

1. On this, see, for example, Pope John Paul II's apostolic exhortation *Reconciliatio et Poenitentia*, no. 17; "Discourse to the International Congress of Moral Theology," April 10, 1986, no. 3, in *Persona, Verità, e Morale: Atti del Congresso Internazionale di Teologia Morale (Roma, 7-12 aprile 1986)* (Rome: Città Nuova Editrice, 1987), p. 12.

2. In a document included in the "Majority Report," the *Documentum Syntheticum de Moralitate Nativitatum*, the majority explicitly repudiated anal/oral sex as absolutely immoral. See text in *The Birth-Control Debate*, ed. Robert Hoyt (Kansas City, MO: The National Catholic Reporter, 1969), p. 76.

3. Charles E. Curran, "Divorce from the Perspective of a Revised Moral Theology," in his *Ongoing Revisions* (Notre Dame, IN: University of Notre Dame Press, 1976), p. 121.

4. *Documentum Syntheticum*, in Hoyt, p. 69.

5. By "conjugal acts which by intention are infertile" the authors of *Documentum Syntheticum* mean marital acts chosen during the wife's infertile period. The authors see no moral difference between the use of "artificial" contraceptives and abstinence from intercourse during the wife's fertile time.

6. *Documentum Syntheticum*, in Hoyt, p. 72.

7. Ibid., p. 75.

8. On this, see the *Schema Documenti de Responsabili Paternitate*, another document included in the "Majority Report," in Hoyt, pp. 88-90.

9. Josef Fuchs, "Naturrecht oder naturalistischer Fehlschluss?" *Stimmen der Zeit* 29 (1988), 409, 420-422; Fuchs, *Christian Ethics in a Secular Arena* (Washington, DC: Georgetown University Press, 1984), p. 75; Fuchs, *Personal Responsibility and Christian Morality* (Washington, DC: Georgetown University Press, 1983), pp. 131, 139.

10. Louis Janssens, "Ontic Evil and Moral Evil," *Louvain Studies* 4 (1972), 144 (reprinted in *Readings in Moral Theology, No. 1*, ed. Charles E. Curran and Richard A. McCormick [New York: Paulist Press, 1979], pp. 72-73); "Norms and Priorities in a Love Ethic," *Louvain Studies* 6 (1977), 231.

11. E.g., Timothy O'Connell, *Principles for a Catholic Morality* (New York: Seabury, 1978), pp. 157-158; Richard Gula, *Reason Informed by Faith: Foundations of Catholic Morality* (New York: Paulist Press, 1989), pp. 282-283.

12. Janssens, "Norms and Priorities in a Love Ethic," 207; O'Connell, *Principles*, pp. 158-159; Gula, *Reason Informed by Faith*, pp. 283-284.

13. On this, see Gula, *What Are They Saying About Moral Norms?* (New York: Paulist Press, 1982), pp. 55-56.

14. Fuchs, *Christian Ethics in a Secular Arena*, p. 72.

15. Janssens, "Norms and Priorities in a Love Ethic," 208.

16. Fuchs, *Christian Ethics in a Secular Arena*, p. 72; see Fuchs, "Naturrecht oder naturalistischer Fehlschluss?" 411, 416, 419; see also Richard McCormick, *Notes on Moral Theology 1965-1980* (Lanham, MD: University Press of America, 1981), pp. 578-579.

17. Fuchs, *Personal Responsibility and Christian Morality*, p. 191; Fuchs, *Christian Ethics in a Secular Arena*, p. 74; Janssens, "Norms and Priorities in a Love Ethic," 210, 216; Gula, *Reason Informed by Faith*, pp. 288-289.

18. Gula, *Reason Informed by Faith*, p. 291.

19. On this, see, for example, McCormick, *How Brave a New World? Dilemmas in Bioethics* (New York: Doubleday, 1981), p. 5.

20. "Premoral" is the term preferred by Fuchs; "nonmoral" is preferred by Schüller, McCormick, and others; "ontic" is used by Janssens and others.

21. See above, note 4.

22. Bruno Schüller, "What Ethical Principles Are Universally Valid?" *Theology Digest* 19 (March, 1971), 24 (translation of "Zur Problematik allgemeinen ethischer Grundsatze," *Theologie und Philosophie* 45 [1970], 4). McCormick's comment on this text is of interest. He writes: "Stated negatively, it [this principle] reads: put in a position where he will unavoidably cause evil, man must discover which is the worst evil and avoid it. Stated positively, this is its formulation: put before two concurring but mutually exclusive values, man should discover which must be preferred and act accordingly. These statements imply that a physical evil can be caused or permitted only if it is demanded by a proportionate good" (*Notes on Moral Theology 1965-1980*, p. 315).

23. McCormick, "Ambiguity in Moral Choice," The Père Marquette Theology Lecture for 1973, as reprinted in *Doing Evil to Achieve Good*, ed. Richard McCormick and Paul Ramsey (Chicago: Loyola University Press, 1978), p. 39.

24. Fuchs, *Personal Responsibility and Christian Morality*, p. 138.

25. For justification of directly intended abortion for a "commensurate" or "proportionate" reason, see Charles E. Curran, *New Perspectives in Moral Theology* (Notre Dame, IN: University of Notre Dame Press, 1974), pp. 190-191; for mercy killing or euthanasia, see Daniel Maguire, *Death By Choice* (New York: Doubleday, 1974).

26. See, for instance, McCormick, *Notes on Moral Theology 1965-1980,* pp. 515-516, 718; Charles Curran, *Contemporary Problems in Moral Theology* (Notre Dame, IN: Fides, 1970), pp. 144-145; *New Perspectives in Moral Theology,* pp. 190-193.

27. McCormick, "Ambiguity in Moral Choice," as reprinted in *Doing Evil to Achieve Good,* pp. 30-31; see also pp. 35-36.

28. Schüller, "The Double Effect in Catholic Thought: A Revolution," in *Doing Evil to Achieve Good,* p. 191. See McCormick, "A Commentary on the Commentaries," ibid., p. 241.

29. Schüller, as cited by McCormick, "A Commentary on the Commentaries," pp. 241, 243.

30. Schüller, "The Double Effect in Catholic Thought," p. 191; emphasis in the original.

31. McCormick, "A Commentary on the Commentaries," p. 241.

32. See, for instance, Gula, *Reason Informed by Faith,* pp. 244-245.

33. See above, notes 6 and 7.

34. Fuchs, *Personal Responsibility and Christian Morality,* p. 138.

35. See above, note 17.

36. McCormick, "A Commentary on the Commentaries," p. 241.

37. Gula, *Reason Informed by Faith,* p. 291.

38. Francis Sullivan, *Magisterium: Teaching Authority in the Catholic Church* (New York: Paulist Press, 1983), pp. 150-151. Sullivan lists Curran, Fuchs, Böckle, Schüller, Häring, and other revisionists as agreeing with this way of putting the matter.

39. Fuchs, *Personal Responsibility and Christian Morality,* p. 129.

40. Ibid., p. 133.

41. Ibid., p. 124.

42. Sullivan, *Magisterium,* pp. 151-152; see Fuchs, *Personal Responsibility and Christian Morality,* p. 140.

43. Fuchs, *Personal Responsibility and Christian Morality,* p. 142.

44. On this, see Maguire, *Death by Choice,* p. 99; Janssens, "Norms and Priorities in a Love Ethic," 217.

45. O'Connell, *Principles for a Catholic Morality,* p. 162.

46. Fuchs, *Personal Responsibility and Christian Morality,* pp. 140-142; Janssens, "Norms and Priorities in a Love Ethic," 217-218.

47. See above, note 17.

48. St. Thomas Aquinas, *In II Sent.,* d. 40, q. un., a. 1, ad 4; *In IV Sent.,* d. 16, q. 3, a. 1b. ad 2; *Summa theologiae,* 1-2, 1, 3, ad 3; *De Malo,* q. 2, a. 4c. See Karl Hoermann, "Das Objekt als Quelle der Sitt-lilchkeit," in *The Ethics of St. Thomas Aquinas,* ed. L. Elders (Vatican City: Libreria Editrice Vaticana, 1984), pp. 122-123, 126-128; Martin Rhonheimer, *Natur als Grundlage der Moral* (Innsbruck

and Vienna: Tyrolia Verlag, 1987), p. 95; and Theo Belmans, *Le sens objectif de l'agir humain* (Vatican City: Libreria Editrice Vaticana, 1980), pp. 214-216.

49. Pope John Paul II, *Reconciliatio et Poenitentia*, no. 17.

50. St. Thomas Aquinas, *Summa theologiae*, 1-2, 20, 2; *In II Sent.*, d. 40, q. un., a. 2.

51. For texts from St. Thomas, analysis, and commentary, see Patrick Lee, "The Permanence of the Ten Commandments: St. Thomas and His Modern Commentators," *Theological Studies* 42 (1981), 431-432; Belmans, *Le sens objectif de l'agir humain*, pp. 62, 109-119, 124, 162, 237; Rhonheimer, *Natur als Grundlage der Moral*, pp. 91-99, 317-345, 367-374.

52. Thus "direct" killing of the innocent is always explained as killing intended by the will either as an end or as a means. See Pope Pius XII, *Discorsi e Radiomessagi di sua Santità Pio XII* 6 (November 12, 1949), 191-192; Pope Paul VI, *Humanae vitae*, note 14; Congregation for the Doctrine of the Faith, *De Abortu Procurato* (November 18, 1974), no. 7, and *Donum vitae* (February 22, 1987), note 20.

53. St. Thomas Aquinas, *In II Sent.*, d. 40, q. 1, a. 1, ad 4; *Summa theologiae*, 1-2, 1, 3, ad 3.

54. See above, notes 27-31.

55. McCormick, "Ambiguity in Moral Choice," as reprinted in *Doing Evil to Achieve Good*, p. 38.

56. Germain Grisez, "Against Consequentialism," *American Journal of Jurisprudence* 23 (1978), 21-72; Grisez, *The Way of the Lord Jesus*, Vol. 1, *Christian Moral Principles* (Chicago: Franciscan Herald Press, 1983), pp. 141-172; John Finnis, *Natural Law and Natural Rights* (Oxford and New York: Oxford University Press, The Clarendon Press, 1980), pp. 118-125; Finnis, *Fundamentals of Ethics* (Washington, DC: Georgetown University Press, 1983), pp. 86-105; John Finnis, Joseph M. Boyle, Jr., and Germain Grisez, *Nuclear Deterrence, Morality, and Realism* (Oxford and New York: Oxford University Press, 1987), pp. 254-261.

57. In *Nuclear Deterrence, Morality, and Realism*, Finnis, Boyle, and Grisez show how the revisionist principle is incompatible with free choice. They note that this principle requires that "two conditions be met: (i) that a morally significant choice be made and (ii) that the person making it be able to identify one option as offering unqualifiedly greater good or lesser evil. But these two conditions are incompatible, and in requiring that they be met simultaneously consequentialism is incoherent" (p. 254). As they show, choice is possible only when there are two or more alternatives. But an alternative exists only when the good it promises is not available in other possibilities. Thus, if condition (ii) is met, condition (i) cannot be, and vice versa.

58. McCormick, "A Commentary on the Commentaries," in *Doing Evil to Achieve Good*, p. 227; see also pp. 251-253.

59. Ibid.

60. McCormick's response has been reduced to absurdity by Finnis in *Fundamentals of Ethics,* pp. 99-105, and it has been severely criticized by Grisez in *Christian Moral Principles,* pp. 161-164. McCormick, so far as I know, has not even attempted to reply to these incisive critiques.

61. Garth Hallett, "The 'Incommensurability' of Values," *Heythrop Journal* 28 (1987), 373-387.

62. Finnis, *Moral Absolutes: Tradition, Revision, and Truth* (Washington, DC: The Catholic University of America Press, 1991).

63. Robert McKim and Peter Simpson, "On the Alleged Incoherence of Consequentialism," *New Scholasticism* 62 (1988), 349-352.

64. Finnis, "The Act of the Person," in *Persona, Verità, e Morale,* p. 172.

65. Bartholomew Kiely, "The Impracticality of Proportionalism," *Gregorianum* 66 (1985), 656-666.

66. In addition to the works by Grisez, Finnis, Kiely, Rhonheimer, Belmans, Lee, and Hoermann already cited in previous notes, see Servais Pinckaers, *Ce qu'on ne peut jamais faire: La question des acts intrinsèquements mauvais. Histoire et discussion* (Fribourg and Paris: Editions Univérsitaires and Editions du Cerf, 1986); John R. Connery, "Catholic Ethics: Has the Norm for Rule-Making Changed?" *Theological Studies* 42 (1981), 232-250; William E. May, "Aquinas and Janssens on the Moral Meaning of Human Acts," *Thomist* 48 (1984), 566-606.

67. On this, see the texts cited in notes 48, 50, 51, and 53 above. Also see Eric D'Arcy, *Human Acts: An Essay on Their Moral Evaluation* (Oxford and New York: Oxford University Press, 1963), pp. 18-25.

68. Sullivan, *Magisterium,* pp. 151-152.

69. On this, see Germain Grisez, "Moral Absolutes: A Critique of the View of Josef Fuchs, S.J." *Anthropos* (now *Anthropotes): Rivista di Studi sulla Persona e la Famiglia* 1(1985),170.

70. Fuchs, *Personal Responsibility and Christian Morality,* p. 129.

71. Grisez, "Moral Absolutes," 172.

72. Fuchs, "Naturrecht oder naturalistischer Fehlschluss?" 409, 420-422; Fuchs, *Christian Ethics in a Secular Arena,* p. 75; McCormick, *Notes on Moral Theology 1965-1980,* pp. 710-711.

73. Janssens, "Ontic Evil and Moral Evil," 144; "Norms and Priorities in a Love Ethic," 231.

74. Sullivan, *Magisterium,* p. 152; Karl Rahner, "Basic Observations on the Subject of the Changeable and Unchangeable Factors in the Church," *Theological Investigations,* Vol. 14 (New York: Herder and Herder, 1976), pp. 14-15.

75. *Gaudium et spes,* no. 29; *Lumen gentium,* no. 19.

76. *Lumen gentium,* no. 13.

77. *Gaudium et spes,* no. 29; *Lumen gentium,* no. 13.

78. See, e.g., Robert Sokolowski, *Moral Action* (Bloomington, IN: Indiana University Press, 1985), p. 152; see also his *The God of Faith and Reason* (Notre Dame, IN: University of Notre Dame Press, 1982), pp. 62-63. Another version of this view is provided by Walter E. Conn, *Conscience: Development and Self-Transcendence* (Birmingham, AL: Religious Education Press, 1981), pp. 209-210.

79. On this, see Chapter Two, above, pp. 47-48.

80. See above, notes 11-15.

81. See above, notes 17-18.

82. On fundamental option and the radical difference between ordinary free choices and fundamental option in the mind of revisionists, see, for instance, Josef Fuchs, *Human Values and Christian Morality* (Dublin: Gill and Macmillan, 1970), pp. 92-112, esp. 96-98.

83. The best critique of fundamental option theory that I know of is that given by Joseph M. Boyle, Jr., "Freedom, the Human Person, and Human Acts," in *Principles of Catholic Moral Life*, ed. William E. May (Chicago: Franciscan Herald Press, 1980), pp. 237-266.

84. Fuchs, *Human Values and Christian Morality*, p. 96.

85. *Gaudium et spes*, no. 39.

86. *Apostolicam Actuositatem*, no. 5.

87. St. Thomas Aquinas, *Summa theologiae*, 1-2, 100, 3, ad 1.

88. Grisez, *Christian Moral Principles*, p. 184.

89. That God is totally innocent of evil and only permits it is taught by the Council of Trent, Session VI, in *Enchiridion Symbolorum*, ed. Henricus Denzinger and Adolphus Schönmetzer (33rd ed.; Rome: Herder, 1983), no. 1556. For pertinent texts from St. Thomas and discussion, see Lee, "Permanence of the Ten Commandments," 455-456.

APPENDIX I TO CHAPTER FOUR

St. Thomas and Moral Absolutes

In Chapter Three, when we examined the thought of St. Thomas on natural law, we saw that he affirmed the truth of moral absolutes or specific norms proscribing as unconditionally contrary to natural law specifiable kinds of human actions. He held, as we saw, that the precepts of the Decalogue, which are immediate or proximate conclusions to the first and common principles of natural law, are moral absolutes. Even God, he held, cannot grant dispensations from them.[1]

Today many revisionists, among them Charles E. Curran, Louis Janssens, John Dedek, and Richard Gula,[2] claim that St. Thomas did *not* affirm the truth of moral absolutes. They claim that he understood the precepts of the Decalogue as "formal" norms, i.e., norms prohibiting actions *already described in morally evaluative terms,* such as *murder* or *unjust killing* or intercourse with the *wrong* person.[3] While acknowledging that St. Thomas affirmed the "transcendental" types of norms that they themselves accept as absolute — such principles as that "good is to be done and pursued and evil is to be avoided," "one ought always act in accordance with right reason," and "one must love God and neighbor" — they claim that he taught that derivative norms, such as those proscribing the deliberate killing of the innocent, are true "only for the most part," i.e., they are useful generalizations but not universally true moral norms.[4] In addition, some claim that since Aquinas considered the end to be the formal element specifying the moral goodness or badness of a human act, it follows that for him an action really willed and done coherently for the sake of a good end must be morally good.[5] Finally, revisionist theologians Janssens and McCormick allege that a passage from St. Thomas's *Quaestiones Quodlibetales* shows clearly that he recognized that an act which, materially considered, involves the deformity of some nonmoral evil, can be made right by circumstances in which the nonmoral goods achieved will outweigh the nonmoral evils involved and make the act to be morally right and good.[6] What is to be said of these claims by revisionist theologians?

To grasp properly the thought of St. Thomas and, in particular, his teaching on the absoluteness of the precepts of the Decalogue, it is essential to grasp the distinction he makes between human acts described in their "natural" species and human acts considered in their "moral" species. Only by understanding this distinction is it possible to appreciate his reply to such objections that the killing of innocent persons is at times morally permissible, insofar as Abraham, a just and good man, was willing to sacrifice his innocent son Isaac. According to Aquinas, killing an innocent person, executing a convicted criminal, and killing an assailant in an act of self-defense are all, in their "natural" species, "acts of killing."[7] But they differ in their "moral" species insofar as only the killing of an innocent person is an "act of killing" in the moral sense and as such morally wicked in itself (*secundum se*)[8] and contrary to the precept of the Decalogue prohibiting killing, whereas the killings involved in executing a convicted criminal and in defending oneself by the measured use of force against an unprovoked attack are partial aspects of actions that are morally good, specified morally by reason of the object of the will's choice as acts of justice and legitimate self-defense and *not* as acts of killing.[9]

The basis for this distinction is that human acts, precisely as "human" or "moral," receive their "forms" not from nature but from human intelligence, which places them in their moral species by discerning their "ends," "objects," and "circumstances." Aquinas insists that *all* these factors must be morally good or in harmony with the precepts of natural law if the whole human act is to be good.[10] He holds that the end and the object are the primary factors giving a human act its moral species insofar as they are the primary realities willed by the agent. The end for whose sake an action is done is a primary source of an act's moral species because humans, as intelligent beings, act in the first place only for the sake of an end.[11] The end is the "more universal form" (*forma magis universalis*) of the whole human act in the same sense in which a genus is said to be the "more universal form" with respect to its diverse species.[12] But the "object" of the external act chosen and commanded by the will is also a primary source of the moral species of the whole human act, precisely because this object is the object of an act of will or of choice. Since it is the "proximate" end that the acting person intends,[13] it must be good if the whole human act is to be good. Thus, for example, a person may choose to give alms to the poor. This is the "object" of an act of the will, for it is the object chosen and commanded by the will. And giving alms is something good. But the end for whose sake one chooses to give alms must also be good — to help the poor, to give glory to God. If one gives alms in order to win praise, the act is morally vitiated by its end. But if one wishes to help the poor (a good end), one cannot choose evil means (an object) to do so. Thus, alleviating the poor by embezzling money or by selling illegal drugs is morally wicked.

With these distinctions in mind, we find Thomas's position on the precepts of the Decalogue to be completely lucid. He holds that these precepts are absolute, or exceptionless. They are not mere formal norms or tautologies prohibiting actions already known to be "unjust," but specific norms proscribing identifiable sorts of human acts as absolutely immoral and contrary to the natural law. The moral objects of the acts identified by these precepts are specified descriptively as "killing the innocent," "coition with someone who is not one's own [i.e., one's spouse]," and "taking what belongs to another."[14] Aquinas teaches that *apparent* exceptions to these norms are in truth *different kinds of human acts, specified by different objects of human choice.* Thus, for St. Thomas, the object of Abraham's act, when he was willing to obey God's command to sacrifice his son Isaac, was not the "killing of an innocent person" but "the carrying out of God's just command." God's command changed the situation, not by voluntaristically dissolving the obligation of the norm that we are not to kill the innocent, but by creating conditions in which the object and hence moral species of Abraham's chosen act was *not* killing the innocent but executing God's justice.[15]

St. Thomas, therefore, affirms the truth of moral absolutes, namely, natural law precepts proscribing acts specified as morally bad by reason of their "objects," i.e., the intelligible subject matter upon which the will's act of choice bears. Among such absolutes are those proscribing the deliberate killing of the innocent, adultery, theft, and fornication.[16] Thus, when he encountered the view of the commentator on Aristotle's *Nicomachean Ethics*, whom we know only as the "Old Scholiast," that adultery (sexual union with a tyrant's wife in this case) is morally permissible when done to save a nation from tyranny, St. Thomas immediately replies: "The Commentator is not to be followed in this; one ought not commit adultery for the sake of any good whatsoever."[17]

As already noted, Janssens and McCormick appeal to a passage in the *Quaestiones Quodlibetales* to prove that Aquinas taught that it is morally right to intend a lesser nonmoral evil for the sake of a greater nonmoral good. They claim that in this passage he teaches that in some circumstances the nonmoral disvalue attached to some kinds of actions (e.g., killing), while remaining, is nonetheless justified by "outweighing circumstances."[18] But in the passage to which they appeal, St. Thomas expressly says that, when the circumstances make the act right — and circumstances *can* change the moral species of an act *if and only if* they enter into the very "object" chosen[19] — the disorder or deformity of the act, rather than remaining as a "nonmoral evil," is *totally taken away*: it is no longer present, so that it cannot be cancelled out by "outweighing" circumstances.[20] To put it another way, the act includes no "nonmoral" evil that is counterbalanced by some greater nonmoral good. Its intelligible content — what is chosen — is something good, not bad.

He illustrates this by referring to killing in self-defense. In legitimate self-defense, the "object" of choice is not something evil but something good: the protection of one's own life from unprovoked attack. The act that one chooses is not an act of killing but an act properly and legitimately called an "act of self-defense." The death of the assailant, while foreseen, is not properly what one is setting out to do: it is not the "object" of one's choice. Rather, it is an unavoidable effect of the chosen act of self-defense, but an effect that is not directly and deliberately willed. More significantly, in the very same text St. Thomas says that there are some kinds of human acts that "have deformity inseparably annexed to them, such as fornication, adultery, and others of this sort, which can in no way be done morally."[21] Apparently, this passage in the text escaped the notice of Janssens and McCormick, for they do not mention it. Yet it is a passage in which St. Thomas affirms what they deny: the truth of moral absolutes and the intrinsic evil of certain sorts of human acts as specified by their moral objects.

The presentation here makes it clear that St. Thomas, despite the claims of revisionist theologians, clearly taught that there are moral absolutes. His thought can be summarized as follows:

1. He teaches that there are acts that are "evil in themselves in their kind" (*secundum se mala ex genere*), which may never be done "for any good" (*pro nulla utilitate*), "in no way" (*nullo modo*), "in no event" (*in nullo casu*) — and gives examples of such acts in morally neutral terms: killing the innocent,[22] committing adultery in order to overthrow tyranny,[23] "putting forth falsehood."[24]
2. He teaches that besides affirmative precepts (which bind generally, *semper*, but not universally, *ad semper*), there are negative precepts which are valid and binding always and universally (*semper et ad semper*), e.g., "at no time is one to steal or commit adultery."[25]
3. He everywhere rejects arguments attempting to solve "conflict" cases by identifying a state of affairs or effect that could seem to be a lesser evil (*minus malum*) than doing an act that is wicked in itself of its kind (*secundum se malum ex genere*).[26]
4. He teaches that it is a revealed truth that evil may not be done for the sake of good, even the highest and greatest good such as salvation.[27]
5. He teaches, as we have seen, that the precepts of the Decalogue, most of which are negative and binding always and universally (*semper et ad semper*) are, when properly understood, subject to no exceptions whatsoever, even by divine dispensation.[28]

The conclusion is evident: St. Thomas affirmed the truth of moral absolutes.

Notes for Appendix I to Chapter Four

1. See St. Thomas, *Summa theologiae*, 1-2, 100, 8.

2. Charles E. Curran, "Absolute Norms in Moral Theology," in his *A New Look at Christian Morality* (Notre Dame, IN: Fides, 1968), p. 83; Louis Janssens, "Ontic Evil and Moral Evil," *Louvain Studies* 4 (1972), 115-156; John Dedek, "Intrinsically Evil Acts: An Historical Study of the Mind of St. Thomas," *Thomist* 43 (1979), 385-413; Richard M. Gula, *Reason Informed by Faith: Foundations of Catholic Morality* (New York: Paulist Press, 1989), p. 292.

For a critique of Dedek, see Patrick Lee, "Permanence of the Ten Commandments: St. Thomas and His Modern Commentators," *Theological Studies* 42 (1981), 422-443. For a critique of Janssens, see William E. May, "Aquinas and Janssens on the Moral Meaning of Human Acts," *Thomist* 48 (1984), 566-606.

3. E.g., Dedek, "Intrinsically Evil Acts," 408-409.

4. E.g., Richard A. McCormick, *Notes on Moral Theology: 1965-1980* (Lanham, MD: University Press of America, 1981), pp. 582-584, 767, no. 52. See Franz Scholz, "Problems on Norms Raised by Ethical Borderline Situations," in *Readings in Moral Theology, No. 1: Moral Norms and the Catholic Tradition*, ed. Charles E. Curran and Richard A. McCormick (New York: Paulist Press, 1978), pp. 164-165. Revisionist theologians constantly appeal to the passage in *Summa theologiae*, 1-2, 94, 4, where St. Thomas speaks of norms that "valent ut in pluribus" but are subject to exceptions "ut in paucioribus."

5. Janssens, "Ontic Evil and Moral Evil," 125-126.

6. The text in question is *Quaestiones Quodlibetales*, 9, q. 7, a. 2. Janssens, "Norms and Priorities in a Love Ethic," *Louvain Studies* 6 (1978), 232; McCormick, "Moral Theology Since Vatican II: Clarity or Chaos?" *Cross Currents* 29 (Spring, 1979), 21.

7. *Summa theologiae*, 1-2, 1, 3, ad 3; see *In II Sent.*, d. 40, q. 1, a. 2, ad 4.

8. *Summa theologiae*, 2-5, 64, 6.

9. Ibid., 2-2, 64, 2, on execution of criminals as an act of justice; and 64, 7, on self-defense. Note that in 64, 7, Thomas says that if a private person deliberately intends the death of the assailant, the act, in its moral species, is changed from an act of self-defense into an immoral act of killing.

10. Ibid., 1-2, 18, entire question.

11. Ibid., 1-2, 18, 1-3.

12. Ibid., 1-2, 18, 7c and ad 3.

13. Ibid., 1-2, 20, 2.

14. Ibid., 1-2, 100, 8.

15. For a detailed examination of relevant texts from St. Thomas on this matter, see Lee, "The Permanence of the Ten Commandments."

16. On killing the innocent, *Summa theologiae*, 2-2, 64, 6; on adultery, ibid., 2-2, 154, 8; on theft, ibid., 2-2, 64, 5 and 6; on fornication, ibid., 2-2, 154, 2.

17. *De Malo*, q. 15, a. 1, ad 15.

18. Janssens, "Norms and Priorities in a Love Ethic," 232; McCormick, "Moral Theology since Vatican II: Clarity or Chaos?" 21.

19. On this, see *Summa theologiae*, 1-2, 18, 10.

20. *Quaestiones Quodlibetales*, 9, q. 7, a. 2: "aliae circumstaritiae possunt supervenire ita honestantes actum, quod *praedictae inordinationes totaliter evacuuntur.*"

21. Ibid.: "quaedam enim sunt quae habent deformitatem inseparabiliter annexam, ut fornicatio, adulterium, et alia huiusmodi, *quae nullo modo bene fieri possent.*"

22. *Summa theologiae*, 2-2, 64, 6.

23. *De Malo*, q. 15,a. 1, ad 5.

24. *Summa theologiae*, 2-2, 69, 2.

25. *Ad Romanos*, c. 13, lect. 2; cf. *In III Sent.*, d. 25, q. 2, a. 1b. ad 3; *In IV Sent.*, d. 17, q. 3, a. 1d, ad 3; *De Malo*, q. 7, a. 1, ad 8; *Summa theologiae*, 2-2, 33, 2; 79, 3, ad 3.

26. *In IV Sent.*, d. 6, q. 1, qua. 1, a. 1, ad 4; *Summa theologiae*, 2-2, 110, 3, ad 4; 3, 68, 11, ad 3; 80, 6, ad 2.

27. *Summa theologiae*, 3, 68, 11, ad 3.

28. Ibid., 1-2, 100, 8; *In III Sent.*, d. 37, q. 1, a. 4.

APPENDIX II TO CHAPTER FOUR

Pope John Paul II and Moral Absolutes

Toward the end of the third chapter of *Veritatis splendor*, in reminding his brother bishops of his and their responsibilities as pastors, John Paul II identifies the "teaching which represents the central theme of this Encyclical," the teaching being restated "with the authority of the Successor of Peter." This is the teaching that reaffirms "*the universality and immutability of the moral commandments*, particularly those which prohibit always and without exception *intrinsically evil acts*" (no. 115).

Here I will present and comment on the teaching of *Veritatis splendor* on the question of intrinsically evil acts and, corresponding to them, absolute or exceptionless moral norms. I will do so by examining John Paul II's teaching on (1) the moral specification of human acts; (2) the criteria for assessing their moral goodness or badness and the truth that moral absolutes, by excluding intrinsically evil acts, protect the inviolable dignity of human persons and point the way toward fulfillment in Christ; and (3) his repudiation of those ethical theories that reject moral absolutes and the notion of intrinsically evil acts as understood by the Catholic tradition. I will conclude by reflecting on the infallibility of the teaching found in *Veritatis splendor*. But before looking at his teaching on the moral specification of human acts, it is important to point out — as noted already in Chapter One — that John Paul II clearly recognizes that freedom of choice is the existential principle of our moral life, and that human acts, precisely insofar as they are freely chosen, "give moral definition to the very person who performs them, determining his *profound spiritual traits*" (*Veritatis splendor*, no. 71; cf. no. 61). It is therefore crucially important to be able to determine, before we freely choose to do something, whether or not the proposed action is morally good. We need to know how human acts are morally specified and the criteria for determining their moral character.

1. The Moral Specification of Human Acts

Pope John Paul II is explicitly concerned with the specification of human acts and the criteria for assessing their moral goodness or badness in the fourth part of Chapter Two of *Veritatis splendor*. After repudiating some contemporary ethical theories, which he identifies as types of "teleologism," as utterly inadequate (and I shall return to this issue below), the Holy Father emphasizes that "*the morality of the human act depends primarily and fundamentally on the 'object' rationally chosen by the deliberate will"* (no. 78, with explicit reference to St. Thomas, *Summa theologiae*, 1-2, 18, 6). Then, in a very important passage well summarizing the Catholic tradition as expressed by St. Thomas, John Paul II writes as follows:

> In order to be able to grasp the object of an act which specifies that act morally, it is therefore necessary to place oneself *in the perspective of the acting person.* The object of the act of willing is in fact a freely chosen kind of behavior. To the extent that it is in conformity with the order of reason, it is the cause of the goodness of the will; it perfects us moral-ly. . . . By the object of a given moral act, then, one cannot mean a pro-cess or an event of the merely physical order, to be assessed on the basis of its ability to bring about a given state of affairs in the outside world. Rather, that object is the proximate end of a deliberate decision which determines the act of willing on the part of the acting person [no. 78].

The "object" of a human act, in other words, is the subject matter with which it is concerned — it is an intelligible proposal that one can adopt by choice and execute externally. For instance, the "object" of an act of adultery is having intercourse with someone who is not one's spouse or with the spouse of another. This is *what* adultery is.

With this understanding of the "object" of a human act in mind, it is easy to grasp John Paul II's conclusion, namely, that *"One must reject the thesis*, char-acteristic of teleological and proportionalist theories, *which holds that it is im-possible to qualify as morally evil according to its species — its 'object' — the deliberate choice of certain kinds of behavior or specific acts, apart from consideration of the intention for which the choice is made or the totality of the foreseeable consequences of that act for all persons concerned"* [no. 79; cf. no. 82].

2. The Criteria for Assessing the Moral Goodness or Badness of Human Acts

With this understanding of the "object" of a human act in mind, it is also easy to grasp the pope's argument, which he himself summarizes by saying: "Reason attests that there are objects of the human act which are by their nature 'incapable of being ordered' to God *because they radically contradict the good of the person made in his image"* (no. 80; emphasis added).

I added emphasis to the last passage cited from *Veritatis splendor* because here the Holy Father is referring to the moral criteria or *truths* that enable us to determine whether a proposed "object" of human choice is morally good or bad. As we saw earlier, in discussing John Paul II's understanding of natural law, he had emphasized that we can love our neighbor only by cherishing and respecting the good of our neighbor, which we do by cherishing and respecting the *goods* perfective of him. As noted earlier, in Chapter Two, John Paul II insists that "the different commandments of the Decalogue are really only so many reflections on the one commandment about the good of the person, at the level of the many different goods which characterize his identity as a spiritual and bodily being in relationship with God, with his neighbor, and with the material world. . . . The commandments of which Jesus reminds the young man are meant to safeguard *the good* of the person, the image of God, by protecting his *goods*" (no. 13). John Paul II, as we have also already seen, affirms that the negative precepts of the Decalogue — "You shall not murder; you shall not commit adultery; you shall not steal; you shall not bear false witness" — "express with particular force the ever urgent need to protect human life, the communion of persons in marriage," and the like (no. 13).

The human acts, specified by their objects, which the Catholic tradition has always recognized as intrinsically evil, are excluded by negative precepts forbidding us to adopt by free choice proposals to damage, destroy, or impede the goods of human persons. These precepts do not, moreover, say that it is wrong to act contrary to a virtue — e.g., to "kill unjustly" or "engage in unchaste intercourse." Rather, these precepts exclude, without exception as the pope reminds us (cf. nos. 52, 67, 76, 82), "specific," "concrete," "particular" *kinds of behavior* (cf. nos. 49, 52, 70, 77, 79, 82) as specified by the object of human choice. Those kinds of behavior — e.g., doing something to bring about the death of an innocent person or engaging in sexual intercourse despite the fact that at least one of the parties is married — are excluded by the relevant negative moral precept without first being identified by their opposition to virtue.

As John Paul II explains, "negative moral precepts . . . prohibiting certain concrete actions or kinds of behavior as intrinsically evil" (no. 67) protect the dignity of the person and are required by love of neighbor as oneself (nos. 13, 50-52, 67, 99). Intrinsically evil acts violate (cf. no. 75) and "radically contradict" (no. 80) "the good of the person, at the level of the many different goods which characterize his identity as a spiritual and bodily being in relationship with God, with his neighbor and with the material world" (no. 13; cf. nos. 78-80). It is impossible, the pope explains, to respect the good of persons without respecting the goods intrinsic to them, "the goods . . . indicated by the natural law as goods to be pursued" (no. 67), the " 'personal goods' . . . safeguarded by the commandments, which, according to Saint Thomas, contain the whole natural law" (no. 79; cf. nos. 43, 72, 78). John Paul II emphasizes that "the primordial moral requirement of loving and respecting the person as an end and never as a mere means also implies, by its very nature, respect for fundamental goods," among which is bodily life (no. 48; cf. no. 50).

3. Moral Absolutes Protect the Inviolable Dignity of Human Persons and Point the Way Toward Fulfillment in Christ

The great truth that absolute moral norms proscribing intrinsically evil acts, "valid always and for everyone, with no exception," is obviously, as John Paul II emphasizes, crucial for the defense of inviolable human rights (no. 97). The Holy Father writes: "These norms in fact represent the unshakable foundation and solid guarantee of a just and peaceful human coexistence, and hence of genuine democracy, which can come into being and develop only on the basis of the equality of all its members, who possess common rights and duties. *When it is a matter of the moral norms prohibiting intrinsic evil, there are no privileges or exceptions for anyone*" (no. 96). The denial of intrinsically evil acts and moral absolutes excluding them leads to the surrendering of the inviolable rights of human persons, rights that must be recognized and respected if society is to be decent.

John Paul II recognizes "the cost of suffering and grave sacrifice . . . which fidelity to the moral order can demand" (no. 93). Nonetheless, he is at pains to point out that the discernment which the Church exercises regarding the "teleologisms" "is not limited to denouncing and refuting them," because they lead to a denial of absolute moral norms proscribing intrinsically evil acts. Rather, in making this discernment, the Church, in a positive way, "seeks, with great love, to help all the faithful to form a moral conscience which will make judgments and lead to decisions in accordance with the truth," ultimately with the truth revealed in Jesus (no. 85). For it is precisely "*in the Crucified Christ that the Church finds the answer*" to the question as to why we must obey "universal and unchanging moral norms" (no. 85). These norms are binding precisely because they protect the inviolable dignity of the human person, whom we are to love with the love of Christ, a self-sacrificial love ready to suffer evil rather than do it.

John Paul II illustrates this great truth by appealing to the witness of martyrs. "The unacceptability of 'teleological,' 'consequentialist,' and 'proportionalist' ethical theories, which deny the existence of negative moral norms regarding specific kinds of behavior, norms which are valid without exception, is confirmed in a particularly eloquent way by Christian martyrdom" (no. 90). The pope then goes on to cite examples: Susanna in the Old Testament, who was ready to suffer death rather than to commit adultery; John the Baptist in the New Testament, who suffered death in witnessing to Herod "the law of the Lord" regarding marriage; and others from the New Testament, not least Jesus himself (no. 93). John Paul points out that "martyrdom, accepted as an affirmation of the inviolability of the moral order, bears splendid witness both to the holiness of God's law and to the inviolability of the personal dignity of man, created in God's image and likeness" (no. 92). Indeed, he continues, "martyrdom rejects as false and illusory whatever 'human meaning' one might claim to attribute, even in 'exceptional' conditions, to an act morally evil in itself. Indeed, it even more clearly unmasks the true face of such an act: *it is a violation of man's 'humanity,'* in the one perpetrating it even before the one enduring it" (no. 92, with a reference to *Gaudium et spes,* no. 27).

Absolute moral norms proscribing always and everywhere acts intrinsically evil by reason of the object of moral choice — to damage, destroy, or impede fundamental goods of human persons — point the way to fulfillment in Christ, the Crucified One who, as Vatican Council II instructs us, "fully discloses man to himself and unfolds his noble calling by revealing the mystery of the Father and the Father's love" (no. 2, with a citation from *Gaudium et spes,* no. 22). "The Crucified Christ" — who gives to us the final answer why we must, if we are to be fully the beings God wants us to be, forbear doing the evil proscribed by absolute moral norms — "reveals the authentic meaning of freedom: he lives it fully in the total gift of himself and calls his disciples to share in his freedom" (no. 85). In a singularly important passage, John Paul II then writes:

> Human freedom belongs to us as creatures; it is a freedom which is given as a gift, one to be received like a seed and to be cultivated responsibly. It is an essential part of that creaturely image which is the basis of the dignity of the person. Within that freedom there is an echo of the primordial vocation whereby the Creator calls man to the true Good, and even more, through Christ's Revelation, to become his friend and to share his own divine life. It is at once inalienable self-possession and openness to all that exists, in passing beyond self to knowledge and love of the other (cf. *Gaudium et spes,* no. 24). Freedom is then rooted in the truth about man, and it is ultimately directed towards communion [no. 86].

As Jesus reveals to us, "freedom is acquired in *love,* that is, in the *gift of self* . . . the gift of self *in service to God and one's brethren*" (no. 87). This is the ultimate truth meant to guide free choices: to love, even as we have been and are loved by God in Christ, whose "crucified flesh fully reveals the unbreakable bond between freedom and truth, just as his Resurrection from the dead is the supreme exaltation of the fruitfulness and saving power of a freedom lived out in truth" (no. 87).

In teaching these absolute norms, the Church is by no means rigoristic or unrealistic. It is simply reminding us of our dignity as human persons and of the dignity we are called to give to ourselves, through our free choices, with the help of God's grace: the dignity of persons who love even as God loves us in the Crucified Jesus. Moreover, in our struggle to live worthily as beings made in God's image and called to communion with him, we are not alone. We can live as God wills us to because he is ever ready to help us with his grace. As the pope reminds us, God never commands the impossible: "Temptations can be overcome, sins can be avoided, because together with the commandments the Lord gives us the possibility of keeping them" (no. 102). This truth, John Paul II recalls, is a matter of Catholic faith. The Council of Trent, he points out, solemnly condemned the view "that the commandments of God are impossible of observance by the one who is justified. For God does not command the impossible, but in commanding he admonishes you to do what you can and to pray for what you cannot, and he gives his aid to enable you" (no. 102, citing from the Council of Trent, Session VI, Decree on Justification, *Cum Hoc Tempore*, ch. 2, DS 1536; cf. Canon 18, DS 1568).

The truth that there are intrinsically evil acts and, corresponding to them, absolute norms admitting of no exceptions, is in no way opposed to human freedom and dignity. To the contrary, it is rooted in the inviolable dignity of the human person made in the image and likeness of God and called, like God himself, to be absolutely innocent of evil, to be unwilling to set his heart, his will, his choice on the doing of evil, i.e., on damaging, destroying, or impeding the goods perfective of human persons. This is the truth to which the martyrs and, above all, the Crucified Christ bear witness. Moreover, with the help of God's never-failing grace, we can indeed forbear the doing of evil.

4. The Incoherence of Ethical Theories Denying the Existence of Intrinsically Evil Acts and Absolute Moral Norms

In the fourth part of Chapter Two of *Veritatis splendor*, in discussing the human act, John Paul II clearly distinguishes between what he calls "teleology" and "teleologism." He affirms that "the moral life has an essentially *teleological character*, since it consists in the deliberate ordering of human acts to God, the supreme good and ultimate end (*telos*) of man" (no. 73). But he contrasts teleology with "*teleologism*": "Certain *ethical theories*," he writes, "called '*teleological*,' claim to be concerned for the conformity of human acts with the ends pursued by the agent and with the values intended by him. The criteria for evaluating the moral rightness of an action are drawn from the *weighing of the nonmoral or premoral goods* to be gained and the corresponding nonmoral or premoral values to be respected. For some, concrete behavior would be right or wrong according to whether or not it is capable of producing a better state of affairs for all concerned. Right conduct would be the one capable of 'maximizing' goods and 'minimizing' evils" (no. 74).

One type of "teleologism" identified by the pope — "consequentialism" — "claims to draw the criteria of the rightness of a given way of acting solely from a calculation of the foreseeable consequences stemming from a given choice." Another variant — "proportionalism" — "by weighing the various values and goods being sought, focuses rather on the proportion acknowledged between the good and bad effects of that choice, with a view to the 'greater good' or 'lesser evil' actually possible in a particular situation" (no. 75). Those holding these theories claim that it is impossible to determine whether an act traditionally regarded as intrinsically evil (e.g., direct abortion) would really be morally evil until one has considered, in the concrete situation, the "premoral" good and evil state of affairs it is likely to cause. They conclude that the foreseeable proportions of "premoral" goods to evils in the alternatives available can at times justify exceptions to precepts traditionally regarded as absolute (cf. no. 75).

John Paul II firmly rejects these theories, declaring that they "are not faithful to the Church's teaching, when they believe that they can justify, as morally good, deliberate choices of kinds of behavior contrary to the commandments of the divine and natural law" (no. 76). He affirms that this way of evaluating human acts "is not an adequate method for determining whether the choice of that concrete kind of behavior is 'according to its species' or 'in itself' good or bad, licit or illicit," because "everyone recognizes the difficulty, or rather the impossibility, of evaluating all the good and evil consequences and effects — defined as pre-moral — of one's own acts" (no. 77).

Here the Holy Father draws attention to the insuperable problem facing advocates of proportionalism and consequentialism: there is no coherent way of "weighing" "premoral" goods and evils. This is a matter that was fully discussed in the text of Chapter Four.

5. The Infallibility of the Teaching Found in *Veritatis Splendor*

John Paul II nowhere in his encyclical introduces the subject of infallibility. However, he teaches elsewhere that the truth of absolute moral norms always and everywhere proscribing intrinsically evil acts is a revealed truth. He repudiates consequentialism and proportionalism not only because they are philosophically and theologically flawed moral theories, but also, and more importantly, because they are *opposed to divine revelation and to the definitive teaching of the Church*. He reminds us that "the faithful are obliged to acknowledge and respect the specific moral precepts declared and taught by the Church in the name of

God, the Creator and Lord" (no. 76), and in reminding us of this he refers explicitly to the solemn teaching of the Council of Trent (cf. footnote 127 in no. 76 of the encyclical, where John Paul II refers to the Council of Trent, Decree on Justification, *Cum Hoc Tempore,* Canon 19, DS 1569; he also refers to the teaching of Clement XI, constitution *Unigenitus Dei Filius* [September 8, 1713] against the Errors of Paschasius Quesnel, nos. 53-56, DS 2453-2456). Later on, he says that "in teaching the existence of intrinsically evil acts, the Church accepts the teaching of Sacred Scripture" (no. 81). He then cites two texts from St. Paul, Romans 3:8 and 1 Corinthians 6:9-10. He refers to the text from Romans, first in a citation from St. Thomas (no. 78, with reference to St. Thomas's *In Duo Praecepta Caritatis et in Decem Legis Praecepta. De Dilectione Dei: Opuscula Theologica,* II, No. 1168, ed. Taurinen [1954], 250), then in the heading to numbers 79-83, and finally in a citation from *Humanae vitae* (no. 14), where Pope Paul VI taught that "it is never lawful, even for the gravest reasons, to do evil that good may come of it (cf. Rom 3:8)" (no. 80). And toward the close of his discussion of intrinsically evil acts in the fourth part of Chapter Two, the Holy Father points out: "The doctrine of the object as a source of morality represents an authentic explication of the Biblical morality of the Covenant and of the commandments" (no. 82).

As Germain Grisez has said, John Paul II's appeal "is to God's authority in revealing, which is the source of the Church's infallibility in believing and the Magisterium's authority in teaching." Grisez goes on to say that "theologians who have been dissenting from the doctrine reaffirmed in this encyclical now have only three choices: to admit that they have been mistaken, to admit that they do not believe God's word, or to claim that the pope is grossly misinterpreting the Bible." He concludes by writing: "In claiming that the received teaching concerning intrinsically evil acts is a revealed truth, the pope also implicitly asserts that it is definable. That implicit assertion will be denied by those rejecting the teaching. This argument is definitely over essentials, and cannot long go unresolved. . . . Only the Magisterium's definitive judgment will settle it" (Germain Grisez, "Revelation versus Dissent," *The Tablet* [October 16, 1993], 1331).

CHAPTER FIVE

Sin and the Moral Life

According to Christian faith, Christ came to save us from sin, and through participating in his redemptive death and resurrection we "die" to sin and rise to a new kind of life as members of the divine family, as adopted brothers and sisters of God's Eternal Word.

But what is sin, and how does it affect our moral life? The purpose of this chapter is to present in some depth the meaning of *personal* sin. Thus, it will not be concerned with the reality of original sin, the sin that affects our lives as children of Adam and as a result of which concupiscence has entered into the human heart.[1] The major concerns of this chapter, therefore, are with (1) the core meaning of sin, (2) the distinction between mortal and venial sin and the basis of this distinction, and (3) the effect of sin on our moral life.

1. The Core Meaning of Sin

The central meaning of sin is set forth in the Scriptures and in the Catholic theological tradition. I shall first examine the teaching of the Scriptures on sin and then discuss the understanding of sin in the Catholic theological tradition.

A. The Biblical Understanding of Sin[2]

The story of the "fall" of Adam and Eve in Genesis (3:1-14) is a dramatic portrayal of the reality of sin and its essential features. Our protoparents deliberately violate a known precept of God (Gn 3:3-6). Their outward act of disobedience is an expression of their inner act of rebellion; they are moved to sin partially by suspicion about God's love for them, partially by frustration over the limits to their liberty imposed by God's precept, and partially by desire for the immediate good, "knowledge of good and evil," promised by the performance of the sinful act. Their rebellious deed harms them (Gn 3:7) and alienates them from God, from one another, and from themselves (Gn 3:8-24). Faced with their sin, they try in vain to defend themselves with specious rationalizations (Gn 3:8-15), but nothing they can do can prevent the disastrous effects of their sin (Gn 3:14-24).

The idea that sin is a perverse revolt against God, so dramatically set forth in the story of the Fall, is central to the Old Testament's understanding of sin. The Old Testament consistently regards sin as a wicked rebellion against the Lord (Nm 14:9; Dt 28:15), a contemptuous spurning of God (2 Sm 12:10; Is 1:4; 43:24; Mi 4:6). When seen from the perspective of God's covenant with his people, sin is recognized as an act of unfaithfulness and adultery (Is 24:5; 48:8; Jer 3:20; 9:1; Ez 16:59; Hos 3:l).[3] When viewed from the perspective of divine wisdom, sin is branded "foolishness" (Dt 32:6; Is 29:11; Prv 1:7). Seen from the perspective of God's holiness, sin is an "abomination" (Lv 16:16; 18:26; Jgs 20:6).

In some passages — for instance, that telling of Uzzah's death for reaching out to touch the ark of the covenant (2 Sm 6:6-7) — sin is somewhat primitively described as the violation, however unintended, of a taboo. But this way of conceiving sin in the Old Testament is very rare. The consistent teaching of the Old Testament is that sin is rooted in human freedom and consists in an abuse of God's gift of free choice (Sir 15:11-20). Sin springs from the "heart" of a person, and as such is an act involving a personal, inner, and enduring wrong (1 Sm 16:7; Jer 4:4; Ez 11:19; Ps 51), a view of sin reaffirmed most clearly in the New Testament (Mt 7:20-23 and par.).

Both Testaments use a rich vocabulary to describe the reality and evil of sin. The three most common words used in the Old Testament to designate sin are *hāttā'*, *pesha'*, and *'awōn*. *Hāttā'*, which literally means "missing the mark," stresses that sin is a willful rejection of God's known will. *Pesha'*, meaning "rebellion," shows how, in sinning, human persons reject God and his love. *'Awōn*, meaning "iniquity" or "guilt," refers to the way sin twists and distorts the sinner's inner being. In the New Testament, the principal terms used to refer to sin are *harmatia* and *harmatēma*, *anomia*, *adikia*, and *skotos*. *Harmatia* and *harmatēma* are like the Old Testament *hāttā'*, and designate sin as a freely chosen deed casting aside God's loving norms for human life. *Anomia* or "lawlessness" was frequently used in the singular to stress that sin consists in a spirit of rebellion and contempt for God and his law. *Adikia*, "injustice," emphasizes that sin is a refusal to accept God and his reign revealed in Christ and to live in the justice that God has given. *Pseudos*, "falsehood," and *skotos*, "darkness," show that sin is an opposition to the truth of God, to Jesus Christ — who is the way, the truth, and the life — to one's fellowmen, and to the truth of being a human person.[4]

Psalm 51, the "Miserere," beautifully summarizes Old Testament thought on the reality and evil of sin. The first verses of this psalm — in which David prays for forgiveness of his sins of adultery with Bathsheba and of having her husband, Uriah, killed — draw together the Old Testament view of sin in a fascinating way. "Have mercy on me, O God, according to thy steadfast love; according to thy abundant mercy blot out my transgressions (*pesha'*). Wash me thoroughly from my iniquity (*'awōn*), and cleanse me from my sin (*hāttā' t*)!

For I know my transgressions (*pesha'*), and my sin (*ḥāṭṭā't*) is ever before me. Against thee, thee only, have I sinned (*ḥāṭṭā'*), and done that which is evil *(ra')* in thy sight" (Ps 51:1-4). Note how David uses all of the principal Old Testament words to identify his sin. By his sins of adultery and murder he had rebelled against God's precepts, deviated from the path they marked out, and made himself wicked and hateful to the Lord. Also note how David acknowledges that sin is a terrible evil precisely because it offends God ("Against thee, thee only, have I sinned"). In saying this, David in no way denies that his sins of adultery and murder were grave affronts to Uriah, but he is stressing that sin is essentially a base affront to God, whose holy will and loving plan for mankind — a will and plan concerned only with the true good of human persons (see Dt 6.24) — is the norm for human action. Finally, in this prayer of repentance David begs the Lord to create in him a new heart, to heal him of his sin (Ps 51:10). In so praying, he stresses another major biblical teaching on sin, namely, that only God can forgive sin and bring the sinner back to life.

The Scriptures understand sin to be essentially an offense against God. Nonetheless, sin does not hurt or harm God in his inner being, for God as the wholly transcendent One can in no way be harmed by the actions of his creatures. Rather, sin harms the sinner (Jb 35:6; Is 59:1-2; Jer 7:8, 19). Still, sin does wound God in his "image," i.e., in the human persons he has made to share in his life. Inasmuch as it is a refusal by sinners to let themselves be loved by God, sin in a certain sense, as the biblical scholar Stanislaus Lyonnet has observed, harms the "God who suffers from not being loved, whom love has, so to speak, rendered 'vulnerable.' "[5]

The New Testament takes up and deepens these Old Testament themes on the reality and evil of sin. Because of its more profound grasp of the loving intimacy that God wills to share with his children, the New Testament deepens the Old Testament understanding of sin as separation from God. The Father so loves us that he sends his only-begotten Son to be with us and for us, actively seeking to reconcile sinners with himself, loving sinners even while he is being repudiated by them. Thus, sin is seen as a refusal of the Father's love (Lk 15), a refusal rooted in the heart, in the free, self-determining choice of the sinner to reject God's offer of grace and friendship. Just as light and darkness have nothing in common, so neither do the life offered to us in Christ and the iniquity of sin (2 Cor 6:3; 1 Jn). Jesus and the devil, belief and unbelief, God and idols are absolutely opposed; so, too, are uprightness and iniquity (2 Cor 6:15-16).

In the New Testament, the concept of sin is closely linked to the concept of conversion. Jesus begins his public life by calling people to repentance (Mk 1:4, 15; Mt 3:7-10; Lk 3:7). As the biblical scholar Johannes Bauer observes, "this presupposes that the men to whom [Jesus' preaching] is addressed have already *turned away* from God. It is precisely in this turning away from God that sin consists. It is disobedience to God (Lk 15:21) and lawlessness (Mt 7:23; 13:41)."[6] Just as we turn to God and cleave to him through the act of conversion, so by sinning we turn away from him.

Another point brought out in the New Testament teaching on sin is that we are lost and slaves to sin without God's help. Left to our own resources, we cannot live long without sin, for it is God who guides us on the path of righteousness (cf. Rom 1-5). If we abandon God through sin, we are like the prodigal son and the lost sheep in the parable of Luke's gospel (Lk 15). But God is our Friend, our Savior, our Redeemer. The very name *Jesus* means salvation, for he is the one sent by the Father to redeem us and to reconcile us to the Father.

The New Testament, in particular the Pauline and Johannine traditions, frequently tends to shift focus from individual sinful acts (*harmatiai, harmatēmata* in the plural) to sin as such *(hē harmatia, hē adikia, hē anomia,* in the singular). According to the gospel of John, Christ has come to take away the *sin* of the world (Jn 1:29; see also 1 Jn 3:5). As Bauer puts it:

> Jesus takes all the sins — that is, the debt of sin — upon himself in order to lead the world home from its state of separation from God. In John the nature of sin as a state of being sundered from God finds its clearest expression. Jesus, who is one with God, is *without* sin (Jn 8:46). He is the light, and the sinners are darkness (Jn 3:19). He is always heard by God, whereas God does not hearken to sinners (9:31). For this reason John refers to sin simply as *anomia* (lawlessness, godlessness) (1 Jn 3:4), that which places man in constant opposition to the will of God. . . . The gospel [of John] has the same message to convey (8:34): The sinner is a son of Satan: "You are of your father, the devil" (8.44).[7]

The same is true of the Pauline literature. Paul treats sin not only as an act but as the common human condition. Without excusing anyone — for sin is a deliberate, willful act — he presents a world in which sin reigns and is overcome only by the reign of Christ and complete submission to him (Rom 5-8). Paul sees in sin a power that has entered into human persons by their voluntary submission to it, ruling in their "flesh" as a kind of pseudo-law. In short, while it in no way minimizes the evil of sinful actions, the New Testament stresses that sin is the unitary reality of one's state of alienation from God, a state brought into being by the individual's many wicked deeds. Sins are sins because they give rise to, prolong, and express life apart from God. The good news of the gospel is that God himself has come to visit his people, to call them to conversion, to reconcile them to himself. He does this by the death-resurrection of Jesus, a saving act in which all men can share by dying to sin in baptism and rising to a new kind of life made possible by God's only-begotten Son's redemptive deed and by the gift of the Holy Spirit, who will be with this re-created people, to lead them along a path of righteousness and honor.[8]

B. The Understanding of Sin in the Catholic Theological Tradition

One way of grasping the understanding of sin in the Catholic theological tradition is to begin with St. Augustine's famous definitions of sin and reflect on them in the light of what St. Thomas, other theologians, and the magisterium have had to say about this subject matter. Two definitions of sin advanced by St. Augustine have become classic. The first says that sin is "anything said, done, or desired contrary to the eternal law."[9] The second defines sin as a "turning away from God and a turning toward the creature."[10]

Some contemporary theologians do not look too favorably on Augustine's first definition of sin. The attitude common to many theologians today is reflected in the following passage from Philip S. Keane, S.S.: "Many traditional moral textbooks defined sin as the breaking of God's eternal law. Moral theologians today do not dispute the fact that we humans need laws or rules, nor do they dispute the fact that when sin takes place, laws are very often broken. What moral theologians do question today is whether lawbreaking should be understood as the most central or formal element in the definition of sin. A very significant percentage of moral theologians [today] would assert that it is inadequate to hold that the essence of sin is breaking God's law."[11]

Evidently, Keane and the theologians whose ideas he articulates (Curran, Häring, McCormick, and others) fear that this Augustinian definition of sin is, or at least seems to be, too "legalistic," insofar as it sees sin as basically the infraction of some externally imposed norm. And the repudiation of "legalism" by these theologians is quite justified. Moral principles and norms are not arbitrary rules imposed upon human liberty: they are, rather, *truths* in whose light good choices can be made. But if we keep in mind the traditional Catholic understanding of "law" as a wise and loving ordering of human persons to the goods — and the Good — perfective of them, we can see the good sense of this Augustinian definition of sin.

Here it is worth recalling the teaching of Vatican Council II that was reviewed in Chapters Two and Three. There we saw that the Council Fathers, recapitulating the thought of Augustine, Thomas, and others, taught that "the highest norm of human life is the divine law — eternal, objective, and universal — whereby God orders, directs, and governs the entire universe and all the ways of the human community by a plan conceived in wisdom and love." Continuing, the Council said, "Man has been made by God to participate in this law, with the result that, under the gentle disposition of divine providence, he can come to perceive ever more increasingly the unchanging truth" (*Dignitatis humanae*, no. 3; cf. *Gaudium et spes*, nos. 16-17). We saw further, in Chapter Three, that the natural law is the way in which human persons "participate" in God's divine and eternal law. Through the natural law, human persons come to an ever deeper understanding of what they are to do if they are to be fully the beings God wills them to be. In short, the eternal law is God's wise and loving plan for the good of human persons, and so great is his love and respect for them that he has made them able to share actively in his loving and wise plan so that they are not only ruled and measured by it but are inwardly capable of shaping their choices and actions in accordance with its truth.[12]

When "eternal law" is understood in this nonlegalistic way, we can understand how sin is, in essence, a morally evil act, i.e., a freely chosen act known to be contrary to the eternal law as this is made manifest in our conscience (*Dignitatis humanae*, no. 3; *Gaudium et spes*, no. 16). As morally evil, the freely chosen act is deprived of the goodness it can and ought to have.[13] As an evil or privation in the moral order, the sinful act blocks the fulfillment of human persons on every level of existence, harming and twisting the person in his or her depths (*Gaudium et spes*, no. 27), damaging human community, and rupturing the relationship that God wills should exist between himself and humankind (see *Gaudium et spes*, no. 13).

Understood as a freely chosen act of self-determination opposed to the eternal law, sin is an act deprived of the openness it can and ought to have to the full good of human persons, the good to which they are directed by God's eternal law, for, as St. Thomas has said so well, "God is not offended by us except in so far as we act against our own good."[14] Sin, in other words, is a deliberately chosen act known to violate the basic norm of human activity, namely, that such activity, "in accord with the divine plan and will, should harmonize with the authentic good of the human race, and allow men as individuals and as members of society to pursue their total vocation and fulfill it" (*Gaudium et spes*, no. 35).

God's eternal law, his wise and loving plan for leading human persons to their fulfillment, is known, in some measure at least, even by unbelievers, for its basic requirements are, as St. Paul taught, written in their hearts (Rom 1:18-22). Less metaphorically put, the requirements of God's eternal law are, as Vatican Council II clearly taught, made known to men and women through the mediation of conscience (*Dignitatis humanae*, no. 3; *Gaudium et spes*, nos. 16-17). Thus, a person who knowingly acts contrary to the truth made known in conscience always deviates from the loving plan of the eternal law and in this way offends and opposes God;[15] and, as St. Thomas says, it is precisely from the perspective of its nature as an offense against God that sin is considered in theology.[16] Indeed, St. Thomas held that even the unbaptized are able, by virtue of their power of self-determining free choice and with the help of God's unfailing grace, to accept God and his law of love or to repudiate him and his law in their first fully human act of self-determining free choice.[17]

In other words, it is right and proper to define sin as anything said, done, or desired contrary to the eternal law.[18] The substance or matter of the sin is the word, deed, or desire; what makes these to be *sin* — i.e., what constitutes the chosen word, deed, or desire as sinful — is the fact that the person, by freely choosing (willing) what he or she knows to be contrary to God's loving plan, gives to himself or herself the *identity* of one opposed to this loving plan — i.e., a sinner.

For the faithful, moreover, God's eternal law is made known not only through the mediation of conscience enlightened by reason but also through the mediation of the revealed and saving truth proclaimed by the Church and accepted in faith. Believers know, or ought to know, that their freely chosen immoral acts not only violate God's loving plan for human existence but also viciously repudiate his offer of life and love. Thus, sin, as an offense against God, takes on a special heinousness for the faithful: it is an act of ungrateful infidelity — and it is for this reason that the prophets regularly compared sin to adultery. By sinning, Christians exchange the life of freedom won for them by Christ for renewed death and slavery (cf. Rom 6 and Gal 5). In addition, since the Christian is irrevocably, for weal or woe, a member of Christ's body — the Church — by reason of baptism (cf. 1 Cor 6), there is an ecclesial element or aspect to every sin of a Christian: sin violates the Christian's responsibility to Christ and to the Church (cf. Rom 14:7-8; Gal 5:13 — 6:10).

The second Augustinian definition of sin as a "turning away from God and a turning toward a creature" brings out further dimensions of sin. This definition emphasizes that sin has a twofold aspect, one positive — the turning toward a creature — and the other negative or, more precisely, privative — the turning away from God. Nonetheless, because of the strong Neoplatonic influence on St. Augustine, this definition needs to be made more precise. Augustine did not, it can be argued, properly appreciate the intrinsic worth of created goods and the role they have to play in God's plan in fulfilling human persons. Unlike Aquinas — and, I should add, Vatican Council II (cf. *Gaudium et spes*, nos. 38-39) — who regarded such created goods as life, knowledge, beauty, and harmonious relationships with others and with God and the like as "ends" or "points" of human existence, subordinate, of course, to the Uncreated Good that God is,[19] Augustine seems to have looked upon such goods as mere "means" to the final end, God. God alone, who is the highest and incommutable good, was, for Augustine, to be "enjoyed"; all created goods, even those intrinsically perfective of human persons, were to be "used." Augustine's thought here, it seems to me and to others, needs to be corrected; the truth of his definition is better expressed if we say that sin is a turning away from God and an *inordinate* or *unmeasured* turning toward a creature.

The turning away from God, as already noted, is the privative aspect of sin, the aspect that makes the sinful choice to be evil or deprived of the goodness it can and ought to have. This same privative aspect was identified in the first Augustinian definition of sin as the violation of God's eternal law; here this privative aspect is specified as an aversion from God himself. The turning toward the creature is the positive element in the sin, for this designates the "good" that entices the sinner and makes the sinful alternative attractive and choosable.

This definition of sin is rich in meaning. No one, as St. Thomas observes, does evil purely for the sake of evil.[20] When we do things that we know are wicked and sinful, that we know are opposed to God's law of love, we are not acting irrationally, for we are seeking to participate in some appealing good. Again, as St. Thomas perceptively notes, the turning away from God and the setting aside of his law of love is not precisely what the sinner is setting out to do in sinning. It is not as though we say to ourselves, "I am going to harden my heart against God." The privative aspect of the sin, in other words, is not the final aim or point of our intentional action; our intent, at least in the sense of our ulterior end in acting, is rather the participation in some appealing good. Thus, the sinner need not "intend," in one of the senses of that term, to offend God and to turn aside from him.[21] The sinner may only be seeking to gratify himself.[22] He may, of course, be willing to turn away from God as a *means* to this gratification; and he surely "intends" to do what he knows is opposed to God's law of love as a *means* to the good in which he seeks to participate. And this is the precise point. The sinner's choice can and ought to be compatible with love of God; it can and ought to conform to the requirements of God's law, the law that directs us to love God above all else and to love our neighbor as ourselves. But the sinner chooses to act in a way he knows is not compatible with this kind of love. He recognizes that choosing to pursue this particular created good here and now necessarily demands that he close his heart, his person, to God's all-encompassing love. Because of this recognition, he realizes that his pursuit of this particular created good here and now means putting love for it ahead of his love for God and neighbor. It is in this way that the sinner "turns away" from God and puts in the place of God some created good.[23]

Reflection on these two Augustinian definitions of sin has revealed something of sin's significance as a contemptuous rebellion against God. But in order to grasp its reality and terrible evil more fully, some observations about the inner core of sin and its social and ecclesial dimensions are needed.

The core of the sinful act is the free, self-determining choice whereby the sinner gives to himself or herself a moral identity — that, namely, of a sinner.

As our Lord makes clear, sin flows from the heart, i.e., from the inner core of a person as a free and responsible being: "For from the heart come evil intentions: murder, adultery, fornication, theft, perjury, slander. These are the things that make a man unclean" (Mt 15:18-19). The external behavior flows from our free choice, and while the external behavior comes and goes, the *being* that we give to ourselves through the free, self-determining choice to engage in this behavior (e.g., adultery) abides within us as part of our identity, our character. As St. Thomas notes (and as we saw in Chapter Two), human action is immanent, not transitive; i.e., it abides within the agent either to fulfill or perfect the agent, if it is morally upright and in accord with God's loving plan, or to damage and harm the agent, if it is morally bad and sinful.[24] Because the inner core of sin is a free, self-determining choice that abides within the person, the reality of sin, traditionally termed the "guilt" or "stain" of sin, remains within the sinner.

In short, we make ourselves *to be* the persons we are by the choices that we freely make. In every sinful choice, we make ourselves to be sinners and guilty in the sight of the Lord.[25] This perduring of sin within the sinner is what is meant by the "state" of sin or condition of sinfulness. Jesus summons us to recognize our sinfulness and to have a change of heart, a *metanoia*, a conversion, which consists in a new self-determining choice whereby, in response to and with the help of God's unfailing and healing grace, we give to ourselves the identity of repentant sinners, of persons who have been reconciled to God. Sin persists in the being of the person who sins, and one morally evil commitment can lead to many morally wicked acts insofar as through the free choice to sin one has disposed oneself to act sinfully. To put this another way: Sin is not simply deviation in isolated pieces of external behavior; it is evil in the existential domain and extends to all that exists by or is affected by sinful choices.

In addition, when the sinner is a baptized person, there is, as was already noted, an "ecclesial" element in sin — the sinner's sin affects not just the sinner but the whole Church. Through baptism, we become one body with Jesus, members of his body, the Church. Thus, as St. Paul stressed so dramatically in 1 Corinthians 6, when a Christian has sex with a whore he joins to her not only his own body but the body of Christ as well; his sin is not only one of impurity but also one of defiling the Church. There is, thus, a sacrilegious aspect to the sinful choices of those who have, through baptism, become one body with Christ.

All this helps us to see the social significance of sin. The sinful choices of individuals, when tolerated and accepted by the society in which they live, soon become the practices of the society. They become embedded in its laws and customs, its way of life, its way of mediating reality to its people. Thus, it is right to consider sin social as well as personal. But we must keep in mind that every social sin originates in — and is perpetrated by — individual persons' sinful choices. Particular persons, as Pope John Paul II has emphasized, are responsible for initiating and maintaining such social evils as the oppression of minorities, unjust wars, the manipulation of communications, etc.[26]

Moreover, while sin is the result of the abuse by created persons of their gift of freedom, "deep within its human reality," Pope John Paul II has reminded us, "there are factors at work which place it beyond the merely human in the border area where man's conscience, will, and sensitivity are in contact with the dark forces which, according to St. Paul, are active in the world almost to the point of ruling it."[27] It is for this reason that only God, the one from whom we turn away in choosing to sin and the one whose loving law we freely choose to cast aside, can rescue us from this dread evil; and, in his mercy, he has chosen to do so by sending us his only-begotten Son who, by fully accepting our humanity and by his redemptive death-resurrection, has conquered sin and its power over us.

2. The Distinction Between Mortal and Venial Sin

The understanding of sin developed in the previous pages applies properly only to what the Catholic tradition has come to call "mortal" or deadly or grave sin (there is, as we shall see, some difficulty in restricting the definition of sin as "anything said, done, or desired contrary to the eternal law" to mortal sin). This understanding, in other words, is realized fully only in the sort of sin whereby human persons cleave inordinately to some created good to the point that they put this good in the place that God is to have in their hearts. It is the sort of sin whereby human persons truly rebel against God and die to divine life, to friendship with God, opposing themselves, by their own free and self-determining choice, to his love and his law.

But do human persons so oppose themselves to God in every immoral act? Common sense and the Catholic theological tradition hold that some immoral acts are not "mortally" sinful, i.e., so opposed to God's law and love that they destroy friendship between God and human persons. Such immoral acts are called "venial" sins, and the core meaning of sin as previously set forth applies to them only analogically. There is, in short, a basic distinction to be made between "mortal" and "venial" sins.

A. Biblical and Magisterial Sources for This Distinction

The Scriptures do not formally distinguish between mortal and venial sins, but both Testaments clearly bear witness to this distinction. The Old Testament required an expiatory offering for sins of human weakness and inadvertence (see Lv 4-5), but it taught that other sins are crimes against the covenant community and God. Atonement for such sins could not be made by an expiatory offering; these sins were punishable by death or by cutting the sinner off from the community (see Lv 7:25; 17:8-10, 14; 19:7-8). In the New Testament, Jesus sharply distinguishes between the "beam" in the hypocrite's eye and the "mote" in the eye of the hypocrite's brother (Mt 7:5), and it is evident that our Lord considers the hypocrite's sin far graver than the sin of the one whom the hypocrite criticizes. Moreover, in the prayer Jesus taught his disciples, he asks them to beg forgiveness for their daily "debts" or transgressions (Mt 6:12; Lk 11:4), while he threatens others with hell's fire for their sins (Mt 23:33). The epistles distinguish between the daily sins of which even those regenerated in baptism can be guilty and those offenses that exclude one from the kingdom of heaven (contrast Jas 3:2 and 1 Jn 1:8 with 1 Cor 6:9-10 and Gal 5:19-21). They also speak of sins that lead to death (Rom 6:16) and call for excommunication from the community (1 Cor 5:13).

Of special interest is a passage in 1 Corinthians in which St. Paul says that people build differently on the foundation that is Jesus Christ. Some build with gold, silver, and jewels, while others build with wood, hay, or straw. On judgment day, each one's work will be tested; one whose building burns because of its poor material can be saved, but only through fire. Others, however, have utterly destroyed God's temple by severing themselves from Jesus; they will be destroyed, not saved (1 Cor 3:10-17). This passage is of special interest because a long theological tradition, beginning with the Fathers and continuing through such medieval theologians as St. Bonaventure and St. Thomas Aquinas, considered it a source for the distinction between mortal and venial sin.[28]

The authoritative teaching of the magisterium also bears witness to the distinction between mortal and venial sin. The Council of Orange (A.D. 529), rejecting Pelagianism, taught that even the upright Christian is guilty of sin (DS 229-230). The Council of Trent in the sixteenth century taught that not all sins deprive one of God's grace; some are venial (DS 1537); the same Council required Catholics to seek the forgiveness of God and the Church through sacramental confession of all mortal sins of which they are aware, whereas such confession is not required of venial sins, although it is recommended (DS 1679-1681). This teaching of Trent on the distinction between mortal and venial sin was reaffirmed by the 1983 Synod of Bishops and by Pope John Paul II in his apostolic exhortation *Reconciliatio et Poenitentia*.

The observations of Pope John Paul II relative to the distinction between mortal and venial sin in this document need to be noted. He first summarizes the biblical testimony (as noted previously here) relevant to this distinction. He then provides a brief summary of the views of Augustine and Aquinas on the subject, and then concludes by saying:

With the whole tradition of the Church, we call mortal sin the act by which man freely and consciously rejects God, his law, the covenant of love that God offers, preferring to turn in on himself or to some created and finite reality, something contrary to the divine will (*conversio ad creaturam*). This can occur in a direct and formal way in the sins of idolatry, apostasy and atheism, or in an equivalent way as in every act of disobedience to God's commandments in a grave matter. Man perceives that this disobedience to God destroys the bond that unites him with his life principle. It is mortal sin, that is, an act which gravely offends God and ends in turning against man himself with a dark and powerful force of destruction.[29]

B. The Classical Theological Understanding of This Distinction

The classical theological understanding of the difference between mortal and venial sin has been articulated most fully and clearly by St. Thomas Aquinas. With the Fathers of the Church, he stressed that mortal sin is irreparable by human power — only God can save us from the spiritual death caused by mortal sin. Venial sin, on the other hand, can be healed from a source within the sinner. What accounts for this difference? According to St. Thomas, the principle of our moral-spiritual life is charity or the love of God, whereby we are ordered to him as our final end. If charity within the person is lost, there is no inner source within the person to repair the harm he or she has done in sinning. Mortal sin destroys charity or the principle of our moral-spiritual life. As St. Thomas put the matter, "those acts are of their kind mortal sins through which the covenant of friendship between man and God and between man and man is violated; for they are contrary to the two precepts of *charity, which is the life of the soul* "[30] (emphasis added).

If charity or love is lost, only God can bring the sinner back to life. Thus, the sin whereby this love is destroyed is properly called "mortal" or deadly.

But St. Thomas held (and, in doing so, summarized the thought of the Fathers and earlier medieval theologians) that the principle of our moral-spiritual life, charity, is not destroyed by some kinds of immoral acts. Since charity is not lost by such immoral deeds, there abides within the sinner himself or herself a healing principle — namely, charity or love — and the person can repent of such immoral deeds by reshaping his or her life in accord with this principle. Such sins, called "venial" because they are "pardonable," are like bodily diseases that can be overcome by the body's inherent vitality, while mortal sins are like lethal bodily diseases that will surely lead to death unless there is saving intervention from some extrinsic source or principle.[31] By sinning mortally, in other words, a person fully turns away from God toward a creature and erects a created good as, here and now, his end. By sinning venially, on the other hand, one does not turn away from God, even though there is some disordered attachment to a created good. All this seems quite sound.

But St. Thomas also maintained that venial sin, which can be called "sin" only in an analogous and derivative sense, is not "against the law" (*contra legem*), "since one who sins venially does not do what the law forbids or fail to do what it requires by a precept; but such a sinner behaves apart from the law (*praeter legem*) by not keeping to the reasonable mode which the law points out."[32]

St. Thomas's position here — namely, that venial sin is not "against the law" but merely "apart from the law" — seems difficult to sustain. While it is true that only mortal sin fully turns us away from God, our last end, it is hard to understand why venial sins are simply "apart from the law" (*praeter legem*) and not "against the law" (*contra legem*). The immorality involved in filching a newspaper from a rack is surely "against" the precept that we ought not to steal. Nonetheless, the main thrust of St. Thomas's thought is clear. Venial sin, while morally evil, does not mean acting in a way that separates us from the love of God, that cuts us off from the ultimate end (God) to which we are directed by God's eternal law.[33]

According to St. Thomas, three conditions are required if a sin is to be mortal or opposed to the love that God pours into our hearts. These are grave matter, sufficient reflection, and full consent of the will.[34] Sins venial by reason of insufficient reflection or lack of full consent are called by St. Thomas sins venial "in their cause," i.e., in the person responsible for them. Such venial sins do not have a determinate kind. Thus, offenses which of themselves are grave — for instance, blasphemy or adultery — can be "venial" (pardonable, reparable) if they are committed by a person who is confused or ignorant about what he or she is doing or whose choice is not adequately free. Other sins, Aquinas taught, are venial by reason of their "object" or subject matter, in contrast to others that are of themselves gravely or mortally sinful. His position — which summarizes well the thought of his predecessors, subsequent theological tradition, and the teaching and pastoral practice of the Church — is that some kinds of human acts are known to be incompatible with the love that should exist between human persons and God and within human society. Thus, for example, blasphemy and idolatry are simply not reconcilable with love of God, while murder, adultery, and the like are completely opposed to love of one's neighbor. Such acts, when freely chosen with adequate knowledge about what one is doing, are mortally sinful. Other kinds of human acts entail some moral disorder, but are not themselves destructive of love of God or neighbor, e.g., aimless chattering, telling a lie that does not harm anyone, etc. These are the "matter" or "object" of venial sin.[35]

St. Thomas identifies grave matter with actions whose "object" is deliberately opposed to love of God and neighbor — the bond of charity that is, as Thomas says, the "life of the soul."[36] This seems to be a good criterion for distinguishing between mortal and venial sins. Yet there is a problem. Why is it that some actions that are morally evil do not constitute grave matter? Charity, after all, is love of divine goodness; but every morally evil act seems incompatible with this love and opposed to it. Similarly, charity is love of one's neighbor and a willingness to serve the neighbor's need. A small lie to my wife — e.g., telling her that I have mailed a letter she asked me to when I forgot (intending to mail it as soon as possible) — seems to violate this love and to be opposed to the charity that should unite me to her. The problem here is similar to the one we saw previously, when venial sin was described as a morally evil deed that was "apart from the law" but not "against the law." In other words, the position taken by St. Thomas that some moral evils constitute "light" matter — insofar as they are compatible with love of God and neighbor and hence are the "stuff" of venial or pardonable sin, whereas others constitute "grave" matter because of their incompatibility with such love and thus give rise to mortal sins — seems reasonable, but there are some perplexities that remain and need to be resolved.

C. Fundamental Option Theories and the Distinction Between Mortal and Venial Sin

In attempting to account for the difference between mortal and venial sin, several contemporary theologians — among them some of the most influential, such as Karl Rahner and Josef Fuchs — have developed the notion of "fundamental" or "basic" freedom and the significance of this freedom for understanding the reality of mortal sin. To understand their position, it is necessary, first of all, to have an accurate idea of what they mean by basic or fundamental freedom. The descriptions of this freedom provided by several advocates of the notion will be helpful here.

One leading proponent of the view, Josef Fuchs, has this to say about "basic" or "fundamental" freedom: "Basic freedom, on the other hand [as contrasted with freedom of choice], denotes a still more fundamental, deeper-rooted freedom, not immediately accessible to psychological investigation. This is the freedom that enables us not only to decide freely on particular acts and aims, but also, by means of these *to determine ourselves totally as persons* and not merely in any particular area of behavior"[37] (emphasis added).

Another proponent of the view says that "there is another dimension to freedom. It is *not* the freedom of choice to do a particular thing or not, a choice of specific objects. It is rather *the free determination of oneself* with regard to the totality of existence and its direction. It is a fundamental choice between love and selfishness, between self and God our destiny. This is often called by recent theologians the fundamental option, an act of fundamental liberty"[38] (emphasis added).

Still another advocate puts the matter this way: "According to this theory man is structured in a series of concentric circles or various levels. On the deepest level of the individual, at the personal center, man's freedom decides, loves, commits itself in the fullest sense of these terms. This is the center of grave morality where man makes himself and his total existence good or evil."[39]

These descriptions of fundamental or basic freedom enable us to grasp the essential features of fundamental freedom as proposed by many contemporary theologians. Joseph Boyle has accurately summarized these features, and it will be helpful to look at his summary. Boyle writes: "First of all, it [fundamental freedom] is exercised at the very core of the human person; thus it is the locus of self-determination and hence of basic moral responsibility. Second, it does not have as its object any particular action or set of actions, but rather its object is the entire self in its relationship to God. Third, the exercise of fundamental freedom is not an action in any normal sense of the word. Something like an option or preference is involved, but this preference is more like a stance or attitude than an act of choosing. Furthermore, there is no explicit awareness of a time when one took one's fundamental stance. . . . It is none too clear exactly what the relationship between free choice and the exercise of fundamental freedom is, but it is clear that one can choose freely in a way inconsistent with the exercise of one's fundamental freedom without altering the fundamental stance established by this freedom."[40]

How is the notion of fundamental freedom related to the distinction between mortal and venial sin? Proponents of fundamental option maintain that a sin is "mortal" only when there is a fundamental option against God and his love (or against some other Ultimate). Mortal sin, in other words, involves the exercise of fundamental or basic freedom. The distinction between grave and light matter is relevant to the distinction between mortal and venial sin insofar as grave matter, according to the proponents of fundamental option, is the sort of thing likely to be an *occasion* for making or reversing one's fundamental option. Actions not likely to change one's fundamental disposition toward or against God are "light" matter. "Grave" and "light" matter can be used to name not only morally evil acts but also morally good ones. Some morally good acts are of "grave" import while others are not.

While grave matter — for instance, killing an innocent person or committing adultery — provides an appropriate *occasion* for reversing or confirming one's fundamental option through an exercise of fundamental freedom, it does not necessarily follow, according to the theologians who hold this position, that a particular act of this kind necessarily entails a repudiation of one's basic commitment to love God and neighbor. Still, proponents of this view recognize that one *can* change one's stance before God in particular acts of free choice. In other words, according to the proponents of fundamental option theory, grave matter is a "sign" that one's fundamental freedom may be at stake. Nonetheless, according to its advocates, one could freely choose to engage in an act that one knows involves grave matter — e.g., committing adultery or deliberately killing an innocent human being — and still not violate one's fundamental option toward God (or some Ultimate). Thus, advocates of this position frequently distinguish between three kinds of sin: venial, in which only light matter is involved or in which one's freedom of choice is inhibited or one's knowledge is not clear; grave sins, which entail grave matter knowingly and freely chosen; and mortal sin, which requires that one exercise one's basic or fundamental freedom by taking a stance totally opposed to God (or some Ultimate).

Proponents of fundamental option theory are correct in recognizing, with Aquinas, that the change from being God's friend to being one opposed to his love is a matter of profound importance and that a basic commitment for God is, as St. Thomas noted, "not easily lost."[41] They are likewise correct in stressing the unity of our moral-spiritual life, refusing to see it as a series of disparate and isolated acts.

Despite these valid insights, theories of fundamental option are beset with insuperably difficult problems, so that they cannot be regarded as the correct account of the difference between mortal and venial sin. First and most important, most theories of fundamental option needlessly shift the locus of self-determination from the free choices we make every day (e.g., my choice to lie to my wife, to commit adultery, to play favorites among my children, to cheat on my income tax) to an alleged act of total self-disposition deep within the person that remains prereflexive, unthematic, and incapable of being articulated explicitly in one's consciousness.[42] Even those versions of fundamental option theory which affirm that fundamental option is a special kind of free choice and not an exercise of a freedom more basic than free choice[43] cannot adequately explain why *some* free choices are self-determining and others are not.

In other words, fundamental option theories, which either relocate self-determination from free choice to an exercise of basic freedom distinct from free choice or hold that we are self-determined only by *some* free choices and not by all of our free choices, fail to take seriously the reality of free choice. As we have seen before, we make or break our lives as moral beings in and through the free choices that we make in our daily lives. We become liars, adulterers, cheaters, murderers, etc., in freely choosing to lie, commit adultery, cheat, kill the innocent, and so forth. As has been said over and over again, at the heart of human actions is a free, self-determining choice, and this choice abides in us until contradictory choices are made. As St. Thomas said, "to act (i.e., to choose to do something) is an action abiding in the agent."[44] Fundamental option theory fails adequately to take into account the *self-determining* significance of the free choices we make in our daily lives.

Proponents of fundamental option admit that some acts are so gravely immoral that freely choosing to do them is *likely* to change a good fundamental option into a bad one. Yet they also claim that in some and perhaps many cases immoral acts involving grave matter (e.g., committing adultery, deliberately killing an innocent person) can be done *with sufficient reflection and full consent* without necessarily changing one's fundamental stance for God.[45] This is very strange. It has led, in practice, to the view that some sorts of acts traditionally considered to be mortal sins if done deliberately and after sufficient reflection (e.g., adultery) are not, in fact, mortal sins but only "grave" ones.

Here it is pertinent to observe, with Pope John Paul II, that the 1983 Synod of Bishops, which met to discuss the theme "Reconciliation and Penance in the Mission of the Church," affirmed that "mortal sin is sin whose object is grave matter and which is also committed with full knowledge and deliberate consent."[46] He went on to observe that "care will have to be taken not to reduce mortal sin to an act of 'fundamental option' — as is commonly said today — against God, intending thereby an explicit and formal contempt for God and neighbor. For mortal sin also exists when a person, knowingly and willingly, for whatever reason, chooses something gravely disordered. In fact, such a choice already includes contempt for the divine law, a rejection of God's love for humanity and the whole of creation; the person turns away from God and loses charity. Thus the fundamental orientation can be radically changed by individual acts."[47]

While *some* versions of fundamental option that do not deny the self-determining character of free choice can be compatible with traditional Catholic teaching and practice, the types of fundamental option theory analyzed here are not. They do not help us understand what factor in addition to grave matter, sufficient reflection, and full consent (i.e., a free choice) would constitute an exercise of basic or fundamental freedom. According to the definitive and irreformable teaching of the Church, solemnly affirmed by the Council of Trent (see DS 1679, 1707), one commits mortal sin when one knowingly and freely chooses to do something condemned by the Church as intrinsically and gravely evil — a teaching reaffirmed, as we have seen, by the 1983 Synod of Bishops and Pope John Paul II. The kind of fundamental option theories presented and criticized here deny this, and Catholics influenced by such theories no longer can identify those sins for which they absolutely must repent and seek forgiveness in the sacrament of penance. It thus follows that these accounts of fundamental option are not compatible with Catholic faith.

Pope John Paul II considers fundamental option theory and mortal sin in the third part of Chapter Two of his encyclical *Veritatis splendor*. There he first recognizes the existential significance of free choice as self-determining (*Veritatis splendor,* no. 68) and the crucial importance of certain choices that " 'shape' a person's entire moral life" (ibid.). He then notes that some theologians today "have proposed an even more radical revision of the *relationship between person and acts.* They speak of a 'fundamental freedom,' deeper than and different from freedom of choice, which needs to be considered if human actions are to be correctly understood and evaluated" (no. 65). These theologians have *relocated* self-determination from the free choices we make every day, including fundamental commitments, to a "fundamental option . . . whereby the person makes an overall self-determination" (no. 65). A distinction "thus comes to be introduced *between the fundamental option and deliberate choices of a concrete kind of behavior*" (no. 65). "The conclusion to which this eventually leads is that the properly moral assessment of the person is reserved to his fundamental option, prescinding . . . from his choice of particular actions, of concrete kinds of behavior" (ibid.).

On this view, the free choice to do an act known to be gravely immoral need not be a mortal sin. For, advocates of this view claim, the free choice to do so may not reverse one's fundamental option, which they regard as distinct from any particular choice to do this or that.

John Paul II judges that "to separate the fundamental option from concrete kinds of behavior means to contradict the substantial integrity or personal unity of the moral agent in his body and in his soul" (no. 67). But even before making this judgment, he rejects contemporary tendencies to relocate self-determination from the free choices we make every day to an alleged fundamental option at the core of our being. He judges this as "contrary to the teaching of Scripture itself, which sees the fundamental option as a genuine choice of freedom and links that choice profoundly to particular acts" (no. 67). He teaches that the "choice of freedom" which "Christian moral teaching, even in its Biblical roots, acknowledges" as fundamental is "the decision of faith, of the *obedience of faith* (cf. Rom 16:26)." This is the free choice, he then continues, citing a passage from Vatican Council II (*Dei Verbum,* no. 5), "by which man makes a total and free self-commitment to God, offering 'the full submission of intellect and will to God as he reveals' " (no. 66). He continues by saying that since faith is a commitment to God that is to bear fruit in works (cf. Mt 12:33-35; Lk 6:43-45; Rom 8:5-10; Gal 5:22), it demands that one keep the commandments of the Decalogue and follow Jesus even to the point of losing his life for Jesus' sake and the sake of the gospel (cf. Mk 8.35) (no. 66).

John Paul II then stresses that this fundamental option — a free choice that can rightly be called a commitment " 'shaping' a person's entire moral life" (cf. no. 65) — "*is always brought into play through conscious and free decisions.* Precisely for this reason, *it is revoked when man engages his freedom in conscious decisions to the contrary, with regard to morally grave matter*" (no. 67).

John Paul II likewise reminds us that the Council of Trent solemnly de-fined as a truth of Catholic faith that "the grace of justification once received is lost not only by apostasy, by which faith is lost, but also by any other mortal sin" (no. 68, with a reference to Session VI of the Council of Trent, Decree on Justification, *Cum Hoc Tempore*, ch. 15, DS 1544; Canon 19, DS 1569). He then reaffirms the teaching of the Church that mortal sin exists "when a per-son knowingly and willingly, for whatever reason, chooses something gravely disordered" (no. 70, with a reference to *Reconciliatio et Poenitentia*, no. 17). It thus follows that "the separation of fundamental option from deliberate choices of particular kinds of behavior, disordered in themselves or in their circum-stances, which would not engage that option . . . involves a denial of Catholic doctrine on *mortal sin*" (no. 70).

D. Fundamental Commitments, the Christian Way of Life, and Mortal Sin

Despite the criticisms just given, advocates of a fundamental option seem correct in holding that the difference between grave and light matter is to be found in the depth to which different kinds of acts disrupt the existential being of a person. Aquinas seems correct in saying that certain kinds of choices include matter known to be completely incompatible with love of God and neighbor and hence destructive of the principle of our moral-spir-itual life, while others entail subject matter which, though immoral and in-compatible with a perfected love of God and neighbor, is reconcilable with such love.

In addition, while the positing of an exercise of "fundamental" or "basic" freedom at the core of one's being whereby one disposes of oneself totally for or against God (or some Ultimate) seems an obscure and unnecessary hy-pothesis, there are certain kinds of free choices, rightly called commitments, that direct a person in a definite way of life — e.g., the choice to become a Christian, the choice to marry, the choice to become a religious or a scholar or a lawyer, the choice to join the Mafia or the Nazis or a drug-trafficking ring. Such commitments, it must be noted, are specific exercises of free choice of which a person is explicitly conscious — they are not some mysterious act so deep within the person that the person cannot, reflectively, make it an object of explicit consciousness.[48] And such commitments do entail basic moral stances on the part of the person, stances for or against what is right and good, stances for or against the loving plan of God.

Thus, as Germain Grisez has noted, it seems reasonable to hold that there is a basic option or commitment for the Christian — namely, the choice to become a Christian through baptism (and, if baptized in infancy, to ratify the baptismal commitment in the sacrament of confirmation or through other acts, for instance, during the liturgy of Holy Saturday).[49] This basic commitment or fundamental option, the act of living faith, is a definite free choice. As the Fathers of Vatican Council II said, "By faith man freely commits his entire self to God, making 'the full submission of his intellect and will to God who reveals,' and willingly assenting to the revelation given by him" *(Dei Verbum,* no. 5; internal citation from Vatican Council I, Dogmatic Constitution on the Faith, ch. 3, DS 3008). The Church, moreover, teaches that faith is the source of all justification and the beginning of our salvation. It teaches that faith is God's gift, and that this gift is accepted by a free human act.[50] Finally, the Church teaches that this definite choice commits a person to a life of good works.[51]

Moreover, from its very beginning the Church has regarded some morally evil acts as absolutely incompatible with the requirements of faith, with the "way of life" to which a person who becomes one with Jesus and who shares in his death-resurrection is committed. As Pope John Paul II has said: "[T]here exist acts which, *per se* and in themselves, independently of circumstances, are always seriously wrong by reason of their object. These acts, if carried out with sufficient awareness and freedom, are always gravely sinful. This *doctrine,* based on the Decalogue and on the preaching of the Old Testament, and assimilated into the *kerygma* of the apostles and belonging to the earliest teaching of the Church, and constantly reaffirmed by her to this day, is exactly verified in the experience of the men and women of all times."[52]

The act of living faith, in other words, has definite specifications, not only with respect to what one is to believe but also with respect to what one is to do and to refrain from doing. Thus, the Church has, from New Testament times to the present,[53] consistently taught that certain specific kinds of acts constitute grave matter and, if knowingly and freely chosen, are mortal sins (fornication, adultery, deliberately killing the innocent, etc., as well as sins directly contrary to faith).[54]

In summary, mortal sin is the sort of sin that involves grave matter, i.e., matter *judged by the Church* to be incompatible with the life to which one is called and to which one commits oneself through the act of living faith. In addition to matter known to be grave, mortal sin requires sufficient reflection and an adequately free human choice, because it is a deed (whose core is a free, self-determining choice) whereby a human person turns away from God toward some created good. Even nonbelievers recognize that morally evil choices involving matter of this kind are utterly incompatible with a commitment to lead morally upright lives, for they have in their hearts the natural law, their own way of participating in God's loving plan for human existence. Venial sin, while immoral and incompatible with perfect love, is "pardonable" either by its matter, which the Church judges is not completely incompatible with the life to which living faith commits one and which upright nonbelievers can recognize as not completely incompatible with their commitment to lead morally upright lives, or by reason of defects of knowledge or of freedom on the part of the sinner.

3. The Role of Sin in Our Moral Lives: The Way of Sin to Death

St. Paul spoke of a "law" that he found in his "members," a "law" opposed to the one that he found in his "mind" (Rom 7:22-23). This "law" of his members inclined him to act in ways that he knew were immoral. The Church and theologians have seen in this passage from St. Paul, in which he expresses a universal human experience, biblical testimony to the reality of concupiscence. Concupiscence, which derives from original sin and inclines us toward personal sin,[55] remains even in those who have been regenerated in the waters of baptism. As a result of original sin and the concupiscence to which it gives rise, we find ourselves in a condition of disintegration and experience terrible tensions within ourselves, being drawn, as Vatican Council II reminds us, toward the good by the native thrust of our will and by the law of God written in our hearts, and being inclined toward evil by reason of the concupiscence that is in us *(Gaudium et spes,* no. 13).

Moreover, in addition to being subject to concupiscence, we are by nature passionate and emotional beings as well as intelligent and willing beings. Our passions, as both the Scriptures (Jas 1:13-14) and human experience bear witness, can at times make sinful choices very appealing to us. They can also make choices that we know are, according to God's law, quite repugnant. As a result, we are tempted, and powerful forces within us (passions under the disintegrating influence of concupiscence) incline us, to consent to what we know to be morally evil.

Furthermore, the sinful acts of individuals, when accepted by society, become a part of that society's way of life. The "world" shaped by sin (cf. Rom 5:12; 1 Jn 5:16; Jn 1:29) obscures values, provides bad example, and frequently pushes us toward sin, and even puts pressure on us to sin.[56]

To add to the sources within us and in the world that prompt us to sin, the devil, the father of lies, "prowls about like a roaring lion seeking whom he may devour" (1 Pt 5:8). As the Scriptures instruct us, he and his legions are at work seeking to lead us into evil.

Nevertheless, the only cause of sin is our own free will, our own self-determining choice deliberately to do what we know is morally bad and in this way set aside God's loving plan. Once we freely yield to temptation, we are subject to further temptation as we seek to integrate our life with the sinful self we have made ourselves to be. This leads us to rationalize our sinful choices.

We are strongly inclined to distort our relationship to God by self-righteousness or, at times, by flight. We even seek to conceal from ourselves our own identity as sinners.

Although venial sin is sin only in an analogous sense, it can prepare the way for mortal sin. It makes us aware of sinful possibilities that might otherwise have remained unknown; it puts us in situations difficult to escape without mortal sin; and it frequently makes attractive the objectives we are tempted to pursue by mortal sin.[57]

The Catholic tradition has also recognized that some sins are "capital," insofar as they are the "heads" (*capita*) or sources of other sins. Since the time of Pope St. Gregory the Great in the eighth century, seven such capital sins have been commonly named: pride (vainglory), covetousness (avarice), lust, gluttony, anger, envy, and sloth. Some of these sins are attitudes that compete with love of God and neighbor. Thus, pride is a disposition to find fulfillment in status and the respect of others; lust and gluttony are dispositions to fulfillment in immediate sensible gratifications; avarice, a disposition to fulfillment in possessions.[58] Other capital sins are ways of rationalizing our sinfulness. Thus, sloth disposes us to put off reforming our moral and spiritual life, resisting the effort needed to give up sinful attachments;[59] envy makes us hate the good of others, whose goodness puts demands on us that we do not like.[60] As a capital sin, anger is a disposition to wipe out especially whatever poses a threat to our sinful self.[61]

According to Catholic faith, every sin can be forgiven during life because of God's surpassing love (DS 349). Still, the Scriptures speak of sins that cannot be forgiven, in the sense that they constitute a terrible offense against the truth and the light, against the Holy Spirit (Mt 12:31-32; 1 Jn 5:16). In speaking of sin in this way, the Scriptures are referring to a sin more radical than most mortal sins, for it is a sin whose nature blocks forgiveness. From the time of Augustine, theologians have provided a list of sins against the Holy Spirit, proceeding from initial impenitence through obduracy, presumption, despair, rejection of known truth, envy of the grace given to others, to final impenitence.[62] Final impenitence leads us to hell, the eternal separation from God begun in this life through our free, self-determining choices to turn from God and his law of love and to cleave inordinately to some created good that, in effect, we put in God's place.

In conclusion: Through our willingness to do what we know is wicked in the sight of the Lord, we open a chasm between ourselves and God. Through rationalization, we make this chasm wider and wider until we can no longer hear his call and discern the word of truth that he has spoken in this world. The gospel is the good news that God himself has come to save us from sin, to be with us and for us, to be our Emmanuel. Only by a self-determining act of conversion, of *metanoia,* of penance, made possible by the saving death and resurrection of Jesus, can we be reunited with our God and rise to a life of holiness, a life of constant conversion and growth in the way of truth and of life. But, in this struggle, we can confidently hope in God, for, as St. Paul so eloquently said, "nothing, neither death nor life, no angel, no prince, nothing that exists, nothing still to come, not any power, or height or depth, nor any created thing, can ever come between us and the love of God made visible in Christ Jesus our Lord" (Rom 8:38-39). Nothing separates us from God; only we separate ourselves from him by rejecting his love and refusing his mercy.

The *Catechism of the Catholic Church* provides a brief but excellent account of sin, one with which this chapter is in conformity, in nos. 1846-1876.

Notes for Chapter Five

1. Good accounts of original sin are found in the following sources: Germain Grisez, *The Way of the Lord Jesus,* Vol. 1, *Christian Moral Principles* (Chicago: Franciscan Herald Press, 1983), pp. 333-360; T.C. O'Brien, "Appendix 2" and "Appendix 3" in St. Thomas Aquinas, *Summa theologiae,* Vol. 26 (New York: McGraw-Hill, 1965), pp. 110-120; C.J. Peter, "Original Justice" and "Original Sin," *New Catholic Encyclopedia* (New York: McGraw-Hill, 1967), Vol. 10, pp. 774-801.

2. On the meaning of sin in Scripture, consult the following: Johannes Bauer, "Sin," in *Sacramentum Verbi* (New York: Herder and Herder, 1971), 3.849-862; J. Lechowski, "Sin (in the Bible)," *New Catholic Encyclopedia,* Vol. 13, pp. 226-241; S. Lyonnet, "Sin," in *Theological Dictionary of the Bible,* ed. X. Léon-Dufour (rev. ed.; New York: Seabury, 1973), pp. 50-55.

3. Some hold that sin is essentially a violation of the covenant. While it is true that sin does violate the covenant once it has been established, it does not follow from this that sin is limited to covenant violations. The Chosen People's idolatry was sinful prior to the establishment of the covenant (Ez 20:7-8), and the prophets vehemently denounced the sins of pagan nations who had no special covenant relationship with God (Am 1:3-2.3). In the New Testament, St. Paul taught that the pagans living outside the covenant are nonetheless guilty of sin, by reason of the "law" written in their hearts, because of their immoral acts (Rom 1:18-22; 2:14-16).

4. On the biblical vocabulary for sin, see G. Quell et al., "Harmatano," in *Theological Dictionary of the Bible,* ed. G. Kittel, trans. G. Bromiley (Grand Rapids, MI: Eerdmans, 1969) 1.267-316.

5. Stanislaus Lyonnet, "Sin," in *Theological Dictionary of the Bible,* p. 553.

6. Johannes Bauer, "Sin," in *Sacramentum Verbi* 3.856.

7. Ibid., 857-858.

8. On this, see Bauer, Lyonnet, and other authors cited in note 2.

9. St. Augustine, *Contra Faustum*, 22.27: "factum, dictum, vel concupitum contra legem aetemani."

10. St. Augustine, *De Libero Arbitrio*, 2.53: "aversio a Deo, conversio ad creaturam."

11. Philip Keane, *Sexual Morality: A Catholic Perspective* (New York: Paulist Press, 1977), pp. 35-36.

12. On this, see Chapter Three, above.

13. St. Thomas Aquinas, *De Malo*, 7, 3.

14. St. Thomas Aquinas, *Summa Contra Gentes*, 3.122.

15. St. Thomas Aquinas, *Summa theologiae*, 1-2, 71, 2, ad 4; 71, 6.

16. Ibid., 71, 6, ad 5.

17. Ibid., 89, 6.

18. Ibid., 71, 6.

19. Ibid., 94, 2.

20. Ibid., 72, 1.

21. Ibid., 72, 1; 3, 1; 75, 1 and 2; 78, 1.

22. Ibid., 71, 2, ad 3; 77.

23. Ibid., 71, 6; 79, 2.

24. Ibid., 57, 4.

25. Ibid., 86, all articles; 87, 6.

26. Pope John Paul II, *Reconciliatio et Poenitentia*, no. 16.

27. Ibid., no. 14. See Rom 7:7-25; Eph 2:2.

28. See St. Augustine, *Expositions on the Psalms*, 81 (80), 19-20; St. Thomas Aquinas, *Summa theologiae*, 1-2, 89, 2. See also Th. Deman, "Péché Mortel et Péché Veniel," *Dictionnaire de Théologie Catholique* 12.225-226.

29. Pope John Paul II, *Reconciliatio et Poenitentia*, no. 17.

30. St. Thomas Aquinas, *Summa theologiae*, Supplement to the Third Part, 65, 4c: "illi actus ex suo genere sunt peccata mortalia per quos foedus amicitiae hominis ad Deum et hominis ad hominem violatur: haec enim sunt contra duo praecepta caritatis, *quae est animae vita*." See also ibid., 3, 89, 6.

31. Ibid., 1-2, 88, 1.

32. Ibid., 88, 1, ad 1.

33. Ibid., 88, 1, ad 2; see 88, 2; 89, 3.

34. Ibid., 88, 2 and 6.

35. Ibid., 88, 2.

36. See texts cited in note 30.

37. Josef Fuchs, *Human Values and Christian Morality* (New York: Macmillan, 1970), p. 93.

38. Richard McCormick, "The Moral Theology of Vatican II," in *The Future of Ethics and Moral Theology* (Chicago: Argus Communications, 1968), p. 12.

39. John Glaser, "Transition Between Grace to Sin: Fresh Perspectives," *Theological Studies* 29 (1968), 261-262. Also see Karl Rahner, "Theology of Freedom," *Theological Investigations*, Vol. 8 (New York: Herder and Herder, 1969), pp. 178-196.

40. Joseph Boyle, "Freedom, the Human Person, and Human Action," in *Principles of Catholic Moral Life*, ed. William E. May (Chicago: Franciscan Herald Press, 1980), p. 250.

41. St. Thomas Aquinas, *De Veritate*, 27, 1, ad 9.

42. Boyle, "Freedom, the Human Person, and Human Action," pp. 237-266.

43. On this, see, for example, Richard McCormick, in *An American Catechism*, ed. George Dyer (New York: Seabury, 1975), pp. 189-190.

44. St. Thomas Aquinas, *Summa theologiae*, 1-2, 57, 4.

45. On this, see Keane, *Sexual Morality*, pp. 38-40; Fuchs, *Human Values and Christian Morality*, pp. 99-100; Timothy E. O'Connell, *Principles for a Catholic Morality* (1st ed.; New York: Seabury, 1978), p. 62.

46. Pope John Paul II, *Reconciliatio et Poenitentia*, no. 17.

47. Ibid.

48. In his *The Critical Call: Dilemmas in Moral Theology* (Washington, DC: Georgetown University Press, 1989), McCormick seeks to defend advocates of fundamental option theory from criticism that this view considers fundamental freedom as an act that is not accessible to consciousness. He stresses that it is not accessible to "explicit" or "thematic" consciousness, but that its proponents recognize it as an awareness or consciousness that is "unthematic." McCormick's response to criticism is totally inadequate. He fails, for example, even to consider Boyle's essay (noted above) or to note that Boyle is clearly aware of the distinction between "thematic" and "unthematic" consciousness. The major difficulty is that most versions of fundamental option theory relocate self-determination from the free choices human persons make to an exercise of freedom that is, to say the least, very obscure.

49. Grisez, *Christian Moral Principles*, pp. 393-398.

50. DS 1528-1532; Vatican Council II, *Dei Verbum*, no. 5; *Dignitatis humanae*, nos. 2, 3.

51. DS 1532-1539; Vatican Council II, *Lumen gentium*, no. 35; *Dignitatis humanae*, nos. 5, 10.

52. Pope John Paul II, *Reconciliatio et Poenitentia*, no. 17.

53. Thus, the Church has always taught, from the days of the *Didache* in the second century on, that such acts as abortion, infanticide, adultery, fornication, and homosexual activity are always gravely wrong. On this, see William E. May,

Moral Absolutes: Catholic Tradition, Current Trends, and the Truth (Milwaukee: Marquette University Press, 1989).

54. See Pope John Paul II, *Reconciliatio et Poenitentia,* no. 17.

55. Council of Trent; DS 1515.

56. On this, see Piet Schoonenberg, *Man and Sin* (Notre Dame, IN: University of Notre Dame Press, 1968).

57. St. Thomas Aquinas, *Summa theologiae,* 1-2, 88, 3; see Grisez, *Christian Moral Principles,* pp. 439-440.

58. *Summa theologiae,* 1-2, 84, 4; 2-2, 118, 7; 148, 5; 155, 4; 162, 8.

59. Ibid., 2-2, 35.

60. Ibid., 2-2, 36.

61. Ibid., 2-2, 158, 2, 6,7.

62. Ibid., 2-2, 1-4.

CHAPTER SIX

Christian Faith and Our Moral Life

According to Catholic faith, Jesus Christ our Lord is the "center and goal of the whole history of mankind" *(Gaudium et spes,* no. 10). Christ is the one who "fully reveals man to himself" (ibid., no. 22). He is the "perfect man" (ibid., nos. 22, 38, 41, 45), in whom "human nature is assumed, not annulled" (ibid., no. 22). He is the one who "by his incarnation has somehow united all men with himself" (ibid.; *Redemptor hominis,* nos. 13, 18). Moreover, all men "have the same nature and the same origin" *(Gaudium et spes,* no. 29; *Lumen gentium,* no. 19), and all have the "same calling and divine destiny," and so, being fundamentally equal both in nature and in supernatural calling *(Gaudium et spes,* no. 29), can be citizens of the one people of God regardless of race or place or time *(Lumen gentium,* no. 13).

Christ is our Redeemer, our Savior, and by uniting our lives with his we can in truth become fully the beings his Father wills us to be. The purpose of this chapter is thus to investigate the meaning of our lives as moral beings who have, through baptism, become "one" with Christ. Its purpose is to see how the "natural law" is brought to fulfillment and completion by the gospel "law" of Christ. To achieve this purpose, the following topics will be pursued: (1) the existential context within which our struggle to live morally good lives is situated; (2) Jesus Christ, *the* foundation of the Christian moral life; (3) the meaning of our baptismal commitment and of our personal vocation to follow Christ; (4) the specific nature of Christian love as the principle of the moral lives of Christians; (5) the Lord's Sermon on the Mount, with its beatitudes, as the "charter of Christian ethics"; (6) the question of specific Christian norms; and (7) the "practicality" of the Christian moral life.

1. The Existential Context of Our Moral Life

St. Thomas offered several reasons why human persons, in order to be fully the beings God wills them to be, need a divinely revealed law in addition to natural law and human law derived from it. Two of these reasons are of particular significance. He noted, first of all, that for the proper direction of human life a divinely revealed law is necessary inasmuch as the final end to which human beings are called — namely, a life of eternal happiness and life with God — is an end that exceeds merely human capacities and that, therefore, a divinely revealed "law" is needed if human actions are to be properly directed. He then observed that a divinely revealed law is needed inasmuch as human judgment is uncertain, especially when it has to do with contingent and particular matters, with the result that different judgments are given about diverse kinds of human action, so that human laws with respect to them are quite different and, at times, contradictory. Consequently, precisely so that human persons might know "without any doubt what ought to be done and what avoided" a divinely given law is needed, one that cannot err.[1] In another text, St. Thomas expands on the second point. There he remarks that divinely-given precepts are necessary even with respect to the acts of the moral virtues, to which man's natural reason inclines him, precisely because the "natural reason of man has been darkened by the concupiscence of sin."[2]

I will first take up the second of the reasons St. Thomas gives for the need of a divinely revealed law, i.e., weakness and incertitude of human judgments about what is to be done and avoided, a weakness and incertitude caused in large measure by the reality of sin and its effects on our lives. I will then consider his first reason for the need of a divinely revealed law, namely, our supernatural calling to live in union with God himself.

First, the reality of sin. Which one of us has not personally experienced the anguish expressed by St. Paul when he exclaimed: "I do not understand my own actions. For I do not do what I want, but I do the very thing I hate. . . . I can will what is right, but I cannot do it. For I do not do the good I want, but the evil I do not want is what I do" (Rom 7:15-19). Paul continued by saying: "My inner self agrees with the law of God, but I see in my body's members another law at war with the law of my mind; this makes me the prisoner of the law of sin in my members" (Rom 7:22-23). Paul's words, which accurately describe a genuine human experience, in no way deny the reality of free choice, for Paul holds himself and others morally responsible for the evil chosen and done (cf. Rom 1:20-32; 2:14-16). But his words do testify to the reality of sin and its impact on our existence as moral beings.

In the passages just cited from Romans, St. Paul focuses on the debilitating effects of sin on our efforts, *conatively*, to do what we ourselves have come to know that we ought to do if we are to be fully the beings God wills us to be. But sin also has a debilitating effect on our endeavor, *cognitively*, to come to know what we are to do if we are to be fully the beings God wills us to be. In short, we live our lives as moral beings within an existential framework wherein we encounter both *disabling* and *enabling* factors or, theologically considered, sin and grace, both in our struggle to *know* moral truth and in our struggle to *do* the good we come to know.[3] My concern here is with the disabling effect of sin on our existence as moral beings.

In the previous chapter, we investigated the meaning and reality of personal sin, of which all of us, if we are honest, are guilty — for "if we say, 'We are free of the guilt of sin,' we deceive ourselves; the truth is not to be found in us" (1 Jn 1:8). In that chapter, we saw that personal sin, unless repented, abides in us as an inclination or disposition to further sin, blinding us to moral truth. Moreover, the sins of individuals, when accepted and endorsed by others, soon become the practices of a society, becoming embedded in its culture, mediating to us false understandings of ourselves and of what we are to do, inviting us — sometimes with pressure — to do what is wicked.[4]

We live, in other words, in a world wounded by sin. In addition to our own personal sins, there is the "sin of the world," i.e., the sinful situation in which we live and in which we come to an understanding of ourselves and of what we are to do. While no one can force us to sin, we can be invited to do so, and, at times, "invited" with considerable pressure. As one theologian, Piet Schoonenberg, S.J., has remarked: "[T]here is an influence of one [person's] freedom upon another. From a free action there proceeds an appeal to which the free action of another may respond. That appeal may operate at once through the cognitive faculties of the other. It can also have a delayed effect in space or time. Today's sin may not only draw others along through seduction but it may also in the same way influence posterity, which has lost its bearings on account of the sins of the fathers."[5]

The sins of others, in other words, can frequently be a source of sin for ourselves. They affect us cognitively and conatively, obscuring values and norms, giving us bad example, and, at times, bad example with pressure.

Indeed, Pope John Paul II has stressed the reality of "social sin." We need to recognize "that, by virtue of human solidarity . . . each individual's sin in some way affects others." Indeed, he continued, "one can speak of a communion of sins, whereby a soul that lowers itself through sin drags down with itself the Church and, in some way, the whole world; . . . with greater or lesser violence, with greater or lesser harm, every sin has repercussions on the entire ecclesial body and on the whole human family" (*Reconciliatio et Poenitentia*, no. 16). Because of "social sin," which ultimately, as Pope John Paul II stresses, is rooted in the *personal* sins of specific individual human persons (*Reconciliatio et Poenitentia*, no. 16), we are "disabled" in our struggle both to discover moral truth and to shape our choices and lives in accord with it.

There is, in addition, the reality of original sin and its effects on our existence as moral beings. Here it will be worthwhile to recall briefly the Church's teaching on this subject. Pope Paul VI well summarized this teaching in his *The Credo of the People of God*. I will first cite his brief but accurate presentation of this teaching and then offer some comments. Pope Paul VI had this to say:

We believe that in Adam all have sinned, which means that the original offense committed by him caused human nature, common to all men, to fall to a state in which it bears the consequences of that offense, and which is not the state in which it was at first in our first parents, established as they were in holiness and justice, and in which man knew neither evil nor death. It is human nature so fallen, stripped of the grace that clothed it, injured in its own natural powers and subjected to the dominion of death, that is transmitted to all men, and it is in this sense that every man is born in sin. We therefore hold, with the Council of Trent, that original sin is transmitted with human nature, "not by imitation, but by propagation," and that it is thus "proper to everyone."[6]

The Council of Trent, at its fifth session on June 17, 1546 (cf. DS 1510-1516), definitively taught that human beings, in the person of Adam,[7] were constituted in justice and holiness. However, it continued, Adam disobeyed God and as a result lost his original justice and holiness, incurring the punishment of death, and was changed for the worse in body and soul. The Council further taught that Adam passed on this sin to *all* human persons and that this sin is transmitted by propagation, not imitation.[8] The harm to human persons wrought by original sin is healed only by Christ our Savior. Even babies, this Council and the Church teach, are guilty of original sin and are therefore in need of baptism so that the salvation won by Christ can be mediated to them.

That even babies are "guilty" of original sin and in need of salvation is the firm teaching of the Church. One of its greatest doctors, St. Augustine, who was himself not baptized as an infant and who, in his *Confessions*, bemoaned this fact, expressed in an unforgettable way the reason for this teaching. The Church, he wrote, confesses that Jesus Christ is the Savior and Redeemer of *all* human beings, no matter their race or age or condition. Infants, who are in no way guilty of personal sin, are still in need of redemption by Christ. As Augustine said, " 'You call his name Jesus.' Why? 'Because he will save his people.' From what? 'From their sins.' Now in the case of a child, he is brought to the Church to make him a Christian, in order to baptize him, supposedly in order that he may belong to the people of Jesus. But of what Jesus? He who saves 'his people from their sins.' If he [the child] does not have anything that can be saved in him, let him be taken away from here. Why do we not say to the mothers: Take these children away from here? Because Jesus is Savior. But if these have nothing in them to be saved from, take them away."[9]

To put it another way, original sin and redemption go hand in hand. If there is no original sin, there is no redemption in Christ. The Church teaches that baptism brings to human persons the grace of Christ, which really takes original sin away (DS 1515). Nonetheless, it holds, there remains even in those regenerated by the waters of baptism, the effect of original sin — concupiscence. Concupiscence (i.e., disordered human desires) — and which one of us is not aware of such? — is not itself sin. But it comes from sin (original sin), and it inclines us toward personal sin (DS 1515), with the result that our minds are darkened — i.e., able only with difficulty to come to know moral truth (the point St. Thomas was making) — and our wills weakened — i.e., strongly inclined to choose contrary to our own best judgments.

Sin — personal, social, original — is a reality in our lives. It cripples us in our efforts to know and do the truth. Because of sin, we at times feel powerless to do the good we know we ought to do. To be fully the beings God wills us to be, we need help, "enabling" factors. One of these enabling factors is the "law" that God himself graciously reveals to us, the law first given to us through Moses and then wondrously brought to fulfillment and completion by Christ, our Lord and Redeemer. This is precisely the point that St. Thomas was emphasizing in the second reason he advanced for the necessity of a divinely revealed law.

But our greatest help, the principal "enabling" factor in our lives as moral beings, is Jesus Christ himself, the Father's supreme gift to his human creatures. Jesus, whom St. Thomas calls "our best and wisest friend,"[10] is indeed "the way, the truth, and the life" (Jn 14:6). He is the one who is "preparing a place" for us in his "Father's house" (Jn 14:2, 3), bringing to us the gift of life eternal in union with his Father. He and his Father, moreover, give to us the Paraclete, the Spirit of Truth, to be with us always (cf. Jn 14:16, 17), to lead us on our journey to our heavenly home, guiding us inwardly to our supernatural end, life everlasting as members of the divine family. The gospel "law" divinely given to us in and through Jesus is, as St. Thomas tells us, in essence the "grace of the Holy Spirit which is given to Christ's faithful."[11] This "law" empowers us not only to know what we are to do if we are to be fully the beings God wills us to be but also to do what we come to know we ought to do, to live as faithful children of God, as persons called to share in God's inner Triune life. And this is precisely the point behind St. Thomas's first reason for the necessity of a divinely given "law."

It is now opportune to examine more deeply *the* foundation of the Christian moral life, namely, Jesus Christ our Lord.

2. Jesus, the Foundation of the Christian Moral Life

Jesus, Vatican Council II instructs us, "fully reveals man to himself" (*Gaudium et spes,* no. 22). He does so because he is the center of human history, the one who holds primacy of place in God's loving plan for human persons and, indeed, for the whole created universe. This is clearly the central message of the New Testament, a message eloquently summarized by St. Paul in his words to the Colossians:

> He [Christ] is the image of the invisible God, the first-born of all creation; for in him all things were created, in heaven and on earth, visible and invisible . . . — all things were created through him and for him. He is before all things, and in him all things hold together. He is the head of the body, the church; he is the beginning, the first-born from the dead, that in everything he might be preeminent. For in him all the fullness of God was pleased to dwell, and through him to reconcile to himself all things, whether on earth or in heaven, making peace by the blood of the cross. And you, who once were estranged and hostile in mind, doing evil deeds, he has now reconciled in his body of flesh by his death, in order to present you holy and blameless and irreproachable before him [Col 1:15-22].

That Jesus is *the* foundation of the Christian moral life is central to the teaching of John Paul II in his encyclical *Veritatis splendor*. In the introduction to the encyclical, the Holy Father calls attention to the passage from Vatican Council II cited above, emphasizing the truth that "*it is only in the mystery of the Word incarnate that light is shed on the mystery of man*. . . . It is Christ, the last Adam, who fully discloses man to himself and unfolds his noble calling by revealing the mystery of the Father and the Father's love" (no. 2). Jesus, in his very person, "fulfills" the law and brings it to perfection and by doing so reveals to man his noble calling. Thus, the moral life ultimately means following Christ. But we follow Christ, John Paul II writes, not by any outward imitation but by "*becoming conformed to him* who became a servant even to giving himself on the Cross (cf. Phil 2:5-8)" (no. 21). Following Christ means "*holding fast to the very person of Jesus*" (no. 19). Indeed, as John Paul II emphasizes: "*The Crucified Christ reveals the authentic meaning of human freedom; he lives it fully in the total gift of himself* and calls his disciples to share in his freedom" (no. 85). On this, see also the *Catechism of the Catholic Church* (nos. 1701-1715).

Jesus is true God and true man. He is true God, for "in him all the fullness of God was pleased to dwell." He is God's eternal, unbegotten "Word" (cf. Jn 1:1). And Jesus is true man, for he is God's eternal Word made flesh, i.e., man (cf. Jn 1:14). "Born of a woman" (Gal 4:4), he is "like his brothers in every respect" (Heb 2:17), "tempted as we are, yet without sinning" (Heb 4:15). Insofar as he is man, Jesus achieves human fulfillment by living a perfect human life, one manifesting God's goodness in a unique and special way: "I glorified you on earth, having accomplished the work you gave me to do" (Jn

17:4). And his Father crowns his work by raising him — and all persons who are united with him — from the dead. Indeed, as St. Paul teaches us, "Christ has in fact been raised from the dead, the first-fruits of all who have fallen asleep. Death came through one man and in the same way the resurrection of the dead has come through one man. Just as all men die in Adam, so all men will be brought to life in Christ" (1 Cor 15:20-22). Again, as man, Jesus is the "first-born of all creation" (Col 1:15), and is completed by creation united under him: God "has let us know the mystery of his purpose, the hidden plan he so kindly made in Christ from the beginning to act upon when the times had run their course to the end; that he would bring everything together under Christ as head, everything in the heavens and everything on earth" (Eph 1:9-10; cf. Eph 1:22-23).

As God, Jesus unites those who are his own to the Father. "The glory which you have given me I have given to them, that they may be one as we are one, I in them, and you in me, that they may become perfectly one" (Jn 17:22-23). Insofar as he is God, Jesus mediates to us a share in his divinity, for "from his fullness we have all received" (Jn 1:16). Indeed, in Jesus we have become "partakers of the divine nature" (2 Pt 1:4). Because his human life, death, and resurrection was the life, death, and resurrection of God's only-begotten Son, those who are united to him are in truth "begotten" anew. They now become literally "children of God," members of the divine family: "See what love the Father has given us, that we should be called children of God; and so we are. . . . Everyone who believes that Jesus is the Christ is a child of God" (1 Jn 3:1, 5:1).

Through baptism, we are truly united to Christ, dead to sin — i.e., no longer under its sway and impotent before it — and risen to a new kind of life, the life proper to God's own children. St. Thomas put the matter this way:

> Through baptism a person is reborn to a spiritual life, one proper to Christ's faithful, as the Apostle says (Gal 2:20), "the life I now live in the flesh I live by faith in the Son of God [who loved me and gave himself for me]." But this life belongs only to the members who are united with the head, from whom they receive sense and movement. And therefore it is necessary that through baptism a person is incorporated into Christ as his member. For just as sense and movement flow from the natural head to its [bodily] members, so from the spiritual head, who is Christ, flow to his members both a spiritual sense, which consists in the knowledge of the truth, and a spiritual movement, which operates through the inspiration of grace. Hence John says (1:14, 16), "We have seen him full of grace and truth, and of his fullness we have all received." And therefore it follows that the baptized are enlightened by Christ regarding the knowledge

of the truth, and they are impregnated by him with an abundance of good works through the infusion of faith.[12]

Jesus is truly *the* foundation of Christian moral life, for the life we now are empowered to live is in reality a *divine* life as well as a human life. Just as Jesus fully shared our humanity and our human life, so we, by being engrafted onto the "vine" which is Christ (cf. Jn 15:1-11), really share his divinity. In him, we are literally divinized, and our life in union with God begins here and now, to be brought to fulfillment in the heavenly kingdom when, "with death conquered the children of God will be raised in Christ and what was sown in weakness and dishonor will put on the imperishable (cf. 1 Cor 15:42, 53); charity and its works will remain (cf. 1 Cor 13:8; 3:14), and all of creation (cf. Rom 8:19-21), which God made for man, will be set free from its bondage to decay" (*Gaudium et spes*, no. 39). Although our life in union with Jesus — and in, with, and through him, with the Father and the Holy Spirit — will reach its fulfillment only on the day of the resurrection, it is absolutely essential to realize that this divine life is already, here and now, present within us. We are, *now*, God's children; the divine nature has been communicated to us. While always remaining human, we really share in Christ's divinity. We are literally "other Christs," truly his brothers and sisters and in, with, and through him, God's very children.[13]

We receive this divine life in baptism, and this divine life is nurtured by the heavenly food God wills to give us, the body and blood of his Son, our Redeemer and Brother, Jesus Christ. From the earliest times, Christian faith has held that eating this food differs markedly from eating other food. When we eat ordinary food, we transform it into ourselves. But when we ingest Jesus' living body, "he makes our mortal flesh come alive with his glorious resurrection life,"[14] precisely because " 'the partaking of the body and blood of Christ does nothing other than transform us into that which we consume' " (*Lumen gentium*, no. 26, citing St. Leo the Great).[15]

As Grisez points out, our union with Jesus is threefold.[16] There is, first of all, our union with him in divine life as children of God. This is the dimension of our union with Jesus that has already been summarized, for it is the union that divinizes us and makes us to be members of the divine family. This aspect of our unity with Christ begins with baptism and is fulfilled and completed when we see God, no longer in a glass and darkly, but face to face (cf. 1 Cor 13:12).

There is, secondly, the *bodily* union between Jesus and his faithful, the members of his Church. This dimension of our union with Christ, while mysterious, is real. It is this aspect of our union with Jesus that is developed in the New Testament, particularly in the gospel of John and in the Pauline literature. In John's gospel, it is expressed by a metaphor comparing the re-lationship of Jesus to his disciples to that of the vine to its branches (Jn 15:1-8). St. Paul develops this dimension of our union with Jesus in those many passages in his writings when he compares the relationship of Christ to his members, the Church, to the living relationship of the body's head to its members. One of the most striking of these passages is found in 1 Corin-thians 6, where St. Paul says: "Do you not know that your bodies are mem-bers of Christ? Shall I then take Christ's members and make them the members of a prostitute? Of course not! Or do you not know that anyone who joins himself to a prostitute becomes one body with her? For the 'two,' it says, 'will become one flesh.' But whoever is joined to the Lord becomes one spirit with him" (1 Cor 6:15-17).[17]

The author of the epistle to the Ephesians compares the bodily union of Christ to his members to the unity in one flesh of husband and wife (Eph 5:22-33). The one-flesh union of marriage, which is most perfectly actual-ized in fruitful marital union integrating the love-giving and life-giving meanings of the bodily union of husband and wife, sheds much light on the bodily union that exists between Jesus and his bride, the Church. It is a life-giving and a love-giving union. Like husband and wife, Jesus and his mem-bers do not lose their individual identity, and they play distinct roles in their nurturing of life and love, yet they are still one. Moreover, because of this bodily union with Christ — a union that will be brought to completion and fulfillment in the resurrection — the members of Jesus' body share *already* in his resurrection life. Thus, Paul says: "If then you have been raised in Christ, seek the things that are above, where Christ is, seated at the right hand of God. Set your minds on things that are above, not on things that are on earth. For you have died, and your life is hid with Christ in God. When Christ, who is our life, appears, then you also will appear with him in glory" (Col 3:1-4).

Third, and finally, there is a unity between Christ and the Christian in human acts. This dimension of the Christian's union with Jesus will be con-sidered more fully in the next section of this chapter. But here I would like to illustrate this union by noting briefly its paradigmatic exemplar, our union with Jesus' redemptive act in the sacrifice of the Mass, which renews his sacrifice of himself to his Father on the cross and in which he and his people unite in praising and thanking the Father. The Council of Trent definitively teaches that the Mass is a true sacrifice, the renewal of our Lord's sacrifice on the cross (DS 1739-1742), while Vatican Council II reminds us that our Lord instituted the Eucharist to perpetuate the sacrifice of his body and blood through the centuries until he comes again (*Sacrosanctum concilium*, no. 47).

Moreover, as the General Introduction to the *Roman Missal* says: "The Church's rule of prayer corresponds to the Church's enduring rule of faith. It teaches us that the sacrifice of the cross and its sacramental renewal in the Mass are one and the same, differing only in the manner of offering. At the Last Supper Christ the Lord instituted this sacramental renewal and commanded his apostles to do it in memory of him. It is at once a sacrifice of praise and thanksgiving, a sacrifice that reconciles us to the Father and makes amends to him for the sins of the world."[18]

How can the sacrifice of the Mass be "one and the same" with the sacrifice of the cross? And how is our action in the Mass united with Christ's own act of giving himself up to the Father? Here it is necessary to recall a most important matter developed in the first chapter, namely, that human acts are not physical events that come and go like the falling of leaves but spiritual realities that abide within the person until contradictory choices are made. For at the heart of our human actions is a free, self-determining choice that abides within us as part of our identity. Jesus' free choice, as a human being, to suffer death for our salvation so that he could carry out the work given to him by his Father did not end with his death. It abides within him as a determinant of his glorious human identity — for Christ *is now* still a human being, the kind of human being we are called to be but with his humanity hypostatically united to his divinity in the unity of his person. This truth is at the heart of the teaching found in the epistle to the Hebrews, which says, "But when Christ appeared as high priest of the good things that have come, then through the greater and more perfect tent (not made with hands, that is, not of this creation) he entered once for all into the Holy Place, taking not the blood of goats and calves but his own blood, thus securing an eternal redemption" (Heb 9:11-12; cf. Heb 9:24-28; 10:5-14).

The Mass today continues to carry out Jesus' redemptive choice. The way of executing this choice differs from the way it was carried out on Calvary, but it is the very same choice, the oblation of his own body and blood for our reconciliation. Moreover, we, his people, participate in this saving action through the mediation of the priest, who does now what Jesus told him to do at the Last Supper. For, as Vatican Council II teaches, the Mass perpetuates the sacrifice of the cross until Jesus comes again, making it present so that we can share in it (*Sacrosanctum concilium,* no. 47). It is precisely for this reason that the Church "earnestly desires that Christ's faithful, when present at this mystery of faith, should not be there as strangers or silent spectators. On the contrary, through a good understanding of the rites and prayers they should take part in the sacred action, conscious of what they are doing, with devotion and full collaboration. . . . Offering the immaculate victim, not only through the hands of the priest but all *together with him,* they should learn to offer themselves" (*Sacrosanctum concilium,* no. 48; emphasis added).

All of Christian life proceeds from and prepares for the Eucharist, the renewal of Christ's redemptive act and the living food of his disciples wherein their union with him is deepened and enriched. Thus, as Grisez has said, "Christians live in order to have prayer and works, joys and sufferings, to bring to the Offertory; having known Jesus in the breaking of the Bread, Christians come forth from Mass and enter into other activities in order to love and serve the Lord. In the Mass . . . the overarching act of each Christian's life as a whole . . . persons already Christian by baptism become fully joined to Jesus by cooperating in his human act and thus linking their lives (made up of their own acts) with his."[19]

In short, Jesus himself is the foundation of the Christian life. His disciples are one with him insofar as they share in his own divine life, are united bodily with him in a union even more intimate than that between husband and wife, and act in union with him by giving themselves, with him, as an offering of praise and thanksgiving to the Father.

3. Our Baptismal Commitment and Personal Vocation

An important passage from Vatican Council II reads as follows:

> At all times and among every people, God has given welcome to whosoever fears him and does what is right (cf. Acts 10:35). It has pleased God, however, to make men holy and save them not merely as individuals without any mutual bonds, but by making them into a single people, a people which acknowledges him in truth and serves him in holiness. He therefore chose the race of Israel as a people unto himself. With it he set up a covenant. Step by step he taught this people by manifesting in its history both himself and the decree of his will, and by making it holy unto himself. All these things, however, were done by way of preparation and as a figure of that new and perfect covenant which was to be ratified in Christ, and of that more luminous revelation which was to be given through God's very Word made flesh.
>
> "Behold the days shall come, says the Lord, and I will make a new covenant with the house of Israel, and with the house of Judah. . . . I will give my law in their bowels, and I will write it in their heart; and I will be their God; and they shall be my people. . . . For all shall know me, from the least of them even to the greatest, says the Lord" (Jer 31:31-34). Christ instituted this new covenant, that is to say, the new testament, in his blood (cf. 1 Cor 11:25), by calling together a people made up of Jew and Gentile, making them one, not according to the flesh but in the Spirit [*Lumen gentium*, no. 9].

As Grisez observes:

> [T]his passage explicitly mentions three aspects of the life of a Christian which follow from its being life within the covenant. First, the Christian lives within the covenant community, the Church; one's Christian life is not primarily that of an individual before God. Second, one enters into the new covenant not by the flesh (by birth as a Jew) but by the Spirit (by the grace of justification which gives living faith). Third, in the new covenant, one receives a law which must be lived, and it is all the more effective because it is written in the heart of every Christian, not merely inscribed on stone or in the Torah.[20]

In this section I will consider the first two aspects of our lives as Christians noted in *Lumen gentium,* namely, the fact that our life in Christ is a corporate one, as people of his covenanted community, the Church, whose entrance into this community is not by flesh but by the Spirit. I will then consider the indispensable role that each one of us is personally called upon to play within this covenant community by discerning and carrying out our own personal vocation. In the next section of this chapter, the third aspect of our lives as Christians — namely, life in accordance with the "law" of love written in our hearts — will be taken up.

The new and more perfect covenant between God and humankind that was established through the saving death and resurrection of Jesus is the covenant between God and those who accept Jesus in living faith and, by so doing, become incorporated into his body, the Church. The Church is the new people of God, and it is made up of those who have been "regenerated" by the waters of baptism into a new family, the family of God's adopted sons and daughters, the brothers and sisters of Jesus Christ.

Our entry into this new covenant is not by flesh but by the Spirit. Our redemption from sin and resurrection to a new life of justification is first and foremost a gift of God, won for us through the redemptive death and resurrection of Jesus, and communicated to us by the Paraclete, the Spirit whom Father and Son send to us to fill our hearts with divine life and love. But, since God has endowed us with freedom of choice so that we can, through free choice, determine ourselves and freely accept his gift of life, he wills that we cooperate freely with his grace and gift of life. Moved by the Spirit, one enters into the new covenant when one accepts by an act of living faith the justifying and redeeming gift of life in Christ.

One becomes a member of Jesus' people, the Church, in baptism, when one "dies" to the old humanity wounded by Adam's sin (cf. Rom 5:12) and "rises" to a new kind of life, the kind made possible by union with the risen

Lord: "We were buried therefore with him by baptism into death, so that as Christ was raised from the dead by the glory of the Father, we too might walk in newness of life" (Rom 6:4). Through baptism, we have "put on Christ" (Gal 3:27) and live in union with him. And at the heart of baptism is a free, self-determining choice whereby one renounces a life of sin and commits oneself to live henceforward worthily as a child of God, a member of Christ's body. Most of us were baptized as infants and, at that time, could not actually make free choices for ourselves. But others, our godparents, stood as our proxies, responding in our name to the call to die to sin and live in a way worthy of God's own children. And, as we grew in the household of the faith, we renewed our baptismal commitment when we received the sacrament of confirmation; and we are given the opportunity to reaffirm this commitment frequently during our lives, particularly during the liturgy of the Easter Vigil.

Baptism, in other words, entails the kind of choice rightly called a commitment. It is, as Grisez notes, *the* fundamental option of the Christian,[21] whereby the Christian freely commits himself or herself to a life in union with Jesus. In and through this overarching choice, the Christian is committed to share in Christ's redemptive work. Our task as Christians is to complete, in our own flesh, "what is lacking in Christ's afflictions for the sake of his body, that is, the church" (Col 1:24). Jesus wills that we, his members, complete the redemptive work that he has begun so that "we all attain to the unity of faith and of the knowledge of the Son of God, to mature manhood, to the measure of the stature of the fullness of Christ" (Eph 4:13), until Jesus "will change our lowly body to be like his glorious body, by the power which enables him even to subject all things to himself' (Phil 3:21). In and through baptism, God pours into our hearts his very own life and love, and in receiving this superabundant gift, bequeathed to us by virtue of Jesus' saving death and resurrection, we in turn commit ourselves to cooperating with our Redeemer in his saving mission.[22]

Indeed, as St. Paul stresses in his letters to the Thessalonians, the first of which probably was written a short twenty years after the death and resurrection of Jesus, our entire life as Christians is to be a preparation for the Parousia, when Jesus will return in glory to bring to final completion his saving mission. It is to this life of preparation that we commit ourselves in baptism. And since through baptism God's love has been communicated to us, making us his holy ones and children capable of walking worthily in the new life to which we have been raised, Paul's prayer is that the Lord may make us "abound and overflow in love toward one another and toward all men," in order to strengthen our hearts "blameless in holiness before our God and Father at the coming of our Lord Jesus with all his saints" (1 Thes 3:12-13); his prayer is that "the God of peace himself may sanctify [us] wholly," so that our whole being, "spirit, soul, and body, may be kept sound and blameless for the coming of our Lord Jesus Christ" (1 Thes 5:23-24). It is precisely because our life in Christ is to participate in his redemptive work, and in this way prepare the way for his glorious second coming, that Paul likewise prays that "God may make [us] worthy of his call, and may fulfill every good resolve and work of faith, so that the name of our Lord Jesus may be glorified in [us] and [we] in him, according to the grace of our God and the Lord Jesus Christ" (2 Thes 1:11-12).[23]

Our life as Christians begins when, in living faith, we accept God's word (1 Thes 1:6; 2:13; Eph 1:13), which the gospels compare to a seed sown in good soil (Mt 13:23; Mk 4:20; Lk 8:15), and which Paul regards as a continually active power in believers (1 Thes 2:13), having an inner power to bear fruit and grow (Col 1:5f; Eph 1:13; 2 Cor 6:1). But it is not enough simply to have received the word. The Christian's baptismal commitment requires him or her to take up the "sword given by the Spirit" and use it as a weapon in the spiritual combat (Eph 6:17).

God is indeed our Savior and Redeemer. It is through his initiative that we are *now*, by virtue of the love he has poured into our hearts, saved (Ti 3:5; Eph 2:5, 8; 1 Cor 15:1). He has sanctified us (1 Cor 1:2; 6:11), filling us with the fullness of Christ (Col 1:10), making us new men and women (Eph 2:15), clothing us in Christ (Gal 3:27) and making us new creatures (2 Cor 5:17), pouring his love into us through the Holy Spirit (Rom 5:5), so that we are indeed called by him and chosen (Rom 1:6; 8:28, 33; 1 Cor 1:24; Col 3:12) and made into his children, the children of light (Eph 5:8; 1 Thes 5:5; 1 Jn 3:1). But God's work in us is not completed by baptism. God continues to save us (1 Cor 1:18; 2 Cor 2:15), to make us holy and blameless (1 Thes 5:23; 3:13). And we are called and empowered by his grace to respond freely and be his co-workers in perfecting our holiness (2 Cor 7:1) by wholeheartedly dedicating ourselves to a life of righteousness and sanctification (Rom 6:19). It is our task continually to "put on the Lord Jesus Christ" (Rom 13:14), casting off the works of darkness and putting on the armor of light (Rom 13:2; Eph 5:8-11). As the children of the God who is love, our call and commitment is to "abide in him" (1 Jn 2:28; 4:13f) and walk in the light and not in darkness (1 Jn 1:7).

By reason of our baptismal commitment, we are, in short, "to be what we are!"[24] We are to image Christ in our lives, to cooperate with him in redeeming others and, indeed, in redeeming the entire cosmos. We are to lead apostolic lives, for like the apostles we, too, are sent into the world in the love and service of the Lord (cf. the final words of the Mass, when we are sent forth to bring God's saving work to others by our own daily deeds).

Such is the meaning of our baptism and our baptismal commitment. Jesus and his bride, the Church, give birth to us as children of God and brothers and sisters of the Lord. By freely accepting this God-given identity, we commit ourselves to walk worthily in the vocation to which we have been called.

Christians have a common vocation or call to sanctity, to perfection: "[A]s he who called you is holy, be holy yourselves in all your conduct, since it is written, 'You shall be holy, for I am holy'" (1 Pt 1:15-16). They therefore must keep the Lord's commandments, for only in this way will they truly love him: "He who has my commandments and keeps them, he it is who loves me" (Jn 14:21; cf. 1 Jn 2:5; 3:24; 4:21). And what are these? "If you would enter life," Jesus tells us, "keep the commandments." And in reply to the rich young man who inquired about them, he replied: "You shall not kill, You shall not commit adultery, You shall not steal, You shall not bear false witness, Honor your father and mother, and, You shall love your neighbor as yourself" (Mt 19:17-18). Christians are to walk in the same way that Jesus walked (cf. 1 Jn 2:6). And to follow Jesus is to make one's own his commitment to redeem: "If any man would come after me, let him deny himself and take up his cross and follow me. For whoever would save his life will lose it, and whoever loses his life for my sake and the gospel's will save it" (Mk 8:34-35). Thus, Christians, in answering God's call and in carrying out their vocation, will shape their lives in accord with the teaching of the Church, their mother and Christ's spotless bride (on this, see Chapter Seven). Above all, to remain faithful to their baptismal commitment and to carry out their vocation, Christians will love even as they have been and are loved by God in Christ: "This is my commandment, that you love one another as I have loved you" (Jn 15:12). In the following section of this chapter, an effort will be made to show how Jesus' command to love even as he loves inwardly transforms and perfects the moral life of the Christian. My point here is that our common Christian vocation requires us to keep the commandments as these are understood within Christ's body, the Church, and to love even as Jesus loves.

But in addition to their common vocation, each Christian has a unique and irreplaceable vocation within the family of God, the Church. Not only are different Christians called to different ways of life in the world — the married life, the priestly life, the religious life, the life of a single person within the world — but within each state of life each Christian has his or her unique role to play in filling up what is lacking in Christ's afflictions and in bringing to completion his work of redemption. Vatican Council II, as Germain Grisez so aptly points out,[25] insists that each one of us has a personal vocation to carry out as a member of Jesus' people. Indeed, as the Council Fathers noted, "by our faith we are bound all the more to fulfill these responsibilities [our earthly ones as Christians] according to the vocation of each one" (*Gaudium et spes*, no. 43). And, as Grisez likewise notes, the personal vocation of each one of us as Christians is emphasized by Pope John Paul II, who seeks to build on the teaching of St. Paul, in his encyclical *Redemptor hominis*. For in that document, the Holy Father wrote:

> For the whole of the community of the People of God and for each member of it what is in question is not just a specific "social membership"; rather, for each and every one what is essential is a particular "vocation." Indeed, the Church as the People of God is also — according to the teaching of St. Paul . . ., of which Pius XII reminded us in wonderful terms — "Christ's Mystical Body." Membership in that body has for its source a particular call united with the saving action of grace. Therefore, if we wish to keep in mind this community of the People of God, which is so vast and so extremely differentiated, we must see first and foremost Christ saying in a way to each member of the community, "Follow Me" [no. 71].

Moreover, in his 1988 apostolic exhortation *Christifideles Laici,* John Paul II had this to say about personal vocation:

> God calls me and sends me forth as a laborer in his vineyard. He calls me and sends me forth. . . . This personal vocation and mission defines the dignity and the responsibility of each member of the lay faithful. . . . To be able to discover the actual will of God in our lives always involves the following: a receptive listening to the Word of God and the Church, fervent and constant prayer, recourse to a wise and loving spiritual guide, and a faithful discernment of the gifts and talents given by God, as well as the social and historic situations in which one lives [no. 58].

Personal vocation is each individual Christian's unique way of following Jesus, of walking in his path. Jesus needs the special contribution each one of us can make to complete his work of redemption. Thus, as Grisez says, "Not only do all Christians share the common vocation to follow Jesus and not only do particular Christians share the vocation to particular states of life, but each Christian also has a personal vocation: his or her unique way of following Jesus."[26]

Thus, by our baptismal commitment we are persons who have chosen to accept God's saving word in faith and to shape our lives in accord with the demands of living faith. As new creatures, begotten anew in Christ Jesus, we are called to a life of perfection, with the responsibility to order our choices and lives in accordance with the commandments of the Lord as these are proposed to us by his bride, the Church (on this, see Chapter Seven). In addition, each one of us has a unique personal vocation, an indispensable role to play in bringing Christ's work of redemption to completion. In order to carry out this role, however, we need help. And Jesus, our best and wisest friend, gives us this help in the form of the "law" of the new covenant, his "law" of love. To this we will now turn our attention so that we can see how this divinely given law fulfills, perfects, and transforms the natural law that we considered in Chapter Three.

4. Christian Love, the Principle of Our Life in Christ

In order to introduce this section, it will be useful, I believe, to note some of St. Thomas Aquinas's observations on the new "law" of the gospel, the law of love. As will be recalled, one of the principal reasons the Common Doctor of the Church advanced for humankind's need of a divinely revealed law, in addition to natural law, if human persons are to be fully the beings God wills them to be, is the fact that they are, in truth, called to an end that surpasses human understanding and human capacity, namely, life eternal with God himself, a life that begins here and now. To enable his children to attain this end and to live worthily as his children, God gave them a "law." This divinely revealed law, given in its preliminary form to Moses and the Chosen People of the old covenant when it was written on stones, was communicated in its fullness to human beings by Jesus, God's Son and our brother, when he established the new and everlasting covenant between God and his people and inscribed this law in their hearts. And, as St. Thomas teaches, what is "most powerful in the law of new covenant, and in which its whole power consists, is the grace of the Holy Spirit, which is given through faith." Therefore, he continues, "the new law is first and foremost the very grace of the Holy Spirit, which is given to Christ's faithful."[27]

This law not only gives us the knowledge of what we are to do if we are to be fully the beings we are meant to be, it also inwardly enables us, St. Thomas says, to *do* everything necessary to live fully as God wills us to.[28] In fact, although we are still capable of sinning (even though we have been reborn in the Spirit) until we are confirmed in glory, the new law given to us in Jesus, "insofar as it is considered in itself, gives us sufficient help so that we can avoid sin."[29] For the new law divinely inscribed in our hearts by God himself is precisely the "law of love."[30]

As we have seen in our study of natural law in Chapter Three, the twofold law of love of God and neighbor is, as St. Thomas and the Catholic tradition maintain, the basic moral norm for discriminating between choices that are morally upright and those that are morally bad. This is the law of love divinely revealed to Moses and the people of the old covenant. Our Lord himself, in answering the question "Which is the greatest commandment of the Law?"

— i.e., the divinely revealed law given to the Chosen People through Moses — referred to key passages in the Old Testament (Dt 6:5 and Lv 19:18), and said, " 'You must love the Lord your God with all your heart, with all your soul, and with all your mind.' This is the greatest and the first commandment. And the second is like to it: 'You must love your neighbor as yourself' " (Mt 23:37-39; cf. Mk 12:28-34; Lk 10:25-29). From this twofold law of love are derived, as we have seen, the Ten Commandments.[31] Moreover, as we have seen, this twofold law of love of God and neighbor can be articulated in a more philosophical way as follows: "In voluntarily acting for human goods, and avoiding what is opposed to them, one ought to choose and otherwise will those and only those possibilities whose willing is compatible with a will toward integral human fulfillment."[32] Jesus himself reaffirms this "law" and its requirements.

But Jesus does more than this, for the "law" he writes in our hearts through the gift of the Holy Spirit in baptism inwardly transfigures and fulfills this law of love. He gives to us a new commandment, for we, his brothers and sisters, risen now to a new life and able, in, with, and through Jesus to call God our Father, must love even as we have been and are loved by God in Christ. "A new commandment I give to you, that you love one another; even as I have loved you, that you also love one another. By this all men will know that you are my disciples" (Jn 13:34-35). Like Jesus, we must be ready to lay down our lives for our brothers and sisters (cf. Jn 15:12-14; 1 Jn 3:16). As Grisez notes, "these characteristics of Jesus' love result from a more fundamental principle: His human love for us is rooted in his divine love, which he receives in being begotten by the Father and which he shares with us. Thus he says, 'As the Father has loved me, so have I loved you; abide in my love' " (Jn 15:9).[33] The demand to love even as we have been and are loved by God in Jesus is what is *new* in the divine law communicated to us by the grace of the Holy Spirit. As God's sons and daughters, Christians must love as God's only-begotten Son-made-man loves.

Moreover, God, who is love (cf. 1 Jn 4:8), pours his own life and love into our being when we, through baptism (and through the renewal of our baptismal commitment throughout our lives), accept his word in living faith. His own life and love are given to us through the Holy Spirit because of the redemptive work of Jesus. And his love, present within us, is *the* principle or source of our lives as his children. Empowered now to walk worthily in the vocation to which we are called, we Christians are now able to love even as Jesus loves. Because this is so, the basic moral norm of love of God and neighbor, philosophically articulated as above, is inwardly transformed. As Grisez perceptively says, "Christian love transforms the first principle of morality into a more definite norm: One ought to will those and only those possibilities which contribute to the integral human fulfillment being realized in the fulfillment of all things in Jesus."[34]

Our moral life is, as we have seen, our way of cooperating with Jesus' redemptive act. In addition, since every act of each Christian's life should contribute to the carrying out of the unique vocation to which each Christian is called, everything in our lives should be transformed by Christian love, the love that God himself pours into our hearts and in which we are to "abide." It thus follows that every one of our personal choices, every act in our lives, should be inwardly shaped by a more-than-human love, by the divine love that God himself communicates to us through his Holy Spirit through the mediation of his eternally begotten Son-made-flesh, Jesus Christ. As the inner principle of the Christian moral life, the love given to us by God himself gives us the power to live as his children, to unite our own personal acts with the saving act of Jesus, and to carry out faithfully our own personal vocation.

In *Veritatis splendor,* John Paul II clearly teaches that love is the principle of Christian life. He stresses that Jesus reveals to us that authentic human "freedom is acquired in *love,* that is, in the *gift of self* . . . the gift of self *in service to God and one's brethren*" (no. 87). This is the ultimate truth meant to guide our choices: to love, even as we have been and are loved by God in Christ, whose "crucified flesh fully reveals the unbreakable bond between freedom and truth, just as his Resurrection from the dead is the supreme exaltation of the fruitfulness and saving power of a freedom lived out in truth" (no. 87). The pope further points out that "those who live 'by the flesh' experience God's law as a burden," while those "who are impelled by love and 'walk in the Spirit' (Gal 5:16) . . . find in God's law the fundamental and necessary way in which to practice love as something freely chosen and freely lived out" (no. 18). Men and women *can,* with God's never-failing grace, "abide" in love (cf. no. 24).

5. The Beatitudes, Specifying the Requirements of Christian Love

According to St. Thomas Aquinas, the Lord's Sermon on the Mount (Mt 5) "contains completely the information needed for the Christian life. In it the inner movements of the person are perfectly ordered."[35] In saying this, St. Thomas was simply reaffirming a Christian tradition going back to the Fathers of the Church. Indeed, as St. Augustine so aptly said, "If a person will devoutly and calmly consider the sermon which our Lord Jesus Christ spoke on the mount, I think he will find in it, as measured by the highest norms of morality, the *perfect pattern of the Christian life*"[36] (emphasis added). Moreover, as Grisez notes, in his *The Credo of the People of God* Pope Paul VI stresses the beatitudes in his summary of Jesus' moral teaching. Our Lord announced and established the kingdom, gave to his disciples the new commandment to love one another as he does, and "taught us the way of the Beatitudes of the gospel: poverty in spirit, meekness, suffering borne with patience, thirst after justice, mercy, purity of heart, will for peace, persecution suffered for justice' sake."[37] By linking the beatitudes so intimately with the commandment to love as Jesus does, Pope Paul infers that the beatitudes can be regarded as the model summary of the uniquely Christian content of Jesus' moral teaching.

In *Veritatis splendor*, John Paul II, following St. Augustine, calls our Lord's Sermon on the Mount the *"magna charta* of Christian morality" (no. 15). In his Sermon on the Mount, Jesus emphasized that he had not "come to abolish the law and the prophets," but rather "to fulfill them" (Mt 5:17). The pope goes on to say that *"Jesus brings the commandments to fulfillment . . . by interiorizing their demands and by bringing out their fullest meaning. . . .* Thus the commandment 'You shall not kill' becomes a call to an attentive love which protects and promotes the life of one's neighbor. The precept prohibiting adultery becomes an invitation to a pure way of looking at others, capable of respecting the spousal meaning of the body" (no. 15).

The beatitudes of the Sermon on the Mount, the Holy Father continues, "speak of basic attitudes and dispositions in life and therefore they *do not coincide exactly with the commandments.* On the other hand, *there is no separation or opposition* between the Beatitudes and the commandments: both refer to the good, to eternal life" (no. 16). They are "above all *promises*, from which there also indirectly flow *normative indications* for the moral life . . . they are a sort of *self-portrait of Christ . . . invitations to discipleship and to communion of life with Christ"* (no. 16). (On this matter, also see the *Catechism of the Catholic Church*, nos. 1716-1729.)

The citation from John Paul II's *Veritatis splendor* provides us with perceptive insights into the way in which the beatitudes relate to Christian love. I shall now, after briefly reviewing some material already discussed in order to provide a framework within which the Sermon on the Mount can be fitted, attempt to offer a more detailed understanding of this issue.

We have also seen that Christian love, the principle of our new life in Christ and the divinely given "law" of the gospel, fulfills, completes, and transforms the natural law. As will be recalled, the basic normative principle of natural law is religiously expressed as love of God and love of neighbor and is philosophically articulated as a readiness to choose and otherwise will those and only those possibilities compatible with integral human fulfillment. Christian love fulfills, completes, and transforms the natural law, so expressed, by further specifying it. We are now commanded to love even as we have been and are loved by God in Christ, and in order to love in this way we, Christ's brothers and sisters, are to choose and otherwise will those and only those possibilities which contribute to the integral human fulfillment being realized in the fulfillment of all things in Christ.

The beatitudes (or blessings), promised by our Lord to his faithful disciples in his Sermon on the Mount, are rooted in the new command that Jesus gave us to love as he loves. In my opinion, the most significant attempt by a contemporary Catholic theologian to show how the beatitudes are related to Christian love is found in the work of Germain Grisez, who seeks in this way to develop the long Christian tradition, affirmed by St. Augustine and St. Thomas, that the Sermon on the Mount is indeed the charter of our lives as Christians. Much of what follows, accordingly, will be my attempt to summarize Grisez's thought on this subject.[38]

In Chapter Three, we saw that the first moral principle of the natural law — the twofold law of love of God and neighbor, of willing integral human fulfillment — was specified by the various "modes of responsibility" insofar as these modes specified ways of choosing that are incompatible with a respect for integral human fulfillment, with a heart open to the goods perfective of human persons and of the persons in whom these goods are meant to flourish.[39] Modes of Christian response, in a similar way, specify the requirements of the gospel law of Christian love, which fulfills and transforms the natural law. These modes of Christian response specify ways of acting that mark a person whose will, enlivened by the love of God poured into his or her heart, is inwardly disposed to act with the confidence born of his or her Christian hope, that integral human fulfillment is indeed realizable in union with Jesus. These are the modes characterizing the life of persons who, by reason of their living faith, are called "blessed" by the Lord, for the modes of Christian response ought, Grisez observes, to be regarded more as blessings than demands.[40] They are internal dispositions, inclining the Christian to do what is pleasing to God. They are Christian virtues, and as rooted in God's gift of his own life and love, they can rightly be considered as "gifts" of his Spirit.

What exactly are these beatitudes? According to Matthew's account of the Sermon on the Mount they are the following: "Blessed are the poor in spirit, / for theirs is the kingdom of heaven. / Blessed are those who mourn, / for they shall be comforted. / Blessed are the meek, / for they shall inherit the earth. / Blessed are those who hunger and thirst for righteousness, / for they shall be satisfied. / Blessed are the merciful, / for they shall obtain mercy. / Blessed are the pure of heart, / for they shall see God. / Blessed are the peacemakers, / for they shall be called the children of God. / Blessed are those who are persecuted for righteousness' sake, / for theirs is the kingdom of heaven" (Mt 5:3-10).

Reflection on the beatitudes helps us understand that they propose norms of Christian life more specific than the commandment to love as Jesus does —

the first principle of Christian morality. Yet they are not so specific as definite norms of Christian life, i.e., norms identifying the precise human choices and acts that one, as a Christian, is called upon to do here and now in carrying out his or her unique personal vocation. They are rather modes of Christian response, internal Christian dispositions or virtues, linked traditionally, as in the thought of St. Augustine and St. Thomas Aquinas, to the "gifts" of the Holy Spirit[41] as enumerated in Isaiah 11:1 — "And the Spirit of the Lord shall rest upon him, the spirit of wisdom and understanding, the spirit of counsel and might, the spirit of knowledge and fear of the Lord" — to which the Christian tradition, relying on the Vulgate translation of Isaiah, added the "spirit of piety."

When the beatitudes are considered within this framework, Grisez believes that the modes of Christian response can be expressed as follows:

1. *To expect and accept all good, including the good fruits of one's work, as God's gift* — for the "poor in spirit" understand that their achievements are only a share, given freely and generously by God, in his fullness. The virtuous disposition is humility; the Christian vice is pride. The corresponding gift of the Spirit is fear of the Lord. . . .

2. *To accept one's limited role in the Body of Christ and fulfill it* — for the "meek" understand that submissiveness to God's will involves no loss or delay to their personal fulfillment. The virtuous disposition is "Christian dedication," while lukewarmness and minimalism are opposed to it. The corresponding gift of the Spirit is piety or godliness, an attitude of filial reverence and dutifulness toward God.

3. *To put aside or avoid everything which is not necessary or useful in the fulfillment of one's personal vocation* — for those who "mourn" (not only contrite sinners but all those who turn from transient goods to fulfillment in Jesus) understand that to be disposed to goodness itself frees one from the pursuit of particular, finite goods for their own sake. The virtuous disposition is detachment; worldliness and anxiety are opposed dispositions. The corresponding gift of the Spirit is knowledge, by which one discerns what belongs to faith and judges everything by its light.

4. *To endure fearlessly whatever is necessary or useful for the fulfillment of one's personal vocation* — for those who "hunger and thirst for righteousness" understand that they have nothing whatsoever to fear. The virtuous disposition is the faithfulness and heroism characteristic of the martyr, though required of all Christians, while weakness of faith and faintheartedness in the face of non-Christian standards are among the Christian vices. The corresponding gift of the Spirit is fortitude.

5. *To be merciful according to the universal and perfect measure of mercy which God has revealed in Jesus* — for those who "are merciful" understand

that they are to be disinterested and selfless as God is. The virtuous disposition is mercy, compassion, service to others on the model of Jesus, while the opposed vice is a legalistic attitude toward others. The gift of the Spirit is counsel. . . .

6. *To strive to conform one's whole self to living faith, and purge anything which does not meet this standard* — for the "pure of heart" understand that in this life charity requires continuous conversion. The virtuous disposition is single-minded devotion to God, including a sense of sin and continuing conversion, while the Christian vice is reflected in mediocrity and insincerity. The corresponding gift of the Spirit is understanding.

7. *To respond to evil with good, not with resistance, much less with destructive action* — for "peacemakers" understand that the effort to live according to divine love must be universally conciliatory. The virtuous disposition is the conciliatoriness which seeks the redemption of enemies; one opposed disposition is the tendency to shun evil instead of carrying on a redemptive ministry to those enslaved by it. The corresponding gift of the Spirit is wisdom, the power of putting in order as peacemakers do.

8. *To do no evil that good might come of it, but suffer evil together with Jesus in cooperation with God's redeeming love* — for "those persecuted for righteousness' sake" understand that one must undergo evil in order to bring the evildoer in touch with perfect goodness. The virtuous disposition is self-oblation, the Christian vice the fragile rectitude of the person who does not wish to sin but seeks fulfillment in this world. Since there are only seven gifts, Augustine assigns none here; however, one might say there is a corresponding gift, unique to each Christian and disposing him or her to offer God the unique gift of himself or herself.[42]

6. The Question of Specific Christian Moral Norms

The natural law — or what can be called the "common morality of humankind" — is brought to perfection and fulfillment by the new gospel law of love. But the natural law is *not*, however, annulled or contradicted by the new law of love. Christian love unequivocally requires that Jesus' brothers and sisters conform their choices and actions to the principles and norms of natural law — the principles and norms, including absolute or exceptionless norms, considered in Chapters Three and Four. Indeed, the Church, Christ's spouse and the bulwark of truth, insists steadfastly on the truth of these principles and norms, of which the Church is the "authoritative interpreter" (cf. *Dignitatis humanae*, no. 14).

As we have seen, faith in Christ and the God-given love poured into the hearts of his faithful inwardly transform the basic principle of natural law and the modes of responsibility that further specify it. The Christian is to choose and otherwise will those and only those possibilities whose willing is compatible with the integral human fulfillment being realized in and through Jesus' redemptive work, the work in which each Christian is personally called to share. Uniting his or her life and actions with the redemptive life and action of Jesus, the Christian responds by choosing in such a way that his or her whole life embodies the virtues characteristic of those called "blessed" by the Lord.

Yet the question remains: Are there specific Christian moral norms, i.e., norms identifying ways of choosing and acting that are uniquely Christian and knowable only in the light of faith? On the one hand, it would seem that there are not, for the specific moral norms knowable by virtue of the basic principles of natural law and its modes of responsibility seem sufficient to order human choices and actions; so why are additional norms necessary? On the other hand, a study of Scripture, in particular the New Testament, and reflection on the material previously set forth in this chapter would seem to indicate that there are moral norms specifically Christian in content. The gospels, in particular the gospel according to Matthew, describe Jesus as presenting a strikingly new and distinctive morality or way of life, one that as a whole surpasses in its content anything found in the Old Testament as well as in any other religion or philosophy. Jesus' command that we forgive our enemies and do good to those who persecute us, although perhaps suggested or foreshadowed in the moral teaching of others, is at the heart of a new and unique way of coping with evil, and all this is illustrated most perfectly in Jesus' own life, passion, and death (Mt 5:38-48; Mk 8:31-33; Lk 9:22). Jesus' disciples are called to carry their cross and follow him (Mt 16:24; Mk 8:34; Lk 9:23). And above all, Christians are to love as Jesus does (Jn 13:34-35). Finally, Paul's whole teaching on the union between Christ and his members implies that Christian love gives rise to specific norms unique to those who by faith live in Christ.

The question of specific Christian norms is the subject of much debate among Catholic theologians today. Many, including Charles E. Curran, Timothy E. O'Connell, Richard McCormick, Josef Fuchs, and Bruno Schüller, deny that there are norms specific to Christians.[43] While these theologians generally acknowledge that Christian faith provides motives and intentions for acting morally that are specifically Christian, they do not see the need for affirming the existence of norms identifying specific sorts of human choices and actions that are uniquely or distinctively Christian in character.[44]

At times, these theologians invoke the authority of St. Thomas Aquinas to support their position, referring to a text in which St. Thomas affirmed that the new law of love added no directives for external actions above and beyond the directives provided by natural law.[45] Despite the fact that St. Thomas did indeed teach this, however, appeal to this text does not resolve the issue even on the grounds of St. Thomas's authority. For St. Thomas also taught quite clearly that there are specific Christian virtues, divinely given to those united to Christ through the outpouring of God's love, and that these virtues are the principles from which specifically Christian ways of acting proceed.[46] He likewise held that Christians are specifically obliged to fast and give alms.[47] The issue was never formally addressed as such by St. Thomas; a resolution of the question on the basis of his thought requires patient interpretation of different texts.

Other contemporary Catholic theologians insist that there are specifically Christian moral norms. Among theologians holding this view are Hans Urs von Balthasar, Josef Ratzinger, Dionigi Tettamanzi, Bernhard Stoeckle, and Germain Grisez.[48] Here as elsewhere, Grisez's thought is, in my opinion, very helpful and insightful, succinctly synthesizing important biblical perspectives and elements noted by some of the other authors mentioned.

The common basis of these authors' claim that there are specifically Christian moral norms is the existential condition of humankind. As we have already seen, because of sin, original and personal, it is difficult for us both to know and to do the good. Thus, even with respect to specific moral norms that are, in principle, knowable in the light of natural law principles, divine revelation is needed. In short, moral truth about *some* matters *can* be securely known without divine revelation, but moral truth about *other* matters can be known *securely* only because God has revealed what truly ought to be done (cf. Vatican Council I, *Dei Filius*, c. 2; DS 3003, 3004, 3005). This, however, does not show the need for norms specifically Christian in content and knowable *only* in the light of divine revelation. But in addition to being fallen and sinful creatures, human persons are *now*, by virtue of Christ's redemptive work and their union with him, *new* creatures, truly members of the divine family and capable of living a new kind of life and, in truth, of sharing in Christ's work of redeeming sinners and the world. Thus, Christian faith can give rise to specific norms proper to the Christian way of life. "It does this," Grisez says, "by proposing options both possible for and appealing to fallen men and women — options which either cannot be conceived without faith or would lack sufficient appeal to be considered in deliberation in the absence of Christian hope. Specific moral norms are generated only when proposals are articulated as appealing possibilities for choice. Thus, by advancing fresh proposals, faith generates specific norms which could not be known without it."[49] Hence, by taking into account the actual existential situation of men and women as fallen and redeemed, Christian faith can and does give rise to specific moral norms. One specific moral norm for the Christian is that he or she "should find, accept, and faithfully carry out [his or her] personal vocation."[50]

In addition, as one carries out one's personal vocation to follow Jesus and to cooperate with him in his redemptive work, new alternatives and possibilities will be suggested as specific ways of implementing this vocation. This is indeed the situation that was seemingly in St. Thomas's mind when he said that "just as sense and movement flow from the natural head to its [bodily] members, so from the spiritual head, who is Christ, flow to his members both a spiritual sense, which consists in the knowledge of the truth, and a spiritual movement, which operates through the inspiration of grace."[51]

To summarize, Christian faith, while in no way annulling or contradicting the principles and norms of natural law, inwardly transforms its basic normative principle by showing how integral human fulfillment is to be realized by cooperating with Christ's redemptive work and likewise inwardly transforms its modes of responsibility into Christian modes of responding in ways characterizing those whom the Lord calls "blessed." In addition, taking realistically into account the existential condition of human persons as wounded by sin but now, by virtue of Jesus' saving act, capacitated to live truly as God's own children, it also proposes specific norms for each Christian as he or she discerns and faithfully implements his or her unique personal vocation to follow Jesus and help bring to completion his redemptive work.

7. The Practicality of the Christian Moral Life

Is the Christian moral life, as outlined in the previous pages, truly capable of being led? Or is it simply an unattainable ideal, utterly unrealistic and incapable of achievement? Is it, moreover, rigoristic in its demands, placing intolerable burdens upon people without considering their weakness and frailty?

In some senses, the Christian moral life is an ideal because to live it requires a determined and lifelong effort in the face of serious obstacles and, at times, personal failure. In this sense, being just and chaste and courageous in our lives is also an ideal. It is likewise an ideal to be honest in one's business dealings, to refuse to cheat on one's income tax when "everyone else" is doing so, and to be a good parent. But simply because it is at times very hard to be just and chaste and courageous, to be honest in our business dealings and social responsibilities, and to be good parents, no one would conclude that these are impossible and unrealizable ideals. The requirements to be just, to be good parents, etc., are binding norms, not electives, for the morally upright person. So too, for the Christian, being all this and, in addition, loving God with our whole heart and soul and strength and our neighbors as ourselves, and, indeed, loving others even as Jesus does are not optional electives but requirements of the new law of love.

To forgive our enemies, to return good for evil, to suffer evil and, by doing so, to share in Jesus' redemptive work are all strictly binding demands of Christian love. To act in this way is *not*, for the Christian, a nebulous ideal to be achieved in some utopia but a requirement of the Christian life and the only realistic way to overcome evil in our lives and in the world.

We are called to be perfect, even as our heavenly Father is perfect. And perfection consists in living a life of Christian love. Our perfection, of course, will not be completed until the resurrection, but it begins *here and now*, because, as a result of God's gracious initiative, we are, by reason of our union with Jesus, already his children. His own life, his love, is within us, and we are to abide in his love (cf. 1 Jn 4:16) and in this way day by day grow in holiness and love by participating ever more deeply in the love that he pours into our hearts.

Christians frequently fail, at times blamelessly, to live as love requires. No one is held to the impossible. One cannot be morally responsible for anything that one cannot truly choose to do, either because it does not occur to one, because one can see no point in doing it, or because one can think of no way to begin doing it. And, at times, each one of us is in this sort of situation, so that it is subjectively not possible to do what Christian love requires. But obstacles of this kind can be overcome as we mature in the faith and come to realize ever more deeply what our baptismal commitment entails.

It is also true that we frequently fail to live Christian lives because of our own neglect and sinful choices. Even Peter, the apostle whom Jesus chose to be the rock on which to build his Church, cowardly abandoned his Lord. And each one of us is painfully aware of our own betrayals of Jesus. But Jesus in his love and mercy is ready to bring us reconciliation and give to us again and again the love that is life if we are willing to repent our sins and accept the forgiveness he wills to give us.

The biggest problem, I believe, in living the Christian life and in carrying out faithfully our personal vocation is that we want to hold back. We refuse to give ourselves to the God of love, to let him take possession of us and come to abide in us. Like St. Augustine, who once said, "Give me chastity, O Lord, but not yet,"[52] we want God's love to abide in us and to abide in it, but not yet — because we know that if this happens we will have to give up some things to which we are attached and which we find attractive despite their irreconcilability with a truly Christian life. Our need is to put first things first — the love of God and of others, even as they have been and are loved by God in Christ. If, with God's never-failing help, we do this, we will mature in Christ and abide ever more deeply in his Father's love.

The Christian moral life, moreover, is *not* rigoristic. It is not a legalistic code of do's and don'ts, arbitrarily imposed upon us from without in order to restrict our liberty. Rather, the life of Christian love is an internal demand of our nature as redeemed by Christ and, in, with, and through him, raised to the level of the divine. For, as we have seen already, in Christ we are divinized, made sharers in his divinity just as he shares our humanity, so that we are in truth his brothers and sisters, children of his Father. By abiding in God's love and cooperating with Jesus in his redemptive work, we will indeed achieve integral human fulfillment; we will become truly the beings God wills us to be.

To put matters another way, if we live up to our baptismal commitment and endeavor day by day to carry out our personal vocation, we will be able to live the Christian life. As the Council of Trent said:

> Therefore, in this way the justified become both the "friends of God" and members of his household (see Jn 15:15; Eph 2:19), advancing from virtue to virtue (see Ps 83:8), renewed (as the Apostle says) day by day (see 2 Cor 4:16), that is, by mortifying the members of their flesh (see Col 3:5) and showing them as weapons of justice (see Rom 6:13, 19) unto sanctification by observing the commandments of God and of the Church. When faith works along with their works (see Jas 2:22), the justified increase in the very justice which they have received through the grace of Christ and are justified the more, as it is written, "He who is just, let him be just still" (Rv 22:11), and again, "Fear not to be justified even to death" (Sir 18:22), and again, "You see that by works a man is justified, and not by faith only" (Jas 2:24). Indeed, the holy Church begs this increase of justice when she prays, "O Lord, give us an increase of faith, hope, and charity" [Council of Trent, DS 1535].

If we are, moreover, to live our lives as faithful followers of Jesus, we need to make use of the aids he wills to give us in our struggle. We cannot live as Christians unless, like Jesus himself, we give ourselves over to prayer, to communion with God, in a colloquy in which we present to him our needs and ask him for his help, praising and thanking him for his boundless goodness to us. We need, above all, to remain close to Jesus by receiving with devotion and love his body and blood in the Eucharist and coming to him in the confessional when we have sinned or have need of advice as to what we ought to do to live as his faithful disciples. Jesus, our best and wisest friend, is the great "enabling factor" of our moral lives, but he cannot help us if we do not let him do so.

Long ago St. Augustine said, "God does not command the impossible, but by commanding he admonishes you that you should do what you can and beg him for what you cannot."[53] At the Council of Trent, the Church made these words of St. Augustine its own (DS 1536). While the Christian life may at times seem to be an impossible ideal, it is possible because of God's grace. For fallen mankind, it cannot be attained; but for men and women who have been regenerated in the waters of baptism and nourished with the body and blood of Christ, it can. For, like Jesus, their one desire is to do what is pleasing to the Father.

"This is the love of God," wrote the author of the first epistle of John, "that we keep his commandments. And his commandments are not burdensome. For whatever is born of God overcomes the world" (1 Jn 5:3-4). Commenting on this text, St. Augustine wrote, "These commandments are not burdensome to one who loves, but they are so to one who does not."[54] St. Thomas referred to this text of Scripture and Augustine's comment on it when he took up the question "Is the new law of love more burdensome than the old law?" He noted that it is indeed more difficult to govern one's inner choices in accord with the demands of Christian love than to control one's external actions. But he went on to say that the difficulty is present when one lacks the inner power or virtue to live the life of Christian love. But, and this is his major point, for the virtuous person, the one into whom God's own love has been poured and who abides in this love, what is seemingly difficult becomes easy and light.[55] Thus, Jesus, who demands that his disciples take up their cross daily and follow him, likewise says, "Take my yoke upon you, and learn from me; for I am gentle and lowly in heart, and you will find rest for your souls. For my yoke is easy, and my burden is light" (Mt 11:29-30).[56]

In addition, we Christians know that even now we share in God's own life; we are, in short, *new* creatures, God's own children and members of his family; we also know that, if we are faithful to the Word communicated to us, our life in Christ will be fully perfected in the life to come, where we will find, transfigured and freed of all imperfection, the fruits of our own human choices and actions (cf. *Gaudium et spes,* nos. 38-39).

In sum, the Christian life is practicable and realistic; but it is so only because of God's unfailing help.

John Paul II clearly spells out in a succinct way the practicality of the Christian moral life when he writes: "To imitate and live out the love of Christ is not possible for man by his own strength alone. He becomes *capable of this love only by virtue of a gift received"* (*Veritatis splendor,* no. 22).

Conclusion

In this chapter, we have seen the basic requirements of the Christian moral life and its uniqueness as well as its distinctiveness. It is this life that the Church proposes to us. In the next chapter, our attention will turn to consider the role of the Church and its teachings in our moral life.

Notes for Chapter Six

1. St. Thomas Aquinas, *Summa theologiae*, 1-2, 91, 4: "Praeter legem naturalem et legem humanam, necessarium fuit ad directionem humanae vitae habere legem divinam. . . . Primo quidem, quia per legem dirigitur homo ad actus proprios in ordine ad ultimum finem. . . . Sed quia homo ordinatur ad finem beatitudinis aeternae, quae excedit proportionem naturalis facultatis humanae . . . ideo necessarium fuit ut supra legem naturalem et humanam, dirigeretur etiam ad suum finem lege divinitus data. Secundo, quia propter incertitudinem humani iudicii, praecipue de rebus contingentibus et particularibus, contingit de actibus humanis diversorum esse diversa iudicia, ex quibus etiam diversae et contrariae leges procedunt. Ut ergo homo absque omni dubitatione scire possit quid ei sit agendum et quid vitandum, necessarium fuit ut in actibus propriis dirigeretur per legem divinitus datam, de qua constat quod non potest errare."

2. Ibid., 2-2, 22, 1, ad 1: "ad ea etiam ad quae naturalis ratio inclinat, sicut sunt actus virtutum moralium, necesse fuit praecepta legis divinae dari, propter maiorem firmitatem, et praecipue quia naturalis ratio hominis obtenebrata erat per concupiscentias peccati."

3. On this, see John Macquarrie, *Three Issues in Ethics* (New York: Harper and Row, 1970), pp. 119-125, where he discusses "enabling" and "disabling" factors in our struggle to know and do the good.

4. Here it is worthwhile to consider what Bernard Lonergan, S.J., has to say with respect to the fact that we enter a world "mediated by meaning." See his *Method in Theology* (New York: Herder and Herder, 1972), pp. 18-25.

5. Piet Schoonenberg, S.J., *Man and Sin*, trans. J. Donceel (Notre Dame, IN: University of Notre Dame Press, 1968), p. 104. See also pp. 112-117, where Schoonenberg discusses the negative effects of bad example, bad example with pressure, and the obscuring of norms and values.

6. Pope Paul VI, *The Credo of the People of God*, no. 16, as found in Candido Pozo, S.J., *The Credo of the People of God: A Theological Commentary*, trans. Mark Pilon (Chicago: Franciscan Herald Press, 1980), p. 103. Pozo's commentary on Paul's teaching, pp. 104-118, is very helpful.

7. The Fathers of the Council of Trent, in setting forth Catholic teaching on original sin, took for granted what is today called "monogenism," i.e., the view that all human persons derive from a single couple, Adam and Eve. Because of evolutionary theory and the evidence in support of it, some contemporary theologians think that monogenism is unlikely and therefore support the view called "polygenism," i.e., the view that at the beginning of the human race stands not a single couple but a population of "many" first parents. Both Pope Pius XII (in his 1951 encyclical, *Humani Generis* [see DS 3897]) and Pope Paul VI (in his "Orig-

inal Sin and Modern Science: Address of Pope Paul VI to Participants in a Symposium on Original Sin," *The Pope Speaks* 11 [1966], 234) warn that polygenism *appears* incompatible with the received teaching of the Church on original sin. But it is not clear that either of these popes intended to propose definitively that monogenism must be held. Consequently, as Germain Grisez has noted (*The Way of the Lord Jesus*, Vol. 1, *Christian Moral Principles* [Chicago: Franciscan Herald Press, 1983], p. 340): "[I]f a Catholic can show how polygenism is compatible with the essential elements of the Church's teaching on original sin, then he or she may admit polygenism on the evidence for it." On this entire issue, Grisez's treatment (ibid., pp. 339-341) is most helpful. Of value, too, are Pozo, *The Credo of the People of God: A Theological Commentary*, pp. 108-112, and O.W. Garrigan, "Monogenism," *New Catholic Encyclopedia* (New York: McGraw-Hill, 1967), Vol. 9, pp. 1063-1064.

8. DS 1513.

9. St. Augustine, *Sermo* 193; *Patrologiae Cursus Completus: Series Latina* (hereafter PL) 38.1334.

10. St. Thomas Aquinas, *Summa theologiae*, 1-2, 108, 4, sed contra: "Christus maxime est sapiens et amicus."

11. Ibid., 106, 1: "Principaliter lex nova est ipsa gratia Spiritus Sancti, quae datur Christi fidelibus."

12. Ibid., 3, 69, 5: "Per baptismum aliquis regeneratur in spiritualem vitam, quae est propria fidelium Christi; sicut Apostolus dicit (Gal 2:20), 'Quod autem nunc vivo in carne, in fide vivo Filii Dei.' Vita autem non est nisi membrorum capiti unitorum, a quo sensum et motum suscipiunt. Et ideo necesse est quod per baptismum aliquis incorporetur Christo quasi membrum ipsius. Sicut autem a capita naturali derivatur ad membra sensus et motus, ita a capite spirituali, quod est Christus, derivatur ad membra eius sensus spiritualis, qui consistit in cognitione veritatis, et motus spiritualis, qui est per gratiae instinctum. Unde Joan. 1 (14) dicitur, 'Vidimus eum plenum gratiae et veritatis, et de plenitudine eius omnes accipimus.' Et ideo consequens est quod baptizati illuminentur a Christo circa cognitionem veritatis, et fecundentur ab eo fecunditate bonorum operum per gratiae infusionem."

13. Grisez develops this truth magnificently in *Christian Moral Principles*, Chapter 24, "Christians: Human Children of God," pp. 573-598, with a wealth of documentation from Scripture, Vatican Council II, St. Thomas, and other sources.

14. Ibid., p. 794.

15. St. Leo the Great, *Sermo* 63; PL 54.3576.

16. Grisez, *Christian Moral Principles*, pp. 463, 472.

17. On this matter, see Pierre Benoit, O.P., *Jesus and the Gospel*, trans. Benet Weatherhead (London: Darton, Longman and Todd, 1979), Vol. 1, pp. 58-67.

18. *Roman Missal*, Introduction, 2.

19. Grisez, *Christian Moral Principles,* p. 554; cf. Chapter 33, pp. 789-806, for a rich development of this idea.

20. Ibid., p. 553.

21. Ibid., p. 551.

22. On this theme, see George T. Montague, S.M., *Maturing in Christ* (Milwaukee: Bruce Publishing Co., 1964), pp. 193-230.

23. Montague gives rich commentary on this Pauline theme in ibid., pp. 15-53.

24. Again, Montague, ibid., pp. 92-100, offers a superb commentary on this matter and on the "constitutive-progressive" texts found in St. Paul. On this matter, cf. also Manuel Miguens, O.F.M., "On Being a Christian and the Moral Life: Pauline Perspectives," in *Principles of Catholic Moral Life,* ed. William E. May (Chicago: Franciscan Herald Press, 1981), pp. 89-110.

25. Grisez, *Christian Moral Principles,* p. 559.

26. Ibid., p. 560.

27. St. Thomas Aquinas, *Summa theologiae,* 1-2, 106, 1: "Id autem quod est potissimum in lege novi testamenti, et in quo tota virtus eius consistit, est gratia Spiritus Sancti, quae datur per fidem Christi. Et ideo principaliter lex nova est ipsa gratia Spiritus Sancti, quae datur Christi fidelibus." An excellent commentary on St. Thomas's teaching on the new law, the very pinnacle of his moral thought, is provided by Servais Pinckaers, O.P., *Les sources de la morale chrétienne: sa méthode, son contenu, son histoire* (Fribourg and Paris: Editions Universitaires and Editions du Cerf, 1985), pp. 174-195.

28. *Summa theologiae,* 106, 1, ad 2: "lex nova est indita homini, non solum indicans quid sit faciendum, sed etiam adiuvans ad implendum."

29. Ibid., 106, 2, ad 2: "lex nova . . . quantum est de se, sufficiens auxilium dat ad non peccandum."

30. Ibid., 107, 1, ad 2.: "lex nova, cuius principalitas consistit in ipsa spirituali gratia indita cordibus, dicitur *lex amoris.*"

31. See above, Chapter Three, pp. 76-80.

32. See above, Chapter Three, p. 101-102; see also Grisez, *Christian Moral Principles,* p. 184.

33. Grisez, *Christian Moral Principles,* p. 604.

34. Ibid., p. 605.

35. St. Thomas Aquinas, *Summa theologiae,* 1-2, 108, 3: "Sermo quem Dominus in Monte proposuit (Matt 5), totam informationem Christianae vitae continet. In quo perfecte interiores motus hominis ordinantur."

36. St. Augustine, *The Lord's Sermon on the Mount,* I.1; trans. John J. Jepson, S.S., in *Ancient Christian Writers,* No. 5 (Westminster, MD: The Newman Press, 1948), p. 11. On this, see also Pinckaers, *Les sources de la morale chrétienne . . . ,* pp. 150-173.

37. Pope Paul VI, *The Credo of the People of God,* no. 12; in Pozo, *The Credo of the People of God: A Theological Commentary,* p. 53.

38. Grisez, *Christian Moral Principles*, Chapter 26, "Modes of Christian Response," pp. 627-659.

39. See above, Chapter Three, pp. 102-105, and especially p. 137, note 116.

40. Grisez, *Christian Moral Principles,* p. 653; cf. pp. 628-629.

41. St. Augustine, *The Lord's Sermon on the Mount*, 1.5, in the Jepson translation, pp. 18-21. St. Thomas Aquinas, *Summa theologiae*, 1-2, 69, 1 and 3. In 1-2, 68, 1, Aquinas distinguishes the gifts from the virtues, maintaining that the gifts are added to virtues and enable one to be led by the Spirit. Grisez, with others, does not see the need to distinguish so sharply between infused virtues and gifts of the Holy Spirit.

42. Grisez, *Christian Moral Principles,* pp. 654-655.

43. For the views of these theologians on this topic see: Charles E. Curran, *Catholic Moral Theology in Dialogue* (Notre Dame, IN: Fides, 1972), pp. 1-23; Timothy E. O'Connell, *Principles for a Catholic Morality* (New York: Seabury, 1978), pp. 199-209, 227; Richard A. McCormick, *Notes on Moral Theology 1965 through 1980* (Lanham, MD: University Press of America,1981), pp. 299-303; Josef Fuchs, "Is There a Specifically Christian Morality?" in *Readings in Moral Theology, No. 2: The Distinctiveness of Christian Ethics*, ed. Charles E. Curran and Richard A. McCormick, S.J. (New York: Paulist Press, 1980), pp. 3-17; Bruno Schüller, S.J., "Christianity and the New Man: The Moral Dimension — Specificity of Christian Ethics," in *Theology and Discovery: Essays in Honor of Karl Rahner, S.J.*, ed. William J. Kelly, S.J. (Milwaukee: Marquette University Press, 1980), pp. 307-327.

44. Thus, Fuchs, for example, clearly acknowledges that Christian faith determines the intentionality, motivation, and way of life that characterizes persons who seek to live as Christians. But he denies that faith specifies moral requirements unknowable without it and whose fulfillment is demanded by Christian love. See Fuchs, "Is There a Specifically Christian Morality?" pp. 14-16.

45. St. Thomas Aquinas, *Summa theologiae*, 1-2, 108, 2.

46. Ibid., 1-2, 51, 4; 63, 3.

47. Ibid., 2-2, 147, on fasting; 2-2, 32, on almsgiving.

48. For these authors, see the following: Hans Urs von Balthasar, "Nine Theses in Christian Ethics," in *Readings in Moral Theology, No. 2: The Distinctiveness of Christian Ethics*, pp. 191-193; Josef Ratzinger, "Magisterium of the Church, Faith, Morality," in *Readings in Moral Theology*, pp. 176-178; Dionigi Tettamanzi, "Is There a Christian Ethics?" in *Readings in Moral Theology . . .*, pp. 20-49; Bernhard Stoeckle, "Flucht in das Humanum? Erwagungen zur Diskussion uber die Frage nach dem Proprium christlicher Ethik," *Internationale katholische Zeitschrift*

(Communio) 6 (1977), 312-324; Grisez, *Christian Moral Principles*, pp. 606-609, 664-666.

49. Grisez, *Christian Moral Principles*, p. 607.

50. Ibid., p. 609.

51. St. Thomas Aquinas, *Summa theologiae*, 3, 69, 5; text cited above in note 12.

52. St. Augustine, *Confessions*, 8.12.

53. St. Augustine, *De Natura et Gratia*, 43.50; PL 44.271.

54. Ibid., 69.72; PL 44.289.

55. St. Thomas Aquinas, *Summa theologiae*, 1-2, 107, 4.

56. On the points developed in this section and also on many others pertinent to the practicability of Christian morality, see Grisez, *Christian Moral Principles*, pp. 683-704.

CHAPTER SEVEN

The Church as Moral Teacher

The purpose of this chapter is to examine the role of the Church as moral teacher. I will begin by examining the nature of the teaching authority or magisterium of the Church and by distinguishing the different ways in which this authority is exercised — i.e., infallibly and irrevocably and authoritatively but not infallibly — and by identifying two ways in which the magisterium proposes truths of both faith and morals infallibly — i.e., either in an extraordinary manner through solemn definitions or in its ordinary, day-by-day exercise of its pastoral mission. I will then show that the magisterium not only can propose but has infallibly proposed specific moral norms through the exercise of the ordinary magisterium. Finally, I will consider the nature of the response that Catholics are to give to authoritative but noninfallibly proposed magisterial teachings on moral questions. In connection with this particular question, I will take up the issue of dissent from Church teaching.

1. Teaching and Pastoral Authority Within the Church

Catholics believe that the Church is the "pillar of truth" (cf. 1 Tm 3:15). Jesus promised his apostles that he would not leave them orphans and that he would send his Holy Spirit to assist them (cf. Jn 14:16-17, 26; 15:26-27; 16:7-15; 20:21-22; Lk 24:49; Acts 1:8; 2:1-4). The role of the Holy Spirit paralleled that of the apostles; both bore witness to Jesus and communicated the truth revealed in him to the first Christian communities (cf. Jn 15:26-27). The Spirit revealed nothing new; rather, he helped the apostles to appropriate God's revelation in Jesus (cf. Jn 16:13-15). Within the Church, the apostles held first place (cf. 1 Cor 12:28), for upon them the Church is established, both now and forever (cf. Eph 2:20; Rv 1:8, 20). The apostles were chosen to receive God's revelation in Jesus, but this revelation was not meant for them alone but for all humankind, to whom Jesus sent them to teach his truth (cf. Mt 28:20). The apostolic preaching, through which the revelation given by our Lord was communicated to the apostolic Church, was, as Vatican Council II affirmed, "to be preserved in a continuous line of succession until the end of time. Hence, the apostles, in handing on what they themselves had received, warn the faithful to maintain the traditions which they had learned either by word of mouth or by letter (cf. 2 Thes 2:15); and they warn the faithful to fight hard for the faith that had been handed over to them once and for all (cf. Jude 3). What was handed on by the apostles comprises everything that serves to make the People of God live their lives in holiness and increase their faith. In this way the Church, in her doctrine, life and worship, perpetuates and transmits to every generation all that she herself is, all that she believes" (*Dei Verbum*, no. 8).

Moreover, within the apostolic college, Peter, the "rock" upon whom Jesus founded the Church (Mt 16:16) and the one to whom Jesus had given the charge to confirm his brothers (Jn 21:15-17), was primary; he was the head of the apostolic college. Catholic faith holds that the authority given by Christ to Peter and the other apostles to teach in Jesus' name still exists in the Church. It is vested in the college of bishops, who are the successors of the apostles; and just as headship within the apostolic college was divinely given to Peter, so too in the college of bishops this headship is, by God's will, given to Peter's successor, the bishop of Rome. Thus, Vatican Council II clearly teaches:

> That divine mission, which was committed by Christ to the apostles, is destined to last until the end of the world (cf. Mt 28:20). . . . Moreover, just as the office which the Lord confided to Peter alone, as first of the apostles, destined to be transmitted to his successors, is a permanent one, so also endures the office, which the apostles received, of shepherding the Church, a charge destined to be exercised without interruption by the sacred order of bishops. This sacred synod consequently teaches that the bishops have by divine institution taken the place of the apostles as pastors of the Church, in such wise that whoever listens to them is listening to Christ and whoever despises them despises Christ and him who sent Christ (cf. Lk 10:16) [*Lumen gentium*, no. 20].

In short, the magisterium, understood precisely as the authority to teach in the name of Christ the truths of faith and "everything that serves to make the People of God live their lives in holiness" (*Dei Verbum*, no. 8) is entrusted to the college of bishops under the headship of the Roman pontiff.[1] It is, moreover, necessary to emphasize, as did St. Thomas Aquinas in the Middle Ages, that this teaching office is essentially and primarily pastoral in nature, charged with the *cura animarum*, the "care of souls."[2] It is not, as some contemporary theologians seem to hold, primarily "jurisdictional" in character, concerned with Church discipline and order.[3] It is concerned rather with *truths* of both faith and morals. Thus, it teaches in Christ's name both truths that must be believed — such as those concerning the nature of God, his inner triune life, the mystery of the union of the divine and the human natures in the one person of Christ, and the like — *and* truths that must be lived, i.e., moral truths, the truths to which human choices and actions must be conformed if they are to be compatible with the life that Christians have received as adopted children of God, as living members of Christ's body, and temples of the Holy Spirit (cf. 1 Jn; 1 Cor 6).

All this has been well summarized by John Paul II in *Veritatis splendor.* Toward the conclusion of the first chapter of this encyclical, the pope reminds his readers that a more-than-human authority has been entrusted by Christ to the apostles and their successors. Explicitly appealing to the centrally important texts from Vatican II already noted, John Paul II says that this more-than-human authority "is apparent from the *living Tradition.*" He then confirms this by citing a key passage from *Dei Verbum*, Vatican II's Dogmatic Constitution on Divine Revelation, which reminds us that *"the task of authentically interpreting the word of God, whether in its written form or in that of Tradition, has been entrusted only to those charged with the Church's living Magisterium, whose authority is exercised in the name of Jesus Christ"* (*Veritatis splendor,* no. 27, with internal citation from *Dei Verbum,* no. 10). His point is that Catholics believe, as a cardinal truth of their faith, that Jesus has not left them orphans and has invested in the magisterium the more-than-human authority to speak in his name on everything that pertains to faith and morals. It is the responsibility of the magisterium to teach the faithful the way to eternal life, the truth that frees us from slavery to sin and enables us to live in union with Jesus.

This magisterium must also, as Avery Dulles has noted, " 'tune in' on the theological wisdom" found in the community if it is to carry out its mission effectively.[4] But it is important to keep in mind that the magisterium has the responsibility and the right to discern where this wisdom lies. Theologians frequently differ among themselves; disputes and debates arise within the Church and within the community of theologians, and the magisterium has the obligation and the God-given charism and authority to settle these disputes when they affect the faith and life of the Church. It is the magisterium's responsibility to distinguish between theological positions that are compatible with the Church's own understanding of what Christian life is all about and those that are not — as Dulles himself acknowledges.[5]

According to Catholic faith, the magisterium, invested in the college of bishops under the headship of the pope, *always* teaches with the authority of Christ — a more-than-human authority. At times, it proposes matters, whether of faith or of morals, infallibly, i.e., with the assurance that what is proposed is absolutely irreformable and a matter to be held definitively by the faithful. Teachings proposed in this way are to be given the assent of faith. At other times, it proposes matters of faith or morals *authoritatively and as true*, but not as absolutely irreformable. Although teachings proposed in this way do not require the assent of faith, they are to be received with "a religious submission (an '*obsequium religiosum*') of will and mind," and all the faithful — including pope, bishops, ordinary lay people, *and theologians* — are to accept these teachings as true.

It is crucially important to recognize that the magisterium can teach infallibly on matters of faith and morals in two different ways. First, a matter of faith or morals can be solemnly defined as such either by an ecumenical council or by the pope when, "as supreme shepherd and teacher of the faithful . . . he proclaims by a definitive act some doctrine of faith or morals" (*Lumen gentium,* no. 25; cf. Vatican Council I, DS 3074). It was in this way, for example, that the Council of Nicaea defined the truth of faith concerning Christ's divinity and that the Council of Chalcedon defined the truth of faith concerning the union of the divine and human natures in the person of Jesus Christ. It was in this way, too, that Pope Pius IX defined the truth of the immaculate conception of the Blessed Virgin Mary and that Pope Pius XII defined that of her glorious bodily assumption into heaven. This way of teaching infallibly is called the *extraordinary* exercise of the magisterium.

Secondly, and it is crucial to acknowledge this, the magisterium can and does teach infallibly on matters of faith *and morals* in the ordinary, day-to-day execution of its pastoral mission if some very specific conditions are fulfilled. The Dogmatic Constitution on the Church (*Lumen gentium*) of Vatican Council II clearly described these conditions. The relevant passage from that document, in which the Council Fathers summarize the constant and received tradition of the Church, reads as follows:

> Although the bishops, taken individually, do not enjoy the privilege of infallibility, they do, however, proclaim the doctrine of Christ infallibly on the following conditions: namely, when, even though dispersed throughout the entire world but preserving for all that amongst themselves and with Peter's successor the bond of communion, in their authoritative teaching concerning matters of faith *or morals*, they are in agreement that a particular teaching is to be held definitively and absolutely [*Lumen gentium*, no. 25; emphasis added; cf. Vatican I, *Dei Filius*, DS 3011].

What the Fathers of Vatican Council II add to this passage is also most important to keep in mind, for they immediately say:

> This is still more clearly the case when, assembled in an ecumenical council, they are, for the universal Church, teachers of and judges in matters of faith *and morals*, whose judgments must be adhered to with the loyal and obedient *assent of faith* [ibid.; emphasis added].

In his 1995 encyclical *Evangelium vitae*, John Paul II made it very clear that the *ordinary and universal* magisterium of the Church has infallibly proposed the truth of three specific moral norms, that, namely (1) "the direct and voluntary killing of an innocent human being is always gravely immoral" (no. 57); (2) "direct abortion, that is, abortion willed as an end or as a means, always constitutes a grave moral disorder" (no. 62); and (3) "euthanasia is a grave violation of the law of God" (no. 65). In unequivocally proposing these three specific norms identifying actions intrinsically evil by reason of their object, John Paul II was *not* issuing an *ex cathedra* or solemn definition, an exercise of the *extraordinary* magisterium. Rather, he explicitly referred to the ordinary and universal magisterium. In proposing the truth of these three norms, John Paul II maintained that the doctrine set forth in them is based on the natural or unwritten law, on Scripture or the written Word of God, is transmitted by the Church's Tradition, and is taught by the ordinary and universal magisterium (see text *of Evangelium vitae*, nos. 57, 62, and 65). He also appended at the end of the paragraphs containing these propositions an *explicit* reference to the text of *Lumen gentium,* no. 25, the text cited previously in this section in which the Fathers of Vatican Council II set forth the conditions under which the bishops, "united among themselves and preserving with Peter's successor the bond of communion, in their authoritative teaching concerning matters of faith *or morals,* are in agreement that a particular teaching is to be held definitively and absolutely." In this way, John Paul II clearly shows us that certain specific moral norms have indeed been infallibly proposed by the universal and ordinary magisterium of the Church.

Not all of the teachings of the magisterium are infallibly proposed. Nonetheless, those teachings of the magisterium on faith and morals that are not proposed infallibly — i.e., presented as definitive and irreformable — are still taught with the authority of Jesus Christ himself. Such teachings are "noninfallible," but it is necessary to understand precisely what this term means. It is a technical one to designate magisterial teachings that are authoritatively proposed, and proposed *as true and certain,* but not taught as absolutely irreformable. Teachings of this kind are not to be regarded as "fallible" teachings, as if they were merely probable opinions or expressions of some "party line" or merely "official" policy. Rather, teachings, whether of faith or morals, proposed in this way are taught by the magisterium as truths that the faithful, including theologians, are to accept and in the light of which they are to shape inwardly their choices and actions. These teachings, precisely because they are taught with the more-than-human authority vested in the magisterium by the will of Christ, express the "mind" of Christ on the matters in question.[6]

Although such teachings, unlike teachings infallibly proposed, do not bind the consciences of Catholics *in faith,* they nonetheless are binding on the consciences of Catholics, requiring from the faithful a "ready and respectful allegiance of mind" (*obsequium religiosum*). When they speak authoritatively but noninfallibly, the "bishops who teach in communion with the Roman Pontiff," so the Fathers of Vatican Council II remind us, "are to be viewed by all as witnesses of divine and Catholic truth; the faithful, on their part, are obliged to submit to their bishops' teaching, made in the name of Christ, in matters of faith and morals, and to adhere to it with a ready and respectful allegiance of mind. This loyal submission of the will and the intellect must be given, in a special way, to the authentic teaching authority of the Roman Pontiff, even when he does not speak *ex cathedra*, in such wise, indeed, that his supreme teaching authority is acknowledged with respect, and that one sincerely adheres to declarations made by him, conformably with his manifest mind and intention, which is made known principally either by the character of the documents in question, or by the frequency with which a certain doctrine is proposed, or by the manner in which a doctrine is formulated" (*Lumen gentium,* no. 25).

The nature of this "ready and respectful allegiance of mind," this "loyal submission of the will and the intellect," will be taken up in the final part of this chapter. The point here is that the authoritative, noninfallibly proposed teachings of the magisterium on matters of faith and morals are to be regarded by all Catholics as expressions of the mind of Christ and are to be accepted as true. Catholics should have a connatural eagerness to accept and embrace these teachings, to make them their own, and to conform their lives to them.

2. Specific Moral Norms Infallibly Taught by the Magisterium

In the previous section, we saw that the magisterium *can* propose moral as well as dogmatic truths *infallibly* by the exercise of the ordinary and universal magisterium when certain conditions — those enumerated in *Lumen gentium* (no. 25) — are fulfilled. We further saw that in *Evangelium vitae* John Paul II affirmed that three specific moral norms had been proposed infallibly in this way.

I believe — and so do other theologians[7] — that the core of Catholic moral teaching, as summarized by the precepts of the Decalogue (the Ten Commandments), precisely *as these precepts have been traditionally understood within the Church,* has been taught infallibly by the magisterium in the day-to-day ordinary exercise of the authority divinely invested in it. We are not deliberately to kill innocent human beings; we are not to fornicate, commit adultery, engage in sodomy; we are not to steal; we are not to perjure ourselves. Note that I say that the core of Catholic moral teaching is summarized in the precepts of the Decalogue *as these have been traditionally understood within the*

Church. Thus, for example, the precept "Thou shalt not commit adultery" has traditionally been understood unequivocally to exclude not only intercourse with someone other than one's spouse (adultery) but also all freely chosen genital activity outside the covenant of marriage. This was precisely the way this precept of the Decalogue was understood by the Fathers of the Church — for example, St. Augustine[8] — by the medieval scholastics, and by all Catholic theologians until the mid-1960's.

Thus, in discussing the sixth commandment, Peter Lombard, whose *Libri IV Sententiarum* was used as *the* basic text in Catholic theology from the middle of the twelfth century until the middle of the sixteenth century, stressed that this commandment required one to forbear from all nonmarital genital activity. Lombard, together with all medieval theologians and, indeed, all Catholic theologians until the very recent past, held that any sexual activity fully contrary to the purposes of marriage and of the sexual differentiation of the species into male and female was gravely sinful and a violation of this precept of the Decalogue.[9]

This is, in addition, the teaching found in the *Roman Catechism*,[10] and the teaching of this catechism on the precepts of the Decalogue is crucially important. The *Roman Catechism*, popularly known as *The Catechism of the Council of Trent*, was mandated by Trent, was written primarily by St. Charles Borromeo, was published with the authority of Pope St. Pius V in 1566, and was in use throughout the world until the middle of this century. It was praised by many popes, who ordered that it be put into the hands of parish priests and used in the catechetical instruction of the faithful. In 1721, Pope Clement XIII published an encyclical, *In Dominico Agro*, devoted to this catechism. In it, he said that there was an obligation to use it throughout the universal Church as a means of "guarding the deposit of faith." He called it the printed form of "that teaching which is common doctrine in the Church."[11] Vatican Council I said that as a result of this catechism "the moral life of the Christian people was revitalized by the more thorough instruction given to the faithful."[12] From all this, one can see the significance of the witness of this catechism to truths both of faith and morals. It is a reputable witness to the ordinary, day-to-day teaching of bishops throughout the world in union with the Holy Father.

According to the *Roman Catechism*, keeping the precepts of the Decalogue is absolutely necessary for salvation,[13] and these precepts unequivocally and absolutely condemn as gravely immoral not only adultery and fornication but all sins of impurity, such as homosexual acts.[14] These precepts also — while allowing human persons to kill animals and other persons to defend their own lives by using lethal force against unprovoked attacks, and while acknowledging that duly authorized public officials could execute criminals and engage in a just war — absolutely condemn the killing of the innocent as well as suicide (or the deliberate killing of oneself).[15] In short, an examination of this catechism, universally used in the Church for many centuries with the approval of popes and local bishops, shows that it taught that observing many specific moral absolutes is unconditionally necessary for salvation. Surely this means that pope and bishops in union with him were "in agreement that particular teachings [namely, those just cited] are to be held definitively and absolutely" (cf. *Lumen gentium*, no. 25).

This teaching of the *Roman Catechism* was in no way changed by Vatican Council II. It was, indeed, firmly reasserted. Recall that this Council, after affirming that matters of faith and morals can be taught infallibly in the day-to-day exercise of the magisterial authority by bishops throughout the world in union with the pope, insisted that this is even more the case when the bishops, assembled in an ecumenical council, act as teachers of the universal Church and as judges on matters of faith and morals. In the light of this clear teaching, it is most important to examine some key statements made by the Fathers of Vatican Council II about *specific moral norms*. An examination of this kind shows, beyond the shadow of a doubt, that the bishops united at Vatican Council II under the leadership of the pope unambiguously insisted that certain specific norms proposed by the magisterium are to be held definitively by the faithful. In doing so, they fulfilled the conditions — set forth in *Lumen gentium* and noted already — under which bishops can propose matters of faith and morals infallibly. For instance, after affirming the dignity of human persons and of human life, they unequivocally brand as infamous numerous crimes against human persons and human life, declaring that "the varieties of crime [against human life and human persons] are numerous: all offenses against life itself, such as murder, genocide, abortion, euthanasia, and willful self-destruction; all violations of the integrity of the human person such as mutilations, physical and mental torture, undue psychological pressures; all offenses against human dignity, such as subhuman living conditions, arbitrary imprisonment, deportation, slavery, prostitution, the selling of women and children, degrading working conditions where men are treated as mere tools for profit rather than free and responsible persons; all these and their like are criminal; they poison civilization; and they debase their perpetrators more than their victims and militate against the honor of the Creator" (*Gaudium et spes*, no. 27).

Some of the actions designated as criminal here are, it is true, described in morally evaluative language, such as "murder," "subhuman," "arbitrary," and "degrading." As so described, such actions are obviously immoral. But other actions unequivocally condemned as absolutely immoral in this passage are described factually, without the use of morally evaluative language, e.g., abortion, euthanasia, willful self-destruction (suicide), slavery, the selling of women and children. Specific moral norms proscribing such deeds are absolute, exceptionless.

Moreover, elsewhere in the same document we find that abortion and infanticide are called "abominable crimes" (ibid., no. 51). In addition, in the same document the Council Fathers, recalling to mind the "universally binding principles of the natural law," brand as "frightful crimes" actions designed for the "reasoned and methodical destruction of an entire nation, race, or ethnic minority" (ibid., no. 79) and declare that "every act of war directed to the indiscriminate destruction of whole cities or vast areas with their inhabitants is a crime against God and man, which merits firm and unequivocal condemnation" (ibid., no. 80).

In view of these luminously clear statements, made by bishops "assembled in an ecumenical council" and "acting as teachers of and judges in matters of . . . morals" (*Lumen gentium,* no. 25), it seems logical to conclude that Catholic moral teaching on the absolute immunity of innocent human life from direct attack is infallibly proposed according to the criteria set forth in *Lumen gentium* (no. 25).

In short, Vatican Council II definitely affirms that the magisterium teaches infallibly on questions of morality when specific conditions are met. I submit that these conditions have been met with respect to the core of Catholic moral teaching as set forth in the precepts of the Decalogue, *as these have been traditionally understood within the Church* (e.g., within the *Roman Catechism*). This conclusion, moreover, is corroborated by examining the teaching of the bishops assembled at Vatican Council II on the absolute inviolability of innocent human life from deliberate, intentional attack.

Moreover, as we saw in Appendix II of Chapter Four, in discussing the teaching of John Paul II on intrinsically evil acts and, corresponding to them, absolute moral norms, John Paul II, while not explicitly invoking infallibility in the encyclical, nonetheless everywhere teaches that the truth of absolute moral norms always and everywhere proscribing intrinsically evil acts is a *revealed truth.* He repudiates consequentialism and proportionalism not only because they are seriously flawed ethical theories but also, and more importantly, because they are *opposed to divine revelation and to the definitive teaching of the Church* (cf. *Veritatis splendor,* nos. 76, 79-83, and texts cited in Appendix II of Chapter Four). His appeal is to God's authority in revealing, which is the source of the magisterium's authority in teaching. He clearly regards the teaching of the Church on the absoluteness of the precepts of the Decalogue, as these precepts have traditionally been understood within the Church, as irrevocable and unchanging, i.e., as infallible.

The *Catechism of the Catholic Church,* solemnly promulgated by Pope John Paul II on the feast of the Immaculate Conception, 1992, clearly reaffirms the teaching of the *Roman Catechism* and of the Catholic tradition on this matter. It teaches that there are explicit kinds of human acts, specified by the object of moral choice, that are *always* morally wrong, precisely because a willingness to choose an object of this kind displays a disordered will, i.e., moral evil (no. 1755). In discussing the precepts of the Decalogue, *as understood within the Catholic tradition and as proclaimed by the magisterium in exercising its responsibility to safeguard the deposit of faith and to expound it faithfully* (cf. *Catechism of the Catholic Church,* nos. 2033-2035), it identifies various kinds of intrinsically evil acts, proscribed by absolute norms: e.g., the intentional killing of the innocent (cf. no. 2273), as in infanticide (no. 2268), abortion (no. 2273), mercy killing or euthanasia (no. 2277); masturbation (no. 2352); fornication (no. 2353); rape (no. 2356); homosexual acts (no. 2357); adultery (nos. 2380-2381); contraception (no. 2370).

The truth that the core of Catholic moral teaching, as found in the Decalogue, is infallibly proposed by the magisterium, moreover, is by no means novel. It was the received teaching of theologians prior to Vatican Council II, as the following citation from the "early" Karl Rahner makes luminously clear:

> The Church teaches these commandments [the Ten Commandments] with divine authority exactly as she teaches the other "truths of the faith," either through her "ordinary" magisterium or through an act of her "extraordinary" magisterium in *ex cathedra* definitions of the Pope or a general council, but also through her ordinary magisterium, that is, in the normal teaching of the faith to the faithful in schools, sermons, and all the other kinds of instruction. In the nature of the case this will be the normal way in which moral norms are taught, and definitions by Pope or general council the exception; but it is binding on the faithful in conscience just as the teaching through the extraordinary magisterium is. . . . *It is therefore quite untrue that only those moral norms for which there is a solemn definition . . . are binding in the faith on the Christian as revealed by God.* . . . When the whole Church in her everyday teaching does in fact teach a moral rule everywhere in the world as a commandment of God, she is preserved from error by the assistance of the Holy Ghost, *and this rule is therefore really the will of God and is binding on the faithful in conscience.*[16]

This section has advanced arguments and evidence to support the conclusion that not only can the magisterium teach infallibly on specific moral issues but that it has actually done so. The core of Catholic moral teaching, which is found in the precepts of the Decalogue, *as these precepts have been traditionally understood within the Church*, has been infallibly proposed, and this core includes specific moral norms. The arguments of revisionist theologians to support their claim that the magisterium has not taught and indeed cannot teach infallibly on specific moral issues are weak and based on false presuppositions.

Despite all this evidence to show that the magisterium can propose and has infallibly proposed specific moral norms, several contemporary theologians claim that not only has the magisterium not done this but that it *cannot* do so. According to these theologians, no specific moral norms taught by the magisterium (e.g., norms forbidding adultery and fornication, the intentional killing of innocent human life, as in abortion) have been infallibly proposed. Charles E. Curran is the best-known American advocate of this position, but it is common to many, including Daniel Maguire, Richard Gula, Richard Mc-Cormick, Francis Sullivan, and others in the United States and elsewhere.[17]

Thus, here I will view briefly and criticize the reasons advanced by these revisionist theologians to support their claim that the magisterium has not taught and indeed *cannot* teach infallibly on specific moral norms. I will then present evidence and arguments to support the view that the magisterium can indeed teach infallibly on specific moral matters and that it has in fact taught in this way.

Revisionist theologians seek to support their claim in several ways. First, they claim that no specific moral teachings of the Church have been solemnly defined, and they appeal to canon law to support this claim. Thus, Curran and his associates, writing in 1969, appealed to paragraph 3 of canon 1323 of the old 1917 *Code of Canon Law* (= canon 749 in the new 1983 *Code*). This paragraph reads: "No doctrine is to be understood to be infallibly defined unless this is manifestly demonstrated." Curran and his colleagues then asserted that it is not manifest that any specific moral norms have been solemnly defined.[18]

The problem with this argument is that it limits "infallibly defined" to "solemnly defined." For Curran and his associates conveniently — so it seems to me and others — ignore what the same canon has to say in the paragraph immediately preceding the one they cite, namely, that "The College of Bishops also possesses infallibility in its teaching when . . . the bishops, dispersed throughout the world but maintaining the bond of communion among themselves and with the successor of Peter, together with the same Roman Pontiff authoritatively teach matters of faith *or morals*, and are agreed that a particular teaching is definitively to be held."[19] As can be seen, this canon — which was included in the 1917 *Code* and repeated verbatim in the 1983 *Code* — sets forth the same teaching about the infallibility of the ordinary magisterium on matters of both faith and morals as did Vatican Council II in paragraph 25 of *Lumen gentium*. In other words, Curran and other revisionist theologians simply do not consider whether any specific moral norms have been infallibly proposed by the *ordinary* day-to-day exercise of the magisterium, according to the criteria clearly articulated by the Fathers of Vatican Council II. Equating infallibly proposed teachings with *teachings solemnly defined*, they fail to take seriously the possibility that some specific moral teachings of the Church have been proposed infallibly by the ordinary exercise of the magisterium.

A second reason advanced by revisionist theologians to support their claim that the magisterium has not taught and indeed *cannot* teach infallibly on specific moral norms is intimately related to their denial of moral absolutes. As we saw in Chapter Four, they contend that specific moral norms are known inductively by the collaborative exercise of human intelligence by persons living together in communities and reflecting on common human experiences.[20] They then conclude that *no* specific moral norms can be absolute because of the ongoing and open-ended character of human experience. As a leading revisionist theologian, Francis Sullivan, puts it, "we can never exclude the possibility that future experience, hitherto unimagined, might put a moral problem into a new frame of reference which would call for a revision of a norm that, when formulated, could not have taken such new experience into account."[21]

From this it follows, the revisionist theologians maintain, that the magisterium simply cannot teach infallibly on specific moral issues.[22]

Since this claim of revisionist theologians was examined in detail in Chapter Four and shown to be seriously flawed, there is no need here to repeat the critique already made.[23] Moreover, and I think that this is both relevant and important, the *Instruction on the Ecclesial Vocation of the Theologian*, issued by the Congregation for the Doctrine of the Faith on May 24, 1990, explicitly affirmed: "Revelation also contains moral teachings which *per se* could be known by natural reason. Access to them, however, is made difficult by man's sinful condition. *It is a doctrine of faith that these moral norms can be infallibly taught by the Magisterium*" (no. 16, with reference to Vatican Council I, dogmatic constitution *Dei Filius*, ch. 2; DS 3005; emphasis added). In short, this claim of revisionist theologians, in addition to being seriously flawed as specious moral reasoning (as shown in Chapter Four), is also *explicitly denied* by the magisterium itself.

Another reason advanced by revisionist theologians to bolster their contention that the magisterium has not and indeed cannot teach infallibly on specific moral issues is again closely linked to their denial of moral absolutes. They allege that so-called "concrete" human nature is subject to radical change and consequently that norms based on concrete human nature (as distinguished from "transcendental" human nature) are subject to change. Thus, the "later" Karl Rahner — i.e., the post-*Humanae vitae* Rahner (the views of the "earlier" Rahner will be discussed below) — claimed that the possible range of infallibly moral teaching extends to "hardly any particular or individual norms of

Christian morality."[24] To support his claim that infallibility is restricted to rather abstract and general norms (he seems to have had in mind norms urging us to do good and avoid evil and to avoid doing actions already qualified as immoral, such as *unjust* killing), he simply asserted that concrete human nature is subject to radical change.[25]

This allegation of revisionist theologians has been examined already, in Chapter Four, and found wanting. It is, therefore, not necessary to repeat this critique of revisionist thought here.[26]

From all this, I conclude that the "arguments" advanced by revisionist theologians to support their contention that the magisterium has not taught and indeed cannot teach infallibly on specific moral issues are specious and question-begging. They have utterly failed even to consider the possibility that some specific moral teachings of the magisterium are, in fact, infallibly proposed insofar as they meet the criteria for infallibly proposed teachings that we find in paragraph 25 of Vatican Council II's *Lumen gentium.* The magisterium, after all, as we have seen, has the authority and obligation to lead the Christian people along a path of holiness and of a life compatible with their baptismal commitment. It can surely indicate negatively what sorts or kinds of human choices and actions are utterly irreconcilable with a life of holiness.

3. What Response Should Be Given to Moral Teachings of the Magisterium Proposed Authoritatively But Not Infallibly?

As we have already seen, Vatican Council II teaches that the faithful, including theologians, are to give to authoritative but noninfallibly proposed magisterial teachings "a ready and respectful allegiance of mind," and the "loyal submission of the will and intellect" (*Lumen gentium,* no. 25). But exactly what does this mean? Many Catholic theologians today agree with Curran that this loyal submission of will and the intellect and this ready and respectful allegiance of mind are compatible with dissent from authoritative magisterial teachings. In 1969, Curran and his associates advanced the view that "it is common teaching in the Church that Catholics may dissent from authoritative, noninfallible teachings of the magisterium when sufficient reasons for doing so exist."[27] This is still the position taken by Curran[28] and by revisionist theologians and is reflected in the textbooks on moral theology, intended to be used in seminaries, written by such authors as Timothy E. O'Connell and Richard M. Gula.[29]

Before examining the reasons that Curran and others advance to support their claim that "Catholics may dissent from authoritative, noninfallible teachings of the magisterium when sufficient reasons for doing so exist," it will be useful to look more closely at the teaching of Vatican Council II on this question. The reason why it is important to do so is the fact that, as William B. Smith has pointed out, "the question of 'Dissent' as presently posed [e.g., by Curran and associates] is of relatively recent vintage."[30] As Smith observes: "A careful review of the standard theological encyclopedias and dictionaries of theology finds no entries under the title of 'Dissent' prior to 1972. Standard manuals of theology did raise possible questions about the rare individual who could not give nor offer personal *assent* to formal Church teaching, and such questions were discussed under treatments of the Magisterium or the Teaching of the Church, examining the status of such teaching and its binding force and/or extent."[31]

Nothing was said explicitly about dissent at Vatican Council II. However, the Theological Commission of the Council did respond to an emendation offered by three bishops in connection with the passage from *Lumen gentium* that has already been cited, namely, that in which the Council Fathers said that "a ready and respectful allegiance of mind" (*obsequium religiosum*) and a "loyal submission of the will and mind" must be given to authoritative but noninfallibly proposed magisterial teachings. The three bishops had raised the theoretical possibility that a learned person, in the face of a doctrine not infallibly proposed, cannot, for well-founded reasons, give his internal assent (*interne assentire non potest*). What should such a person then do? The reply of the Theological Commission was that in such instances the "approved theological treatises should be consulted."[32] As Smith observes, "it should be noted that the question posed to the Commission concerned the *negative* inability to give positive assent . . . which is not at all the same as a *positive right* to dissent."[33]

If these "approved theological treatises" are examined, one discovers, as Germain Grisez has shown in detail,[34] that no approved manual of theology ever authorized dissent from authoritative magisterial teaching. Some of them treated the question of *withholding internal assent* by a competent person who has serious reasons for doing so. The manuals taught that such a person ought to maintain silence and communicate the difficulty he experienced in assenting to the teaching in question to the magisterial teacher (pope or bishop) concerned.[35] In other words, these "approved theological treatises" — to which the Theological Commission of Vatican Council II referred concerned bishops for guidance on the matter — in no way supported public dissent from authoritative but noninfallibly proposed magisterial teaching. They spoke, not of *dissent*, but of *withholding assent*, which is something far different from dissent.

In fact, as Smith points out, the "early" Karl Rahner, in an article prepared for a theological commentary on the documents of Vatican Council II, had this to say in a commentary on the text from *Lumen gentium* (no. 25) that we have been considering: "This magisterium . . . whose authority . . . varies wide-ly . . . must be accepted with the basic respect due to the office in general and with an inner assent to its declarations. The text does not mention the possi-bility that in certain cases, 'obedient silence' is enough, but since this is com-monly held, it is certainly not excluded."[36]

In sum, Vatican Council II said nothing about a right to dissent. Its Theo-logical Commission, in answering a question raised by only three bishops, referred them to approved theological manuals. These manuals in no way sup-ported a right to public dissent from magisterial teaching. Rather, they noted that competent individuals might *withhold assent* from teachings that are not infallibly proposed and might maintain an "obedient silence," while commu-nicating their reasons for withholding assent to appropriate magisterial au-thorities.

Consequently, when Curran and others (for instance, Gula) claim that approved theological manuals support public dissent from noninfallibly pro-posed magisterial teachings,[37] their claim turns out to be erroneous. Gula con-tinues to make this claim,[38] but Curran, who originally made it, was forced to admit that "the perspective of the manuals concerning assent and dissent suf-fers from serious philosophical and theological limitations." According to him, "the manuals' analysis of the nature of assent is inadequate, and quite oblivi-ous to the central questions raised by Newman in his *Grammar of Assent*."[39]

Curran's position here is simply amazing. Whatever may be said of it, it surely constitutes a repudiation of his earlier claim that the manualists testify to a common teaching justifying dissent. I cannot here go into an analysis of Newman's teaching in his *Grammar of Assent*. But I do think it is pertinent to note that Newman in no way asserted a right of Catholics to dissent from authoritative teachings of the magisterium. Quite to the contrary, for he wrote, in speaking of conscience, that "the sense of right and wrong, which is the first element in religion, is so delicate, so fitful, so easily puzzled, obscured, per-verted, so subtle in its argumentative methods, so impressible by education, so biased by pride and passion, so unsteady in its course that, in the struggle for existence amid the various exercises and triumphs of the human intellect, this sense is at once the highest of all teachers, yet the least luminous; *and the Church, the Pope, the hierarchy are, in the divine purpose, the supply of an urgent demand*."[40]

In the light of all this, I submit that the appeal by Curran and others to pre-Vatican II manuals of theology and to John Cardinal Newman to support their claim that public dissent from noninfallibly proposed magisterial teach-ings is legitimate is simply spurious and should hence be summarily dismissed.

Curran and others also claim that their affirmation of a right to public dissent is warranted in view of Vatican Council II itself. They claim, in other words, that Vatican Council II itself supports dissent. Pressed to show how this claim is corroborated by conciliar documents, however, they acknowledge that there are no explicit conciliar texts supporting public dissent. But they go on to say, as Curran does, that "the very existence of the Council" supports dissent and that post-Vatican II ecclesiology contemporizes the classic 'right to dissent' in a dialogic context."[41] Continuing, Curran maintains that "*Lumen gentium, Gaudium et spes*, and the *Decree on Ecumenism* of Vatican II articulate an ecclesiological atmosphere that differs basically from the rather hierarchical character of *Humanae vitae.*"[42]

What can be said of this? First of all, we have already seen that there is no "classic right to dissent" found in pre-Vatican II theology. Second, nothing that the Council itself said supports a right to dissent, a point frankly admitted by Avery Dulles, who wrote that "the Council in its formal teaching did not advance the discussion of dissent beyond where it had been in the previous generation."[43] In fact, the revisionist theologians who support dissent from Church teaching now find fault with the ecclesiology of Vatican Council II! Thus, one of them, Richard McCormick, now claims that it is "widely, even if quietly, admitted in the [revisionist] theological community that this paragraph [no. 25 of *Lumen gentium*] represents a very dated and discussable notion of the Church's teaching office."[44] So it thus seems to me that Curran's appeal to the "ecclesiology" of the documents of Vatican Council II to support public dissent from authoritative magisterial teaching is simply specious. As far as his appeal to the "ecclesiological atmosphere" of the conciliar documents is concerned, I think that the response of one scholar suffices to show its flimsiness: " 'Ecclesiological atmosphere' — one expected a theological conclusion and suddenly found oneself in metaphysical meteorology."[45]

Revisionist theologians also claim that public dissent from magisterial teaching is warranted by the fact that in the past such teachings have been in error,[46] by the fact that dogma cannot develop unless such dissent is recognized,[47] and so forth. All these arguments have been examined at length by others, particularly by Grisez, and found wanting. As Grisez notes, there have been real errors in positions taken by the magisterium in the past, but in such instances the questions at issue were primarily ones of discipline or government, not doctrine (e.g., decrees of the Biblical Commission between 1905 and 1915).[48] When the questions at issue are doctrinal or moral (e.g., slavery, the question of religious liberty), it is arguable whether there were any errors when one considers precisely what was asserted by the magisterium in different contexts.[49] Grisez likewise shows that sound development in doctrine does not require dissent in order to take place.[50]

The position taken by Curran and other revisionist theologians is that frequently authoritative magisterial teaching on moral issues is in fact erroneous (e.g., the teaching on the inherent wickedness of contraception, the absolute immorality of all intentional killing of innocent human life, the absolute immorality of all freely chosen genital acts outside the marital covenant) and that the faithful are at liberty to dissent from such teachings whenever they have sufficiently good reasons for doing so. This position also claims that the views of theologians cannot simply be ignored, and that when large numbers of them teach that Catholics are free to set aside authoritative but noninfallibly proposed magisterial teachings and substitute for such teachings the views of theologians, the faithful act rightly in dissenting. Thus, Curran, to support his dissenting views on such issues as contraception, appealed to the fact that "over 750 theologians in North America have signed a theological statement of support for me."[51] Hence, an appeal to theological peers is a final appeal by revisionist theologians to support their advocacy of dissent from authoritative but noninfallibly proposed magisterial teachings.

What is to be said of this? It can be said immediately that this is simply a self-serving appeal, and that it has been formally repudiated by the magisterium. Thus, in an official response on March 13, 1975, to a similar appeal to theological opinion as a legitimate source to justify dissent from Church teaching on contraceptive sterilization, the Congregation for the Doctrine of the Faith had this to say: "The Congregation, while it confirms this traditional doctrine of the Church [on the absolute immorality of contraceptive sterilization], is not unaware of the dissent against this teaching from many theologians. The Congregation, however, denies that doctrinal significance can be attributed to this fact as such, so as to constitute a 'theological source' which the faithful might invoke and thereby abandon the authentic magisterium, and follow the opinions of private theologians which dissent from it."[52]

In other words, the claim made by Curran and others that "it is common teaching in the Church that Catholics may dissent from authoritative, noninfallible teachings of the magisterium when sufficient reasons for doing so exist" is spurious, supported only by weak and tendentious arguments.

Moreover, this claim has recently been even more firmly rejected by the magisterium itself. In the 1990 *Instruction on the Ecclesial Vocation of the Theologian*, to which reference has already been made, the Congregation for the Doctrine of the Faith takes up this matter in detail. The document, in doing so, provides a helpful commentary on the nature of the "religious submission of soul" or of "will and mind" that the Fathers of Vatican Council II said is to be given by the faithful, including theologians, to such authoritative but noninfallibly proposed magisterial teachings.

The *Instruction* clearly distinguishes between *questions* that theologians may raise about such teachings (nos. 24-31) and *dissent* from such teachings (nos. 32-41). It judges that questioning can be compatible with the "religious submission" required, but it firmly and unequivocally repudiates dissent from these teachings as incompatible with this "religious submission" and irreconcilable with the vocation of the theologian. Dissent from infallibly proposed teachings is *a fortiori* excluded.

The *Instruction* begins its discussion of the difference between questioning and dissent by stressing that "the willingness to submit loyally to the teachings of the Magisterium *per se* not irreformable must be the rule" (no. 24). It is most important to note this. Any questioning of these magisterial teachings must take place within the context provided by the religious submission of will and mind that is owed to those who hold a more-than-human authority within the Church. To be legitimate, questioning of noninfallibly proposed magisterial teachings must be rooted in a spirit of religious docility; an attitude of hostility toward the magisterium is excluded from the beginning.

Given this spirit of docility, however, the *Instruction* recognizes the possibility that a "theologian may, according to the case, raise questions regarding the timeliness, the form, or even the contents of magisterial interventions of this kind" (no. 24). Although such questions may cause tensions to arise between theologians and the magisterium, these tensions "can become a dynamic factor, a stimulus, to both the Magisterium and theologians to fulfill their respective roles while practicing dialogue," so long as they "do not spring from hostile and contrary feelings" (no. 25). But, and this is very significant, "there should never be a diminishment [in the theologian] of that fundamental openness loyally to accept the teaching of the Magisterium as is fitting for every believer by reason of the obedience of the faith," a readiness manifested by the theologian's willingness, "if need be, to revise his own opinions and examine the objections which his colleagues might offer him" (no. 29). Note that the *Instruction* obviously considers it proper for theologians to publish their "questions," for it speaks of their obligation to take seriously into account objections leveled against their views by other theologians and to revise their positions in the light of such criticism — and this is normally given only after a theologian has made his questions known by publishing them in professional theological journals.

The teaching of the *Instruction* on this matter is sound and helpful. As one can see, it confirms the position taken by the "approved authors" to whom those Fathers of Vatican Council II were referred who wanted further guidance on the meaning of the "religious submission," demanded by *Lumen gentium*, to be given authoritative but noninfallibly proposed magisterial teachings. What this means is that theologians have the right, with respect to such teachings, to raise questions and propose alternatives that may seem opposed to them, *provided* that they are willing (a) to submit their conclusions to the criticism of their fellow theologians, (b) to revise their opinions in the light of this criticism, and (c) ultimately to accept the judgment of the magisterium. Ordinarily, I believe, theologians raise questions of this kind when they can appeal to other magisterial teachings that are more certainly and definitively taught with which they think the teaching questioned is incompatible.

Questioning of this kind is judged by the Congregation to be in accord with the religious submission of will and mind required by *Lumen gentium*. But one is not, if one is to be faithful to Christ and to the Church, to assert that what the magisterium teaches is in fact false and that the faithful are at liberty to reject this teaching and for it substitute their own opinions or the opinions of theologians. But this is precisely what theological dissent entails.

The *Instruction* is very clear on this matter. After briefly describing the factors remotely or indirectly influencing dissent (no. 32), it notes the different forms dissent has taken. The most radical seeks to change the Church according to a protest patterned after political society. But "more frequently," the *Instruction* observes, dissent involves the claim that "the theologian is not bound to adhere to any Magisterial teaching unless it is infallible," and that the "theologian would accordingly be totally free to raise doubts or reject the non-infallible teaching of the Magisterium, particularly in the case of specific moral norms" (no. 33). Here the *Instruction* quite accurately describes the kind of dissent that has taken place over the past quarter century. Its description of dissent is similar to that given of it by Curran and his associates in 1969 and cited above, namely, that "Catholics may dissent from authoritative, noninfallible teachings of the magisterium when sufficient reasons for doing so exist." But Curran and his colleagues claimed that this was "common teaching in the Church," whereas the *Instruction* rightly repudiates this claim and holds that dissent of this kind is utterly irreconcilable with Church teaching and the vocation of the theologian. The faithful ought never to prefer the opinions of theologians, however learned, to the authoritative teaching of those who have been invested with the more-than-human authority to teach in Christ's name.[53]

More recently, John Paul II in *Veritatis splendor* emphasizes that "*dissent, in the form of carefully orchestrated protests and polemics carried on in the media, is opposed to ecclesial communion and to a correct understanding of the hierarchical constitution of the People of God*" (no. 113). If theologians dissent in this way, he continues, "the Church's Pastors have the duty to act in conformity with their apostolic mission, insisting that *the right of the faithful* to receive Catholic doctrine in its purity and integrity must be preserved" (no. 113). In addition, he insists that "no damage must be done to the *harmony between faith and life: the unity of the Church* is damaged not only by Christians who reject or distort the truths of faith but also by those who disregard the moral obligations to which they are called by the Gospel (cf. 1 Cor 5:9-13)" (no. 26).

Theologians, as theologians, are not "pastors" within the Church. They have not been given the mission, with both the responsibility and the right, to instruct the faithful in "all that serves to make the People of God live their lives in holiness and increase their faith" (*Dei Verbum*, no. 8). This mission has been entrusted exclusively to those who succeed to what is communicable in the apostolic office, i.e., it has been entrusted to the divinely instituted pastoral magisterium of the bishops in union with and under the headship of the Holy Father, Peter's successor and Christ's vicar. When they usurp the pastoral office, theologians act wrongly and do a grave disservice to the Church. But this is precisely what is done when they allege that they have a "right" to dissent from the authoritative teachings of the magisterium, replacing them with their own opinions and encouraging the faithful to set aside what pope and bishops teach in Christ's name and put in its place their own views.

The issue, ultimately, is this: Who speaks for the Church? Who has the authority to speak in the name of Christ and to settle disputes that may arise within his family? The Catholic answer to this question is that this authority is vested, by the will of Christ himself, in the pope and bishops in communion with the Holy Father. This body has the responsibility to judge on everything that affects the holiness and life of those who have, through baptism, become one with Christ. While it is legitimate for Catholics, including theologians, to raise questions about some teachings that are not irreformably or infallibly proposed, it is not right for them to arrogate to themselves the office entrusted by Christ to the pope and bishops in union with him. It is not legitimate for them to assert that what these teachers proclaim in Christ's name is definitely false, that their teachings can be set aside, and that views contradicting them can be adopted as practical norms of Christian life. It is *a fortiori* seriously wrong when theologians encourage the faithful to depart from teachings that have been infallibly proposed. And, as we have seen, the core of Catholic moral teaching, as found in the precepts of the Decalogue, as these have been traditionally understood within the Church — as excluding absolutely and unexceptionally all intentional killing of the innocent, all freely chosen genital sex outside the marital covenant, etc. — has been infallibly proposed.

The moral teachings of the magisterium are to be looked upon not as legalistic rules but as precious truths intended to enable the faithful to come to know who they are and what they are to do if they are to be fully the beings God wants them to be: his faithful children, ready to walk worthily in the vocation to which they have been called, ready to follow the call to participate in Christ's redemptive work.

A concise presentation of the Church as Mother and Teacher of the moral life is found in the *Catechism of the Catholic Church*, nos. 2030-2051.

Notes for Chapter Seven

1. "The task of authentically interpreting the word of God, whether written or handed on, has been entrusted exclusively to the teaching office of the Church, whose authority is exercised in the name of Christ" (*Dei Verbum*, no. 10).

2. St. Thomas Aquinas, *In IV Sententiarum*, d. 19, q. 2, a. 2, qua. 2, ad 4.

3. See, for example, Avery Dulles, S.J., *The Survival of Dogma* (New York: Doubleday, 1973), p. 102, where he emphasizes the "jurisdictional" supremacy of bishops. In the same work (p. 108) and in his presidential address to the Catholic Theological Society of America in 1976, "The Theologians and the Magisterium," *Catholic Theological Society of America: Proceedings of the Thirty-First Annual Convention* 31 (1976), 235-246, he *seems* at times to see the role of the ecclesial magisterium as being concerned with "good order" in the Church and not so much with the truth. However, in other places (e.g., *Survival of Dogma*, p. 100) he clearly acknowledges that the magisterium of bishops in union with the pope has the final "say" on matters of faith and morals insofar as they express the mind of Christ.

4. Dulles, *Survival of Dogma*, p. 108.

5. Ibid., p. 100. Also see Dulles's essay, "*Successio apostolorum — successio prophetarum — successio doctorum:* Who Has the Say in the Church?" *Concilium*, Vol. 148 (New York: Seabury, 1981), p. 62, where he says: "Without unified authoritative leadership, the Church would disintegrate into a plurality of movements having, indeed, a certain common inspiration but incapable of adopting a clear corporate stand on any controversial issue" (p. 62).

6. On this, see notes 1 and 3 above. Also see the helpful essay of Ronald E. Lawler, O.F.M. Cap., "The Magisterium and Catholic Moral Teaching," in *Persona, Verità, e Morale: Atti del Congresso internazionale di Teologia Morale (Roma, 7-12 aprile, 1986)* (Rome: Citta Nuova Editrice, 1987), pp. 217-233.

7. E.g., Germain Grisez, John Ford, S.J., et al. Here a key text is Germain Grisez and John Ford, "Contraception and the Infallibility of the Ordinary Magisterium," *Theological Studies* 39 (1978), 258-312. See also Grisez's "Infallibility and Specific Moral Norms."

8. St. Augustine, *Quaestiones in Ex.* 9, PL 31.622.

9. Peter Lombard, *Libri IV Sententiarum*, III, d. 37, c. iv.: " 'non moechaberis,' id est, 'ne cuilibet miscearis excepto foedere matrimonii.' A parte enim totum intelligitur. Nomine ergo 'moechiae' omnis concubitus iilicitus illorum membrorum ... debet intelligi." See also ibid., IV, d. 28, c. ii. On this matter, see Ronald Lawler et al., *Catholic Sexual Ethics: A Summary, Explanation, and Defense* (Second Edition: Huntington, IN: Our Sunday Visitor, Inc., 1998), pp. 46-67.

10. *Roman Catechism,* translated and annotated by Robert Bradley, S.J., and Eugene Kevane (Boston: St. Paul Editions, 1983).

11. Cited by Bradley and Kevane in their introduction to the *Roman Catechism,* p. vii.

12. *Documents of Vatican Council I,* trans. John F. Broderick, S.J. (Collegeville, MN: Liturgical Press, 1971), p. 38.

13. *Roman Catechism,* p. 351.

14. Ibid., pp. 420-422.

15. Ibid., pp.411-413.

16. Karl Rahner, S.J., *Nature and Grace: Dilemmas in the Modern Church* (London: Sheed and Ward, 1963), pp. 51-52.

17. Charles E. Curran, Robert E. Hunt, and the "Subject Professors," with John Hunt and Terence Connelly, *Dissent in and for the Church: Theologians and "Humanae Vitae"* (New York: Sheed and Ward, Inc., 1969), p. 26; cf. Curran, "Humanae Vitae: Ten Years Later," *Commonweal* 105 (July 7, 1978), 429; Daniel Maguire, "Morality and the Magisterium," *Cross Currents* 18 (Winter, 1968), 41-65; Richard Gula, *Reason Informed by Faith: Foundations of Catholic Morality* (New York: Paulist Press, 1989), pp. 209-210.

18. Curran et al., *Dissent in and for the Church,* p. 63. Curran and his associates erroneously give the number of the relevant canon as 1223. The correct number is 1323 in the 1917 *Code.*

19. *Code of Canon Law* (1983 ed.; Rome: Typis Polyglottis Vaticanis, 1983), canon 749, no. 2. See also Vatican Council I, DS 3011.

20. Francis Sullivan, S.J., *Magisterium: Teaching Authority in the Church* (New York: Paulist Press, 1983), pp. 150-151. Sullivan notes that Curran, Franz Böckle, Bruno Schüller, Bernard Häring, and many other theologians agree with this way of expressing the matter.

21. Ibid., pp. 151-152.

22. Ibid. See also pp. 166-173 and 215-216, where Sullivan claims that specific moral issues are beyond the range of infallible teachings. Sullivan's claim has been devastatingly criticized by Germain Grisez, "Infallibility and Specific Moral Norms: A Review Discussion," *Thomist* 49 (1985), 255-271. Moreover, James O'Connor has conclusively shown that Sullivan's interpretation of the famous "Relatio" of Bishop Gasser at Vatican Council I — an interpretation central to Sullivan's claims — is quite mistaken. On this latter point, see James O'Connor, *The Gift of Infallibility* (Boston: St. Paul Editions, 1986).

23. See above, pp. 157f.

24. Karl Rahner, S.J., *Theological Investigations,* Vol. 14, *Ecclesiology, Questions in the Church, the Christian in the World,* trans. David Bourke (New York: Seabury, 1976), p. 14.

25. Ibid., pp. 14-15. An excellent and devastating critique of Rahner's anthropology is provided by Cornelio Fabro, *La svolta antropologia di Karl Rahner* (Milan: Rusconi, 1974), especially pp. 87-121.

26. See above, pp. 157f.

27. Curran et al., *Dissent in and for the Church*, p. 26.

28. See his *Free and Faithful Dissent* (Kansas City, MO: Sheed and Ward, Inc., 1987), passim.

29. Gula, *Reason Informed by Faith*, pp. 207-217; Timothy E. O'Connell, *Principles for a Catholic Morality* (New York: Seabury, 1978), pp. 93-97.

30. William B. Smith, "The Question of Dissent in Moral Theology," in *Persona, Verità, e Morale*, pp. 235-254, at p. 233. Smith's essay is most worthwhile. He published a somewhat expanded version under the title "Is Dissent Legitimate?" *Social Justice Review* 77.9 and 10 (September/October, 1986) 164-169, 181.

31. Ibid., p. 235.

32. *Acta Synodalia Concilii Oecumenici Vaticani Secundi*, III/8 (Rome: Typis Polyglottis Vaticanis, 1976), no. 159, p. 88.

33. Smith, "The Question of Dissent," p. 239.

34. Grisez, *The Way of the Lord Jesus*, Vol. 1, *Christian Moral Principles* (Chicago: Franciscan Herald Press, 1983), pp. 853, 867-869 (notes 38, 39, 40, 41, and 42); cf. pp. 873-874.

35. See Smith, "The Question of Dissent," p. 239.

36. Rahner, in *Commentary on the Documents of Vatican Council II*, ed. Herbert Vorgrimler, trans. K. Smyth, Vol. 1 (New York: Herder and Herder, 1967), p. 209; cited by Smith, "The Question of Dissent," p. 239.

37. Curran et al., *Dissent in and for the Church*, p. 26.

38. Gula, *Reason Informed by Faith*, pp. 208, 218 (note 9).

39. Curran et al., *Dissent in and for the Church*, pp. 47-48.

40. John Henry Cardinal Newman, *Letter to the Duke of Norfolk*, cited by the bishops of Ireland in their pastoral letter on conscience, 1975, *Conscience and Morality*, no. 20.

41. Curran et al., *Dissent in and for the Church*, p. 119.

42. Ibid., p. 124.

43. Dulles, *The Resilient Church* (New York: Doubleday, 1977), p. 109.

44. Richard A. McCormick, S.J., *Notes on Moral Theology 1965-1980* (Lanham, MD: University Press of America, 1980), p. 667.

45. Grisez, *Christian Moral Principles*, p. 874.

46. In *Readings in Moral Theology, No. 3, The Magisterium and Morality*, ed. Charles E. Curran and Richard A. McCormick (New York: Paulist Press, 1985), a number of revisionist theologians, among them Daniel Maguire and Bruno Schüller, argue that dissent is warranted because of "errors" in past magisterial

teaching, particularly, so they claim, on the subject of religious liberty. See pp. 29-30, 45-46.

47. Gula, *Reason Informed by Faith*, pp. 207-216.

48. Grisez, *Christian Moral Principles*, pp. 883-885.

49. Ibid., pp. 891-894, 899-900.

50. Ibid., pp. 901-902.

51. Curran, *Origins* 15 (8/20/86), 667-680.

52. Congregation for the Doctrine of the Faith, "Responsa ad quasita Conferentiae Episcopalis Americae Septentrionalis circa sterilizationem in nosocomiis Catholicis," March 13, 1975, in *Acta Apostolicis Sedis* 68 (1976)

53. On this, see St. Thomas Aquinas, *Quodlibetum* IX, q. 8: "[W]e must abide by the pope's judgment rather than by the opinion of any theologian, however well versed he may be in divine Scriptures."

CHAPTER EIGHT

Christian Moral Life and John Paul II's Encyclical *Veritatis Splendor*

In this chapter, I will first provide a detailed exposition of the teaching of John Paul II in this encyclical and then review some of the major reactions from theologians, pro and con, which it elicited. In presenting the teaching of the encyclical, I will make use of the very fine commentary given by Dionigi Tettamanzi, formerly a professor of moral theology in Italy and now cardinal archbishop of Genoa. After this presentation of the encyclical, I will consider some reactions to it.

DETAILED EXPOSITION OF POPE JOHN PAUL II'S TEACHING

The encyclical *Veritatis splendor*, specifically addressed to "all the bishops of the Catholic Church," is divided into an introduction, three chapters, and a conclusion.

The Introduction and an Overview of the Document

In his Introduction, the pope clearly expresses his reasons for writing this encyclical. It is to exercise his teaching authority by confronting the crisis that has developed in theological-moral reflection during the postconciliar period. His declared intention is to set forth clearly "certain aspects of doctrine which are of crucial importance in facing what is certainly a genuine crisis, since the difficulties which it engenders have most serious implications for the moral life of the faithful and for communion in the Church, as well as for a just and fraternal social life" (no. 5). In fact, he affirms that today "it seems necessary to reflect on the whole of the Church's moral teaching, with the precise goal of recalling certain fundamental truths of Catholic doctrine, which . . . risk being distorted or denied." He notes that "within the Christian community itself" we are faced not simply by limited and occasional dissent but by "an overall and systematic calling into question of traditional moral doctrine, on the basis of certain anthropological and ethical presuppositions. At the root of these presuppositions is the more or less obvious influence of currents of thought which end by detaching human freedom from its essential and constitutive relationship to truth" (no. 4). In order to confront this crisis head-on, the pope

269

proposes "to set forth, with regard to the problems being discussed, the principles of a moral teaching based upon Sacred Scripture and the living Apostolic Tradition, and at the same time to shed light on the presuppositions and consequences of the dissent which that teaching has met" (no. 5).

Each of the three following chapters has its own specific theme. The first, entitled "Christ and the Answer to the Question About Morality," is a prolonged commentary and meditation on the question asked of Jesus by the rich young man in the gospel according to Matthew (Mt 19:16-21). Its purpose is "to bring together the essential elements of revelation in the Old and New Testament with regard to moral action" (no. 28). The second, by far the longest and most intellectually challenging of the document, is called "The Church and the Discernment of Certain Tendencies in Present-day Moral Theology." It is doctrinal in nature, and in it John Paul II takes up "certain fundamental questions regarding the Church's moral teaching," discusses the "issues being debated by ethicists and moral theologians," and, in responding to erroneous views, presents "the principles of a moral teaching based upon Scripture and Tradition." The third chapter, called "Moral Good for the Life of the Church and of the World," emphasizes that Catholics must turn to Jesus and be faithful to him in order to accept, live by, and hand on the moral truth taught by the Church. It stresses the significance of the witness to moral truth given by martyrs and the importance for the contemporary world of the Church's fulfilling her role as moral teacher. It also points out the responsibility of teachers and priests and, in particular, bishops, for sound moral teaching.

There is a profound interior unity to the encyclical. As Dionigi Tettamanzi has said: "This unity is undoubtedly given by the fundamental question concerning the relationship between freedom and truth, or better, by the living word of Jesus Christ: 'You shall know the truth, and the truth will set you free' (Jn 8:32). The whole encyclical is a constant 'listening' to the word of our Lord, a loving and courageous 'meditation' on the meaning and requirements of this word, a 'proposal' and an 'appeal' to follow Christ in order to find in him the full answer to our hunger and thirst for truth and freedom" (D. Tettamanzi, "Introduzione e guida alla lettura," in *Lettera Enciclica di S.S. Papa Giovanni Paolo II Veritatis Splendor: I fondamenti dell'insegnamento morale della Chiesa. Testo integrale con introduzione e guida alla lettura di S.E. Mons. Dionigi Tettamanzi* [Casalle Monferrato: Edizioni Piemme, 1993], p. 13).

Chapter One: Christ and the Answer to the Question About Morality

As noted already, this chapter is a prolonged meditation on the dialogue between Jesus and the rich young man as found in Matthew 19:16-21, the dialogue that begins when the rich young man asks Jesus, "Teacher, what good must I do to have eternal life?" (Mt 19:16).

A. Principal Ideas Set Forth in Chapter One

In my opinion, the leading ideas of this chapter are: (I) the religious and existential significance of the young man's question; (II) the sovereignty of God over the moral order, which he makes known to man through the natural law, through the Decalogue, and above all through his only-begotten Son made man; (III) the essential link between eternal life and the commandments; (IV) the "fulfillment" of the law in Jesus and the universal call to perfection, made possible only by union with Jesus; (V) moral life, unity in the Church, and revelation; and (VI) the more-than-human authority of the Church's magisterium in the moral order. All of these ideas are developed more fully in subsequent chapters of the encyclical.

I. The Religious and Existential Significance of the Young Man's Question

John Paul II insists, "For the young man the question is not so much about rules to be followed, but *about the full meaning of life.* . . . This question is ultimately an appeal to the absolute Good which attracts and beckons us; it is the echo of a call from God who is the origin and goal of man's life" (no. 7). It is *"an essential and unavoidable question for the life of every man,* for it is about the moral good which must be done, and about eternal life. The young man senses that there is a connection between moral good and the fulfillment of his own destiny" (no. 8). The question is indeed "a *religious question* . . . [T]he goodness that attracts and at the same time obliges man has its source in God and indeed is God himself" (no. 9).

II. The Sovereignty of God Over the Moral Order

As the pope says, in responding to the young man's question Jesus makes it clear that its answer "can only be found by turning one's mind and heart to the 'One' who is good. . . . *Only God can answer the question about what is good, because he is the Good itself. To ask about the good,* in fact, *ultimately means to turn towards God,* the fullness of goodness" (no.9; cf. nos. 11, 12).

Moreover, "God has already given an answer to this question: he did so by creating man and ordering him with wisdom and love to his final end through the law which is inscribed in his heart (cf. Rom 2:15), the 'natural law' . . . [which] 'is nothing other than the light of understanding infused in us by God, whereby we understand what must be done and what must be avoided. God gave this light and this law to man at creation' [a citation from St. Thomas]. He also did so in the history of Israel, particularly in the 'ten words,' the *commandments of Sinai.* . . . The gift of the Decalogue was a promise and sign

of the *New Covenant,* in which the law would be written in a new and definitive way upon the human heart (cf. Jer 31:31-34), replacing the law of sin
which had disfigured that heart (cf. Jer 17:1)" (no. 12).

III. The Essential Link Between Obedience to the Commandments and Eternal Life

After affirming that God alone is good, Jesus tells the young man, "If you
wish to enter into life, keep the commandments" (Mt 19:17). "In this way," the
pope says, "a close connection is made *between eternal life and obedience to God's
commandments:* God's commandments show man the path of life and they lead
to it. From the very lips of Jesus, the new Moses, man is once again given the
commandments of the Decalogue. Jesus himself definitively confirms them and
proposes them to us as the way and condition of salvation" (no. 12).

The first three commandments of the Decalogue call "us to acknowledge
God as the one Lord of all and to worship him alone for his infinite holiness"
(no. 11). But the young man, replying to Jesus' declaration that he must keep
the commandments if he wishes to enter eternal life, demands to know "which
ones" (Mt 19:18). As the pope notes, "He asks what he must do in life in order
to show that he acknowledges God's holiness" (no. 13). Responding to this
question, Jesus reminds him of the precepts of the Decalogue concerned with
our neighbor (no. 13). These precepts, John Paul II affirms, are rooted in the
commandment that we are to love our neighbor as ourselves, a commandment
expressing *"the singular dignity of the human person,* 'the only creature that God
has wanted for its own sake' " (no. 13, citing *Gaudium et spes,* no. 24).

At this point the pope develops a matter of crucial importance for the
meaning of our lives as moral beings, namely, that we can love our neighbor
and respect his dignity as a person only by cherishing the goods perfective of
him and by steadfastly refusing to damage, destroy, or impede these goods.
Appealing to the words of Jesus, John Paul II stresses that "the different commandments of the Decalogue are really only so many reflections of the one
commandment about the good of the person, at the level of the many different goods which characterize his identity as a spiritual and bodily being in
relationship with God, with his neighbor, and with the material world. . . .
The commandments of which Jesus reminds the young man are meant to
safeguard *the good* of the person, the image of God, by protecting his *goods"*
(no. 13). Continuing, John Paul II stresses that the negative precepts of the
Decalogue "express with particular force the ever urgent need to protect human life, the communion of persons in marriage" and so on (no. 13).

IV. The 'Fulfillment' of the Law in Jesus; the Universal Call to Perfection

Jesus not only reconfirms the law given to Moses — the "ten words" — but he also is the one who gives us the Sermon on the Mount, the "*magna carta* of Christian morality" (no. 15). In the Sermon on the Mount, Jesus stressed that he had not "come to abolish the Law and the Prophets," but rather "to fulfill them" (Mt 5:17). John Paul says that "Jesus brings God's commandments to fulfillment . . . by interiorizing their demands and by bringing out their fullest meaning" (no. 15). The beatitudes of the Sermon on the Mount "speak of basic attitudes and dispositions in life and therefore *do not coincide exactly with the commandments.* On the other hand, *there is no separation or opposition* between the Beatitudes and the commandments: both refer to the good, to eternal life" (no. 16). They are "above all *promises,* from which there also indirectly flow *normative indications* for the moral life. . . . [T]hey are a sort of *self-portrait of Christ . . . and . . . invitations to discipleship and communion of life with Christ*" (no. 16). The moral life, John Paul II emphasizes, means ultimately the following of Christ. But we follow him not by any outward imitation but "by *becoming conformed to him* who became a servant, even to giving himself on the Cross" (cf. Phil 2:5-8) (no. 21). Following Christ means "*holding fast to the very person of Jesus*" (no. 19).

The pope insists that the invitation to the rich young man to come and follow Christ (Mt 19:21) (no. 19), the summons to be as perfect as the heavenly Father is perfect (cf. Mt 5:48), to "be merciful, even as your Father is merciful" (Lk 6:36), and the *new* command to love one another even as Jesus loves us (cf. Jn 15:12) are addressed to everyone (no. 18).

And it is possible to be conformed to Jesus, to hold fast to him, to love as he does, only because of God's grace (no. 22; cf. no. 11). "To imitate and live out the love of Christ is not possible for man by his own strength alone. He becomes *capable of this love only by the virtue of a gift received*" (no. 22; cf. no. 24).

V. Moral Life, the Unity of the Church, and Revelation

John Paul II declares that "no damage must be done to the harmony between faith and life," and then adds, "*the unity of the Church* is damaged not only by Christians who reject or distort the truths of faith but also by those who disregard the moral obligations to which they are called by the Gospel (cf. 1 Cor 5:9-13)" (no. 26). The Holy Father emphasizes that "from the Church's beginnings, the Apostles . . . *were vigilant over the right conduct of Christians,* just as they were vigilant for the purity of the faith and the handing down of the divine gifts in the sacraments" (no. 26).

VI. The More-than-human Authority of the Magisterium on Moral Questions

In concluding Chapter One, John Paul emphasizes this point by citing key texts from documents of Vatican Council II, among them the Dogmatic Constitution on Divine Revelation (*Dei Verbum*). Here is one lucid text: "The task of authentically interpreting the word of God, whether in its written form or in that of Tradition, has been entrusted only to those charged with the Church's living magisterium, whose authority is exercised in the name of Jesus Christ" (no. 10; cited in VS, n.27).

B. Dionigi Tettamanzi's Analysis of Chapter One

In his excellent commentary on *Veritatis splendor,* Tettamanzi focuses on two major themes: (I) the Christocentric nature of the moral life according to John Paul II and (II) the ecclesial character of Christian moral life.

I. The Christocentric Meaning of Our Moral Life

Throughout this encyclical, and particularly in Chapter One, Jesus Christ is portrayed as the living and personal "law" of the moral life. Tettamanzi writes:

> The first chapter sets forth the essential christocentric meaning of the moral life on every page. To Christ is posed the question about morality, and it is from Christ that the answer to this question comes. It is an answer set forth in Christ's "teaching": "It is he who opens up to the faithful the book of the Scriptures and, by fully revealing the Father's will, teaches the truth about moral action" (no. 8). But there is more: Jesus' answer is one that coincides with his "person," because *Jesus Christ himself is "the answer,"* precisely because the moral life ultimately can be (1) *defined* as a "following of Christ," specifically in the sense of sharing in his life of loving obedience to his father in the gift of himself on the Cross (cf. nos. 19-21); receives (2) its *norm* from Christ himself, namely, the New Law with the gift of his Spirit: "Jesus himself is the loving 'fulfillment' of the Law inasmuch as he fulfills its authentic meaning by the total gift of himself: *he himself becomes a living and personal law,* who invites people to follow him; through the Spirit he gives the grace to share his own life and love and provides the strength to bear witness to that love in personal choices and actions (cf. Jn 13:34-35)" (no. 15). . . .
>
> *Faith,* insofar as it is a following of Christ, necessarily entails a *moral content*: the moral life in its roots "involves holding fast to the very person of Jesus, partaking of his life and his destiny, sharing in his free and loving obedience to the will of his Father" (no. 19). . . . As St. Augustine, whom John Paul II cites, puts it so well: "we have become not only Christians, but Christ. . . . Marvel and rejoice: we have become Christ!" (cited in VS, no. 21). Jesus Christ is thus the constitutive form of every moral commandment. From this emerges the absolute newness and utter originality of Christian morality: it is at once a gift and a task, *grace and*

commandment: "Love and life according to the Gospel cannot be thought of first and foremost as a kind of precept, because what they demand is beyond man's abilities. They are possible only as a result of the God who heals, restores and transforms the human heart by his grace" (no. 23).[1]

II. The Ecclesial Dimension of Christian Moral Life

This, Tettamanzi shows, flows logically from the Christocentric nature of the moral life. Christ, in truth, lives in his body the Church to whom he has given the Spirit as its life-giving principle and guide. Thanks to the Church and to the sacraments entrusted to her, Christians share in the new life of Christ in obedience to his Father and in the gift of self to his brothers and sisters: "*Christ's relevance for people of all times is shown forth in his body, which is the Church.* For this reason the Lord promised his disciples the Holy Spirit, who would 'bring to their remembrance' and teach them to understand his commandments (cf. Jn 14:26), and who would be the principle and constant source of a new life in the world (cf. Jn 3:5-8; Rom 8:1-13)" (no. 25).

Thus, the Church has the God-given task of faithfully handing on Christian moral doctrine: the bond between faith and the moral life is intrinsic and unbreakable (cf. VS, nos. 26-27).[2]

Chapter Two: The Church and the Discernment of Certain Tendencies in Present-day Moral Theology

This chapter contains an important introduction (nos. 28-34) and four parts: (I) "Freedom and Law" (nos. 35-53); (II) "Conscience and Truth" (nos. 54-64); (III) "Fundamental Choice and Specific Kinds of Behavior" (nos. 65-70); and (IV) "The Moral Act" (nos. 71-83).

Introduction

In the introduction (nos. 28-34) to this chapter, John Paul II lucidly states its purpose and identifies the major issues to be considered in it. Since I think that Dionigi Tettamanzi has provided an excellent analysis of this introductory part of the chapter, here I will offer a summary of his presentation.[3]

Chapter Two is dedicated to a "discernment" of certain tendencies in contemporary theology in the light of "sound doctrine." As John Paul II says, "In addressing this Encyclical to you, my Brother Bishops, it is my intention to state *the principles necessary for discerning what is contrary* to 'sound doctrine,' drawing attention to those elements of the Church's moral teaching which today appear particularly exposed to error, ambiguity or neglect" (no. 30).

More precisely, this chapter is concerned with a critical discernment, one "capable of acknowledging what is legitimate, useful and of value [in these tendencies], while at the same time pointing out their ambiguities, dangers, and errors" (no. 34).

The discernment carried out by John Paul II bears on a nest of diverse and complex issues; but they are reducible to *one fundamental question,* that of the *relationship between human freedom and the truth*: "The human issues most frequently debated and differently resolved in contemporary moral reflection are all closely related, albeit in various ways, to a crucial issue: *human freedom*" (no. 31). "If we wish to undertake a critical discernment of these tendencies ... we must examine them in the light of the fundamental dependence of freedom upon truth, a dependence which has found its clearest and most authoritative expression in the words of Christ: 'You will know the truth, and the truth will set you free' (Jn 8:32)" (no. 34).

The problem of the relationship between freedom and the truth is approached by John Paul II under *two perspectives*: (1) from the perspective of "*the law*," the law of God, either in its universal formulation (nos. 35-53 = Part One of Chapter Two) or in its application to personal, concrete situations, through *conscience* (nos. 54-64 = Part Two); (2) from the perspective of "*freedom*," either at the level of its actuation (fundamental choice and particular choices) (nos. 65-70 = Part Three) or at the level of its terminus (the moral act) (nos. 71-83 = Part Four).

An attentive reading of this chapter shows clearly that *the "moral" problem* of the relationship between freedom and the truth is above all and eminently an "*anthropological*" question, having to do with the very *identity* of the human person. The Holy Father explicitly brings this out in the final paragraph of the chapter. There he is referring directly to the question of the morality of human acts, but he finds it necessary to emphasize that ethical issues presuppose and express an anthropology: "As is evident," he writes, "in the question of the morality of human acts, and in particular the question of whether there exist intrinsically evil acts, we find ourselves faced with *the question of man himself*, of his *truth* and of the moral consequences flowing from that truth. By acknowledging and teaching the existence of intrinsic evil in given human acts, the Church remains faithful to the integral truth about man; she thus respects and promotes man in his dignity and vocation" (no. 83).

In the perspective of Christian moral doctrine, *anthropology is intimately linked with theology and with Christology.* The man with whom the encyclical is concerned is the man made in God's image, the man who finds his true meaning "only in the mystery of the Incarnate Word" (cf. *Gaudium et spes*, no. 22, cited in VS, no. 2). It follows from this that the acceptance or refusal of the ethical doctrine developed in the encyclical is directly dependent on the acceptance or refusal of its anthropological doctrine.

I. Freedom and the Law

The central idea developed here is that there can be no real conflict between human freedom of choice and the moral "law." There can be no true conflict because the moral "law," which has God as its author, is not a set of legalistic impositions but rather a set of *truths* meant to help human persons make good moral choices and in this way fulfill themselves and achieve the dignity of persons who, freed from subservience to feelings and in a free choice of the good, pursue their true end (cf. no. 42). John Paul's concern here is to articulate a true understanding of the autonomy proper to man and to repudiate theories that so exalt human freedom that they end up in the subjectivistic notion that men are creators of the moral order, of what is good and bad (cf. nos. 35-37). The pope notes that some of these ideas have had some influence "in the sphere of Catholic moral theology" (no. 36) and that some theologians have sharply distinguished "an *ethical order*, . . . human in origin and of value for *this world* alone, and an *order of salvation*" (no. 37). He rejects these views as incompatible with Catholic faith and then provides (nos. 38-45) an articulation of natural law rooted in the Catholic tradition as expressed by Sts. Augustine and Aquinas and Vatican II. This holds that natural law is our intelligent, active participation in God's divine, eternal law, his "wise and loving plan" for human existence. As John Paul II says, "*the moral law has its origin in God and always finds its source in him*," but at the same time "by virtue of natural reason, which derives from divine wisdom," it is also "*a properly human law*" (no. 40). This law, too, we must remember, is "fulfilled" and "perfected" by the law of grace, the new law of love.

John Paul II in this part confronts the charge, commonly made by revisionist theologians, that the traditional understanding of natural law and, in particular, the magisterium's understanding, is "physicalistic" or "biologistic" (no. 47). John Paul II declares that this claim "does not correspond to the truth about man and his freedom," that it "contradicts the *Church's teachings on the unity of the human person*," who, "in the unity of body and soul . . . is the subject of his own moral acts" (no. 48). Since the definitive teaching of the Church (cf. Council of Vienne, constitution *Fidei Catholicae*; Fifth Lateran Council, papal bull *Apostolici Regiminis*; and Vatican Council II, *Gaudium et spes*, no. 14) maintains that the human person "entails a particular spiritual and bodily structure," it follows that "the primordial moral requirement of loving and respecting the person as an end and never as a mere means also implies, by its very nature, respect for certain fundamental goods" (no. 48), goods such as bodily life and marital communion (cf. no. 13). What John Paul II says here also needs to be seen in light of what he said in Chapter One (no. 12), about respecting the *goods* of human persons.

John Paul II explicitly repudiates here as "*contrary to the teaching of Scripture and Tradition*" (no. 49) the view of those who "reduce the human person to a 'spiritual' and purely formal freedom" and thus misunderstand the moral meaning of the body and human acts involving it. Likening this view to "certain ancient errors . . . always . . . opposed by the Church" (e.g., Manicheism), he then appeals to the teaching of Paul in 1 Corinthians 6:9-19 on the gravity of such sins as fornication and adultery and to the teaching of the Council of Trent, which "lists as 'mortal sins' or 'immoral practices' certain specific kinds of behavior the willful acceptance of which prevents believers from sharing in the inheritance promised to them" (no. 49).

In the concluding number (no. 53) of this part, John Paul II examines the claim that, because of human historicity, specific moral norms are not immutable but change under varying historical and cultural situations. He repudiates this as a type of relativism utterly incompatible with Christ's affirmation, in his teaching against divorce, of the permanent validity of God's plan from "the beginning" and also with the unity of human nature which all human beings share with Christ who "is the same yesterday and today and forever" (no. 53).

II. Conscience and the Truth

Here the Holy Father is at pains to show that conscience, in its precise sense, is a *practical judgment* "which makes known what man must do or not do, or which assesses an act already performed by him" (no. 59). It is, he continues, "a judgment which applies to a concrete situation the rational conviction that one must love and do good and avoid evil [the first principle of natural law]. . . . But whereas the natural law discloses the objective and universal demands of the moral good, conscience is the application of the law to a particular case; this application of the law thus becomes an inner dictate for the individual, a summons to do what is good in this particular situation. Conscience thus formulates *moral obligation* in the light of the natural law; it is the obligation to do what the individual, through the workings of his conscience, *knows* to be a good he is called to do *here and now*. The universality of the law and its obligation are acknowledged, not suppressed . . ." (no. 59). Conscience is *not* a "*decision* on how to act in particular cases" (no. 55). It is rather "*the proximate norm of personal morality*," but its dignity consists in its capacity to disclose the *truth* about moral good and evil, the truth "indicated by the 'divine law,' *the universal and objective norm of morality*" (no. 60; cf. no. 63).

John Paul II repudiates the view of those who separate or even oppose the "teaching of a precept [e.g., the precept not to commit adultery], which is valid in general, and the norm of the individual conscience, which would in fact make the final decision about what is good and what is evil" (no. 56). On this view, only the individual conscience can ultimately decide whether an act generally wrong might be fitting in the concrete situation. The pope notes that "on this basis, an attempt is made to legitimize so-called 'pastoral' solutions contrary to the teaching of the Magisterium, and to justify a 'creative' hermeneutic according to which the moral conscience is in no way obliged, in every case, by a particular negative precept" (no. 56).

Because the dignity of conscience consists in its ability to disclose the truth, conscience "expresses itself in acts of 'judgment' which reflect the truth about the good, and not in arbitrary 'decisions.' The maturity and responsibility of these judgments — and . . . of the individual who is their subject — are not measured by the liberation of the conscience from objective truth, in favor of an alleged autonomy in personal decisions, but, on the contrary, by an insistent search for truth and by allowing oneself to be guided by that truth in one's actions" (no. 61). There is, consequently, the obligation, in conscience, to "form" one's conscience — i.e., "to make it the object of a continuous conversion to what is true and to what is good" — and obviously "Christians have a great help for the formation of conscience *in the Church and her Magisterium.* . . . [T]he authority of the Church, when she pronounces on moral questions, in no way undermines the freedom of conscience of Christians. This is so not only because freedom of conscience is never freedom 'from' the truth but always and only freedom 'in' the truth, but also because **the Magisterium does not bring to the Christian conscience truths which are extraneous to it; rather it brings to light the truths which it ought already to possess, developing them from the starting points of the primordial act of faith**" (no. 64). I added boldface here because of the great significance of this text.

III. Fundamental Choice and Specific Kinds of Behavior

Concern here centers on the relationship between free choices of specific kinds of behavior (e.g., to commit adultery, to cheat on income taxes) and a person's fundamental option "for or against the Good, for or against the Truth, and ultimately for or against God" (no. 65). John Paul II first notes that human freedom is rightly regarded as being "not only the choice for one or another particular action" but "is also, within that choice, a *decision about oneself*" (no. 65). In other words, in and through the free choices we make, we *determine ourselves* (this is indeed the reason why the young man's question has existential and religious significance and is about the meaning of life). The pope also says that it is correct to emphasize the "importance of certain choices which 'shape' a person's entire moral life, and which serve as bounds within which other particular everyday choices can be situated and allowed to develop" (no. 65). In other words, he recognizes the crucial moral significance of certain kinds of choices that can rightly be called "commitments," and he later identifies the fundamental choice or option or commitment of the Christian, namely, the choice to accept Christ in living faith and to commit one's life to him and his redemptive work.

But John Paul II goes on to point out that some theologians today "have proposed an even more radical revision of the *relationship between person and acts*. They speak of a 'fundamental freedom,' deeper than and different from freedom of choice, which needs to be considered if human actions are to be correctly understood and evaluated" (no. 65). These theologians in effect *relocate* self-determination from the free choices we make every day, including fundamental commitments or "options" in this sense. Rather, for them, "the *key role in the moral life* is to be attributed to a 'fundamental option,' brought about by that fundamental freedom whereby the person makes an overall self-determination, not through a specific and conscious decision on the level of reflection, but in a 'transcendental' and 'athematic' way" (no. 65). A distinction "thus comes to be introduced *between the fundamental option and deliberate choices of a concrete kind of behavior*" (no. 65). "The conclusion to which this eventually leads is that the properly moral assessment of the person is reserved to his fundamental option, prescinding . . . from his choice of particular actions, of concrete kinds of behavior" (no. 65).

The pope rejects this move, declaring that "to separate the fundamental option from concrete kinds of behavior means to contradict the substantial integrity or personal unity of the moral agent in his body and in his soul" (no. 67). In fact, he judges the attempt to relocate self-determination from specific free choices to an alleged fundamental option at the depth of our being as "contrary to the teaching of Scripture itself, which sees the fundamental option as a genuine choice of freedom and links that choice profoundly to particular acts" (no. 67). He teaches that the "choice of freedom" — which "Christian moral teaching, even in its biblical roots, acknowledges" as fundamental — is the "decision of faith, of the *obedience of faith* (cf. Rom 16:26)." This is the free choice, he continues (citing Vatican I and Vatican II), "by which man makes a total and free self-commitment to God, offering 'the full submission of intellect and will to God as he reveals" (no. 66). Since faith is a commitment to God that is to bear fruit in works (cf. Mt 12:33-35; Lk 6:43-45; Rom 8:5-10; Gal 5:22), it demands that one keep the commandments of the Decalogue and follow Jesus even to the point of losing his life for Jesus' sake and the sake of the gospel (cf. Mk 8:35) (no. 66).

John Paul II then emphasizes that this fundamental option of the Christian — a specific free choice that can rightly be called a commitment "shaping" a person's entire moral life (cf. no. 65) — "*is always brought into play through conscious and free decisions. Precisely for this reason, it is revoked when man engages his freedom in conscious decisions to the contrary, with regard to mor-*

ally grave matter" (no. 67). He goes on to recall the teaching, solemnly defined by the Council of Trent, that "the grace of justification once received is lost not only by apostasy, by which faith itself is lost, but also by any other mortal sin" (no. 68). He then reaffirms — in opposition to some contemporary theologians — that mortal sin exists "when a person knowingly and willingly, for whatever reason, chooses something gravely disordered" (no. 70). It thus follows that "the separation of fundamental option from deliberate choices of particular kinds of behavior, disordered in themselves or in their circumstances, which would not engage that option, . . . involves a denial of Catholic doctrine on *mortal sin*" (no. 70).

IV. The Moral Act

Here John Paul takes up the criteria (truths) necessary to assess man's freely chosen acts correctly. He distinguishes between "teleology" and "teleologisms." "The moral life," he writes, "has an essentially *teleological character*, since it consists in the deliberate ordering of human acts to God, the supreme good and ultimate end (*telos*) of man" (no. 73). But this teleology is not the same as *teleologism:* "Certain ethical theories," he writes, "called '*teleological*,' claim to be concerned for the conformity of human acts with the ends pursued by the agent and with the values intended by him. The criteria for evaluating the moral rightness of an action are drawn from the *weighing of the nonmoral or premoral goods* to be gained and the corresponding nonmoral or premoral values to be respected. For some, concrete behavior would be right or wrong according to whether or not it is capable of producing a better state of affairs for all concerned. Right conduct would be the one capable of 'maximizing' goods and 'minimizing' evils" (no. 74).

One type of "teleologism" identified by the pope — "consequentialism" — "claims to draw the criteria of the rightness of a given way of acting solely from a calculation of foreseeable consequences deriving from a given choice." Another variant — "proportionalism" — "by weighing the various values and goods being sought, focuses rather on the proportion acknowledged between the good and bad effects of that choice, with a view to the 'greater good' or 'lesser evil' actually possible in a particular situation" (no. 75). Those holding these theories claim that it is impossible to determine whether an act traditionally regarded as intrinsically evil would really be morally evil until one has considered, in the concrete situation, the "premoral" good and evil states of affairs it is likely to cause. They conclude that the foreseen proportions of "premoral" goods to evils in the alternatives available can at times justify exceptions to precepts traditionally regarded as absolute (cf. no. 75).

John Paul II firmly rejects these theories, declaring that they "are not faithful to the Church's teaching, when they believe they can justify, as morally good, deliberate choices of kinds of behavior contrary to the commandments of the divine and natural law" (no. 76). He first shows that "the weighing of the goods and evils foreseeable as the consequence of an action is not an adequate method for determining whether the choice of that concrete kind of behavior is 'according to its species,' or 'in itself,' morally good or bad, licit or illicit" because "everyone recognizes the difficulty, or rather the impossibility, of evaluating all the good and evil consequences and effects — defined as premoral — of one's own acts: an exhaustive rational calculation is not possible. How then can one go about establishing proportions which depend on a measuring, the criteria of which remain obscure?" (no. 77).

But this is not the major problem with "teleologisms," whether "consequentialism" or "proportionalism." The pope goes on to emphasize that "*the morality of the human act depends primarily and fundamentally on the 'object' rationally chosen by the deliberate will*" (no. 78). In a very important passage, well summarizing the Catholic tradition as expressed by St. Thomas Aquinas, the Holy Father writes as follows:

> In order to be able to grasp the object of an act which specifies that act morally, it is therefore necessary to place oneself *in the perspective of the acting person*. The object of the act of willing is in fact a freely chosen kind of behavior. To the extent that it is in conformity with the order of reason, it is the cause of the goodness of the will; it perfects us morally. . . . By the object of a given moral act . . . one cannot mean a process or an event in the merely physical order, to be assessed on the basis of its ability to bring about a given state of affairs in the outside world. Rather, that object is the proximate end of a deliberate decision which determines the act of willing on the part of the acting person [no. 78].

Here John Paul II shows that the "object" primarily specifying an act morally is precisely what one "chooses." It is the "object" of one's choice, of what one freely wills *to do*, and by freely willing to do *this specific deed*, one makes oneself to *be* the kind of person willing to do this. Thus, if the object of my choice is knowingly to have intercourse with someone other than my spouse, I freely choose to commit adultery and make myself *to be* an adulterer. But note that the "object" is *not* a mere physical event, a "piece" of behavior in the external world. It is a *moral object* only because it is the object of a human will act, the act of choice. To put matters another way, the pope here is saying that a human act is not a "thing" having a nature of its own *independent of any human will act*. A human act, precisely as human and moral, flows from a person's "heart," from a person's will. This is why human actions have an existential and religious significance and why they are primarily specified by the object *chosen.*

With this understanding of the "object" of a human act in mind, it is easy to grasp John Paul II's argument, which he himself summarizes by saying: "Reason attests that there are objects of the human act which are by their nature [as specific kinds *of freely chosen* objects] 'incapable of being ordered' to God, because they radically contradict the good of the person made in his image" (no. 80).

From this, it likewise follows the reality of *intrinsically evil acts*: these are human acts specified by objects incapable of being ordered to God for the reason cited — e.g., the intentional killing of an innocent human being, abortion, mercy killing, adultery etc. Corresponding to these intrinsically evil acts are moral absolutes — i.e., specific moral norms that identify in descriptive (not morally evaluative) terms possible objects of human choice which are *always* immoral and hence never to be freely chosen because one willing to do them is willing to make himself to *be* an evildoer.

This is a key teaching — indeed, the central theme — not only of this part of Chapter Two but of the entire encyclical.

Chapter Three: Moral Good for the Life of the Church and of the World

Introduction

Here I will center on six themes taken up by John Paul II in this chapter, namely: (1) the relationship between human freedom and the truth; (2) the intimate, inseparable unity of faith and morality; (3) the inseparable relationship between respect for personal dignity and a refusal to engage in intrinsically evil acts; (4) the absolute need for God's grace to lead a morally upright life; (5) the service of moral theologians; and (6) the responsibilities of bishops.

Interestingly, in his "guida" for readers of the encyclical, Dionigi Tettamanzi singles out six major themes in this chapter, and the six he identifies overlap pretty much with the six that struck me. The six themes identified by Tettamanzi and then developed by him are the following:

1. The relationship between the moral life and the Church's mission of *evangelization*, or, better, given the secularized world in which we live, of *re-evangelization.* But, Tettamanzi emphasizes, this entails essentially communicating the *truth* about man.

2. The Christocentric character of evangelization and of the moral life: It is only in the *crucified Christ* that the full truth of man is revealed.

3. The unconditional respect due to human persons requires absolute moral norms prohibiting always and everywhere intrinsically evil acts, i.e., acts intentionally opposed to the goods perfective of human persons.

4. Respect for what is morally good and the defense of absolute moral norms serve the *true liberty of every man and of all men.* The moral teaching of the Church on issues both of personal morality and of social ethics are rooted in the same truths about man.

5. In order to fulfill her mission of evangelization, the Church must be both Mother and *Teacher,* reminding men of their dignity and of the truths meant to guide their freedom.

6. The mission of evangelization and of teaching the truth about the moral good pertains to all the baptized, but special tasks are committed to theologians and to bishops.[4]

Before taking these things up briefly I want to call attention to a passage (in no. 115) — in a section where John Paul II is specifically speaking to his brother bishops, reminding them of their responsibilities — because in it the pope explicitly identifies the *principal truth* at the heart of the encyclical. He writes as follows:

> Each of us knows how important is the teaching which represents the central theme of this Encyclical and which is today being restated with the authority of the Successor of Peter. Each of us can see the seriousness of what is involved, not only for individuals but also for the whole of society, with the *reaffirmation of the universality and immutability of the moral commandments,* particularly those which prohibit always and without exception *intrinsically evil acts.*

I. The Relationship Between Human Freedom and the Truth

The pope proclaims: "*The crucified Christ reveals the authentic meaning of freedom; he lives it fully in the total gift of himself* and calls his disciples to share in his freedom" (no. 85). He then writes most perceptively about the meaning of human freedom, saying:

> Human freedom belongs to us as creatures; it is a freedom which is given as a gift, one to be received like a seed and to be cultivated responsibly. It is an essential part of that creaturely image which is the basis of the dignity of the person. Within that freedom there is an echo of the primordial vocation whereby the Creator calls man to the true Good, and even more, through Christ's revelation, to become his friend and to share his own divine life. It is at once inalienable self-possession and openness to all that exists, in passing beyond self to knowledge and love

of the other. Freedom then is rooted in the truth about man, and it is ultimately directed towards communion (no. 86).

The ultimate truth meant to guide our choices is that we are to love, even as we have been and are loved by God in Christ, whose "crucified flesh fully reveals the unbreakable bond between freedom and truth, just as his Resurrection from the dead is the supreme exaltation of the fruitfulness and saving power of a freedom lived out in truth" (no. 87).

II. *The Intimate and Inseparable Unity of Faith and Morality*
Because of contemporary secularism and the separation of faith from morality (even on the part of some Catholic theologians), it is urgent, John Paul II emphasizes, "to rediscover the *newness of faith and its power to judge* a prevalent and all-intrusive culture. . . . It is urgent to rediscover and to set forth once more the authentic reality of the Christian faith, which is not simply a set of propositions to be accepted with intellectual assent . . . [but] is a lived knowledge of Christ, a living remembrance of his commandments, and *a truth to be lived out*" (no. 88). Faith "possesses a moral content. It gives rise to and calls for a consistent life commitment; it entails and brings to perfection the acceptance and observance of God's commandments" (no. 89). Indeed, it is through our daily moral life that our faith becomes a "confession," a "witness" before God and man. Living faith, our fundamental option, must bear fruit in works of charity and "of authentic freedom which is manifested and lived in the gift of self, *even to the total gift of self*, like that of Jesus" (no. 89).

III. *The Relationship Between Respect for Personal Dignity and Refusal to Engage in Intrinsically Evil Acts*
In teaching that some objects of human choice are intrinsically evil and that the norms proscribing them are absolute and without exception, the Church serves the truth. Ultimately, the *Crucified Christ* provides the answer to the question: Why must we obey "universal and unchanging moral norms"? (no. 85). He does so because he gave his life — himself — to manifest his love for the persons made in God's image and called to divine life. He *suffered* evil rather than do it. And so do the martyrs. John Paul II insists that martyrdom is senseless unless there are absolute moral norms prohibiting intrinsically evil acts, for the martyrs suffered death rather than freely choose to do evil. He writes that "martyrdom, accepted as an affirmation of the inviolability of the moral order, bears splendid witness both to the holiness of God's law and to the inviolability of the personal dignity of man, created in God's image and likeness" (no. 92). Indeed, "martyrdom rejects as false and illusory whatever 'human meaning' one might claim to attribute, even in 'exceptional' circumstances, to an act morally evil in

itself. Indeed, it even more clearly unmasks the true face of such an act: *it is a violation of man's 'humanity,'* in the one perpetrating it even before the one enduring it" (no. 92).

Moreover, as the pope points out, were there no absolute moral norms prohibiting intrinsically evil acts (i.e., acts intentionally opposed to human goods), there would be no inviolable human rights (nos. 96-97).

IV. The Absolute Need for God's Grace to Live a Morally Upright Life

The Church's teaching on human dignity and, precisely because of the inviolable dignity of the human person, on moral absolutes always and everywhere prohibiting the free choice of acts intentionally opposed to the *goods* of human persons is *not,* as some maintain, rigoristic or harsh. Although at times it may *seem* humanly impossible to avoid *doing evil* to prevent some alleged greater evil, God never abandons us and will give us the grace to resist any temptation. If we ask our Father for bread, he will not give us a stone (cf. no. 102).

V. The Service of Moral Theologians

John Paul II addresses this issue (nos. 110-113) and declares, "*Dissent,* in the form of carefully orchestrated protests and polemics carried on in the media, *is opposed to ecclesial communion and to a correct understanding of the hierarchical constitution of the People of God*" (no. 113). Should theologians not desist from dissent, "the Church's Pastors have the duty to act in conformity with their apostolic mission, insisting that the *right of the faithful* to receive Catholic doctrine in its purity and integrity must be respected" (no. 113).

VI. The Responsibility of Bishops

John Paul II emphasizes the duty of bishops to be vigilant in seeing that the word of God is faithfully taught (nos. 115-117); he passes on to them his evaluation of "certain trends in theology today," reminds them of the seriousness of the "central theme" of the encyclical (the immutability and universality of absolute moral norms), and urges them to help proclaim the truth about man.

In the conclusion of the encyclical, the Holy Father calls on Mary for help; she understands sinful man and loves him, and she will not let him be beguiled by false doctrine.

REACTIONS TO THE ENCYCLICAL[5]

Here I will consider (1) the book entitled *The Splendor of Accuracy: An Examination of the Assertions Made by Veritatis Splendor,* edited by Joseph Selling and Jan Jans,[6] perhaps the most hostile response to the pope's teaching, but representative of the way dissenting theologians sought to discredit it; (2)

the principal objection raised by Richard McCormick, S.J., to the encyclical, along with Martin Rhonheimer's very excellent critique thereof; and (3) the very perceptive and helpful reflections of Joseph A. DiNoia, O.P.

The Selling-Jans Book: *The Splendor of Accuracy*

In their introduction, the editors claim that neither they nor the contributors to the volume "wish or intend that this study be understood as a challenge or rebuke to the teaching of the magisterium in the encyclical" (p. 10). Notwithstanding this rhetoric, the book, as its title unmistakably implies, is definitely intended as a "rebuke" to *Veritatis splendor.*

The volume begins with a long essay, "The Context and Arguments of *Veritatis Splendor*" (pp. 11-70) by Joseph Selling.[7] Selling says that in *Humanae vitae* Pope Paul was forced to take "a position that *somewhat mildly* rejected the use of contraception as a morally acceptable option for married couples" (p. 14; emphasis added). I draw attention to Selling's analysis of *Humanae vitae* because it illustrates the way he appraises papal encyclicals and indicates his approach to *Veritatis splendor.*

Selling finds particularly troublesome John Paul II's teaching regarding human acts and their moral assessment — in particular, the pope's thesis that the morality of human acts depends primarily on the "object" rationally chosen and that the choice of some objects is always incompatible with love of God and neighbor because acts specified by these objects — e.g., the intentional killing of innocent human beings — are intrinsically evil. According to Selling, John Paul II teaches that we can determine the morality of human acts "purely on a consideration of the 'object' of those acts," that is, as he continues, *"the physical activity performed"* (p. 49, note 38; emphasis added).

This claim here is astonishing. He attributes to John Paul II the view that the "object" putting a human act into its moral species is *the physical activity performed,* and that one can judge the morality of a human act without relating it to the will of the human person. But, as we have seen already, John Paul II does *not* say this, but to the contrary clearly says: "By the object of a given moral act, then, *one cannot mean a process or an event of the merely physical order,* to be assessed on the basis of its ability to bring about a given state of affairs in the outside world" (no. 78; emphasis added).

But what is most instructive here is that Selling falsely attributes to John Paul II a position regarding the moral assessment of human acts which the pope explicitly rejects in the very encyclical the "accuracy" of whose assertions Selling claims to be examining. Selling further claims that John Paul II's thought in *Veritatis splendor* seems to have been influenced by what he regards as the nefarious and novel theory of "basic goods" set forth in the writings of Germain

Grisez, John Finnis, and some other contemporary moral theologians (p. 67, note 2). Whether the encyclical, in fact, was influenced by this theory is not the substantive issue, but rather Selling's claim that it is, along with his characterization of this theory. According to Selling, if we examine this "basic goods" theory, looking "below the surface," we will discover that according to it (and, apparently, according to John Paul II who, Selling claims, is influenced by this theory) "it is completely 'natural' . . . to accumulate possessions beyond one's needs, to stratify society according to natural tendencies to lead and to follow, to destroy or at least to neutralize one's enemies, etc." (p. 68). Never have I seen such a mendacious, utterly atrocious falsification of the moral theory developed by Grisez and Finnis, and here, by implication, attributed to Pope John Paul II.

Similar misrepresentations of the encyclical are found in other essays in this volume — namely, those of Gareth Moore, Louis Janssens, Bernard Hoose, and Jan Jans. The only essay included that does not attack and misrepresent the encyclical is that of Brian Johnstone.

In sum, this work, which is clearly intended as a "rebuke" of John Paul II and *Veritatis splendor*, belies its own title. It is by no means an "accurate" examination of the encyclical, and its major "assertions" falsely impute to John Paul II positions he explicitly rejects and mendaciously misrepresent the moral thought of theologians known for their defense of magisterial teaching on moral absolutes and intrinsically evil acts.[8]

Richard McCormick's 'Some Early Reactions to *Veritatis Splendor*' and Martin Rhonheimer's Critique of McCormick[9]

McCormick complains that "the encyclical misunderstands and misrepresents the teleological tendencies it describes" (p. 496). According to him:

> Not a single theologian would hold that a good intention could sanctify what has already been described as a morally wrong act. And that is what the encyclical says proportionalists do. Revisionist writers should both reject and resent that. Since this matter is central, let me pursue it here. The pope is saying that certain actions can be morally wrong from the object (*ex obiecto*) independently of circumstances. As the German theologian Bruno Schüller, S.J., one of the most influential of the proportionalists has shown, that is analytically obvious *if the object is characterized in advance as morally wrong*. No theologian would or could contest the papal statement understood in that sense. But that is not the issue. The key problem is: What objects should be characterized as morally

wrong and on what criteria? Of course, hidden in this question is the further one. What is to count as pertaining to the "object"? [p. 497].

McCormick' s charge here is most serious. If John Paul II has indeed misrepresented the position of proportionalists, he has done them a grave injustice and ought publicly to apologize for having done so.

McCormick maintains that on a central issue, the meaning of the moral "object," the encyclical woefully misrepresents proportionalist thought and offers only a "narrow" understanding of "object."

With Joseph Fuchs, whom he quotes, McCormick "insists that it is the act in its fullness (with concrete circumstances and foreseeable results) that is the one object of decision. The object of the ethical decision for an action is, therefore, not the basic (e.g., physical) act as such (in its ethical relevance, such as killing, speaking falsehood, taking property, sexual stimulation), but the entirety of the basic act, special circumstances, and the chosen or (more or less) foreseeable consequences" (p. 500). I find this text interesting because it seems that it shows that John Paul II has indeed accurately identified the proportionalist position, for according to its leading practitioners, Fuchs and McCormick, in order to determine the moral "object" of an act, one must take into account the "totality" of the act, including its foreseeable consequences, etc. Moreover, this quotation implies that those opposing proportionalism, like John Paul II, identify the moral object with the "physical act." However, John Paul II had *explicitly rejected* this understanding of the moral object in *Veritatis splendor* (no. 78), as we have seen.

Let us look more closely at McCormick's analysis of the "central issue," i.e., the meaning of *moral object*. He agrees that the "object" plays a key role in determining the morality of an act. John Paul II had referred to it as "a freely chosen kind of behavior." McCormick focuses on "behavior." How, he asks, do we determine what kind of behavior it is, i.e., how do we determine the moral object? In these pages of his essay (pp. 503-504), however, he does not do much to help us identify the object. He claims that Rhonheimer, Grisez, and others (who agree with the pope) would think that one has described the object by identifying the behavior chosen (e.g., the choice to kill a person or to speak a falsehood), whereas proportionalists like Knauer and Fuchs (and himself) would say that one can identify the object only by referring to the *reason* (= further intention) why the act was chosen (e.g., organ transplant). Failure to refer to this reason, he says elsewhere, simply yields an object "narrowly conceived." McCormick, however, has little to say that helps us identify the moral "object." He simply asserts that there are disagreements about the matter and that the only way to solve it is "by appeal to experience" (p. 504).

A masterful critique of McCormick's response to *Veritatis splendor* is given by Martin Rhonheimer in his article "Intentional Actions and the Meaning of Object: A Reply to Richard McCormick."[10]

McCormick, Rhonheimer notes, is obviously correct in saying that "intention tells us what is going on," but as Rhonheimer then shows, the Jesuit theologian is vague in identifying what is meant by "intention." He refuses "to speak about 'actions' or about intention involved in the choice of concrete actions; he . . . only talks about intention as related to foreseeable consequences, thereby describing and continuously redescribing 'actions' from the standpoint of a value-balancing observer; in this way he arrives at what he calls the 'expanded notion of object'" (p. 245).

Rhonheimer first comments on McCormick's way of "expanding" the moral object so that in describing it he can do so in terms of the reasons or anticipated consequences the physical behavior will bring about. He notes that McCormick cleverly conceals the problems his "expanded notion" of the object involves by "adopting examples that, in themselves, are precisely *not* examples of 'expanded objects'" (p. 254). Among the examples Rhonheimer gives to illustrate this, one involves the external behavior of drinking whiskey to get drunk and the same external behavior to avoid pain of an operation by anesthetizing oneself. The "objects" freely chosen are different, and we get them not by McCormick's method of expansion but by taking into account the agent's present intention: what he is here and now choosing to do.

Rhonheimer then takes up in detail McCormick's charge that the encyclical "misrepresents" proportionalist thought. He observes that proportionalists will not see or concede what their opponents emphasize — namely, that the object freely chosen and willed morally specifies an act — precisely because they omit "focusing on what is going on in the acting and choosing person, precisely where moral evil comes about. Proportionalists are concerned with the reasons one might have to bring about certain states of affairs as the consequence of one's doings. . . . That is why consequentialists discuss . . . the question of whether it could be right to execute the innocent, instead of simply asserting: to execute an innocent person for whatever reason is *evil* by its object" (pp. 261-262). Continuing, he then says in a lucid and important passage:

> . . . precisely what proportionalists do not want to acknowledge is this: according to the encyclical's quotation of no. 1761 of the *Catechism of the Catholic Church*, "there are specific kinds of behavior that are always wrong to choose, *because their choice entails a disorder of the will, that is, moral evil*," and that, according to *Veritatis splendor*'s key sentence in no. 79, "*one must therefore reject the thesis*, characteristic of teleological and proportionalist theories, which holds that it is impossible *to qualify as moral-*

ly evil according to its species — its "object" — the *deliberate choice of certain kinds of behavior or specific acts, apart from a consideration of the intention for which the choice is made or the totality of the foreseeable consequences of that act for all persons concerned.*" Obviously, the encyclical goes right to the point, and McCormick's reaction, along with similar reactions, confirms that the Pope was right [p. 262].

This is intimately connected to what McCormick considers the gravest error of *Veritatis splendor*, namely, its "misrepresentation" of proportionalism when it declares (in no. 76): "Such theories [proportionalism and consequentialism], however, are not faithful to the Church's teaching, when they believe that they can justify, as morally good, deliberate choices of kinds of behavior contrary to the commandments of the divine and natural law." McCormick repeatedly says that with this the encyclical gravely misrepresents the proportionalists' view, falsely claiming "that [the proportionalist position] attempts to justify *morally wrong actions* by a good intention."

But this, as Rhonheimer goes on to show, "is simply not true." He continues by saying:

> McCormick's complaint would be justified if the Pope held the same understanding of the nature of divine and natural law that is proper to revisionist moral theology. Unlike the proportionalists, however, the encyclical holds that in natural and divine law there are included certain negative precepts that refer *universally* to certain kinds of behavior that one may never choose. The encyclical does not reproach proportionalist theologians for wanting to justify by good intention what is already determined to be morally wrong. The reproach is that proportionalism is a theory by which, in concrete cases, you can justify as morally right what the Church teaches to be universally, *semper et pro semper*, wrong. The Pope therefore reproaches proportionalism for denying that there are certain negative precepts that refer *universally* to certain kinds of behavior that one may never choose (killing the innocent, adultery, fornication, theft, contraception, abortion, lying, etc.) [p. 262].

What the encyclical rejects is the proportionalist notion of expanded object that allows one *in every concrete case* to "redescribe" concrete actions, reducing the commandments of law simply to forbid certain immoral *attitudes*, but not *choices* of determined and intentionally describable *behaviors* or *acts*. Therefore, Rhonheimer says, "*Veritatis splendor* does not here affirm something about the *formal* structure of proportionalist moral judgment (imputing to the proportionalists a theory that seeks to justify the principle, 'one may do evil so that good may come about'); the reproach is a *material* one, that is, that proportionalism is a theory according to which such universal negative norms *cannot* exist, so that, according to this theory, one comes to declare to be morally right what natural and divine law, according to the Church's teaching, declares to be morally wrong and evil" (p. 263).

Rhonheimer then provides interesting citations from another major proportionalist, Josef Fuchs, including one from his essay in *Moraltheologie im Abzeits* (a collection of essays attacking the encyclical), where Fuchs speculates that in the future the command "You shall not commit adultery" could change because of "rare exceptions, on the grounds of highly important reasons and with mutual consent" — although, of course, this should not be called "adultery" if by this term one designates an action already known to be immoral (pp. 263-264).

Rhonheimer's essay contains many rich insights regarding the "intentional content" of a human act — the content designated by the term "object" — but here my purpose was to show how Rhonheimer undercuts McCormick's criticism of *Veritatis splendor*.

J. A. DiNoia's '*Veritatis Splendor*: Moral Life as Transfigured Life'[11]

DiNoia sees great significance in the fact that John Paul II signed *Veritatis splendor* on the feast of the Transfiguration of our Lord. He then begins his essay with a citation not from *Veritatis splendor* but from *Pastores dabo vobis* concerning the great mystery of the Christian religion: the fact that God's Son became man "and gives to those who welcome him 'the power to become the children of God' (Jn 1:12)." Our destiny is to be part of the Trinitarian family, a destiny that begins with our baptism (pp. 1-2).

"An overriding objective of *Veritatis splendor* is to affirm that the Christian moral life makes sense only within this understanding of our calling to 'life on high in Christ Jesus' (Phil 3:14). . . . We must be transformed into people who can enjoy this high destiny" (p. 2). But how does this transformation come about? In *Veritatis splendor*, John Paul II affirms that it is by becoming conformed to Christ, becoming like him. The ultimate aim of a morally upright life is "to render us fit for the eternal company of the triune God. We become good by seeking the Good" as the encyclical makes clear in its exegesis of the encounter of Christ with the rich young man, with which it begins. And we seek the Good by keeping the commandments, and it is only in Christ that we can discover and be enabled to do this (pp. 2-3).

The major question with which John Paul II is concerned in the encyclical is why we should act morally at all. And the answer "is framed in terms of our destiny in Christ to enjoy communion with the triune God and with each in God" (p. 3). *Veritatis splendor* rejects legalism in morality and emphasizes that "happiness is the flourishing of a life lived in seeking the good in order to realize and enjoy personal communion with the triune God and with other persons in God" (p. 4).

The first great truth of the moral life, according to John Paul II, is "the truth of God himself, as embodied in the person and teaching of Jesus. If we want to live in the truth, we must be conformed to the Truth who is Christ himself." To enjoy communion with the triune God, we must become fit for it, and we do so only because of the grace of Christ and "specifically through the transformation that this grace makes possible" (p. 5).

It is here, DiNoia maintains, that the central significance of the mystery of the Transfiguration emerges. He asks why Christ allowed his disciples to behold his glory. He then turns for help to St. Leo the Great, who gave two reasons: first, to remove the scandal of the cross from the hearts of the apostles; second — and more significantly — by allowing his disciples to witness his glory, he revealed to them our future glory as well, to show us what would become of us. DiNoia proposes that we look at the encyclical from this perspective. DiNoia calls attention to passages in which John Paul II makes it clear that Jesus is himself the ultimate pattern and principle of the good moral life, and that it is in being conformed to him that the image of God in us is made perfect. This conformation is no mere conformity; it is the realization of our own personal identity, made possible by our freely choosing to lose our lives for his sake, and Jesus boldly asserted that this is the case. He can make this assertion because "only the inexhaustibly rich *perfect* Image of God who is the Person of the Son could constitute the principle and pattern for the transformation and fulfillment of every human person who has ever lived" (pp. 6-8).

Since we are persons, we must freely embrace the personal communion offered us by the triune God. Christ's grace enables us to do so *freely*. Christian freedom "is a participation in God's freedom — the God-given capacity to enter in a personal way in the realization of our own true happiness. . . . It follows that . . . our actions count for something in each action, and in some actions more than others, we become good or fail to. . . . In the moral life . . . we are growing into fitness, or failing to, for the consummation of our already initiated communion with the Father, Son, and Holy Spirit" (pp. 8-9).

DiNoia ends by relating the bearing of the encyclical to the theme of "Faith and Challenges to the Family." He does so by showing how the family is in a true sense an image of the Trinitarian communion itself insofar as "our transformation into Christ is always in part experienced within the context of our relationships with other persons in whom grace is similarly at work. In this way the family is central to both our understanding and experience of communion and transfiguration" (p. 9).

Conclusion

John Paul's encyclical *Veritatis splendor* addresses in depth some of the most critical issues that are central to an introduction to moral theology. In this book, these subjects have been examined as thoroughly as possible for a work of this kind.

Notes for Chapter Eight

1. Dionigi Tettamanzi, "Guida alla lectura," in *Enciclica Veritatis splendor*, Italian edition (Rome: Piemme, 1993), pp. 16-19.

2. Ibid., pp. 19-21.

3. Ibid., pp. 22-25.

4. Ibid., pp. 39-46.

5. On this matter, see my essay "John Paul II, Moral Theology, and Moral Theologians," in *Veritatis Splendor and the Renewal of Moral Theology*, eds. J.A. DiNoia, O.P., and Romanus Cessario, O.P. (Chicago: Midwest Theological Forum, 1995), pp. 211-239. See also my article, "Theologians and Theologies in the Encyclical," *Anthropotes: Rivista di Studi sulla Persona e la Famiglia* 10.1 (1994), 41-59.

6. Kampen, The Netherlands: Kok Pharos Publishing House; Grand Rapids, MI: Eerdmans, 1994.

7. Selling wrote a doctoral dissertation in which he argued that in *Humanae vitae* "Pope Paul never really intended to condemn every form of artificial birth control for the mature, responsible, loving married couple" ("Moral Teaching, Traditional Teaching, and *Humanae Vitae*" [a summary of Selling's *The Reaction to Humanae Vitae: A Study in Special and Fundamental Theology*, S.T.D. dissertation, Catholic University of Louvain, 1977], *Louvain Studies* 7 [1978], 43).

8. A more extended critique of this work can be found in my article "The Splendor of Accuracy: How Accurate?" *The Thomist* 59 (1995), 465-483.

9. McCormick's essay originally appeared in *Theological Studies* 55 (1994), 481-506.

10. Rhonheimer's essay, originally published in *The Thomist*, has been reprinted in *Veritatis Splendor and the Renewal of Moral Theology*, pp. 241-270. All page references will refer to the essay as found in this book.

11. DiNoia's essay is found in *Veritatis Splendor and the Renewal of Moral Theology*, pp. 1-10.

Christian Moral Life and the *Catechism of the Catholic Church*

At the Extraordinary Synod of Bishops in January 1985, called to commemorate the twentieth anniversary of the conclusion of Vatican Council II, the Synod Fathers expressed the desire that a catechism or compendium of Catholic doctrine on faith and morals be prepared according to the mind of the Council. Pope John Paul II wholeheartedly endorsed this desire and appointed a committee of bishops to draft the catechism. On October 11, 1992, Pope John Paul II issued his apostolic constitution *Fidei depositum,* authorizing publication of the *Catechism of the Catholic Church,* and on the feast of the Immaculate Conception, December 8, 1992, the text of the *Catechism,* which had been written in French, was formally presented to the public by the Holy Father.

The French text was soon translated into the major modern languages, with the English-language text appearing in 1994 after serious debate over the first draft of the translation and correction and emendation of it. In 1997, the official Latin text of the new *Catechism,* containing minor corrections and revisions of the original French text, was made public, and these corrections and revisions were subsequently incorporated into the various vernacular editions.

The *Catechism* contains four principal parts. Part One, entitled "The Profession of Faith," offers an extensive synthesis of the truths of the Catholic faith as set forth in the Creed. Part Two, entitled "The Celebration of the Christian Mystery," presents the liturgy and sacraments of the Church. Part Three, called "Life in Christ," is concerned with the Christian moral life. Part Four, with the title "Christian Prayer," sets forth the indispensable role of prayer in the life of the Christian and focuses on the petitions of the Lord's Prayer. Each part is subdivided into sections, chapters, and articles, and each paragraph of the entire *Catechism* is numbered, for a total of 2,865 numbered paragraphs. Helpful summary sections, called "In Brief," are given at the conclusion of each article, into which the various parts, sections, and chapters are divided.

As noted already, Part Three of the *Catechism* is devoted to a consideration of the Christian moral life. In the introduction to his encyclical *Veritatis splendor* (1995), Pope John Paul II stated that one of the reasons delaying the final preparation and promulgation of this encyclical was that "it seemed fitting for it to be preceded by the *Catechism of the Catholic Church*, which contains a complete and systematic exposition of Christian moral teaching" (no. 5). Thus, in his encyclical, which deals with "*certain fundamental questions regarding the Church's moral teaching*, taking the form of a necessary discernment about issues being debated by ethicists and moral theologians," the Holy Father refers frequently to "the Catechism 'as a sure and authentic reference text for teaching Catholic doctrine" (ibid., no. 5, with an internal citation from his apostolic constitution *Fidei depositum*, no. 4).

Here I will offer a synoptic view of the *Catechism*'s teaching on the Christian moral life, presenting in somewhat more detail aspects of its teaching particularly relevant for an introduction to moral theology. My purpose is not to provide an in-depth theological analysis of this teaching.

1. A Synopsis of the *Catechism*'s Teaching on the Christian Moral Life

One can gain a synoptic view of the *Catechism*'s teaching on the Christian moral life simply by glancing at its contents. This part of the *Catechism* contains two main sections. The first section is called "Man's Vocation: Life in the Spirit" (nos. 1699-2051). This section includes a short introduction (no. 1699) and three chapters, namely, "The Dignity of the Human Person" (nos. 1700-1876), "The Human Community" (nos. 1877-1948), and "God's Salvation: Law and Grace" (nos. 1949-2051). The chapter on the dignity of the human person contains a brief introduction (no. 1700) and eight articles: (1) "Man: The Image of God" (nos. 1701-1715); (2) "Our Vocation to Beatitude" (nos. 1716-1729); (3) "Man's Freedom" (nos. 1730-1748); (4) "The Morality of Human Acts" (nos. 1749-1761); (5) "The Morality of the Passions" (nos. 1762-1775); (6) "Moral Conscience" (nos. 1776-1802); (7) "The Virtues" (nos. 1803-1845); and (8) "Sin" (nos. 1846-1876). The chapter on the human community embraces a brief introduction (no. 1877) and three articles: (1) "The Person and Society" (nos. 1878-1896); (2) "Participation in Social Life" (nos. 1897-1927); and (3) "Social Justice" (nos. 1928-1948). The chapter on God's salvation through law and grace is broken up into a short introduction (no. 1949) and three articles: (1) "The Moral Law" (nos. 1950-1986); (2) "Grace and Justification" (nos. 1987-2029); and (3) "The Church, Mother and Teacher" (nos. 2030-2051).

The second section of Part Three, on the Ten Commandments, begins with a lengthy introduction (nos. 2052-2082), and is then divided into two chapters. Of these, the first, entitled "You Shall Love the Lord Your God with All Your Heart and with All Your Soul, and with All Your Mind" (nos. 2083-2195), contains three articles dealing, respectively, with the first commandment (nos. 2084-2141), the second commandment (nos. 2142-2167), and the third commandment (nos. 2168-2195). Its second chapter, called "You Shall Love Your Neighbor as Yourself" (nos. 2196-2557), is naturally subdivided into seven articles, dealing, respectively, with the fourth commandment (nos. 2197-2257), the fifth commandment (nos. 2258-2330), the sixth commandment (nos. 2331-2400), the seventh commandment (nos. 2401-2463), the eighth commandment (nos. 2464-2513), the ninth commandment (nos. 2514-2533), and the tenth commandment (nos. 2534-2557).

From the above, we can grasp the scope of the *Catechism*'s presentation of the Christian moral life. But a listing of its contents does not help us to understand its spirit and its way of conceiving the Christian moral life. I believe that two bishops who were members of the committee charged with drafting the document afford an initial insight into the spirit of the *Catechism*'s understanding of the Christian moral life. One of them, Jean Honoré, archbishop of Tours in France, commenting on the first section of Part Three of the *Catechism* — "Man's Vocation: Life in the Spirit" — observed that the bishops were aware

> of the pitfall to be avoided in presenting and describing Christian life in terms of a code of morality, as a treatise of good behavior. . . . The ultimate sense could only be the one radiating from the Beatitudes, and the motivation none other than that of the *sequela Christi* (following Christ), a *sequela Christi* seen not only as the imitation of a model viewed from the outside, but as a true *identification* with Christ's inner being, consisting entirely in a relationship and submission to the Father, and in the perfection of witnessing by a life belonging entirely to him. . . . This is the heart of the insight that was to introduce and give unity to the chapter on morality: the faith of the disciple, expressed in the Creed, celebrated in the sacraments, is revealed in the witness of life and the response given to the Gospel's call to perfection.[1]

The second, David Everyman Konstant, bishop of Leeds in England, commenting on the second section of Part Three — "The Ten Commandments" — and anticipating the objection that by giving the commandments such prominence there is the danger that Christian morality will be perceived as a set of negative injunctions, stressed that "the purpose of the commandments in general, as they come to us [through the living Catholic tradition], is not to restrict freedom but to open the way to a truly liberated life. To do this it is necessary to mark off those ways which lead by the route of illusory satisfactions, to falsity and to death." Continuing, he cited the text of the *Didache* (I, 1) wherein it is affirmed that "there are two ways, the one leading to life, the other to death, and between the two there is a great difference." He then went on to point out that "the commandments do not stand in splendid isolation. . . . [Rather], as a framework for moral catechesis they provide the structure into which other themes [those of grace, of the Beatitudes, of the virtues, of sin and forgiveness, of life in the Spirit and in the community of the Church] are woven."[2]

Dionigi Tettamanzi, for long one of the most outstanding moral theologians in Italy and now cardinal archbishop of Milan, provides further insights into the meaning of the Christian moral life as set forth in the *Catechism*. Cardinal Tettamanzi has written, perceptively, "the *Catechism* immediately places us within the context of life, of the new life given by faith and by the sacraments and that requires the free and generous response of Christians. We read at the very beginning of Part Three, dedicated to the Christian moral life, the following: 'Coming to see in the faith their new dignity, Christians are called to lead henceforth a life "worthy of the gospel of Christ" (Phil 1:27). They are made capable of doing so by the grace of Christ and the gifts of the Holy Spirit, which they receive through the sacraments and through prayer' (no. 1692)." Continuing, Tettamanzi says, "there is no separation between Christ and the Christian moral life because for the believer morality is not, above all, the effort of a person to constitute himself, but it is a gift of grace, a gift of imitating and following Jesus Christ, his sentiments, his virtues, his life. The 'come, follow me,' signifies the invitation to believe in Christ and to live by following him, acquiring in particular his new commandment, 'This is my commandment, that you love one another as I have loved you' (Jn 15.12). The point of departure for the Christian moral life is to recognize who man is, his vocation, his dignity and destiny."[3]

I will now attempt to present more fully the essential core of the teaching of the *Catechism of the Catholic Church* relevant to an introduction to moral theology.

2. Essential Meaning of Christian Morality According to the Catechism

We can best grasp the essential understanding of Christian morality as set forth in the *Catechism of the Catholic Church* by focusing attention on the following issues: (a) the moral life as a dynamic endeavor on the part of human persons to become fully the beings God wills them to be; (b) our absolute dependence upon God to enable us to become fully the beings he wills us to be; (c) the God-given authority of the Church as Mother and Teacher; and (d) what we must do in cooperation with God's grace in order to become fully the beings God wills us to be.

A. The Moral Life as an Endeavor on the Part of Human Persons to Become Fully the Beings God Wills Them to Be

The first chapter of the first section of Part Three of the *Catechism* focuses on the dignity of the human person and in its first article takes up the theme that man is indeed the image of the all-holy God. The very first paragraph of the first article (no. 1701) of this chapter begins with a beautiful citation from Vatican Council II's Pastoral Constitution on the Church in the Modern World, *Gaudium et spes* (no. 22), one constantly on the lips of Pope John Paul II, namely, that "Christ . . . makes man fully manifest to man himself and brings to light his exalted vocation" (cf. *Catechism of the Catholic Church*, no. 1710).

This chapter then develops the truths that human persons, created in the image and likeness of God, are gifted with intelligence, whereby they can come to know the truth, and with free choice, whereby they can determine their own lives by their own choices (nos. 1704-1706, 1711-1712, 1730-1748). In addition, it reminds us that, because of original sin, we are inclined toward evil and subject to error (nos. 1707, 1714), but that God, in his great mercy, has sent us his only-begotten Son to redeem us from sin and to enable us, dead to sin through baptism and made new creatures in Christ, to live worthily as children of God, called to be members of the divine family and to life eternal in union with him (nos. 1708-1709, 1715).

Indeed, the *Catechism* centers attention on the beatitudes, the "blessings," spoken by Jesus in his Sermon on the Mount (Mt 5:3-12), emphasizing that these great promises of our Lord make clear to us the actions and the attitudes that should characterize Christian moral life (nos. 1716-1717, 1725-1726). Along with the Decalogue, the "ten words" of God himself so central to salvation history and to the apostolic catechesis, the beatitudes of our Lord's Sermon on the Mount describe for us the path leading to God's kingdom (no., 1724; cf. nos. 1728-1729). Indeed, as Christoph Cardinal Schönborn, who was responsible for the final drafting of the *Catechism*, has said: "Jesus' Sermon on the Mount is the great guidebook to living happily. The eight Beatitudes address ways that make man 'blessed,' bring him a happiness that is more than being cheerful. . . . The life experience of so many Christians, saints both known and unknown, testifies that a life led according to the Sermon on the Mount means even now — in the midst of many sorrows and sufferings — incomparable happiness, an anticipation of eternal joy (cf. *Catechism*, no. 1723)."[4]

The first three articles of the first chapter of the first section of Part Three, in short, portray the Christian moral life as a dynamic endeavor on the part of human persons to become fully the beings God wills them to be: his own children, brothers and sisters of Jesus, the one who was obedient to death and whose only will was to carry out the wise and loving plan of his heavenly Father for human existence.

B. Our Absolute Dependence Upon God to Enable Us to Become Fully the Beings He Wills Us to Be

As already noted, the initial articles of the first chapter of the first section of Part Three remind us of the truths that, as beings made in God's image, we are endowed with intelligence — whereby we can discover the truth, including moral truth — and with freedom of choice, whereby we determine our own lives and selves. They likewise remind us that, because of sin, we are prone to evil and to error, and that it is only by participating in the redemptive death and resurrection of Jesus that we are enabled to live worthily as God's children and in this way become fully the beings he wills us to be. These great truths are developed in greater detail in Article 2 of the third chapter of this section, the article devoted to justification and grace. There it is made clear to us that we do not justify ourselves, but that it is God in his goodness who reconciles sinful men and women to himself by the gift of the Holy Spirit, poured into the hearts of all those who, through baptism, participate in the saving death and resurrection of Jesus (cf. nos. 1987ff). It is only through the gift of the Holy Spirit, which Christ merited for us by his life of obedience and his self-sacrificing death on the cross, that we are able to share in his redemptive act, to be converted from sin to accept — freely — God's gift of justification (nos. 1987-1995).

By the power of the Holy Spirit, sanctifying grace — a sharing in God's divine nature — is poured into our hearts so that we are made holy and enabled to live worthily as God's very own children (nos. 1996-2000; cf. nos. 2017-2027). Precisely because we are now truly God's children, who share in the divine nature just as his Son shares fully our human nature, we are called to a life of perfection, of holiness (nos. 2012-2016; cf. nos. 2028-2029).

Our responsibility is to cooperate with the grace freely given us by the most merciful God. We can do nothing of our own to merit eternal life, to merit membership in the divine family. But God made us to be the kind of beings we are, intelligent and free, precisely because he willed that there be beings to whom he could *give* his own life. He freely offers us this life in Jesus through the Holy Spirit, and inwardly moves us freely to accept his offer, but he will not force himself upon us. We are free to sin, to choose death rather than life, but as our best and wisest friend God is always with us, with his never-failing offer of grace, to enable us to become, freely, the beings he wills us to be. This is the core message of Article 2, "Grace and Justification," of the third chapter of the first section of Part Three.

C. The God-given Authority of the Church as Mother and Teacher

This matter is taken up in Article 3 of the third chapter of the first section of Part Three. The *Catechism* first notes that it is *in* the Church, the communion of all the baptized, that Christians fulfill their vocation, one that requires them, as St. Paul says (cf. Rom 12:1), to offer their bodies as holy and acceptable sacrifices to God (nos. 2030-2031).

The *Catechism*, following the teaching of Vatican Council II, emphasizes that the magisterium of the Church, invested in the college of bishops under the headship of the Roman pontiff, has the God-given authority and responsibility to teach in Christ's name the saving truths of faith and morals (nos. 2033-2034). Moreover, it affirms that the charism of infallibility extends to those elements of Catholic doctrine, including those concerning the moral life, without which the saving truths of the gospel cannot be safeguarded, faithfully presented, and observed (no. 2035). In fact, the *Catechism* insists, the authority of the magisterium extends to *specific* precepts of the natural law insofar as the observance of these precepts is required by our Creator and is necessary for our salvation. In proclaiming these truths of natural law, the magisterium exercises a truly prophetic role for humankind (no. 2036). The faithful, the *Catechism* teaches, have the *right* to be instructed according to the mind of the magisterium, and they have the *duty* to shape their lives in accordance with its authoritative teaching (no. 2037). All the faithful should have an attitude of filial love for the Church, their Mother and Teacher (no. 2040).

D. What We Must Do in Order to Become Fully the Beings God Wills Us to Be

The *Catechism* insists that human persons, precisely because they are endowed with freedom of choice, are, as it were, the mothers and fathers of their own acts (cf. no. 1749). They are obliged to choose in accordance with the truth if they are to be fully the beings God wills them to be.

Article 1, "The Moral Law" (nos. 1950-1986), of the third chapter of Part Three, is devoted to an articulation of the great *truths* of the moral order in accordance with which good moral choice can be made. Here the *Catechism*, following Vatican Council II (and St. Thomas and the Catholic tradition), insists that God's divine and eternal law, his wise and loving plan for human existence, is the highest norm of human life and action (no. 1950; cf. no. 1975). But God has enabled his rational creatures, men and women, to participate actively in this wise and loving plan through the natural law (no. 1954; cf. no. 1978). The natural law is universal and immutable (nos. 1956, 1958). Although the application of the natural law can vary according to circumstances (no. 1957), this law is nonetheless one that unites human persons and imposes upon them common principles and norms that always retain their substantive value (no. 1958). Moreover, it is no easy task to grasp the precepts of the natural law in a clear and immediate way; in our actual condition, as persons wounded by sin, God's grace and revelation are necessary for sinful human persons to come to know rightly the religious and moral truths needed for an upright moral life (cf. no. 1960).

The natural law is fulfilled and perfected by the new law or evangelical law (no. 1965). In essence, this law consists in the grace of the Holy Spirit poured into the hearts of the faithful through faith in Christ (no. 1966). The faithful, who are called to develop within themselves (with the help of God's never-failing grace) the dispositions marked out by the beatitudes of the Lord's Sermon on the Mount (no. 1967), must likewise keep God's commandments (no. 1968). By reason of their union with Christ, Christians are summoned to love even as they have been and are loved by God in Christ, with a healing, redemptive, sacrificial love (nos. 1970-1972).

In discussing the morality of human acts in Article 4 of the third chapter of the first section of Part Three, the *Catechism* makes it clear that the sources for the morality of a human act are the *object chosen* (what one is doing here and now), the *end* for whose sake the object is chosen, and the *circumstances* in which the action takes place (no. 1750) — and that *all* of these elements must be morally good — i.e., in accordance with moral truth — if the whole human act is to be morally good (no. 1755). The *Catechism* clearly identifies the object as the subject matter of the human act as willed and chosen by the agent (e.g., freely chosen intercourse with one's wife [the marital act], freely chosen intercourse with one's daughter [incest]) (no. 1751). It insists that a good intention, in the sense of the intention of the *end* for whose sake an object is chosen (and *intended* as an object of one's free choice) cannot justify the means chosen if this means is evil (immoral) by reason of its object (no. 1753). It likewise clearly affirms that there are specific kinds of acts, specified by their freely chosen objects, that are *always* wrong for one to choose — e.g., fornication — precisely because the willingness to choose an object of this kind displays a disordered will, i.e., moral evil (no. 1755). In other words, the *Catechism* clearly teaches that there are some kinds of human acts, specified by the object of choice, that are intrinsically evil, and that, corresponding to such acts, there are absolute moral norms, admitting of no exceptions.

In the second section of Part Three of the *Catechism*, devoted to a consideration of the Ten Commandments, various kinds of intrinsically evil acts, proscribed by absolute moral norms, are clearly identified: the intentional killing of innocent human persons (cf. no. 2273), as in infanticide (no. 2268), abortion (nos. 2271), mercy killing or euthanasia (no. 2277), and suicide (no. 2281); masturbation (no. 2352); fornication (no. 2353); rape (no. 2356); homosexual acts (no. 2357); adultery (no. 2380-2381). The *Catechism* clearly proclaims, along with Pope Paul VI, that contraception, described as every action which, either in anticipation of the conjugal act, during its accomplishment, or in the development of its consequences, proposes either as end or means to impede procreation, "is intrinsically evil" (no. 2370).

There can be no doubt that the *Catechism* firmly upholds the Catholic tradition that there are some kinds of human acts, specified by the objects freely chosen, that are intrinsically evil and proscribed by absolute moral norms. A willingness to do acts of these kinds is utterly incompatible with Christian life, with the life of God's very own children.

More positively, Christians are called, as we have seen already, to love with the redemptive, healing, and reconciling love of Jesus, a love utterly at odds with a willingness to do evil so that good may come about, and to shape their whole lives in accordance not only with the Ten Commandments but also with the internal dispositions marked out by the beatitudes. To choose in accordance with the truth and to be unwilling freely to do evil is what *we* must do if we are to become fully the beings God wills us to be and enables us to be through the grace of the Holy Spirit, won for us by his Son's life of obedience to the Father's holy will.

Notes for Appendix

1. Jean Honoré, "Catechism Presents Morality as a Lived Experience of Faith in Christ," *Reflections on the Catechism of the Catholic Church,* compiled by Rev. James P. Socias (Chicago: Midwest Theological Forum, 1993), pp. 139-140.

2. David Everyman Konstant, "The Ten Commandments Provide a Positive Framework for Life in Christ," in *Reflections on the Catechism of the Catholic Church,* p. 146.

3. Dionigi Cardinal Tettamanzi, *Viaggio nel Nuovo Catechismo* (Casale Monferrato: Edizioni Piemme, 1993), p. 38.

4. Christoph Cardinal Schönborn, *Living the Catechism of the Catholic Church,* Vol. 3, *Life in Christ* (San Francisco: Ignatius Press, 2001), pp. 17-18.

INDEX

absolutes — SEE moral absolutes

Adler, Mortimer, man's difference from other animals — 66 (note 5; henceforth, "note" and "notes" will be referred to as "n." and "nn.," respectively)

Ansaldo, Aurelio, on Grisez-Finnis-Boyle and their critics — 115, 139 (n.143)

Anselm, St., theology as faith seeking understanding — 37 (n. 1)

Aquinas — SEE Thomas Aquinas, St.

Armstrong, R.A. — 125 (n. 2); primary and secondary precepts of natural law in Thomas Aquinas — 129 (n. 40), 130 (n. 41)

Ashley, Benedict, critique of Grisez-Finnis-Boyle — 115ff, 139 (n. 144)

Augustine, St., definitions of sin — 189f, 191f, 208 (nn. 9-10); free choice — 45, 66 (n. 7); gifts of Holy Spirit and beatitudes — 232, 243 (n. 41); giving self to God — 237, 244 (n. 52); need for grace — 238, 244 (nn. 53-54); Neoplatonic influence on, and sin — 191; original sin — 214, 241 (n. 9); Sermon on the Mount and Christian moral life — 230, 231, 242 (n. 36); sixth commandment — 251, 265 (n. 8)

baptism, fundamental option for Christian — 203f; nature of baptismal commitment — 221-227, cf. 279-281; unites Christians with Jesus — 217ff; and *Veritatis splendor* — 202, 279f

Bauer, Johannes, on sin in New Testament — 187f, 207 (n. 6), 208 (n.8)

Beasley-Murray, G.R., covenant — 39 (n. 14)

beatitudes, and gifts of Holy Spirit — 231ff; modes of Christian response specifying requirements of Christian love — 232f, 243 (n. 42); and *Veritatis splendor* — 273

Bible and moral theology — 31-37

Belmans, Theo, on Thomas Aquinas's understanding of human acts — 167 (n. 48)

Böckle, Franz, proportionalism of — 145, 166 (n. 38), 266 (n. 20)

Bonaventure, St., distinction between mortal and venial sin — 195

Boyle, Joseph, critique of fundamental option theories — 169 (n. 83), 199, 209 (nn. 40, 42); free choice — 67 (n. 10); fundamental freedom — 199; incommensurability of human goods — 153, 167 (n. 56); major writings — 134 (n. 77); SEE ALSO Grisez-Finnis-Boyle and 134-138 (nn.77-132)

Bradley, Robert, significance of *Roman Catechism* — 266 (nn. 10-11)

Brueggemann, Walter, radical injunctions of the covenant — 34, 39 (nn. 15-16)

"Caiaphas" principle — 143f

capital sins — 206

Catechism of the Catholic Church, and beatitudes — 299f; Christian moral life — 295-303; Church as Mother and Teacher — 264, 300f; conscience and the moral life — 65; Decalogue and Christian moral life — 302f; eternal law — 93, 301; free choice — 47, 301; grace, need for — 300; human action, morality of — 302; human action, significance of — 48, 252; human vocation — 296; Jesus, foundation of Christian moral life — 216, 299; Jesus fully reveals man to himself, 299; intrinsically evil acts — 164, 254, 303; love, law of — 303; magisterium, authority of — 264, 300f; moral absolutes — 164, 303; moral law — 301f; natural law — 93, 301; Sermon